How Chinese Women Rise –

What we can learn from Chinese women with successful careers
in top management

How Chinese Women Rise –

What we can learn from Chinese women with successful careers in top management

Dr. Bettina Al-Sadik-Lowinski

Bibliographical information held by the German National Library
The German National Library has listed this book in the Deutsche Nationalbibliografie (German national bibliography); detailed bibliographic information is available online at http://dnb.d-nb.de.

1st edition - Göttingen: Cuvillier, 2018

© CUVILLIER VERLAG, Göttingen, Germany 2018
Nonnenstieg 8, 37075 Göttingen, Germany
Telephone: +49 (0)551-54724-0
Telefax: +49 (0)551-54724-21
www.cuvillier.de

  ISBN 978-3-7369-9808-7
  eISBN 978-3-7369-8808-8

Acknowledgements

For Lara and Luc

The inspiration and support I received from so many people made a vital contribution to my research in China and my decision to proceed to the next stage – this book. I have had the privilege of coaching numerous female executives of many nationalities, who inspired me to write the book. My special thanks go to the 35 amazing female Chinese top executives who participated in the Shanghai Women's Career Lab research project. They offered me their time, gave me their trust and have stayed in touch. Thank you all for your solidarity and support!

Gary Wang, CEO of MindSpan Executive Coaching in Shanghai, generously introduced me to his network and put me in contact with several interview partners. Gundula Fichtler, a former market research executive, supported me with her incisive thinking and honest feedback. Anette Schrage, a German advertising executive who now lives in Canada, and Ian Lawrance, an Australian management consultant, gave feedback on the content and language. My mentors Dick Stroem from Sweden and Sharleen Dyre from Japan provided constant encouragement, as did my close friends Isabel Schlemmer, Karin Rach and Professor Jutta Rump from the Institute of Employability in Germany.

My supervisors Professor Gregory Wegmann and Professor Samuel Mercier from the University of Burgundy gave me continuous support, feedback and inspiration. My special thanks go to Yue Shen, Senior HR Director in Shanghai, who represented the Shanghai Women's Career Lab research participants at my thesis defence in France and also helped me to communicate our results in China.

Last but not least, I would like to thank my family – my husband, my parents and my sister, who are always there for me, and my children Lara (12) and Luc (9), who showed great interest and curiosity in every step of my work and made me feel very proud. This book is for them.

Preface

One day, while running a coaching certification course in Shanghai, an idea I had been mulling over for years suddenly took concrete form, and I began studying the careers of women who had achieved particular success in top management. China offered an abundance of such women. The focus of my investigation was to find out how so many Chinese women are able to reach top management in multinational companies.

The question of how to get more women into senior positions in politics and business comes up regularly in the media, only to then disappear again. There are also a lot of how-to guides for women on the best way to achieve career success. In the same spirit, many companies and governments are committed to helping get more women into senior management. There have been a host of initiatives aimed at increasing the proportion of women in management roles, such as diversity projects that specifically support women. One much-discussed option that has been attempted in Europe for many years is the use of quotas. Thanks to these company and government policies, the proportion of women in senior management positions worldwide has steadily increased down the years. However, there is considerable geographic variation, and some of the world's leading economies – including Germany and Japan – still tend to come quite low down the rankings. Progress has been slow and protracted, something that is often attributed to the historically relatively short phase in which women have been able to work as managers.

According to various sources, China has a higher proportion of women in executive positions than Western industrialised nations such as the USA, France and Germany. In light of this fact, I asked myself whether China has its own "success formula" for female executives. Could these Chinese women serve as case studies who show the internal and external factors that must be in place for women to rise to the management levels of international corporations? Are there strategies that make these Chinese women more successful?

In my work as an executive coach and trainer in China, the first thing that struck me was the self-assurance and ease with which Chinese women occupy very senior roles at multinational companies. I also encountered a far higher proportion of women in senior positions in China than I had in my native country of Germany, in my husband's native country of France or in Japan, where I also worked for a number of years. That sparked my curiosity. What was different here than at home and in other countries that I was professionally acquainted with and where I had also met some very talented women? The idea of investigating this phenomenon more closely gradually took form, and I decided to study the careers of female Chinese executives. Thanks to the network I had built up through my work as an executive coach, I was able to achieve something that represents an insurmountable challenge for many researchers in China: namely, to establish contact with many impressive female Chinese senior executives who were willing to support me and my research by participating in a study. I was greeted with a wave of great solidarity – from supportive men and women from across the world, but above all from Chinese women. That was how this book came about. The idea of the Shanghai Women's Career Lab was born – a unique, multi-year research project in which 35 female Chinese top executives participated. They held management roles at 26 different multinational companies in China, spanning a wide variety of industries and with head offices in Germany, France or the USA. The female Chinese executives were willing to take part in in-depth, exploratory qualitative interviews with myself for my research project.

My own previous career in management at international corporations allowed me to observe and support many women as they pursued their careers. Some rose through the ranks faster than others, many disappeared when children came along, and others got "stuck" in middle management. Later on, I coached numerous women from many different countries, and worked with them to explore in greater depth some of the issues specifically faced by female executives but not by my male clients. The women often described similar issues, but there were also differences according to nationality, environment and culture. I gained the impression that the Chinese women were unlike many of the women I had previously worked with. Whereas the German and Japanese women often had issues resulting from critical social attitudes towards female executives, the challenge of combining work and family, or difficulties dealing with male colleagues, such issues were rarely mentioned by the Chinese women, who were instead primarily concerned with issues of leadership style and career planning in an international context. These personal observations from many years' work with female executives, especially Chinese women, fed into my work on this book.

My starting point was to ask what factors enabled these women to rise to management levels in multinational companies in China. I quickly realised that I did not want to compare the women in my study with men, but rather to focus on their unique career paths and experiences in their specific environment. I resolved to take a gender-neutral perspective free of gender stereotypes, which my German socialisation sometimes did not make any easier. "Gender is not an issue" was how the female Chinese executives replied whenever I broke my resolution and reverted to my preconceived notions. It still makes me chuckle to remember.

The book draws on experiences from a country of vast dimensions, which encompasses the Mosuo minority (one of the world's few matriarchies), traditional interpretations of Confucian values and efforts towards equality rooted in Communist worldviews. The women's paths converged on Shanghai, the international megacity and China's leading economic hub.

I learned a lot from the Chinese women and the things they reported in the interviews, and I would like to share this knowledge with other women throughout the world and with men who want to support women's careers. My interviewees have managed to do what many women across the world are attempting – to rise to senior executive levels at global corporations. How they described themselves and the paths they have taken is the chief topic of this book. By analysing their career paths I have identified what the 35 women have in common, and in this book I present these findings to other women and interested readers in a digestible form. The book is intended to open up alternative perspectives for women and experts who support women in their careers, and to stimulate discussion and reflection. Companies and policy experts will discover inspiration from the Chinese perspective that they can incorporate into their own strategies for supporting women. In addition to background information and research findings from China, the book also offers a career model and career typology that readers can use to strategically address the issues facing them. To anticipate the book's conclusions: a strong desire to keep learning and a strong drive to achieve success are the two constants that run through all the women's accounts. Everything I learned about China's successful female executives, as documented in this book, is owed to a wave of exemplary solidarity.

Contents

1. How women rise –
female Chinese executives as global role models

How different readers can benefit from the findings of the Shanghai Women's Career Lab – What readers can expect from the book

Contrary to what we might expect, China has a higher proportion of women in senior executive roles than almost any other country in the world, far outstripping many Western countries – even though there's not a gender quota in sight. According to figures published in 2014, 38% of senior management roles in China are held by women, far more than in the USA (20%) and Germany (16%) and the global average of 24% (Thornton, 2014). Although other sources report slightly different figures (due to different data collection methods and definitions), the overall picture remains the same: more women attain senior management positions in China than in Western countries. This is surprising given that most publications paint a more negative picture of Chinese women in top management. The data showing a high proportion of Chinese women in senior management prompt the questions of whether Chinese women pursue particular career strategies that make them successful and whether their environment is more favourable for female executives than in other countries. Could female Chinese executives and their careers even serve as role models for other women and societies? The primary focus of the book is to describe the career experiences of successful female Chinese senior executives as fully as possible. The central question addressed here is: what do women need to conquer top management levels? Above all, what skills, behaviours and personality traits do women need to get to the top of global corporations? The Shanghai Women's Career Lab research project offers unique insights into the career determinants and career experiences of a specific group: 35 extremely successful, fascinating Chinese women who have already made it to the top levels. The focus of the project was to establish what distinguishes Chinese women who are able to conquer top management levels. To answer this question, the book draws on the study participants' accounts of critical determinants of their career development and their own experiences during their progression to a senior management role at a multinational company in China. They also provide examples of the attitudes and behaviours that highly successful women exhibit and utilise on their way to the top. A related question concerns the conditions that are needed for more women to get into top management positions globally. These questions require complex, multifactorial treatment. Four major areas appear to be relevant at first glance – society, economic context, family situation and the women themselves. With respect to society, the key questions are how people respond to women in senior management roles and whether societal influences tend to help or hinder women's progression to such roles. Economic conditions and mechanisms define the women's main sphere of activity, and exert both a direct and indirect influence on the proportion of women in top executive roles. But ultimately, it is the women themselves who have to adapt themselves and their actions to the challenges, requirements and responsibilities that senior management positions bring with them. The research that this book is based on aimed to achieve a better understanding of the situation of women in top management roles in China and thereby reveal new avenues for women who are pursuing careers, for policy experts who want to bring about lasting social change and for CEOs who want to support women in their organisations. The idea is to facilitate strategies in China and other countries, so that in future more women can make it into senior executive roles. One possible incidental result could take the form of explanatory models for why, according to published figures, China has such a high proportion of women in senior management roles.

If you glance at the literature on careers, it is striking that even today most books and publications focus primarily on men's careers and on traditional hierarchical career paths. There are only a handful of studies looking exclusively at the careers of women in management. This may be due to the fact that women only recently began to enter senior levels at companies. It is thus also unsurprising that many of the existing studies compare women's careers with men's, as it were making men's careers a benchmark against which to measure women's. Such approaches suggest that women need to be like men in order to get to the top of companies and achieve career success in the traditional form. Various factors are compared, such as women's career orientation and motivation or their image as leaders by contrast with men. As a result, findings on these matters in the existing literature are rather patchy. The Shanghai Women's Career Lab investigated the career paths of 35 female Chinese top executives who work at multinational companies in China (mainly in Shanghai) and the determinants that have influenced their careers. The overall aim was to explore and analyse critical determinants, and to describe the women's career paths and classify them in a typology. The research focuses equally on external and individual factors that contribute to career success and on factors that limit or have a negative impact on success. It also takes account of women's experiences, attitudes and individual perceptions. The findings of the Shanghai Women's Career Lab are not designed to offer generalising conclusions about the situation of working women in China. Rather, the idea is to achieve a deeper understanding of the experiences and views of a highly select group of Chinese women in senior management who already were very successful in their careers. The emphasis is on understanding the actual career strategies of these female Chinese executives, who have had successful careers at global corporations, and on sharing their lessons with other women and business experts.

How can the findings of the Shanghai Female Career Lab serve different readers?

The book intends to provide inspiration and guidance to women, enabling them to plan their careers in a more informed manner. It is thus aimed at women anywhere in the world who are interested in international research on careers, who are starting or in the middle of their own career, or who want to support other women in their careers. This book differs from conventional career guides for women in a number of respects. Firstly, it offers an overview of academic research into women's careers. Secondly, it allows readers to develop an alternative perspective on the issues facing them in their own careers by reflecting on the findings about successful Chinese women. There is not just one way for women to pursue a successful career in top management, but many. By describing successful Chinese women's career strategies, the book aims to offer readers new perspectives that allow them to develop or modify their own career strategies. The second main group that the book is aimed at is managers who have recognised that helping more women to reach senior management positions will give their company a competitive edge in the medium to long term. That's as true for companies based in China as for ones in other parts of the world. Ventolini and Mercier (2015) describe how the management of careers becomes a strategical parameter for organisations in order to stay competitive. In order to implement successful strategies over the long term, companies need the best and most effective executives – in short, the right executives. Accordingly, promoting successful female (as well as male executives) is a key priority for all globally acting companies – within China and all over the globe. In future, there will be no getting around the need for even stronger promotion of women. Multinational companies with offices in China are faced with a particular challenge: "There is little literature which includes Chinese women managers in the research data, even though women's work in China is becoming more and more important." (Aaltio, 2007). Tatli, Vassilopoulou, and Özbilgin

(2013) also describe talent shortages and untapped female potential in China. Chinese university graduates increasingly prefer Chinese employers. The competition for the best managers presents HR departments at multinational companies in China with the challenge of how to attract more untapped female potential to their company and retain it successfully. These multinational companies are directly competing not just with private Chinese companies, but also with state-owned enterprises. In the context of international competition and the slowing down of Chinese growth, the question of how to select the right managers is even more critical than in the past. The findings aims to support companies' strategies for promoting women by providing holistic results that shed light on the determinants of successful careers for women. It attempts to paint a comprehensive picture of the situation of the Chinese women who participated in the Shanghai Women's Career Lab. The descriptions given by the women and the interpretations derived from these descriptions may help company leaders and HR specialists both in China and beyond to develop a deeper understanding of the situation of women in senior management roles.

Last but not least, anyone who wants to bring about social and political changes that lead to lasting improvements in conditions for women and their careers will find this book a catalyst for ideas and discussion. Although social and political debates do not make up the core of the book but are included only where they are touched on in the interviewees' reports, the findings nonetheless provide plenty of material for discussion and alternative perspectives. Countries which still have very low proportions of women in senior management, such as Germany, could also make use of the results to draw conclusions regarding their own country-specific issues. A glance at the global situation shows that there is not just one right way to support women and create more favourable societal conditions.

What can readers expect from this book?

The approach that the current book takes to this wide-ranging topic is explained in chapter 2. Given that the topic of careers and career determinants can be variously interpreted from different perspectives, it is important to make clear right at the start which perspective is being adopted here, and to explain the model that the book's argument and structure are based on. In the research that the book is based on, this model functioned as a "roadmap" (Creswell, 2014) that guided the analysis of existing literature and research. It was also used to generate and analyse the data from the Shanghai Women's Career Lab. The description of the model is followed by an overview of the career determinants that have been investigated by previous research and the resulting theoretical perspectives developed by different researchers. Career patterns are the result of these determinants, and so studying external and individual determinants is of great importance when seeking to understand female managers' career paths.

In Chapter 3, readers can then learn what is meant in scholarship by the term "career" and the concept of "career success" that is often associated with it. The variety of definitions makes clear the different perspectives that researchers bring to the concept of "career". This is especially important given the fact that career theory as a discipline in its own right is still relatively young and primarily influenced by the Anglo-American context. Careers are influenced by a variety of contextual factors, for example socio cultural aspects, family situations and the labour market. The focus of this book is to investigate the specific features of women's careers in China. Accordingly, it primarily presents research approaches that are relevant to describing women's careers. More traditional concepts offer explanations of the forms that careers used to take in the past, while more recent career models explain the forms they take today. Subsequent discussion then focuses on the context in which the Chinese women pursued their careers: namely, the liberalisation of the entire economy and the emergence of a new labour market.

Chapter 4 introduces the Shanghai Women's Career Lab, the research project from which the new findings documented in this book derive. It explains who the participants were, how they were recruited and how the study was conducted. For the project, 35 female top executives were interviewed and 800 pages of transcripts were collected. This material was then analysed using a theory-based methodology. Many researchers consider it difficult to conduct studies in China, since doing so crucially depends on being able to gain access to the right target groups. The Shanghai Women's Career Lab was able to achieve this successfully thanks to the author's extensive network from her work as an executive coach. The "right target group" in this case consisted of female senior executives, who were selected in line with the definition set out in this book. There is also a discussion of why Shanghai is such an ideal location for researching the careers of women in top management positions. Finally, there is a concise summary of the key points of the method used in the qualitative study.

Chapter 5 presents the key findings from the Shanghai Women's Career Lab. It looks at how female Chinese executives describe external career determinants. Selected external determinants for female careers are presented according to the Female Career Model that is being used here. Each subsection begins with a summary of existing research on the respective determinant. Where there are existing findings in previous research on the Chinese context, these results are specifically incorporated. However, due to a lack of published research on China, many aspects are analysed on the basis of Western research. After that, the findings from the interviews are presented, i.e. the concrete results of the Shanghai Women's Career Lab. In relation to external determinants, the focus is on historical and cultural conditions, the labour market context, the influence of the family and the role of mentoring and networks. The historical and cultural framework comprises Confucian values and traditions. Their significance for women's careers is described on the basis of findings from the literature. One significant determinant of women's careers is the political developments in China and the government's efforts to bring about equality of opportunity, which constitute the legal framework within which women pursue their careers. These efforts have also influenced Chinese society and its image of female executives. Hence, the issue of the local image of women in senior management roles is presented, inter alia, in relation to the "Think manager – think male" phenomenon from the perspective of the literature. The specific situation of women in Chinese management is described by reference to figures, the question of whether a glass ceiling exists and a general inquiry into the issue of equality of opportunities for female Chinese managers. The next subsection then addresses the question of whether and to what extent women's careers are influenced by their families. Three components are analysed: women's families of origin, women's own family situation (with a particular focus on the factor of motherhood) and the role of women's partners. Finally, the research considers mentoring and networking, which are important external career determinants. The literature shows that there are particularly pronounced differences between the effects of mentoring on men and women. Against the backdrop of guanxi principles, networking has a special significance in the Chinese context. These principles are firmly embedded in society and so are of far greater importance for careers than networking as understood purely in Western terms.

Chapter 6 then addresses the individual success factors that facilitate advancement to senior management. The primary question here is what skills and personalities these Chinese women needed in order to rise up the ranks. A longer section addresses the connection between personality and career success. Psychologically oriented research identifies the personality dimensions more strongly associated with career success. These include dimensions such as conscientiousness, leadership and achievement motivation, openness to contact, team orientation, emotional stability and flexibility, which are taken from the Big Five, the Business-Focused

Inventory of Personality (BIP) and other theories. In this context, aspects of exercising power, dealing with conflict and competitive behaviour are described in relation to career success. Finally, the section turns to the question of what image best helps women to progress in their careers. The subsequent subsection looks at female leadership styles, since leadership behaviour is a key factor in career development at companies. Most researchers investigate the specific features of women's leadership behaviour in comparison with more characteristically male leadership behaviour. Differences and distinct traits that researchers tend to ascribe to female executives are identified, alongside findings about leadership behaviours that make women especially successful in their careers.

Chapter 7 looks at Chinese women's career advancement in relation to career paths. It starts by considering existing research findings on women's career patterns. The career paths of the 35 participants in the Shanghai Women's Career Lab are then described and interpreted. The chapter begins by clarifying what the concept of "career" means to the women in this study. In the career paths analysis, the individual stages of the women's careers are recorded in chronological order. The analysis is subdivided into three parts: "The start of the women's careers", "Moving up" and "Future career goals". The analysis covers geographic mobility, reasons for changing roles, decision-making processes and alternatives to actual career choices, and both planned and unplanned career decisions. It also investigates the career effects of the choice of company type in China. Particular attention is paid to the challenges that the women have faced in the course of their careers.

The book culminates in chapter 8 with a typology describing the typical career patterns of the research group. The typology incorporates findings about career development determinants and the results of the career paths analysis. The result comprises five groups of patterns that are typical for the Shanghai Women's Career Lab.

The main findings of the Shanghai Women's Career Lab are summarised and discussed in chapter 9. The focus here is on encouraging readers to learn and reflect, based on the experiences of the female Chinese top managers. The chapter offers suggestions for women in their careers and for the other target groups mentioned before. The particular emphasis is on the question how to support more women into senior management roles. These suggestions can be applied against the backdrop of the increasing competition for top talent at multinational companies in China or, in the wider global context, against the backdrop of the question of how to promote the advancement of female executives to top hierarchical levels and management boards at companies. These recommendations are also based on a discussion of the study participants' views about the future for female Chinese executives and the Chinese economy.

The concluding chapter (10) addresses the question of whether Chinese women can serve as global role models for women's careers.

2. The Female Career Model

How female executive careers are analysed in this book – Determinants of women's career success

---

Determinants of female career success

Career development is influenced by a variety of contextual factors. Careers are subject to the reciprocal influences of social conceptions of work and employees' expectations with respect to their careers. Many empirical studies attempt to include multiple levels in their research in the form of defined determinants. The challenge for researchers is to adequately reflect the complexity of these influences. Several studies have examined the impact of very specific constructs such as leadership motive patterns and mentoring. But very few have investigated a range of personal and situational determinants. According to Tharenou, Latimer, and Conroy (1994), determinants of managerial advancement have not been well established. Very few comprehensive theories of managerial advancement have been developed for women.

Various researchers (Tharenou et al., 1994; Ragins, 1989; Fagenson, 1990; Kirchmeyer, 1998; Melamed, 1996; Lyness and Thompson, 2000; Eddelston, (2004); Mayrhofer et al., 2005; Judge et al., 1995) have classified the determinants of career success according to a variety of different, but largely compatible, categorisations. Many of these studies attempt to identify whether certain determinants have more influence than others on the success of women in management, what combination tends to promote success and whether factors can have different effects for men and women. Eddelston (2004) claims that research that examines predictors of career success for both women and men has been inconclusive and contradictory in its findings.

Figure 1 presents a selection of categories of determinants that researchers have studied. Below, some studies on determinants of women's careers and these studies' main findings are presented.

Determinants of career success	Selected authors
Human Capital	Tharenou (1994), Eddelston (2004), Kirchmeyer (1998), Melamed (1996), Arthur (1996)
Personality traits Marketability	Kirchmeyer, Ragins (1997), Mayrhofer (2005), Melamed Eddelston
Motivation career centrality career motivation achievement motivation career impatience	White (1995), Judge (1995), Eddelston, Arthur White, Lyness (2000) Judge, White White, Lyness, Judge, Kirchmeyer, Melamed Eddelston
Opportunity Structure Macro Societal/Demographic	Judge, Arthur, Melamed, Mayrhofer
Career Choices	Melamed
Organisational intermediate organisational training and development micro job level	Melamed, Lyness Tharenou Melamed, Lyness
Interpersonal/Social Capital Mentoring Networking Supportive Relationships	Eddelston, Judge, Amdurer (2014), Ragins Eddelston, Judge, Mayrhofer Eddelston, Mayrhofer Judge, Amdurer
Family	Eddelston, Ragins, Mayrhofer, Kirchmeyer Melamed, Judge, Lyness, Ragins, Tharenou

Figure 1: How researchers categorise "Career determinants" (examples from selected studies)

A gender-specific career model showing different components of career determinants was developed by Tharenou et al. (1994). According to the findings, early educational encouragement, training and development can affect career development by developing knowledge and ultimately facilitate promotion of female executives into higher ranks.

Kirchmeyer (1998) subdivides career determinants into the categories human capital, individual, interpersonal and family. Human capital refers to the personal investment one makes to enhance one's value in the workplace. In contrast to Tharenou et al., Kirchmeyer found that education and work-related experience seem to have a stronger influence on men's progression. Women's accomplishments are attributed to luck or external factors such as affirmative action. Individual determinants relate to one's capacity to manage and include personality traits and other psychological factors. Research confirms that male managers are believed to possess more of the necessary traits than female ones. A high level of femininity (more empathetic, expressive traits) is only associated with low effectiveness for female supervisors. The third category describes interpersonal determinants. These involve supportive relationships at work such as mentoring, networking and the support of superiors. The last category, family, looks at the influence of spouses and children on careers. Kirchmeyer focused on these categories of variables, based on earlier findings suggesting that they may affect men's and women's careers differently.

Three main groups of determinants for career success are the focus of research by Melamed (1996). The first group includes human capital factors and is defined as mental abilities, education, experiences and personality traits. The second group is career choices, which include first job choice and later career moves. Occupational choice is, according to Melamed, probably the most important career decision and one of the most influential determinants of career success. It involves career move decisions and questions such as how long to stay with one employer, mobility and relocation, and career breaks. The third group in this model focuses on opportunity structure and includes macro-societal factors such as market, climate and unemployment, and issues at the micro-job level such as occupation, prosperity and growth. The macro-societal level concerns demographic changes within society such as crisis periods that affect labour market demand. The intermediate level (organisational) accounts for organisational features. Internal mobility is influenced by job vacancy rates and organisational career ladders, size and structures. According to Melamed, the main barriers standing between women and senior management are negative stereotypes at companies that assume that women lack the necessary management skills or are less promising *per se* for management roles due to their gender. Traits that are perceived as characteristic of senior executive roles tend to be traditional and hence typically male. Another major barrier, Melamed believes, is corporate sanctions of career breaks due to maternity leave. A third barrier is gaps in legislative systems, which have meant that it is practically impossible for women to assert their entitlement to equality.

In their career model Eddelston et al. (2004) examine how personal and situational factors dynamically influence men's and women's managerial career success. The model includes a number of individual difference factors, career-related beliefs and career-enhancing outcomes that influence the level of success. Owing to the boundaryless perspective, which theorises "knowing why", "knowing how" and "knowing whom" as important predictors of career success, Eddelston incorporates career impatience (knowing why), marketability and willingness to relocate (knowing how) and mentoring efficacy and exposure to powerful networks (knowing whom). Individuals with career impatience want career progression and are ambitious in their careers. According to Eddelston, they are more likely to take active steps to ensure that they achieve career success. Marketability is an important factor in boundaryless careers and refers to a strong belief that one is attractive and marketable in the workplace. This may encourage individuals to seek out career-enhancing opportunities.

Several facilitators of career are categorised in the career model of Lyness and Thompson (2000). A good track record, development of strong relationships, proactive management of one's own career and setting of career goals, mentoring and developmental job assignments are the factors that influence careers according to this approach. Findings suggest that a good track record may be more important for female than for male managers as it could help to overcome gender stereotypes. Developing relationships refers to the finding that women who are promoted to the highest levels seem to have close ties to strategic sponsors. According to the researchers, setting clear career goals leads individuals to take the initiative with respect to obtaining challenging job assignments and taking more career risks. The proactive approach of managing one's own career is therefore seen as an important facilitator of career advancement in this study. Women encounter greater barriers to obtaining mentors than men, such as a lack of cultural fit and being excluded from informal "old boys' networks", and it is more important for them to have a good track record and develop relationships in order to facilitate their advancement. Women themselves often believe that they are not suited to male-dominated senior management roles or that women face stereotypical prejudices. Successful women were less likely than successful men to report that mentoring facilitated their advancement. Developmental experiences and career histories were similar for female and male executives, but men had more overseas assignments and women had more assignments with non-authoritative roles. One solution the researchers suggest, quoting the review by Ragins (1997) on mentoring women, is to have female mentors for female managers.

A comprehensive, gender neutral model with different layers was developed by Mayrhofer et al. (2005): at the core of the model are career patterns and career success, which are subject to various influences. These career patterns are tangibly and directly affected – to a greater or lesser extent – by these determinants. The first layer, "Person", includes personality traits such as the Big Five, leadership motivation and perceived self-efficacy. The next layer, "Context of origin", includes a person's family of origin and the social relations they are currently embedded in. "Work context" includes the working environment in which individuals operate. It also describes the labour market and the organisation at which they work. The outer layers comprise the social and cultural context and, finally, the global context. As was described earlier, different researchers bring a variety of different perspectives to bear on determinants in relation to women's careers in management. The topic of careers is a complex one in its own right, and is caught between various influences. In the view of certain researchers, women's careers are even more complex because they are subject to a variety of role-based, social and gender-specific influences that do not affect men's careers or do not do so to the same extent.

The Female Career Model

The theories described above make clear that there are many determinants of women's careers and that these determinants can affect the success of a woman in her managerial career in a number of ways. For the Shanghai Women's Career Lab, it was necessary to find an approach that took as much account as possible of the topic's complexity, while also structuring the findings in a digestible form. The Female Career Model described below forms the "roadmap" for the reader and shows the perspective that is adopted in the remainder of the book. The model does not claim to be complete and some of the determinants mentioned above are not considered here, or only to a minimal extent. The model is close to the layers model developed by Mayrhofer et al. (2005), but is not identical to it. In order to reduce complexity, Mayrhofer's chosen image of hierarchical "layers" that influence, condition and interact with one another has been replaced by a more "bin"-like analysis in which determinants are viewed in greater isolation from each other. The organisational perspective and associated influences are only examined in passing in this model, and only in cases where they emerge out of the women's descriptions. This means that the following overview of the influences on the careers of women in management in China is a selection based on the specific perspective of this model.

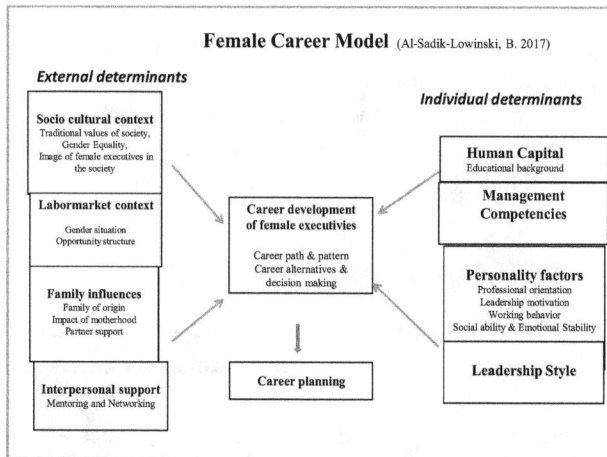

Figure 2: The Female Career Model

The Female Career Model focuses on external determinants and individual influences on the careers of Chinese female senior executives that result in different career paths and plans. These paths and patterns are regarded as being tangibly affected – to a greater or lesser extent – by determinants. They have both descriptive and evaluative components. The external influences are ones that impact on women's careers from the outside in the form of overarching conditions. They derive from the cultural traditions of Chinese society, the labour market situation, specific aspects of gender policy, familial situations and interpersonal support. Interpersonal support refers to personal support systems such as networks, mentors and supportive superiors. Taken together, these factors form the external framework within which the women's careers unfold. The individual influences are made up of aspects that are specific to the participants, grounded in their personal backgrounds and personalities, and linked to their career paths. They include their educational backgrounds, particular skills, aspects of their personalities that are relevant to their careers and their specific leadership styles.

Career paths are associated with individual assessments of career success, which can be expressed through various factors, such as individuals' personal level of satisfaction and the position they have achieved in an organisation's hierarchy. Paths describe the particular positions a person has held over the course of their career and the choices they have made. On this basis, career typologies are developed that exemplify the careers of the Chinese women who participated in the research. The Chinese context is essential to each "bin" of the territory of this model. In addition, the model is also informed by findings from the existing literature on women's careers and critical career determinants that are not limited to particular countries.

The next section begins with an overview of publications on women's careers, both in general and specifically in China. This is followed by a discussion of the individual determinants included in the model in the light of both existing findings and the results of the Shanghai Women's Career Lab.

3. Women's career in research and in a Chinese context

Definition of "career" – Career and career success – Women's careers and career theory – Career theory in flux and how it is taking account of women's careers – Careers before and after the opening of China to the global market – Existing research on the careers of female Chinese executives

Definition of "career"

The concept of career is defined from a range of perspectives by various researchers, leading to diverse definitions. The term "career", at least when it refers to a person's occupational history, is almost always linked to the idea of progression and rising up the ranks of a hierarchy; in this context, "career progression" and "being successful" are often used synonymously. The notion of career describes the professional stages and roles an individual has progressed through. It should be noted that the meaning of "career" in mainland Europe and the German-speaking countries differs from that in the English-speaking world. In the Anglo-American context, "career" is used to describe all possible forms that an individual's working life may take. The term is neutral, simply referring to someone's occupational history without necessarily implying a particular degree of success. Depending on the context, "career" can mean a person's work history and, in some cases, their professional development. An individual's "career" describes the work-related stations and positions they traverse. In German-speaking countries, by contrast, at least in the context of a person's professional development, the term "career" is nearly always associated with the idea of professional progress and rising within a hierarchy; here, "building a career" and "being successful" are often used synonymously.

Rump (2003) observes that there is a degree of uncertainty when it comes to defining the concept of career. Currently, there appears to be something of a lacuna or vacuum. This indicates a paradigm shift. Nonetheless, the term "career" (at least in the German sense) currently still tends to be used in connection with careers in leadership and rising up the management ladder. So the term "career" and conceptions of careers still include a notion of hierarchy. Auer (2000) proposes three conceptions of "career": "advancement-oriented career", "career as employment over the course of time" and "career as a universal form of life". As is clear just from the descriptions, these conceptions show there has been a shift in how the notion of career is understood: it is now also regarded as depending on individual motives. That is to say, individuals define the status that their career has in their life plan. The process is dependent on social changes, such as globalisation, and the uncertainty created by these constant changes, which make it harder to develop career plans. There are diverse interpretations, definitions, opinions and views regarding the concept of career. What is probably still the most frequently cited definition describes a career as "the unfolding sequence of a person's work experience over time" (Arthur, Hall, and Lawrence, 1996). This definition does not make reference to success, but success is nonetheless central to descriptions of careers. Hall distinguishes between "career as professional progression", "career as vocation", "career as a lifelong sequence of role-based experiences" and "career as the sum of positions that an individual holds over the course of their professional life" (Arthur et al., 1996). In the first of Hall's conceptions, the focus is once again on professional advancement. "Career as vocation" refers to professions that are categorised as a career goal in their own right: that is, professions that enjoy such a high status (due to the high level of qualification and lengthy training that they require) that further career progression no longer seems essential. On the third conception of career, by contrast with the first, the emphasis is on individual evaluation of particular stages of a person's career. The fourth conception looks at the individual positions that a person has held during their working life. The central theme of Hall's definition is work and the significance it can have for individuals, organisations or societies. Equally central is the factor of time, which is intrinsic to the concept of a career. Accordingly, "career" should be regarded as a concept that reflects changes in context. As careers develop, they are subject to a number of factors pulling in different directions: on the one hand, the reciprocal influences of companies or organisations and social conceptions of work; and on the other, employees' individual expectations with respect to their career and their actual well-being. They cannot be conceived without a social context, and so context at various levels plays a crucial role. Many empirical studies attempt to include multiple levels in their research (Mayrhofer, Meyer, and Steyrer, 2005).

A further distinction can be made between objective and subjective careers. An "objective career" refers to the individual positions a person has held during their working life, while a "subjective career" refers to the evaluative perspective from which individuals interpret their (working) life as a whole. This definition can also be applied to definitions of career success. "Objective career success" refers simply to the concrete and factually measurable course of an individual's professional life over time, including (for example) salary development, progression through different departments and hierarchical levels within a company or changing to a new employer altogether. Career success is often equated with progression within a corporation and assessed in terms of personal income, hierarchical level and promotions (Kirchmeyer, 1998). Research on careers has focused on the traditional Western definition of success as climbing up the corporate ladder and seeking extrinsic reward (Tu, Forret, and Sullivan, 2006). Longitudinal studies have defined career success as the number of promotions or the level of salary increase within a defined period, whereas cross-sectional studies have used objective measures such as current hierarchical position or salary, or subjective measures such as perceived career success and job satisfaction. More recent research includes individual attitudes towards careers. It defines career success as the positive psychological or work-related outcomes or achievements one has accumulated as a result of one's work experience (Judge, Cable, Boudreau, and Bretz, 1995). So a "subjective" career refers less to concrete aspects of an individual's career and more to the psychological processes by means of which agents make their personal assessments of their own career (Arthur et al., 1996). The category "subjective career" can include things such as individuals' perceptions of the potential career options that are available to them, which in some circumstances may greatly diverge from the possibilities that are actually available. Individuals' satisfaction with their career path and profession also belong to this subjective dimension of career (Mayrhofer et al., 2005). "Career" refers both to a system of positions that an individual has held throughout their life, and to the internal feelings, attitudes and beliefs that a person might hold about these positions. An occupation is a career if the individual associates their self-identity, self-definition and self-concept with it (Jackson, Hodge and Ingram 1994).

From a gender-specific perspective, it can be observed that men's and women's careers were traditionally viewed differently. Men used to have relatively static career paths after completing education or training. By contrast, women's careers historically consisted of short, temporary phases that filled up the time before marriage and motherhood. Some researchers have defined the role of housewife as a career option, while others have argued that this occupation should not be viewed under the aspect of "career" since it comprises unpaid work. Henning and Jardim (1987) view careers from a gender-specific perspective. They believe that men and women have different conceptions of careers. In their view, women regard self-fulfilment and growth as central aspects of their careers, while men are more likely to see careers as a continuous sequence of jobs. The traditional linear developmental and hierarchical conception of career in the literature is, according to Patton and McMahon (2014), not adequate to explain women's perceptions of careers and their experiences of their working lives. It can be seen that the concept of career varies for women depending on their life context and life stages. The career development of women is found to be more complex due to a socialisation process that has emphasised the dichotomy of work and family. Following this perspective, women's careers can be defined as meaningful "life experiences" which vary according to the heterogeneity of women and their biographies. For the purposes of this book, definitions of "career" that take account of both the current paradigm shift in general and the specific perceptions of women are of particular interest.

Career and career success

The notion of career success and what it can be understood to mean are important in connection with the topic of careers. Effectiveness, in combination with subjective and objective dimensions, plays a key role in relation to career success. Effectiveness emphasises the achievement of goals. It is assumed here that every individual knows what goals their career aims at. The constructs of utility, satisfaction and happiness play a role in this connection. The key benchmarks of success that individuals measure themselves against are subsumed under the concept of subjective career success. These benchmarks often comprise different aspects of happiness and contentment. Objective career success includes external signs of career success, such as income, position, promotions, the prestige of a job, number of staff and level of budget responsibility. Central aspects of career success include career orientation and career motivation. Career orientation integrates individual career wishes and motives, and influences a person's choice of profession and the ways in which they evaluate their work. It thus relates to the particular conceptions that a person has of their career. This means that individuals pursue different career goals depending on their individual career orientation. Their career orientation is determined by their value-judgements regarding their careers, their motives and their specific goals. Richardson (1974) carried out empirical studies showing that career orientation can be viewed as a multidimensional construct in which work motivation and values are central components. For example, for one person financial incentives and a high level of responsibility might be the deciding factors behind their choice of occupation, while other people might place emphasis on self-fulfilment and the working environment when making decisions about their career. An individual's entire career plan, and not just parts of it, can depend on their career orientation. One person, for instance, might regard it as important to spend their entire career in a particular sector or field, while others might only be able to identify with a more varied career.

Career motivation is the aspect of career orientation that relates to an individual's intentions and willingness to exert effort in the context of their career. Aberle (1994) distinguishes between extrinsic, intrinsic and extra-professional career motivation. High extrinsic motivation means that an individual is focused on career advancement. They seek out challenges and have high achievement motivation. Intrinsic career motivation, by contrast, focuses on the work itself. Intrinsically motivated individuals look for work that they regard as important and valuable and that corresponds to their interests. There are also extra-professionally motivated individuals, who primarily concentrate on life outside work. Researchers have debated the extent to which men and women differ in terms of career motivation. Later sections of this book will explore the topic of career motivation in greater depth. What is important to note at this stage is that the meaning of work is as potent for women as it is for men. Astin (1984) takes the view that men and women have the same career motivations. However, men and women make different career decisions because their early socialisation experiences and structural opportunities are different.

Sociologists suggest that careers should be regarded as social roles that are defined by society and link individuals to the social structure through subjective and objective aspects of status transitions. This idea suggests that the notions of career and career success have different meanings for men and women. Women managers have been found to view career success more as a process of personal development which involves interesting, challenging work and balance with the rest of their life. Women's own definition of success may have less to do with the externally defined, traditionally male corporate criteria, and more likely to rely on internal criteria such as a sense of personal achievement, integrity and balance (Melamed, 1996). Women's ideas of career success are influenced by their socialisation and the constraints they perceive as likely to affect their careers in organisations where they still often remain the minority (Sturges, 1999).In order to be able to describe the main career patterns in the research group this book looks at subjective and objective elements of success as well as at career motivation. Career patterns are understood as the outcome of various determinants.

Women's careers and career theory

Theories and testing of women's career development continue to draw heavily on frameworks and conceptions derived from male conceptions of work and careers. This needs to be viewed in light of the fact that career theory is still a relatively young discipline that is continuously developing against the backdrop of a constantly changing world of work. From a historical perspective, women only began to play a comparable role to men in the context of the labour market at a relatively late stage, and this is reflected in theoretical concepts that have traditionally been more geared towards men. The approaches taken by different researchers vary not just according to their choice of perspective but also against the background of a changing labour market and changes brought about by globalisation. In the context of social change, individual career patterns and strategies undergo constant transformation. Since these social transformations first began, a large number of career-related constructs have been discussed and debated in the field of career theory. Consequently, there is a wealth of perspectives on the topic of careers. These perspectives come from a whole host of disciplines, including psychology, sociology, economics, anthropology, political science and history, each of which approach concepts of careers from different perspectives and develop highly distinct models of them. Career theory can be defined as "the body of all generalizable attempts to explain career phenomena." (Arthur et al., 1996). The focus is on situation-specific explanations of career outcomes derived from personal experience or local practice.

Reviews of career theory consistently suggest that the field primarily consists of psychological and sociological views. Sonnenfeld and Kotter (1982) identify four types of career theory: sociological theories, psychological theories, hybrid forms combining both, and more recent career theories that also incorporate political and economic dimensions. Sociological approaches study the impact of social determinants on career success. Constructs such as career patterns and paths (Lepine, 1992; Lyness and Thompson, 2000; O'Neil, 2004), career stages and environmental influences on careers (Ragins, 1998) are usually central. Psychological approaches focus on static dispositional differences and their impact on people's careers. They include constructs such as career choice, orientation, motivation (Betz and Fitzgerald, 1987) and aspiration (Farmer, 1985) as well as issues of self-development (Gallos, 1989) and self-efficacy (Hackett and Betz, 1989). Hybrid forms, which combine sociological and psychological approaches, investigate career stages and associated decision-making processes. Process theories (Super, 1957, 1980; Levinson, 1978) study careers and their development over time. These models focus on individuals' development throughout their lives and observe the interplay between self-conception, society and career development. Changing needs and experiences are associated with different career stages, as is the factor of age.

In their meta-analysis of 76 articles, O'Neil et al. (2008) identified four patterns that have cumulatively contributed to the current state of the literature on women's careers: women's careers are embedded in women's larger life contexts; families and careers are central to women's lives; women's career paths manifest a wide range and variety of patterns; and human and social capital are critical factors for women's careers. This meta-analysis shows that in order to study women's careers, a combination of sociologically focused observations of path and environmental influences, process-oriented approaches and psychology-based research are needed in order to draw up a complex picture that approximates reality. There is some debate about the necessity of gender-distinct career theories (Osipow and Fitzgerald, 1996). Some authors offer specific reasons for studying the genders separately (O'Neil, Hopkins, and Bilimoria, 2008) and others suggest that a women-specific research focus is required because women's career development is considerably more complicated due to barriers imposed by the gendered social context (Betz and Fitzgerald, 1987). The next section begins by describing the historical development of career theory, as this is helpful for categorising the extent to which approaches are relevant to an analysis of women's careers. Selected research approaches relevant to women's careers are then presented and their significance for the present study described.

Career theory in flux and how it is taking account of women's careers

As described earlier, career theory historically developed primarily in the Anglo-American world. It is also a fairly young discipline. For a long time, research on management within the field of career theory focused exclusively on the experiences of men, since there were virtually no women in management roles. It is only in recent years that it has been possible to observe greater participation by women in top management worldwide (though there are still fewer women than men). Consequently, research exclusively concerned with the careers of women has only started to appear in recent years (Powell, 2011).

The origins of career theory are often traced back to Taylor (1913), whose work *The Principles of Scientific Management* categorised different types of work and took the view that not every individual was suited to every task. At this time, women tended to occupy the role of housewives and mothers, and for a long time studies looked at them exclusively in this capacity. Until the 1980s, working life was typified by a distinctive corporate culture, and research focused on traditional careers, where employees were closely tied to a particular company. Research concentrated on the conceptions that were predominant on the labour market: working for a single company your whole life and male-dominated corporate careers that were associated with a ladder-like ascent up a hierarchy. During the 1980s and 1990s, theorists attempted to specifically consider women's careers while still using the traditional framework of the male-oriented approach. Newer, more innovative concepts of career that also include political and economic dimensions attempt to respond to changed organisations, drivers of change such as globalisation and the rise of new information technologies. In the mid-1980s, career theory started examining the changes in career paths and career strategies that resulted from these factors. It also took into account the increasing number of women in employment. The previously dominant model of upwards mobility, according to which a person's career usually proceeds in an upwards direction and is limited to just one or two organisations, was replaced by theories of the patchwork career (Bloemer, 2005), the protean career (Hall, 2004) the boundaryless career (Arthur and Rousseau, 1996) and the kaleidoscope career (Mainiéro and Sullivan, 2005). All these theories move away from classical careers and emphasise individuality and autonomy, in contrast to standard working arrangements based on long-term, full-time employment. The new approaches in career theory all share a shift in responsibility for individuals' careers away from organisations and onto the individuals themselves. These approaches also look at how individuals find internal sources of fulfilment through their careers. All of these concepts stress the increasingly fragmented and often discontinuous nature of careers. They also suggest the need for new theory to take account of the expanded occupational opportunities now open to women and the choices these opportunities bring with them, and to explicitly address the lives, experiences and issues of women in the workforce.

Most literature from the field of career theory is based around a dichotomy between, for instance, the bounded and the boundaryless career (Arthur and Rousseau, 1996; DeFillippi and Arthur, 1994; Sullivan, 1999) or the traditional and the protean career (Hall, 2004). Arthur's boundaryless career contrasts with the organisation-based "bounded career". In his theory, modern careers progress across multiple organisations or networks in succession, and career decisions are influenced by individual career goals rather than organisational goals. Sideways moves and temporary backwards steps are typical features of this form of career. Another feature is frequent changing between organisations. DeFillippi and Arthur (1994) describe the three factors "knowing why", "knowing how" and "knowing whom" as the competencies of the boundaryless career. The first refers to the sense of purpose that a person attaches to their career, the second to their professional expertise and the third to their network. The general definition of a boundaryless career does not make reference to individuals' psychological experience of their careers. Fondas (1996) describes the connection between boundaryless careers and women's careers. Boundaryless careers require goals to be achieved through cooperation, sharing influence, and building relationships and connections with others. According to Fondas, the traits that are needed are not those culturally ascribed to men. In the boundaryless context, managing and organising requires people to focus on helping and developing others and to teach people without dominating them. All of these are traditionally identified as feminine traits. Having traditionally had fewer experiences with the demands and constraints of the career ladder, women may feel more familiar with the demands and constraints of ladderless, boundaryless careers instead. Traditional female experience may therefore make it easier to understand the boundaryless career. Women have longstanding experience of developing careers that balance work and non-work activities, and therefore may represent this aspect of boundaryless careers. Mainiero and Sullivan (2005) write that although the concept of the boundaryless career has only become widespread in the last decade, the model has been used by women for decades out of necessity. The needs of caring for others have led women to pursue discontinuous, interrupted and even "sideways" careers. Gangrose (2005) identifies gender differences in the concept of the boundaryless career. Some empirical studies have shown that women more often experience interorganisational mobility, whereas men more often experience intra-organisational mobility. A differential impact was found on the spouses of individuals with boundaryless careers. The spouses experienced a negative impact on pay and upward mobility. This effect was the same for male and female spouses.

Unlike Arthur's concept of the boundaryless career, which looks at individual career paths, Hall's concept of the protean career concentrates on psychological aspects. By contrast with advancement-oriented career concepts, the concept of protean careers not only takes account of highs and lows and early and late development, but gives the shifts between these stages a central, defining place (Hall and Mirvis, 1996). In protean careers, individuals have a guiding commitment to particular personal career values, such as upwards mobility or a particular occupation, or to personal values that the individual defines as a part of their own identity and growth (Gangrose, 2005). A protean career is characterised by openness to new challenges and an interest in a continuous process of learning. From this perspective, a career is regarded as a "series of learning cycles" directed towards a long-term process of development. Hall (2004) defines the protean career as a career in which the person, not the organisation, is in charge, the core values are freedom and growth, and the main success criteria are subjective (perceived success) rather than objective (position, salary). The protean career is therefore primarily based on self-direction in the pursuit of perceived success in one's work. In a protean career, it is possible that a guiding value could be integrated into the multiple sub identities of women, such as wife, mother and career woman, so as to create a balanced life overall. This value could be different from values related to the traditional commitment to a single organisation.

According to Gangrose (2005), the most recent approach to conceptualising careers disconnects them from organisations altogether. In the knowledge and information technology industries, careers are becoming extra-organisational. In such careers, the individual has a contract or temporary position at one organisation after another and is essentially self-employed. The ultimate boundaryless career is developing, with professional networks and staffing agencies becoming the main extra-organisational career development vehicle for both men and women in this new career type. Like older approaches, the newer career theories described here must decide how much account needs to be taken of aspects of careers that are specific to women. Not all researchers are convinced that a separate theory for women's career behaviour is necessary. Patton et al. (2014) addresses this question in her review of existing literature and describes the ongoing debate among researchers. Fitzgerald and Weitzman (1992) have argued that the career development of women, although not fundamentally different from that of men, is demonstrably more complex due to a socialisation process that has emphasised the dichotomy of work and family.

Mainiero and Sullivan (2005) developed a theoretical model with a particular view to women's careers. Their kaleidoscope career model (KCM) provides a framework for understanding women's career choices. This model emphasises that women make holistic choices that take account of relationships, constraints and opportunities. The researchers conclude that women's family lives and working lives are interconnected. According to the model, women shift the pattern of their careers by rotating different aspects of their lives and arranging their relationships and roles in new ways. The authors state that each action is evaluated in light of the impact a decision might have on women's relationships, rather than based upon isolated actions as an independent actor. This research found that women's career decisions were made through the lens of relationalism. This means that women factor the needs of their children, spouse and parents into their careers. 41.1% of the women in the research said that they made career changes due to family demands. 42.7% followed their spouse to another geographical destination. In the kaleidoscope model, the three key parameters of authenticity, balance and challenge are active signposts throughout a woman's career. They shift according to the women's life phase. The ABC model of kaleidoscope careers demonstrates career shifts in response to the character and context of the women's lives according to the three key factors. While men tend to follow a sequential pattern, focusing first on careers and then on their families in later life, the researchers found that women tend to simultaneously focus on relationships throughout their careers, taking all three parameters into consideration. The theories that have been described here, such as the theories of boundaryless, protean and kaleidoscope career are of relevance for analysing career patterns and paths of the Chinese executive women. Later chapters will return to these theories.

Women's careers in a Chinese context

The interviewed women's careers in management took place against the background of China's economic development, making it a central external determinant. In the following, an outline is presented of the key changes that provided the framework for the interviewees' career development over time. The history of China's economy is unique, transforming from a socialist planned economy to a market system under the leadership of the Communist Party (Tagscherer, 1999). The success of such a transformation and hence also economic development depend, *inter alia*, on how ready executives are for the challenge posed by these changes. In general, it can be said that China's reforms and liberalisation have accelerated economic growth and created many jobs and career opportunities for women.

Until the start of the reform movements in the late 1970s, the Chinese economy was in effect completely isolated from the global economy. For thirty years, the state had given the Ministry of Foreign Trade a monopoly on foreign trade and foreign currency, preventing Chinese businesses and consumers from having direct contact with the global market. The year 1978 represents a historic turning point in China's economic history. It marked the start of a radical new direction for economic policy and the gradual integration of the country into the global economy (Fernandez and Underwood, 2006). Since then, China has undergone a fundamental transformation, which can be divided into three different strategic phases. The first phase, from 1979 to 1989, was characterised by the strategy of import substitution. The second phase, from the late 1980s to the Asian financial crisis of 1997/98, was typified by a hybrid strategy of import substitution and a focus on exports following the principle of dynamic protectionism. The last, completely new phase, which is still ongoing, began with the conclusion of the bilateral World Trade Organisation (WTO) negotiations between the USA and China in 1999, which paved the way for China to join the WTO (Cho, 2005). The three core principles of the new strategic direction are a socialist market economy, an opening-up to the outside world and continued leadership by the Communist Party. The goals of the reforms have gradually expanded in scope over the course of time. What started out as an attempt to repair defective areas of the previously dominant planned economy led to market-based reform elements being incorporated into the creation of a planned commodity economy and eventually, in 1992, to the decision to develop a new market system: the socialist market economy (Taubmann, 1994).

Alongside various reforms, including to the agricultural sector, collective companies and services, a policy of opening up the economy in order to accumulate resources was formulated. This policy was initially manifested in the form of four special economic zones (including Shenzhen) that were set up between 1980 and 1981. On the basis of flexible economic policy and various tax breaks, these selected regions were intended to create incentives for foreign direct investment and to promote export-focused industrial development. 14 more coastal cities, including Shanghai, followed in 1984. Inner-city economic and technical development zones were designated so as to attract additional investment and support the establishment of Chinese-international joint ventures. In the years that followed, more regions were gradually opened up to foreign economic activity and designated as zones of various types (Yeung and Shen, 2004). The distribution of economic growth has varied in different geographical regions, with high levels of development in Pacific coastal regions such as Shanghai. China's economic dynamism in the years after the reforms increased the interest of foreign direct investors. Following the reforms, new companies with foreign investment sprang up throughout the country. Foreign direct investment was initially possible in the form of contractual joint ventures/equity joint ventures, and later in the form of wholly foreign-owned enterprises (WFOEs) and mergers and acquisitions (Klenner, 2006). The first 20 joint ventures were founded in 1980; by the end of 1987, there were already 3,900 of them. Current estimates run to over 400,000 foreign companies (China Daily, 2013). The importance of foreign companies for Chinese foreign trade increased steadily in the 1990s. Between 1991 and 1999, exports by foreign companies grew by twice as much as those of domestic ones. This demonstrates the high level of dynamism that was one of the factors attracting many employees during this period (Cho, 2005). China's policy of opening up to the world formally culminated in 2001, when the People's Republic of China joined the WTO. As a condition of membership, the government agreed to a compulsory programme of further economic liberalisation measures. It also agreed to fully open up the Chinese market in accordance with WTO rules. Since then, China has been one of the world's leading recipients of foreign direct investment, taking over the top spot from the USA for the first time in 2002. China's overall economic growth continues unabated, albeit currently at a lower rate. Whereas in the first years after the economic reforms and between 2008 and 2011 real growth was in or around the double figures (9–10%), since 2011 growth has sunk to below 8% and was forecast at 6.9% in 2015 (IMF, 2015).

Careers before and after the opening of China to the global market

The labour market reforms began by targeting the so called "iron rice bowl" system (*tie fanwan*), in which jobs were guaranteed for life. The system had been enacted in the 1950s to protect agricultural workers, but was soon extended to all urban workers too. Until 1998, the state assigned employees to state-owned or collectively owned enterprises (SOEs or COEs) by quota. Since 1949, working life in China had been structured around work unit systems known as *danweis*. Workers were employed for life, and their unit was responsible for providing social security services. They were members of either SOEs or COEs, and were usually in the same unit as their parents. As well as determining the work context, as virtually closed-off systems the units also extended deep into their members' social lives. Nepotism complemented ideology as a selection and placement criterion because of the general belief that family members could be trusted and should be helped (Gangrose, 2005). One peculiarity in China was that jobs could be inherited (*dingti*). The members of the *danweis* enjoyed job security and various benefits such as guaranteed housing, health cover and childcare. It was almost impossible to switch units, and only with the approval of one's superiors (Leung, 2002). The *danwei* that a worker was assigned to was responsible for the *hukou* household registration system, which was introduced in 1958 to regulate and prevent migration within China. The aim was to ensure social order. A person needed official permission for a change of residence. In the mid-1970s, the system went so far as to prevent married partners from rural regions from moving to live with their spouses in the city. Nowadays, *hukous* can be purchased. For example, if someone wants to live in a 100 m^2 apartment in Shanghai, they can buy a *hukou* for around 200,000 USD (Tagscherer, 1999). These *hukous* are a different colour from those of Shanghai locals.

In the 1980s and 1990s, a series of regulations and measures was introduced that helped to create a labour market. They included the 1986 employment contract law (*laodong hetongzhi*), which meant that new employees could only be appointed on fixed-term contracts. In 1992, lifetime employment contracts were converted into fixed-term ones. In the early 1990s, the Chinese were given the right to choose their own jobs for the first time. To do so, they had to reach an agreement with their employer to terminate their existing contract, though to begin with not all employers were willing to do this. Where previously seniority and political loyalty had been the things that really counted on the labour market, from this point forward qualifications and motivation also became competitive factors.

With the introduction of the social market economy, the Chinese economy divided into three segments: the state sector, the collective sector (COEs) and the private sector. The state sector now comprises state-owned enterprises (SOEs), which include large industrial companies, state agencies and ministries, and party offices that are fully under government control. The number of foreign companies rose sharply in the 1990s and made up the majority of Chinese exports. They quickly became an attractive alternative to state agencies for employees. Studies show that foreign companies enjoyed a high status among executives who were open to change. According to one study, in 1993 over a million individuals from the management sector registered at job exchanges (Warner, 1996). Competition between foreign companies for qualified executives, as well as competition between foreign companies and state/private ones, has defined the labour market ever since (Bosse and Schüller, 1998). The opening-up from a planned economy to a market-based one brought with it a rise in unemployment, something that was unknown during the age of *danweis*. Women in low-skilled occupations were disproportionately affected by unemployment. The government attempted to counteract this with various projects aimed at supporting female workers. However, for women in management roles the impact of the global economy on companies and the labour market (for example, during the Asian financial crisis of 1997/98) was probably more relevant.

Existing research on the careers of female Chinese executives

Hildebrandt and Liu describe female manager's careers in comparison with U.S. female and female from other Asian countries in a research with 150 female Chinese managers that was run in 1988, at a time when the reforms just started, as following: "Chinese female managers have little job mobility, pursue careers appraised by the party...work the most hours per week and recommended the political/ideological path as the fastest route to the top". This prompts the question of whether the picture of Chinese women in management painted by Hildebrandt and Liu in 1988 still holds true over 30 years later and what effect the far-reaching transformation of the Chinese economy has had on women's careers. A look at previously published research reveals a variety of answers to this question.

China poses a difficulty for career research in that it has only been possible to speak of career development in China in the defined sense since the country's economic reforms. Prior to the reforms in the 1990s, careers in China were defined by the socialist system, with individuals being given roles by the state. With the opening of the labour market, managers started to make their own career choices and were interested in developing their human capital. Little is known about what factors may influence the career outcomes of Chinese managers. This means that the existing literature is limited by two different constraints, and as a result there is very little research on women's careers in senior management in China. Strikingly, there are a few studies that approach the topic from both sociological and psychological perspectives and only a handful of studies address selected determinants of women's careers.

One comprehensive, widely quoted study on women in management is *Women Managers in the People's Republic of China* (Korabik, 1993), which focuses on the impact of the reforms in China at that time and is based on 19 interviews with female managers and four interviews with male managers. Korabik concluded that many of the social and economic changes in China have furthered the advancement of female Chinese executives. She believed in 1993 there were still many obstacles to equality in the occupational and domestic spheres. Of the small number of studies on women's careers in China that exist, research on women's careers in China have mainly been conducted in the accountancy, consulting, IT and hotel industries. There are also studies that were carried out in state-owned companies and with female entrepreneurs. Of the eight studies presented here, five are comparative studies of men and women, and one is a cross-cultural study of women in Asia and the USA. Only two of the studies were specifically concerned with career determinants and work-family issues. There are indications that certain determinants have a greater impact on women's careers than on men's in China, just as in other countries. The studies also consider the degree to which gender-specific phenomena such as the glass ceiling can be regarded as relevant to the case of China.

Below, there now follows a selection of English-language publications from after 2000 that look at female management careers in China.

Interviews with six women in senior management form the basis of a study by Liu (2013). The study investigates factors that impede or facilitate women's advancement to senior management roles in China. Results regarding the existence of a glass ceiling were mixed. However, participants tended to confirm that one does exist. Organisational barriers that favour men and exclude women from traditional networking were believed to make advancement more difficult. Individual barriers were seen in the internalisation of cultural beliefs that the authors interpret as contributing to lower self-esteem among women. Overall, women were seen as being less ambitious about advancing into senior management. According to the respondents in this study, the main factors that enabled them to advance were strong leadership and conflict management skills and a highly interactive leadership style. Another factor was strong relationships of trust with their superiors. The women's advancement was also helped by their strong focus on learning. The final positive factor that was mentioned was the women's supportive family environments. With a focus on the IT sector, Aaltio and Huang (2007) pose a variety of questions concerning career experiences, cultural, institutional and organisational values, barriers to careers, work-life balance and the cultural concept of the ideal woman. The findings suggest that Chinese women in IT are high-achievers with a high level of ambition. Participants reported taking pleasure in career advancement and the goal of making full use of their potential. The major barriers facing women that were reported in this study were work-family conflicts within Chinese culture, which emphasises *guanxi* and close societal ties. Two career scripts were found. The "high future expectations" type wants to let people know that they can be as good as men, while the "strong belief in own capacities" type believes that talent and competence are more important than networking relations for building a career. All the women reported work-life conflicts.

Cooke and Xiao (2013) researched women's careers in accounting and consulting firms in China from an institutional, cultural, economic and gender-organisational perspective. The results were interpreted against the background of various views. The study contributes to the understanding of women's work and careers in China in a period of economic and social transformation. The aim was to collect detailed information and identify factors that influence female auditors' careers and their choices between work and family commitments. As well as finding a high proportion of women in the auditing profession, the research presented the opinions and beliefs of the male and female managers who were interviewed. According to the study participants, although they could observe almost no gender inequality in regard to type of work and salaries, they did see differences in men's and women's career paths: for example, men took on bigger projects and tasks involving travel. Cooke attributes this to the fact that traditional gender stereotypes appear to be reflected in the way that work is organised. She conjectures that this is due to Confucian values concerning gender roles, which tend to assign women to familial tasks. Another finding was that men are regarded as having higher career motivation than women. Other differences were observed in men's and women's relation to power and politics, which men were regarded as being more focused on.

Yun (2011) researched women's engineering careers in the Chinese hotel sector, where women have accounted for 60% of all positions since 1995. The study included men and women and described how women make a quick start to their careers and get promoted earlier but very rarely reach management level. The author concludes that a "glass ceiling" exists for women in the hotel industry in China. Work-family conflicts, gender stereotypes and gender-based labour division are important obstacles in women's career development in the Chinese hotel sector.

Tu et al. (2005) conducted a study with Chinese managers in southern China on the relation between demographic, human capital, motivational and organisational characteristics and objective career outcomes. This study found that women and top-level decision-makers were more likely to have high incomes. These results did not support the findings of previous research in the US by Judge et al. (1995), who found that individuals who were older, male, married and did not have an employed spouse had greater compensation. On the authors' interpretation, possible explanations for the differences in their findings with respect to Chinese managers are related to specific cultural features such as nepotism and Confucian principles such as the connectedness of people. Career satisfaction was reported to be higher in middle management functions than in line management ones, which led to the interpretation that for the Chinese study participants satisfaction may derive from sources other than work.

In their cross-cultural leadership study on women in China, India, Singapore and the US, Preus, Braun, and Knipfer (2015) investigated how women emerge as leaders in the different countries and how success factors and barriers compare. They concluded that achievement orientation, learning orientation and role models emerged as crucial success factors for the career advancement of female managers. The most salient barrier overall that came up in their study pertained to the care-giver roles of female executives. But unlike the women from other countries, only one in three of the Chinese managers in the study explicitly mentioned conflicts between their caregiver role and their managerial role. The majority put a strong emphasis on their career. With respect to leadership style, the Chinese subgroup mentioned a strong task-oriented leadership style where leaders tell subordinates what they are expected to do.

A study of state-owned companies with male and female managers (Leung, 2002) examines career strategies and coping strategies in cases of career disappointments. Interview participants described the importance of party membership for their ca-reers and the resurgence of traditional gender values in state-owned companies af-ter the reforms. Although women reported a high level of satisfaction with their careers to date, mid-career women in particular felt less satisfied. They report that they have fewer developmental opportunities, receive less support from their man-agers and experience more discrimination than men. Older women believed that they are subject to rigid control systems administered by men. The perceived rea-son for this is the network relations (*guanxi*) of older male managers, who cultivate male networks.

A comparative study of the IT sector by Justin (2008) examines the entrepreneurial orientation and venture performance of female Chinese entrepreneurs in compari-son with male ones. The main difference emerged in the willingness to take risks, which is more likely to be ascribed to female entrepreneurs. In contrast to many accounts in the literature, the female entrepreneurs' growth orientation was just as high as the men's. Also in the IT sector a Xian and Woodhams (2008) interviewed seven women and concluded that deeply embedded values encourage a rejection of planning and proactivity in women's career management.

In summary, it can be said that the findings in the literature on the complex topic of female careers are varied and sometimes contradictory. They tend to suggest that influences such as social role models, cultural values and male-dominated networks make it more difficult for Chinese women to pursue a career in manage-ment. Higher career and power orientation is also ascribed to men, though findings on this are variable and not unanimous. Work-life conflicts are reported in studies with female Chinese managers, just like almost everywhere in the world. Certain personality traits and trusting relationships with superiors are regarded as beneficial to careers. All the studies make clear that careers must be viewed against the background of a variety of determinants that increase or decrease career success. Alongside influences that affect men and women equally, there are some that appear to have a greater or different impact on women's careers. This is taken into account by the Female Career Model, which investigates the key determinants. The Shanghai Women's Career Lab focuses on how women themselves view the career determinants and their own careers, which developed in the context of the rapid changes in China.

4. The Shanghai Women's Career Lab

Methodology at a glance – Participants in the Shanghai Women's Career Lab – Recruiting for the lab – Interviewing – Shanghai: multinational research setting

Methodology at a glance

The Shanghai Women's Career Lab was a unique research project carried out in China from 2014 until 2017, in which a total of 35 women in executive positions at multinational companies participated. The results formed the basis for a doctoral thesis submitted at the University of Burgundy in France (Al-Sadik-Lowinski, 2017). All interviews, the analysis and interpretation were carried out by the author herself, i.e. there were no other interviewers. Methodologically, the empirical research took a qualitative, explorative approach that was based on the conceptual framework – the reference model presented at the beginning of the book. The research design took the form of a multiple case study, the data collection instrument comprised semi-structured, problem-centred interviews and the analysis was based on qualitative reductive content analysis following Mayring (2010). Figure 3 shows the individual elements that make up the "blueprint" for this research.

Research questions	Theory-based
Conceptual framework	Developed from theory
Research methodology	Qualitative, conceptual framework-based, empirical, explorative
Research design	Multiple case study
Data collection instrument	Semi-structured, problem-centred interviews (single person)
Sampling strategy	Theoretical sampling
Data collection process	How, where, transcription process
Analysis of data	Qualitative structured content analysis
Analysis of researcher's role	Open discussion about researcher's bias

Figure 3: Methodology of the Shanghai Women's Career Lab

The aim of the research in the Shanghai Women's Career Lab was to achieve a deeper understanding of the experiences and views of the executive women, for which a qualitative design is a good choice. Given the primary aim, namely to understand the career determinants of female Chinese executives and the connection between these determinants and the women's career development, there is a clear advantage in looking at these determinants holistically. The main focus of any qualitative research is to understand, explain, explore, discover and clarify the circumstances, feelings, perceptions, attitudes, values, beliefs and experiences of a group of people (Kumar, 2014). The emphasis is on specific cases, and the phenomenon is embedded in its context. Individual perspectives are incorporated rather than being stripped away. Influences on careers are here not understood in isolation, but as part of a complex whole. Another advantage of using a qualitative design for this research project was is the capacity to reveal complexity (Miles and Huberman, 2013). The explorative approach makes it possible to paint a picture of the different influences and their interaction with and implications for career paths. The target of the Shanghai Women's Career Lab was not to understand one, but multiple realities. The research is based on 35 multiple cases (Yin, 2014) and therefore has a strong data basis.

The total number of interviewed women (35) is big for a qualitative research but does not allow generalisations to be made. That is not necessary for the purposes of the present research for this book, since it does not aim to produce statistically representative results. However, quasi-statistical analyses have been carried out in subcategories where it seemed to make sense to do so. Hence, it appears to be possible to relate the results to wider questions about the careers of female executives in China on the basis of the theoretical sampling process presented here. Moreover, this systematising analysis is able to make a meaningful contribution to current debate and provide stimulus for theory and practice.

Participants of the Shanghai Women's Career Lab

Most of the 35 women in the research (72%) were aged between 36 and 45 at the time of the interviews. Around 14% were aged between 46 and 50. The oldest participant was 63 years old and still active despite an average female retirement age of 55 in China. Only three of the women were under 36; the youngest participant was 32 years old. The women's group in the Shanghai Women's Career Lab hence covers a wide age range.

Table 1: Age distribution in the group

Age	Number of Participants
30–35	3
36–40	10
41–45	16
46–50	5
51–60	0
>60	1

The 35 participants were recruited from 26 companies with headquarters in the USA (13 companies), Germany (7 companies) or France (6 companies). Companies from other countries were not included. In total, 12 industries are represented, meaning the study participants represent a good cross-section of very different sectors. The women were employed even in a wider range of industries during their career paths. Hence, the research group represents a good cross-section of different sectors. This means that, unlike studies such as Aaltio et al. (2007) on the situation of women in the IT-sector or Yun (2011) on the situation of women in the hotel industry, it is not the aim here to draw conclusions about the specific features of a particular industry. Rather, the aim was to have a wide spread of interviewees from across different industries.

Table 2: Industries of the companies where participants work

Industries	Number of companies
Food and Beverage	5
Luxury goods	1
Pharmaceutical	5
Household	2
Paper/Office equipment	3
Fashion	2
Automotive	2
Consulting	1
Travel	1
Material	1
Electric	2
Steel	1
Total number of companies	**26**

The women for the lab were selected according to the definition of "female senior executive", which was formulated in advance. This means that a theoretical sampling was used to ensure that the "right" women were selected in accordance with the research questions. A comparison of different studies of women in management and statistics on the frequency of women in senior management roles shows that there are different interpretations of the term "senior management", which correspond to different hierarchical levels. Some researches on women in management concentrate on the highest position in a company, that is, the CEO, Board Member, President or General Manager, as women are least represented in these roles worldwide. Other studies lack a specific definition of what precisely is meant by top or senior management. Moreover, it needs to be clarified whether multinational companies are taking a global or a local perspective, as this can result in completely different definitions of the term "senior management". In this study, a "senior executive" is defined as a role that involves a high level of decision-making power, a high level of responsibility for staff and/or budgets and belonging to a high hierarchical level within a company. The following criteria were applied to the selection:

The first selection criterion was that the Chinese interviewees were working at multinational companies at the time of the interview. All but one of the women were working at multinational companies with offices in Shanghai at the time of the interviews, but had worked all over China and overseas in the courses of their careers. The women's hierarchical position, as expressed in their job title, was the next selection criterion. For the purposes of this study and definition, "senior management" includes all local hierarchical levels from General Manager (GM) and President through to Senior Director. In the language of HR, this means level 1, level minus 1 and, in few cases that conform to the underlying definition, level minus 2. Level 1 refers to the company's highest hierarchical level, i.e. GM or equivalent. Level minus 1 generally refers to members of the company's management team and include C-level like Chief Operating Officer (COO) or Chief Financial Officer (CFO). At multinational companies, roles that could be categorised as level minus 2 include department heads with high levels of responsibility and decision-making powers. Examples in the study group include HRDs for major business units or regional directors with over a thousand total reports. Accordingly, the following hierarchical titles were deemed to meet the selection criterion for the definition of "senior executive" used in this study: President, General Manager (GM), Vice General Manager (VP-GM), Chief Financial Officer (CFO), Chief Operating Officer (COO), Vice-President (VP), Senior Director, Director. There is a high number of national HRDs among the interviewees, making up the largest group of job titles. This reflects the fact that most HRD posts in China are held by women. In 2013, for example, 61% of Chinese HRDs were women (Thornton, 2013). Grant Thornton also estimates that 81% of Chinese CFOs are women. This was not reflected in the group, which only included three CFOs. Six of the women hold GM, President or Vice-President posts, and three have responsibility for Asia in their departments. The interviewees included both women with purely local responsibilities and ones with responsibility for the whole of Asia.

Table 3: Titles of participants in recent position

Title in recent position	Number of participants
Vice-GM	1
President	2
GM	4
VP	6
Regional CAO	1
CFO Asia	1
CFO	2
Asia Director	1
Regional Sales Director	1
Senior Director	1
National HRD	10
Director	5
Total:	**35**

As a third criterion, the women were also asked about their reporting lines. The aim of this question was to ascertain which hierarchical level their job title corresponded to (since every company has different classifications) and how close the women were to the company's head management. The study participants needed either to be at the head of the organisation, to be part of the head management team themselves, to be reporting directly to head management or, for those with responsibility for the Asia region, to be reporting to corresponding management levels at the company's head office. The fourth sampling criterion comprised the following points: the scope of decision-making power, the degree of influence on company strategy, personal responsibility, budget responsibility and number of staff. This list of criteria primarily served to assess whether the title of "director" sufficed for inclusion in the study group even where an individual was not part of a company's head management team.

All but three of the interviewees had staff reporting directly to them at the time of the interview. The three women without any direct reports have strategic roles, are members of the head management team and had previously had staff reporting to them directly on multiple occasions over the course of their career. In response to the question about direct reports, 17 women said that they are currently directly responsible for 4–8 staff, while nine are directly responsible for 9–14. These figures correspond to the number of direct reports that would normally be expected of an executive in a major company. When asked about the overall number of staff they were responsible for, that is, not just direct reports but also the levels below, answers ranged up to 8,000 (as well as "not sure"). During their careers, the women had been responsible for varying numbers of staff, sometimes more than in their current role. Examples included roles in sales or training with huge numbers of employees.

The precise selection process, in line with a theoretical sampling approach, made it possible to form a research group for the Shanghai Women's Career Lab that satisfies the definition of "senior executive" given above.

Recruiting for the Shanghai Career Lab

All participants for the Shanghai Women's Career Lab were recruited via professional contacts made by the author in the course of her work as executive coach and management trainer. Following the snowball principle, the participants in turn recommended other women. Other contacts came via a board member at the German Chamber of Commerce in Shanghai, the owner of China's largest executive coaching provider (MindSpan) and other professional networks. The success of the recruitment efforts can be attributed to several factors. One factor of definite importance was that the author was trusted by people she had met through her work as a coach in China, which meant that they were willing to provide recommendations. Another related factor is the high quality of the recommendations made by people with good connections in Shanghai's multinational companies. These factors made it easier to establish contact and develop trust. A final, crucial factor was the Chinese women's solidarity, which made the large number of interviews possible. The original aim was 15–20 interviews, but it was actually possible to carry out 35 interviews during the scheduled period. The author's work as an executive coach and her status as a doctoral candidate made it easier to build up trust during the recruitment process and in the critical phase at the start of the interviews. Personality and "chemistry" certainly also played a role. The fact that a woman with a corporate background was leading the research project and carrying out the interviews also made it easier to establish contact.

Interviewing in the Shanghai Career Lab

The interviews were characterised by open, flexible, personal communication, and usually took place at the offices of the companies where the women work. All the interview, which took place in Shanghai between October and December 2014, were approx. 2.5 hours long and were transcribed immediately afterwards. No third parties were present; if they had been, this would have influenced the results due to the need for strict confidentiality. The interviews were mostly conducted in English, except for five that were held in German at the request of the women. By far the language skills of these women were sufficient for the requirements of the interview. All participants had a very high level (very good or fluent) in their chosen language. It was deliberately decided not to conduct interviews in Chinese, since this would have necessitated the use of an interpreter, which might have affected the trust that was established over the course of the interview. The interviews were structured around a script in the form of a list of topics (problem-centred interviews). The script was based on the conceptual framework, the model presented at the beginning of the book, as this represents a "provisional explanatory model" (Becker, 1993) containing assumptions and suppositions about determinants and interactions relevant to motivations and behaviour that were drawn from the literature, prior interviews and the author's personal experiences. Hence, the interviews were conducted in a structured, systematic way while simultaneously enabling maximum flexibility to allow scope for other issues that were not considered in advance. Figure 4 shows the main points of the interview script.

Interview script:

Background information: study aims, confidentiality, content agreement

1. **Statistics:** *age, marital status, children, highest academic degree, languages, overseas experience*
2. **Family background:** *own childhood, parents occupation*

3. **Career development:** *description of main career stages, from career entry to the present day(number of companies, positions, planned and unplanned steps)*

4. **Individual influences on career development**

• Motivation for reaching a senior management position (reward, role of status, definition of success, work–life balance, downsides to career)
• Major strengths and capabilities (leadership style, power orientation, dealing with competition, vision and innovation, self-confidence)
• Experiences of conflicts during career

5. **External influences on career**

•Family influences (description of upbringing, support for career from family/partner, influence of motherhood on career)
• Experiences of mentoring and networking
• Company type: multinational company (Why? Alternatives, impact of cultural differences)
• Historical/cultural and gender-related influences (opinions about published figures,* influence of Confucian beliefs on women's careers, personal beliefs about gender equality,** opinion about glass ceiling)

5. **Hopes for own professional future** *(economic future of China and impact on women's careers)*

6. **Closing statement:** *please complete the sentence "In the future, female Chinese executives will ... "*

Initial question: data from 2013 (Grant Thornton) shows that 51% of positions in senior management in China are held by women. The global average is 24%. How would you explain this?
*** Initial question: on a scale of 1 to 10, how do you rate gender equality in China? (1 = not equal at all, 10 = fully equal)*

Figure 4: Interview script

Individual interviews were carried out with the participants, which focused both on their experiences and attitudes, and their perceptions and interpretations of these experiences. It was possible to go into unexpected information in more depth and enquire into any critical points that came up in the course of the interviews. Since the order that the topics were discussed in depended to some extent on each individual's answers, not every interview took the same course. Moreover, new issues that came up during the interviews were spontaneously incorporated in an appropriate manner, provided that they seemed relevant to the context of the study. This means that the script was open to being modified, revised and developed like suggested by Lamnek (1995).

The questioning technique used in interviews was very important. The kind of knowledge produced in the interview depends to a considerable extent on the wording of the questions and the ability to sense the immediate meaning of an answer, and the horizon of possible meanings that is opened up, is decisive. This requires a knowledge of and interest in the research topic and the human interaction of the interview as well as a familiarity with modes of questioning (Kvale, 2007). The interviews conducted for this research benefited from the authors experience as an executive and the contextual understanding resulting from this experience. They also profited in particular from her experience as a coach and many years of practising questioning techniques.

Shanghai – multinational research setting

Shanghai is of particular significance for the Female Career Lab, as all but one of the participants were working there at the time of the interviews, and some of the women also grew up there. Through her access to an extensive executive network, especially in Shanghai, the author was able to achieve something that many researchers in China are unable to and recruit a significant number of female senior executives for interviews – indeed, she managed to recruit even more than was originally planned. Today, Shanghai is China's leading business hub due to its economic performance, infrastructure and advanced industrialisation. To understand better the setting of the Shanghai Women's Career Lab, it is helpful to know more about Shanghai's history.

The mega city started out as a small fishing and trading settlement named Hudu and developed into one of the world's biggest trading ports after the signing of the Treaty of Nanking in 1842. By 1864 Shanghai was China's biggest port. By the early 20th century, over 50% of all China's foreign companies were already based in the city. Shanghai was divided into three parts for almost 100 years: the Chinese territory, the French Concession and the international district (the latter settled by the USA and Britain). Due to its key national importance for domestic supply, Shanghai was not chosen as one of the first free trade zones in 1980. Only the founding of the Pudong zone in 1990 set the course for Shanghai to enter the competitive international market, where it has achieved sustained success. The government developed the objective of expanding the city into one of the leading international commercial and financial centres in the Asia-Pacific region. The city's geo strategically favourable position relative to neighbouring countries and its access to a plentiful workforce from the Yangtze Delta, as well as factors such as the large number of scientists, engineers and skilled workers, make it an especially attractive business location. Shanghai has had a modern school system ever since 1905, which replaced the traditional Confucian education system. Since 1980, it has been compulsory for everyone to complete nine years of education (Nyaw, 1996). By 1949, Shanghai already had 41 universities (around 20% of China's total). By 2005, it had 60 universities, including CEIBS, which in 2007 was listed at number 11 on a global ranking of business schools. It also had over 815 research and development institutions (Staiger and Brunhild, 2006).Foreign direct investment rose rapidly from 1.259 billion USD in 1992 to over 6.850 billion USD in 2005 (Wei, and Leung, 2005). The top investors were Japanese companies, followed by investors from Hong Kong, Germany, America and other nations, which established ties with the local economy. By the end of 1997, over 230 of the world's 500 largest companies had offices in Shanghai; by 2003, this figure had risen to over 300. In 2016, more than 836,000 foreign companies had offices in Shanghai, with over 573 choosing Shanghai for their regional head office. This clearly illustrates Shanghai's economic importance for China and the city's high level of economic internationalisation. The city offers a combination of international cosmopolitan business culture and local Chinese business culture, and is therefore an interesting location to study women's careers in management. In particular, it is an ideal research setting to find out how women rise into top management positions in a multinational environment. Although the research lab was confined to women who were working in Shanghai at the time of the interviews, the women's career paths spanned various different Chinese cities, including some in the north of the country.

5. Results from the Shanghai Women's Career Lab: How environment influences women's careers

Cultural and social context of women's careers in China – Confucian values and their importance for Chinese women's careers – The image of female executives in China – Equal or unequal? The situation of female Chinese executives – Proportion of women in senior management roles – Is there a glass ceiling phenomenon in China? – The influence of social origin, family situation and motherhood – The role of mentoring, networking and guanxi

In the following sections, the results of the Shanghai Women's Career Lab are presented. However, it is first necessary to give general introduction to existing findings on each of the determinants included in the model. Figure 5 in the appendix presents an overview of all cited studies. Where it has been possible to draw China-specific findings on the determinants from the literature, direct reference is made to these findings. However, some of the determinants have only been studied in China to a limited degree or not at all. In these cases, the outline restricts itself to general findings from Western research. The results are supported by original quotations from the interviewees, which for reasons of confidentiality have been anonymised.

Cultural and social context of female careers in China – Confucian values and their importance for Chinese women's careers

Almost all published studies on the situation of women in China, both those that are general in nature and those that specifically concern the careers of women in management, make reference to the influence of history and culture on Chinese society. The factor that many publications link most closely to Chinese culture and the situation of women is the teachings of Confucius. In publications on women in management, Confucian traditions are interpreted from gender-based or feminist perspectives. More extensive discussion of the impact of traditional values on present-day management practices can be found in literature on careers and management. Both perspectives are presented in the following, since both influences appear relevant to women in management.

Discussions and interpretations of Confucian teachings and their influence on equal opportunities for women in China vary greatly. The topic is very complex. For thousands of years, a patriarchal social order was maintained in China in accordance with Confucian values and traditions. However, the country's cultural legacy is a mixture of four systems: the teachings of Lao Tse, Buddhist philosophies, legalist traditions and Confucian values (Gangrose, 2007). According to Wegmann and Ruviditsch (2015) only the Confucianism has conserved a notable influence in China. Since the literature primarily links the role and situation of women in China to the influence of Confucius, this will be the focus of the subsequent discussion to the exclusion of the other influences.

Confucianism refers to the philosophical and religious tradition in China that originated with Confucius (551–479 BC) and his teachings, and was subsequently interpreted and developed by various schools and disciples. The core of the teachings is a model of social relationships that defines values and rituals for the Chinese family and is intended to emanate from the family sphere to society as a whole.

The "filial piety" philosophy, as it is known, is generally interpreted as stating that women are subordinate to men, just as the young are subordinate to the old and the citizen to the sovereign. These three obedience rules helped maintain the patriarchal social order in China for thousands of years. The prominent Han Confucian master, Dong Zongshu, maintained that between the two principles that govern the universe, "the *yang* is superior and *yin* is inferior ... the husband is *yang* ... and the wife is *yin*" (Li, C., 2000). Generally, these rankings are interpreted as placing the husband hierarchically above the wife. The *Analects*, a collection of writings by Confucius' followers, recount his conversations with his students. They were recorded for the first time around 600 years after Confucius' death and then repeatedly revised and reinterpreted. Some interpretations describe women as useless or as a negative influence on a man's household at various points (Li, Y., 2000).

Li, C. (2000) wrote a highly detailed study on "Confucianism and feminist concerns" in which she observes that, in general, all authors agree that extreme practices based on Confucian values historically led to the oppression of women in China. Interpretations of Confucius resulted in oppressive discrimination against women. Extreme practices such as the buying and selling of women, violence against women and killing female infants were justified against the background of Confucian teachings. The practice of foot binding, which was banned in 1902 but continued for a long time afterwards, was widespread in China. Other historical examples include the way that widows were treated in the country (Li, C., 2000). Li further argues that early Confucians (such as Mencius) were less supportive than later ones of interpretations of the teachings that degraded women. Since the 20th century, most contemporary proponents of Confucian teachings have once again been supportive of equal rights for women, but there is relatively little published research in this area. This shows that interpretations of Confucius' teachings regarding the role of women have changed time and again over the course of history.

Many Western interpretations operate with stereotypes derived from the teachings and paint a picture of universally oppressed Chinese women as victims without rights. In the literature, the influence of Confucian values on women's careers is generally not the main focus of existing studies on the situation of Chinese women but rather serves as an interpretative framework, and accordingly it often remains a matter of interpretation too. Almost all Western gender studies research, as well as studies originating in China, interpret this tradition as having a mainly negative influence on women in general, and conclude on this basis that it impacts negatively on the situation of Chinese women in management.

Various researchers (Frank, 2001; Liu, 2013; Korabik, 1993; Yung, 2011) describe the negative effects of the influence of Confucian traditions on female executives in their work. Two main strands can be distinguished, which will be addressed in greater detail in later sections of this study. Firstly, the researchers describe negative social stereotypes regarding the suitability of women for senior management, which they trace back to Confucian traditions. Secondly, they describe how cultural socialisation impacts negatively on women's self-esteem (Liu, 2013; Cooke and Xiao, 2013) and hence their effectiveness. The researchers identify negative attitudes towards female managers as being especially prominent in rural regions, where Confucian value systems remain dominant to this day. In consequence, women are prevented from obtaining top roles in these regions. Du (2014) focused a research on the question how Confucianism and gender diversity are related. The findings suggest that the proportion of women directors in boardrooms is significant lower for firms surrounded by a strong Confucian atmosphere.

Blanchard presents a different perspective. Instead of seeing women in China as a homogeneous group that can all be described in the same way, she argues for a more nuanced account (Blanchard and Warnecke, 2010). Several other authors have followed this call for greater nuance. Lin (1939) describes how, in reality, Chinese women were not historically oppressed by men. Women had a prominent position of power within the family. According to Ko (1994), women had a role as household managers that gave them many opportunities to actively influence the fate of their family. The strong role of mothers-in-law and various examples of female Chinese rulers such as Ci Xi, Lü Zhi and Wu Zetian show a different picture of Chinese women – one which contrasts with the many historical accounts that present Chinese women exclusively as victims. Mann (1997) goes one step further and holds stereotyped studies responsible for presenting Chinese women as oppressed victims of a traditional culture who can only be liberated by means of Western values and education. Woo (1998)describes two fundamental values of Confucian teachings that can also be found in feminism – equal opportunities to learn, and an open-minded, flexible attitude to life. Confucians and feminists share a „strong caring orientation ... [both] focus on the tender aspect of human relatedness ... [both] advocate the conception of human beings as socially connected individuals, not as disinterested, separate individuals ... both ethics emphasize situational and moral judgment as well as character-building, instead of rule-following" (Li, C., 2000).

Aside from gender-based perspectives, various authors have published works concentrating on the relevance of Confucius for present-day management practices and values, without specifically addressing women's issues. Hall (1976) describes three key Confucian values that are ubiquitous in Chinese business life. The three key values comprise obligation-based relationships, continuous learning and a focus on practical worldly existence, rather than the spiritual realm. Four of the five relationship types that remain of great relevance to management practices involve a superior-subordinate status, where each party has duties comparable to those in a benevolent parent-child relationship. Relationships between men and women also fall under this pattern. These relationships can be viewed against the background of coaching or mentoring practices, which are firmly anchored in Chinese management practices. The Boundaryless Career (Arthur and Rousseau, 2001) describes how Chinese executives can improve or damage their reputation (lose face) by following Confucian principles. In business life, the influence of nepotism (favouritism of relatives), the importance of networks and the value of lifelong learning are closely linked to Confucian traditions (Arthur and Rousseau, 2001). Li (2013) describes Chinese traditional thinking and the core values derived from it. According to Li's work, there are three features of ancient Chinese thinking: holistic and naive thinking, fuzzy and processual thinking and indirect and long-term thinking. These features manifest, according to Li, in terms of five core values which have an impact on management practices in China regardless of gender. The core values are harmony (*he*); the doctrine of the mean (*zhongdong*); hierarchy, seniority and loyalty (*zhong*); personal connection and relationships (*guanxi* and *renqing*); and face (*mianzi* and *lian*).

The five values are briefly explained below, as they are an important element of the cultural influences on management in China. A more precise understanding of the background to these values would require a more in-depth exploration of their cultural origins. Such explorations are undertaken later in this study at points where relevant to the results. *He* is a highly desirable state and refers both to the harmony between human beings and nature and the harmony within human society. This Chinese concept is based on traditional holistic thinking around a core that is tightly bound by the ethical principles of both vertical (social hierarchy) and horizontal (*guanxi* and *face*) relationships. Managers are expected to give up individual needs in favour of group needs when the two conflict. *Zhongyong* refers to the fundamental Confucian ideal of balance, moderation and appropriateness. The principle of *zhongyong* significantly affects Chinese management styles, for example forms of communication and negotiation, relationships between bosses and managers and among employees, and leadership styles. The ideal of *zhongyong* originated from traditional "fuzzy thinking" (Li, 2013) which advocates a harmonious and balanced relationship between superiors and subordinates. It also recommends that managers adopt a relatively mild, lenient and gentle leadership style and a soft and conflict-free communication and negotiation style. Hierarchy, showing respect to older people and loyalty are important values in Chinese organisations. Superiors are expected to treat subordinates well and subordinates are expected to be loyal to their supervisor in return. Traditionally, Chinese employees show respect for hierarchy and accept the hierarchical nature of the superior-subordinate relationship. Trust and commitment play a key role in interpersonal relationships in China, and a system of reciprocal obligations known as *guanxi* is the Chinese term for a system of reciprocal obligations, with *guan* standing for door or gate while *xi* means to tie up in relationships (Wegmann et al. 2015). This system is key to building long-term relationships in society and management circles on the basis of customs and social norms. In management, *guanxi* can play a central role in various business situations and in dealing with organisational problems. The later section on "Networking" looks at the importance of *guanxi* in greater depth. Saving or making *face* is the last of the five traditional Chinese core values which translate into management practices. *Mianzi*, the social face, represents prestige or reputation and can be obtained through social status. *Lian*, the moral face, stands for the respect of the group for an individual with a good reputation. "In Confucian society, face is both a goal for achieving noble personhood and a means for ensuring the harmony of interpersonal relationships" (Li, 2013). For management practices, this value means that direct criticism is seen as damaging, and therefore conflict resolution rather than confrontational styles can be observed.

The question of whether and, above all, to what extent women in management are influenced by Confucian values nowadays cannot be clearly answered on the basis of the literature. Two general tendencies can be identified in the discussion: the dominant image of women who are oppressed by Confucianism, and feminist interpretations that attempt to paint a more complex picture that goes beyond stereotypes. It has also been shown that traditional values represent the basis for Chinese management practices. These values are not gender-specific and also apply to female executives.

How female Chinese executives view the influence of Confucian values on their career paths

As was described earlier most researchers believe that historical and cultural factors continue to be important external determinants of female managers' careers in China. They claim that Confucian culture has an impact on Chinese women's career prospects (Frank, 2001; Liu, 2013; Korabik, 1993; Yun, 2011). The vast majority of accounts describe the impact as being generally negative. The researchers argue that cultural values derived from Confucian teachings continue to have a directly negative or inhibiting effect on women's careers. As has been shown, opinion is divided on whether or not a state of equal opportunities has really been achieved in Chinese management in recent times. Many authors point out persisting inequalities (Frank, 2001; Liu, 2013; Korabik, 1993; Yun, 2011). Only a few authors paint a more positive picture regarding Confucian values (Blanchard et al., 2010; Ko, 1994; Woo, 1998) or emphasise the importance of traditional values for present-day Chinese management practices independently of the gender debate (Li, 2013; Arthur and Rousseau, 2001).

The interviewed women were therefore asked whether, based on their own experiences, they think traditional Confucian values have influenced their own career paths. When asked about the influence of Confucian values on their career development, a large majority of the female managers interviewed were in agreement: they do not see any direct connection between their own careers and Confucian values, and do not believe these values have had any negative influence on their personal career development. "Not relevant for my career" was the most frequent spontaneous response to this question. Further discussion of the topic revealed the women's knowledge of old Confucian values and yielded various explanations for why the women regard them as irrelevant to their own careers. These explanations can be summarised into five different lines of argument.

1. That's all in the past now

According to this line of argument, the portion of the old traditions relating to the role of women has been superseded by recent political developments in the country towards equal treatment of women. The Cultural Revolution is seen as a break with these traditions. According to this view, the image of women has fundamentally changed since then, with the massive scale of action in the period of the Cultural Revolution resulting in rapid changes in how women are seen. These changes are unanimously seen as positive. Responses such as "China, the most liberated country in the world" provide a clear counter to the more pessimistic assessment found in the literature regarding the situation in China for women in general and female managers in particular.

> M., CFO: "This is a very, very small portion of the social structure which came from very early China. But obviously, due to the Cultural Revolution China, is the most liberated country in the world, maybe the Cultural Revolution was bad, but one good thing it has done is to liberate the ladies' brain. They basically destroyed all the old culture including the old Confucian stuff. So I never had even anything in my brain about this."[1]

> S., CFO: "During the period of President Mao we had the Revolution. The Cultural Revolution. In fact thanks to that Confucius, all the theories of Confucius have been considered as bad during that period. So all those people, my parents' generation had been brainwashed already. I think that in their head it is not more like that. The men shouldn't be higher than a woman. Some way the Revolution helped to balance more the power of the men and the women."

The women are hence in agreement with the accounts from the literature that describe the advances in equality between men and women that have been achieved as a result of policies diametrically opposed to Confucian traditions that have been enacted in China since 1949. They see these policies as having more influence on their careers than the subset of Confucian traditions that are claimed to have resulted in Chinese women historically having a lower status. However, when giving

---

[1] The following interview quotes are given with the interviewees' initials (in line with their wishes as indicated in their consent statements) as well as their job title at the time of the interview and can be found in the interview transcripts.

their personal assessments of the influence of Confucian values on careers, the women mentioned regional differences within China. In the view of the interviewed women, old and discriminatory interpretations of Confucius are no longer relevant in big cities, especially Shanghai, but they may still be influential in the north of the country and in rural regions. This is in line with Wegmann et al. (2015) who point of the regional differences in China with its large territories.

S., HRD: "Confucius is not special for gender. He's philosopher of behaviour. Maybe he will say female should do thing more inside of house. Men should do things outside the house. But for our generation we don't think so. Not that kind of difference for the career. Maybe there's a connection. Because it's a traditional saying and traditional philosophy still have influence but I would say not in big cities – Shanghai, Beijing, and Guangzhou. But for the north region more small cities there will be more influence about the history."

2. Confucius was wrong about the role of women

Another subgroup among the study participants argued that Confucius' view that women have a subordinate role is fundamentally wrong. This echoes Lin (1939) and Ko (1994), who argue against conventional interpretations from a feminist perspective and show that women traditionally had a dominant status, especially in the family. The women in the study group believe that interpretations of Confucius according to which women are generally subordinate to men would entail a division of society into men who work and women who stay at home. The women are critical of the housewife model, where women only work at home and are financially dependent on their partners. They tend to view women who choose this path negatively. It does not conform to their image of society or their socialisation.

Q., GM: "Misunderstanding is in the original Confucius idea; the female is in an inferior position. And I think that the government had played deliberate role in removing these old values and concepts to say that it's wrong. Female and male are equal. Female should also work and be independent. So it's kind of a bit eliminated this idea of inferiority. But for sure not completely. I think it's more in the city. But for example in the countryside because of the agricultural environment definitely still lots of issues for putting female inferior. But I think in the city it's quite successful."

Nonetheless, two of the interviewees observed that there has recently been a trend that could allow the old values to come creeping back. They gave the example of a recent discussion about raising children; one side of the debate takes the view that, for the sake of their children, it is better for women to be housewives.

3. Gender discrimination is a global phenomenon

The women who take this view regard the challenges that women face in their careers as a global problem, not one specific to China. They deny the connection to Confucius and note that every country has ancient traditions that have resulted in discrimination against women. This line of argument views Western interpretations of the negative influence of Confucius as a possible attack on China's image, which the women reject. The interviewees see the Chinese context as being just like that of the USA or Europe, with certain country-specific differences, and do not believe the causes of challenges for women in management are linked to Confucian traditions in particular. This is consonant with the conclusions of Mann (1997), who regards stereotypes in research as responsible for presenting Chinese women as victims of old traditions.

> G., Director Customer Service: "Well, I would not contribute that to Confucius. I would say it's just a general gender positions all over the world. It's just general. It's just happening everywhere. It's not very specific or very overwhelming in China that Confucius playing a role there. Confucius is only one of the indicators of that general thinking about women and men stuff. But it actually exists. It's just that we happen to have a thing called Confucius in China. Maybe you don't have an equivalent thing in Germany or the U.S., but that doesn't mean that it does not exist."

4. Confucius is interpreted incorrectly

Some of the interviewees believe that the core of Confucian traditions is made up of different, very positive values that apply to men and women in equal measure. They take these positive values as points of reference for their own lives and management styles. A particular emphasis is placed on balance, striving for harmony, respect for older people and superiors, and hard work. These women interpret Confucian values as generally positive and as unconnected to any debate about gender. For them, the values are about achieving balance, harmony and respect. They believe that both men and women strive equally to uphold these values, and view them positively as a guiding model.

> C., HRD: "That not only impacts female, but also impacts being humble, respect authority, work hard, it's thousands of years of culture that influences our thinking. More general. Not specifically related to females."

The explanatory approach offered by the women has parallels in the literature. As described earlier, Arthur and Rousseau (2001) and Hall (1976) show the connection between Chinese business values and cultural Confucian values. Three core values occupy a central place: obligation-based relationships, continuous learning and a focus on practical worldly existence. A capacity and a willingness to learn, the cultivation of relationships with people, the development of moral maturity and a general caring orientation are regarded as positive aspects of Confucian values. In this respect, the study participants' responses tally with the kinds of interpretations of the relevance of Confucian values for Chinese management offered by Arthur et al. and Hall. Four of the five types of relationship described by Confucius involve superior-subordinate statuses. This pertains not just to relationships between men and women, but also governs the nature of the relationship between bosses and employees. Both parties have clear tasks, roles and positive duties towards each other. In this connection, the women also reflected on the strengths and potential disadvantages that emerge from these core values, for example the striving for harmony and respect for "face" described by Li (2013) . It became clear that the women see Confucian traditions as being more relevant to general management practices and less so to the specific context of gender.

> *J., CAO: "One of the ... most important things is to have the harmony. This you learned also from our government. We would like to have a harmonize society which is same, like don't be too sharp. Then this of course will have a huge influence. For example why we are not really brave enough to say what we want. If you want something else then another person then there is no harmony. The other thing is that the majority of Chinese, not only women, men are the same, are not really brave enough or not willing to face the conflict directly if there is an issue. Whatever you are doing I don't agree. But I can't say that to you because then it would create conflict then I will ... talk to you but I don't really say the problem, but I try to build kind of relation. Can we go to dinner? Have a chat? We were thinking hopefully we can build a little bit private relationship then you give me face, I give you face. Then I can sort the conflict. They don't really go directly to confront this kind of thing."*

Other women described along similar lines how the teachings impart positive values for conduct in companies, and how female managers in particular follow these values. They said that they themselves specifically augment these capacities with intercultural skills so that they can communicate well with people from other countries and develop an understanding for other business cultures and foreign management practices. Hence, what is relevant for the women is the connection between their own management practices, which bear a strong Confucian imprint, and Western ones. The women believe that the subjugation of women to men is either an aspect of Confucian traditions that is no longer applicable today or that it only pertains to achieving harmony within the family, and hence has no observable effect (discriminatory or otherwise) in the management context. They assign Confucian values to the family sphere and believe that these values strengthen women's role within the family. This view corresponds to the accounts of Ko (1994), Lin (1939) and other feminist theorists.

5. Co-existence in society

Another view was put forward by just one interviewee, who explained how the old Confucian values co-exist in society with Communist values of equality between men and women. According to this view, at its core Chinese society remains very male-dominated and men are given a stronger role, but at the same time the Cultural Revolution has anchored an ideal of equality in society that has encouraged women to be just as active in their careers as men. As a result, so the argument goes, nowadays many women compete as equals. The study participant believes that Confucian values continue to influence companies too, and speaks of a subliminal conflict. She claimed that both tendencies co-exist in society despite being exact opposites. Wegmann et al. (2015) describes this co-existence in the context of Chinese managers in general who combine traditional values and more pragmatic approaches in a paradoxal way.

> H., VP: "I think it coexists. Deep down, the fundamental society links to the Confucius, the Chinese traditions. That's still very male-dominated. But I think the ironic thing is the Communist influence on the culture is the Communism has broad perfect gender equality. It encourages women in the Revolution to be as active as men. I think that's the influence from the Communist."

The women are aware that many researchers view Confucian values as having a mainly negative impact on women's careers. Li (2000) concludes her study by saying that "works cannot be said to have told the whole story about Chinese women". Like Blanchard and Warnecke (2010), her work describes the influence of Confucian culture on Chinese women and formulates various perspectives on the question of whether Chinese women are more oppressed by patriarchal structures than women in other countries. Most of the women who participated in the study reported that they have not experienced any negative consequences of interpretations of Confucian teachings. They believe the portion of the teachings that relates to the role of women tends to be confined to the past. They described Confucian values as offering generally positive models of conduct for society as a whole. They also reported the mostly positive influence that the traditions have had on their leadership styles. They regard it as a challenge to combine their Confucian-influenced management styles with different, Western management styles.

One finding of the Shanghai Women's Career Lab is that most of the women who were interviewed do not believe that Confucian traditions have any discriminatory or negative effects on their careers nowadays, though regional differences are ascribed to northern China. The traditions are seen as relevant to management practices, since they influence Chinese management styles in a gender-neutral way. According to some of the women, at multinational companies these practices need to be adapted to Western practices on a case-by-case basis depending on the respective context.

Think manager – think male? The image of female executives in China

As well as the cultural and political context, there is also the question of the general social acceptance of women in senior management in China. A number of researchers from across the world have studied the image of female executives, with some studies looking specifically at China. Gender stereotypes represent beliefs about the psychological traits that are characteristic of members of each sex. According to stereotype, "masculine" traits such as independence, aggression and dominance are more pronounced in men, while women have "feminine" traits such as being nice, tactful and sensitive to the feelings of others. These gender stereotypes have been studied and remain constant over time. Gender roles describe the behaviour ascribed to, and felt to be appropriate for, each gender. According to these stereotypes, the man's role is to work and the woman's place is at home with the family (Powell, 2011). The level of gender egalitarianism, the extent to which differences in gender roles have been minimised and the degree of support for equal rights vary between cultures (Powell, Francesco, and Ling, 2009). There are a variety of findings on China in the literature with regard to these issues; these findings span the full range of possibilities and include some contradictory results. Educated women do not see themselves as being "the moon reflecting the sunlight" (De Mente, 1999), that is to say as serving a supportive role for men, but rather as being "half the sky", that is to say as having an equal and contributing role. The fact that women continue to be less represented in senior management than men is often ascribed to cultural stereotypes. The connection between Confucian traditions and associated values is also repeatedly mentioned in the literature in relation to the image of female executives. A saying by a Confucian master, "It is a virtue if a woman doesn't have ability", is frequently cited in this connection.

In her research on Chinese students' perceptions of women in management, Frank (2001) concludes that women tend to be less accepted as they move up the management hierarchy. The female participants themselves said that they were more likely to distrust fellow women in senior management roles and preferred male superiors. Frank concluded her research with Chinese students by stating that "it will not be easier for Chinese women to succeed than for US women". In other studies, female executives are characterised as unfair, hard to work with and narrow-minded (Rajerison, 1996). Rajshekhar, Scherer, Sanchez et al (2011) found in their research with students in the US, Chile and China that Chinese men and women displayed the lowest perception of women as managers. Also Sincoff, Owen and Coleman (2009) describe that women were perceived less favourable by Chinese and US male. Chinese women as well as U.S. female were less negative in their perceptions. Ng and Pine's research (2003) in the hotel sector shows the same trend. This picture is consonant with the results of studies from the USA, which show that American women prefer male superiors. Overall, women managers were rated less highly and regarded as less competent, less active, slower, weaker, more subordinate and acquiescent. Frank interprets Chinese women as having a subliminal feeling of inferiority, which results in them judging their fellow women more harshly. According to Frank, their socialisation promotes insecurity and shyness. Korabik (1993) already covered this aspect in detail, writing that the social perception that "men are more able" expresses women's negative sense of their own effectiveness. She too notes that Chinese women internalise cultural perspectives that view women as inferior and that this could have an effect on their motivation to be successful in management. However, according to Judd (1990) the prominence of negative attitudes towards female executives tends to be regionally confined to rural areas. At the same time, female managers were rated as more people-oriented: friendlier, gentler, more lenient and more team-focused overall. This is consonant with many other studies, which show that female managers are more supportive, emotionally open and sensitive than men (Patterson, 1997). Gunkel, Lusk, Wolff et al. (2007) did not confirm stereotypical expectations of women and men with respect to work-related factors in their research.

Probably the best-known studies on the image of female executives are those by Schein (2007, 1996). She investigated the phenomenon she termed "Think manager – think male" over a period of several years, beginning in 1970. The early studies indicate that one cause of difficulties for women in management is gender stereotypes about managerial roles. According to the studies, US men regarded women in the corporate environment as generally less qualified. The characteristics required for success in management were ascribed to men. Despite having a different hypothesis, another study on leader stereotypes by Powell and Butterfield (1989) reached the same result. A good manager was described in terms of predominantly masculine traits. Schein (1996, 2007) found that middle managers in China are more likely than those in other nations to believe that successful managers possess "those characteristics, attitudes and temperaments more commonly ascribed to men". Organisational definitions of competence and leadership are still predicated on traits stereotypically associated with men – tough, aggressive, decisive. Schein's research found that Chinese men and women rate the image of female managers more negatively than participants from other nations. Other research shows that, by contrast, women ascribe the traits required by managers to both genders (Brenner, Tomkiewicz, and Schein, 1989; Schein, 1989; Doge, Gilroy, and Fenzel, 1995). Studies with management students also found that women see both genders as equal with respect to the skills and traits needed to work successfully in management. International comparisons show that it is mainly Chinese men who equate male attributes with management skills. Chinese women, by contrast, see a connection between female traits and the prerequisites for achieving success in management (Schein, 1994). So are leadership stereotypes still relevant to women's management careers? Eagly (2007) answers this question with a resounding yes. Female executives still need to deal with an image of their role that sees it as incompatible with female traits. This image places them at a disadvantage: if they have more feminine attributes, they suffer from not living up to this managerial role model; if they compete with men by having more masculine attributes, they suffer instead from not living up to the female gender role.

According to a survey of 940 men and women from Shanghai, Beijing and Guangzhou published in *China Daily* (China Daily, 2001), the new, current conception of the ideal woman in China is that of the "high-flying professional" who is simultaneously a successful family mother. In the survey, approval for women who were both mothers and competent employees was three times as high as for pure career women.

How research participants see the image of female top managers in China

The women in the Shanghai Women's Career Lab were asked about their experiences in their social environment regarding their own image and the image of women in senior management in general. They regard China's social environment as mainly positive for career women, and have positive experiences of their image as senior executives. This image is associated with success, high incomes and dedication. According to the women, a successful, senior role brings social respect and acceptance, as well as a strong position in the family. In the eyes of society, if a woman achieves success in her career this represents a success for the entire family. The interviewees believe this image is rooted in China's history of universal female employment. Women's socialisation is geared towards employment until retirement age, and hence aligned towards potential careers. The housewife role has previously been exceptional in Chinese society. According to the interviewees, discussions about the role of housewives are a new trend in China, one that only began recently in response to questions about how to raise children properly and the role of grandparents as primary caregivers.

> *A., HRD: "In the past it was a shame not to work. Not to work is like being a parasite, and women will be inferior if they do not work, you will be only an accessory of a men rather than an independent person."*

The following positive terms regarding the role and image of female executives were mentioned:

- Commonly accepted, positive image (9)
- Better (image) than men (3)
- Strong (5), aggressive/assertive (6), confident, hard-working (2)
- Good education (1), capable (2)
- More intelligent, can organise and plan well (3)
- Powerful (2), admired (2)
- Successful (4)
- Caring for her family (1)

The terms "positive" and "commonly accepted" were mentioned multiple times in relation to the image of female executives. In the view of the study participants, women actually enjoy a better image than men in the working environment. This image is based on qualities such as hard work, assertiveness (strong, aggressive) and good organisational skills. Mothers are also admired for being so organised and dealing with two sets of demands, which brings additional social recognition. One interviewee described how mothers in particular receive a high degree of solidarity and support from colleagues and families. However, there were also a few reports of scepticism concerning career mothers' dedication to their children, resulting in a more ambivalent assessment of their image.

By contrast with the mainly positive accounts, a few views were mentioned in which career women were seen as failing to conform to the image of feminine women. Single women in particular only experience their image as career women as positive with reservations, since they fear that potential partners might regard them as too strong, which would reduce the likelihood of marriage. The term "left-over women" describes single career women who are past marrying age. Since only a few single women participated in the study, these descriptions, which were made by only one (single) woman, remain exceptions. This aspect was also picked up again in the evaluations "has no life" and "makes sacrifices". From an external perspective, it is said that women who aspire to CEO roles will either choose not to have children for the sake of their career or will be unable to spend much time with their children. Hence, it is believed that female CEOs are forced to make sacrifices in relation to motherhood. More critical observations regarding the image of career women in China were less common in the research group. Those that there were related to factors such as the jealousy and insecurity triggered by women in top positions. The "*nu qiang ren*" (dragon lady) phenomenon comprises the fear of strong women and associated value judgements: for example, that such women are "difficult to deal with". Only a handful of the women reported that employees prefer male bosses. Critical responses regarding the image of female executives were as follows:

- Bossy (1), critical (1), detail-oriented (1)
- Leftover women, not so feminine (4)
- Has no life, makes sacrifices (4)
- Dragon lady/*nu qiang ren* (1), difficult to be with (1), feared (2)
- Society does not like them (2)

The women's answers regarding the image of female executives in China suggest that there are a lot of positive views and not many critical ones in their environments. The positive views can be understood against the background of traditional family systems in which women's career success is regarded as a positive value since it helps to strengthen the entire family. There also appears to be a tendency in the group to rate female managers more positively than male ones. This contradicts the results in the literature by Frank (2001), Rajerison (1996) and Korabik (1993), who found that women were not thought capable of management tasks. The stereotypical image of men as more capable managers than women was not reflected in these women's accounts. Judd (1990) presents explanations according to which these attitudes are more common in rural regions. Schein (1996) describes how Chinese women tend to see a positive connection between the requirements of management and female traits. According to Schein, it is Chinese men who internalise more negative stereotypes. The women interviewed for this study did not differentiate between views expressed by men or women. However, their own views come from a female perspective, supporting Schein's finding that women in China are more likely than men to see female managers as capable of managerial tasks.

In contrast to most published research, it can be concluded from the descriptions here that Chinese women encounter a predominantly positive image of their role in society and in companies. Unlike in other studies, the descriptions tend to accord with the image of the "high-flying professional" from the survey carried out by *China Daily* (2001). According to the survey results, career women who are also mothers represent the Chinese ideal for women.

China labor market context for female careers: Equal or unequal?
The situation of Chinese female executives

As well as looking at Confucian traditions, the literature also describes and assesses political changes in relation to the situation of women in China. Some of these changes are diametrically opposed to the Confucian cultural traditions that have been described. The well-known feminist and gender studies scholar Li, Y. (2000) describes the May Fourth Movement, which emerged from protests against China's political and economic system in the period from 1910 to 1920, as the country's first feminist movement. It has been possible to observe specific positive effects on equality of opportunity in China since the founding of the People's Republic of China in 1949. The state played a leading part in establishing greater equality by dismantling the feudal system that it is generally agreed oppressed women. Various steps were taken to achieve this goal, involving legislative, administrative and economic mechanisms (Gangrose, 2005). At the legislative level, the state introduced Article 6, which established the basis for improving women's status: "Women shall enjoy equal rights with men in political, economic, educational and social life." (Li, Y., 2000, p. 31). The two most important laws were passed in 1950: the Land Reform Law and the New Marriage Law, which *inter alia* gave women the right to divorce. This was part of a plan intended to bring more women into employment. Subsequently, the employment rate of Chinese women rose sharply. The state continued to introduce regulations and laws that established new rights for women or protected existing ones, with the aim of creating equality of opportunities (Cooke, 2001). The media also disseminated the idea of equal opportunities (Keith, 1997; Jiang, 2000). Examples of measures that were introduced include maternity leave, quotas for women's jobs and state planning of posts for female workers near their husbands during the period from the 1950s to the 1970s. The number of nurseries and crèches in rural regions multiplied during this time.

Mao Zedong's speech with the much-quoted phrase "Women can hold half the sky" became the expression of a new equality movement, and is characteristic of the determination with which the government proclaimed this goal. A high, almost equal proportion of women in employment was achieved, and this was maintained even during the chaotic years of the Cultural Revolution (1966–1976). However, the drastic changes since the Cultural Revolution have had two opposing effects. On the one hand, the literature describes rapid political progress on many aspects of gender equality. But on the other hand, there have also been tendencies that discriminate against women, such as the killing of female infants as a consequence of the one-child policy. According to feminist theorists, women's issues were masculinised during the period of the Cultural Revolution, and women were treated as identical to men despite often having different life circumstances. This masculinisation went against their actual interests. The slogan "Whatever men can do, women can do too" and uniform clothing for men and women were an expression of the views that prevailed at that time (Wang, 1997). The high proportion of women in employment, which far outstrips other industrialised nations in the West and the global average, can be seen as the result of the last 50 years of action by the state. Today, the model of dual employment (where both partners work) is the socially accepted norm in China. The question remains of to what extent laws and regulations are applied in practice. There are many studies debating how much they actually contribute to equality of opportunity (Keith, 1997; Potter, 1999). Stockman, Bonney, and Sheng (1994) see more equality of opportunity in China than in Western nations and describe a continuous decrease in inequality since the establishment of the current Communist government in the mid-1980s: "Chinese institutions are seen to have a higher level of gender equality than Japan, the UK and the USA, with permanent full-time work being the norm for all adults and a high degree of egalitarianism in family roles". Opposing positions point to the underrepresentation of women in senior government roles and conclude, *inter alia*, that women in China still do not have as much power as men (Xi, 1985). Korabik (1993) also concludes that the government measures can only be seen as partial successes on the road to full equality. The transformation of China's economy into a social market economy and the ensuing liberalisation have restricted the state's influence on issues of equality. The unemployment rate rose with the transition from a planned to a social market economy. Women were especially disadvantaged, since proportionally many of them lost their employment and they found it harder to find new jobs. In summary, however, it can be observed that China's political leadership has taken a variety of measures that have continuously improved the situation of women. However, the literature notes critically that while policies have focused on protecting women's rights and increasing the proportion of women in employment, protecting and improving the quality of work prospects has only been of secondary importance (Cooke, 2001). The extent to which political measures directly influence the careers of women in management positions in China ultimately remains an open question, but it can be discussed and interpreted in context. Ultimately, the sociocultural environment in which women operate is marked by an ambivalence between traditional interpretations of Confucian values and political efforts to establish gender equality.

There are no findings that conclusively and unequivocally settle the question of whether the situation for female managers in China is equal or not. The literature on this topic primarily comes from the field of gender studies, which deals with women in general. The aim of gender studies is to point out inequalities. Inequalities between men and women in the Chinese work context can be observed in three main areas: maternity leave, differences in retirement age and the recruitment of staff. These factors result in differences in earnings and in the way men and women are treated in the event of dismissals. The principle of equal salaries for men and women in China was introduced in 1949 with the planned economy. At that time, over 90% of women were employed, far more than in Western nations (Croll, 1995). The introduction of the socialist market economy, which began in 1978 and was completed around 1992, marked the start of the labour contract system. Companies had more freedom and power to set their own salary systems (Naughton, 1995).

Since the mid-1990s, increasing numbers of publications have studied differences in salary between men and women in China (Zhang, Han, Liu, and Zhao, 2008; Kim, Fong, Yoshikawa, Way, Chen, Deng, and Lu, 2010; Hannum, Yupin, and Meian, 2013). There is a consensus that a wage gap exists between men and women that has increased in the past two decades. Chi and Li (2008) show that in 1978, Chinese women only received 84% of men's salaries. By 2004, the gap had widened to 76%.This trend has been confirmed, *inter alia*, by Gustafsson and Li (2000), based on a household study carried out by the Chinese Academy of Social Sciences. However, according to this study, the gender wage gap was higher in highly competitive industries and the private sector, and lower in collective and state sectors. Women's salaries also differed according to their familial status.

Married women had higher salaries in state-owned enterprises, while in joint ventures they earned up to 12% less than unmarried women (Hughes and Maurer-Fazio, 2002). For Chinese women, being married does not necessarily mean earning less; depending on the company type, it can have the opposite effect. However, having children aged under six is a key factor behind differences in salary. The study also shows that less-educated women face the most discrimination. Well-educated women in more senior roles earn salaries that come very close to those of their male counterparts. Xiu and Gunderson (2013) conclude from their study, which also examined previously unexplained differences in salaries, that Chinese women face salary discrimination purely based on their gender too. In a study by the All-China Women's Federation (statistics on Chinese women, 1949–1989, tabl. 3–36 in Liu, 2000), executives and managers were one of the five occupational groups investigated by the study where women earned less than men.

As well as gender-specific factors, maternity leave and pension regulations also play a role, resulting in the differences in earnings described above. In China, maternity leave means that the mother's full salary generally continues to be paid for a period of 98 days. There are also other regulations that protect mothers in the workplace, for example regulations on breastfeeding. Maternity leave is regarded as a cost factor and hence as a risk by Chinese companies, in part due to the fact that many of them do not have insurance. This has a negative effect on women's periods of employment. Child-rearing responsibilities are one cause for the dismissal of women: around 46% of all dismissals are made in the group of women aged 25 to 35. In a study of 908 companies, 9.8% of managers said that they are generally more prepared to dismiss women than men (Cooke, 2001), meaning women are more quickly affected by rounds of dismissals than men. The number of women in employment sank by 7% during the restructuring of Chinese state-owned enterprises between 1995 and 1998. In what are termed "other economic sectors", a category which also includes foreign companies, the number of women in employment sank by 5% in the same period (Jiang, 2000). Over the course of time, previously high rates of women's employment underwent changes. Using the example of married women, Ding, Dong, and Li (2009) show how employment fell from 92% in 1988 to just 74% in 2002.

Meanwhile, differences in China's pension regulations mean that a highly qualified woman's career may be around 15 years shorter than that of a less qualified man. Since 1951, women have retired at an average age of 50 (blue-collar workers) or 55 (white-collar employees). In the course of the economic reforms of the 1980s, it even became normal for female workers to retire before 50 in order to free up jobs for younger, unemployed people. The women then normally take on childcare responsibilities in the family. Unlike in the West, where women return to work in their mid-40s after raising children, it is a social norm for many women to retire at 50 at the latest, especially in the low-wage segment. In exceptional cases, women can work till 60 or later if they are essential to their companies due to their qualifications (Guo, 2000). These regulations mean that women have less time to develop their careers than men. Another consequence of these regulations is lower pensions. Women who are dismissed also receive lower compensation than men because they have generally been employed for a shorter period of time.

There are also differences between men and women when it comes to recruitment. One reason is differences in the perceived suitability or unsuitability of men and women for roles. Another reason (as described above) is that employers anticipate the possibility of a woman becoming pregnant or retiring early, which is a disadvantage in the eyes of the company. Cooke (2001) describes how many employers have a picture of men as being better suited as workers, more mobile and able to work for longer. Recruiting women is associated with higher costs, and women overall are deemed to be less suited to many tasks. Although Chinese law prescribes equal treatment of women, many researchers believe that the implementation of equal treatment remains patchy. The recruitment of women varies according to industry, job type and the associated stereotypes. Cooke notes that only 30% of scientists and only 21.3% of technical specialists are women, but that the proportion of women is rising in the spheres of politics, medicine and science. In politics, women's careers remain tokenistic. Whyte (1984) concludes that women tend to be employed in the low-wage segment and on short-term contracts in the services industry, with preference given to young, attractive women.

In summary, while Chinese law prescribes absolute equality for men and women in relation to employment, other regulations, such as those governing early retirement and maternity leave, could result in unequal treatment. Moreover, it remains unclear how successfully mechanisms for enforcing legal equality requirements are applied. "Gender equality is an important part of corporate social responsibility", remarked Xu Feng, chair of the Shanghai Women's Federation, at the Shanghai International Forum for Women's Development in October 2014, "and we count on organisations to take the lead and give talented female staff the support and career opportunities they deserve". Accordingly, gender equality remains an ongoing concern for China, just as it does for the rest of the world.

Assessments of equality of opportunity from the research group

The best known gender researcher of China (Liu, 2014)[2] states to the question of equality in China: "The saying 'Women are half the sky' acknowledges two things – the importance and contribution of women for the Chinese society and their position in the modern China. If you ask me if women can carry half of the sky, my answer is yes. If you ask me if women in China should carry more than half the sky, I doubt. The Chinese women already carry more than half the sky – this has to be said. We are now coming to a point to discuss more actual questions related to the consequences of this development on women's lives and the society in general."

This section discusses the research participants' subjective judgements regarding equality of opportunity in management in China compared with men, based on their experiences. The women were first asked to verbally rate equality of opportunity for women on a scale from 0 to 10, where 10 means that opportunities for men and women in senior management are completely equal and 0 means there is no equality of opportunity at all. The women were then asked to justify their choice. Not all of the interviewees expressed their assessment in the form of a number. The answers of the 27 women who gave a number were as follows:

Table 4: Rating of gender equality in management

Rating	number of participants
more than 10	3
10*	9
(*but only for big cities	5)
9	1
8 to 9	5
7 to 8	4
6 to 7	4
4 to 5	1
total answers	27

Most of the women feel equal to men in their companies and careers, and some of them even feel superior to them. They described advantages that, as women, they have over men. The gap between 8 or 9 rather than the maximum value of 10 was

2 Authorised quote from a presentation given by Professor Xiaojiang Liu, China's leading researcher on gender issues, at the German Consulate, Salon Yongfu Lu, in October 2014.

mostly justified by reference to regional differences between the country and the cities. The following explanations of the assessments were given:

According to some women, equal opportunities primarily exist in China's bigger cities, such as Shanghai, where women now sometimes have more opportunities in senior management than men. The better opportunities for women at multinational companies result in part from the fact that the GMs (usually from overseas) trust Chinese women more than their male counterparts.

> *M., CFO: "There is no single answer. In big cities it is quite equal. In rural areas less equality. In multinational companies no preference of male or female."*

> *J., Asia Purchasing Director: "In some cases the female has more equality. In big cities it is quite equal."*

> *A., VP: "I think it is equal, also the pay. In China women do not stay at home like in other countries."*

> *C., HRD: "Today women are more powerful than men in China. Also girls today are already much better from school onwards."*

Alongside the predominantly positive assessment of equality of opportunity, some isolated remarks were more critical. According to these remarks, equality of opportunity is dependent on the level within a company and on women being willing and realistically able to combine the requirements of top management (such as frequent travel) with their roles in their families.

> *H., VP: "Middle management it is 100% equal. Top management I think it is 6 of 10. It is not equal because the women do not want these positions. The requirements are too much – like travelling. Total equality is an illusion until the day that men can give births. I think our role in raising a family educating our children is important. But the manifestation of that role is totally not equal."*

There is less agreement regarding equality at the very highest level in a company, namely the CEO or GM role. Some of the women reported that this role is primarily reserved for men. Others were emphatic that there is also equality of opportunity at this level, but that only a few women seriously strive to attain the top job. These views correspond to the responses discussed in the previous section. The group was split into two camps regarding the GM role.

A minority of the women who participated in this study believe that equality of opportunity is generally limited in China. These more critical voices believe that motherhood and maternity leave have a limiting effect.

> *C., HRD: "It is quite equal. But the fact of getting pregnant and the four months' maternity leave might be an issue that lead to preference of male."*

> *C., President: "Gender is no issue. Same as in the US. It really depends if a women has children and gets support for raising them. I don't think that culturally people are biased toward women being inferior to men. I really don't think that kind of mentality exists in the US or here. But it's the expectation the family have on you. The very practical issues that you have to balance."*

Only two of the women who were interviewed believe that equality of opportunity is restricted because of general differences between men's and women's suitability for senior management roles that result in a smaller talent pool of women capable of filling these posts. In their view, women are often more perfectionist than men and come across as less self-assured. One participant thought that many women have other life goals, such as marrying a wealthy man. She also mentioned the challenge women face in keeping up with male rituals such as going for drinks in the evening. One woman who works in sales refuted the latter example by reference to her own experiences and "ability to hold her drink".

> *K., HRD: "Our Company has 30–40% of female directors, not very high. So I give 6–7 of 10. One reason might be that the talent pool of female is historically still smaller. But in the schools today there are more girls succeeding now. Another reason might be that women tend to be perfectionist and do not have enough self-confidence. Male thinks they are ready for the top position if they have 60%."*

> *E., GM: "I give 8 of 10 because sometimes business rituals are difficult for women – like drinking in the evening and so. Also many women do not want a career but just marry a rich man."*

The women were also asked how they think equal opportunities in China compare internationally. The women who have previously worked or lived in Germany spontaneously made comparisons with Germany. They noted that it is much more difficult for women to get into senior management in Germany than in China. They also mentioned motherhood and the obligations it entails as factors that make it more difficult for German women to rise to senior executive roles. Accordingly, Germany received ratings of 3–4 or 5 on the scale from 0 to 10. The same women ranked China at 8–9 out of 10. One respondent gave Switzerland a rating of 4.

China is also ascribed greater equality of opportunity than its neighbours Japan and Korea. Two interviewees mentioned the USA. One of the women believes that there are more women in top positions in China than in the USA, while the other thinks the USA and China fare equally well with respect to equal opportunities for women in senior management.

> *Z., IT-Director: "In Germany it is negative and you are not reliable if you send your child away to the grandmother. For Chinese this is normal. In Germany it is much harder to obtain a leadership role."*

> *J., GM: "There are much less senior manager in Germany, therefore I feel that Germany is more male-dominated."*

In summary, it can be observed that the group takes a mainly positive view of equal opportunities at multinational companies in Shanghai. Only a few researchers have reached the same conclusions (for example, Stockman, Bonney, and Sheng, 1994). Unlike most studies and publications, some of the study participants thought women have better opportunities for senior executive roles than men. However, it was disputed whether Chinese women have equal opportunities with regard to CEO and GM roles, which are usually held by men from overseas. This is also reflected in the figures in the literature, which show that in China (just like in the rest of the world) it continues to be uncommon for CEO positions to be held by women. The interviewees reported that motherhood and the special demands it places on women have a limiting effect on their careers. Again, this matches the literature. The effects of early retirement on women's career development were only mentioned by one woman, who is close to retirement age, in a later part of the study. In the course of their explanations and the interviews, the women did not spontaneously discuss possible salary gaps between men and women or differences in recruitment, which are frequent topics of inquiry in the literature presented earlier (Chi and Li, 2008; Gustafson and Li, 2000; Cooke, 2001).

Overall, the women in this study group presented a more positive picture of equal opportunities for women in management than would be expected on the basis of the published literature. However, their answers cannot be generalised for China as a whole but primarily relate to large cities. Accordingly, Shanghai appears to offer a particularly positive environment for women's careers.

Proportion of women in senior management roles in China

Studies on the proportion of women in management often contain contradictory data and interpretations. Adler and Izarelis (1988) state that although women worldwide represent over fifty percent of the world's population, in no country do women represent half, or even close to half, of the corporate managers. International researchers remain positive about the development of women in management functions, but this tends to relate to successes in middle management. Powell (2011) found that worldwide data shows an increase of women in management. Despite these trends, female managers are concentrated in lower management levels and hold positions with less authority than men. According to Eagly (2007), the number of female managers has "skyrocketed", even though women remain rare in some executive roles. Women now constitute a majority of managers in many areas.

Different data sources show different proportions of women in senior management, both globally and in China. This is due to different definitions of what is meant by "management role" or "senior management". It is necessary to distinguish between data regarding company management roles or functions on a company's board or executive committee and data regarding senior level functions. The latter term often refers collectively to a number of different hierarchical levels. Some data sources show different figures that could easily be misinterpreted, but the data does show a common trend. The various data sources are relatively unanimous with respect to the more general interpretation that, in international comparison, China has a relatively high proportion of women in management roles. In 2014, 64% of women were in the Chinese labour force compared to 78% of the men. Although the number has gone down since 2010, when it stood at 74%, in worldwide comparison Chinese women still have a very high employment rate (Catalyst, 2016). The World Economic Forum reported in 2010 that over 50% of all professional entry level positions in China are held by women. Lam, McGuiness, and Vieto (2013) present data showing that in 2008 around 8.3% of GMs in private Chinese companies and around 5% in Chinese state-owned enterprises were women, and compare these figures with the figure of 4% female GMs in the 1,000 top companies in the USA. Figures from 2014 show that women represented 10.7% of board members and 3.2% of GMs at companies in China (Credit Suisse Research Institute, 2014). A study by McKinsey (2012) shows a proportion of 8% women on boards and 9% women on executive committees, which was below the figures for Europe and the USA. Other figures show a 21% proportion of women on Chinese boards compared with a global average of 19% (Thornston, 2014). According to the World Economic Forum 2015, women accounted for just 17% of all legislators, senior officials and managers in China. Only 18% of firms in China have according to these data women as top managers. De Jonge (2014) discovered in a study which included data from China and India that women did better than average in firms within the financial service sector and in firm with larger work-force size.

Worldwide data show that top level one executive position in companies are only rarely held by women. China thus conforms to the global picture, in which CEO and GM roles continue to be dominated by men. In studies on the proportion of women in senior management roles, on the other hand, China is one of the world leaders. Thornton (2014) calculates a proportion of 39% for 2013, which places China at the top of the world rankings for that year alongside Russia and certain Baltic states. The study shows an average 38% proportion of women in senior management roles at companies over the last eight years. An international comparison by Catalyst researchers showed that women hold 16% of executive functions and just 2% of CEO positions at Fortune 500 companies. According to the Thornton study that has been conducted annually since 2004, the 2013 global average was 24% and the average over time is 22%. By comparison, in the same study the USA came out with 20%, France with 23% and Germany with just 16%. The study's findings on the proportion of women in Chief Financial Officer (CFO) and Human Resource Director (HRD) roles in China are striking, at 81% and 61% respectively. This picture is confirmed by a study carried out by Hays (Hays Asia Salary Guide, 2015), according to which the proportion of women in senior management roles in China is 36%, compared with an Asian average of 29%.

The various figures show that in international comparison, China has a very high proportion of women in senior management. However, the proportion of women at the very highest executive level (CEOs) is like in all countries worldwide lower compared to men. The high proportion of women in China is found in the second executive level directly below the CEO and in management team positions, which here include CFOs, COOs and HRDs. So the claim that only a few women make it to the "O" level in China may be only true with qualification, and generally only with respect to the role of CEO. China is amongst the leading countries concerning women's participation in senior management functions.

Figures from the Shanghai Career Lab:
estimates of the number of women in senior management

In order to gauge the study participants' estimates of the proportion of women in senior management roles in China, they were presented with figures from a 2013 Grant Thornton study in order to stimulate their reflections. According to the original data first published by Thornton, 51% of senior management roles in

China were held by women. The interviewees were told the figure of 51% and the study that it came from, but no other details about how the figure was calculated, and asked how high they would estimate the proportion of women in management to be.[3]

Most of the women estimated that the figure is indeed 51% or higher, and regard this as confirmed by their actual experiences. Only a minority of the women (eight in total) doubted the figure and estimated the true proportion of women in management to be lower. The women's estimates ranged from 20% to 65%, meaning their views are just as varied as the figures on this topic from different sources presented in chapter 2. Those who were more critical of this figure primarily pointed to strong regional differences within China, with the north still seen as a male-dominated region with a lower proportion of women in top positions (which would reduce the overall proportion). Another reason given in favour of a lower figure concerns the most senior executive level in companies (CEO/President). The women believe that there is a lower proportion of women at this level. In this connection, they indicated that there is a high proportion of women in the level directly below (that is, the level of the management team, VPs, directors, etc.). The third reason the women gave for doubting the high figure is not focused on corporate management as such but considers the lower overall proportion of women in senior Chinese government functions. The women who doubted the figure thought it is probably explained by the fact that the study it came from only included southern cities such as Shanghai and multinational companies. They believe that the high figure could be correct for those cities and companies. According to the women, in Shanghai in particular women have traditionally been seen as the stronger sex. All the women confirmed that there is a female majority in the management teams and senior executive levels at their companies.

The majority of study participants confirmed that the figure of 51% corresponds to their actual experiences in their working environment, and some of them think the true figure could be even higher. The women attribute the high proportion of women in senior management that they have observed in their own professional lives to four factors: equality policies; women's strong education and skills; supportive family environments; and the type of company, namely multinational corporations. According to the women, China's equality policies have resulted in eve-

---

[3]   At the end of 2014, Grant Thornton retrospectively corrected the originally published value of 51% to 38%. Upon enquiry, the authors cited survey errors as the reason for this change. In the interviews, the originally published value was used to stimulate the women's views. It is important to note that using the corrected value of 38% might have led to different responses.

ryone working, both men and women. The interviewees believe that Chinese socialisation excludes the option of staying at home and being a housewife, which is
more common in some other countries. Housewives are viewed more critically or
seen as confined to a small, upper-class stratum, and are a new phenomenon for the
country. Choosing not to work or to only work part-time does not exist as a role
model for women, according to the study participants. In this context, they repeatedly emphasised the equal status of men and women, and attributed it to Communism and Mao. The year 1949 and Mao's phrase "half the sky" were mentioned
several times. The women believe that Communism has overcome Confucianism
on the equality front, and that the dominant model in China is a culture where both
men and women earn an income (unlike in the West, where women often stay at
home). The second often mentioned factor behind the high proportion of women in
management is the strong support women receive from their families with childcare, which allows them to develop their careers. According to the interviewees,
the one-child policy made it easier for women to concentrate on their careers, since
it is relatively easy to look after a single child. They believe that Chinese women
are generally keen to return to work even after becoming mothers, as otherwise
they would quickly get bored. The fact that women are socialised to work and to be
self-reliant and financially independent is seen as a reason for the high proportion
of women in management. The third factor that was repeatedly mentioned as a reason for the high proportion of women in management is the women's skills that
make them successful in management roles. The women compared these skills
with those of male managers. According to the interviewees, Chinese women overall have been better educated and more industrious than men for many years. Chinese women were described as ambitious, hard-working and strong communicators. They are also regarded as better at adapting to other cultures than men. The
interviewees regard a trend towards mobility among women as another aspect that
supports the high figure. By contrast, they believe men tend to be spoiled and lack
independence. In their view, one consequence of the one-child policy was to produce a generation of men who are generally perceived in negative terms. As only
children, boys were extremely spoiled and never developed independence. There
are also very good, successful men who do not fit this image, but the women believe that such men only spend a short time as managerial employees before pursuing other career goals such as becoming independent entrepreneurs. Consequently,
they are uncommon at multinational companies. The interviewees also believe that
male GMs of multinational companies see women less as rivals and are more
likely to support and promote them than men. They believe that Chinese men are at
an overall disadvantage at multinational companies, while women benefit from

greater trust. They also note that certain markets have industry-specific benefits for women. The retail and luxury fashion markets were mentioned as sectors where women have particularly good opportunities. Most of the group believe that a high proportion of women in senior management is a reality in present-day China, especially at multinational companies. From their experience, most of the interviewees regard the figure of 51% as quite realistic. However, there is clear agreement among the women that the picture is different in northern China, with lower proportions of women.

The group does agree, though, that there is no equal proportion of men and women at GM level in multinational companies. They believe that it is entirely possible for women to become a CEO or GM in China, and that this is supported by society. However, in their view the fact that many women strive to achieve a work-life balance and to combine work and family stands in the way of their becoming CEOs. From their point of view, there also seems to be discrimination against Chinese in general that stands in the way of them reaching the highest level in multinational companies. This point will be addressed in a later section.

Is there a glass ceiling phenomenon in China?

The much-discussed notion of a "glass ceiling" attempts to explain why women are represented in junior and middle management across the world but are only rarely able to rise to the very highest levels of senior management (Henn, 2012). A glass ceiling is according to the majority of definitions an invisible barrier faced by women (but not men) for reaching top management levels that can only be surmounted with difficulty. According to this explanation, this is one of the reasons why women are excluded from circles of power. Stereotypical expectations about behaviour, informal organisational structures, memberships, networks and informal rituals are other aspects of the glass ceiling that have been studied by various researchers in this context. According to Liu, S. (2013) the number of years somebody spends in a role can serve as an indicator of when they have reached a glass ceiling in their career. According to Ragins (1998), around 92% of female executives in the USA attest to the existence of a glass ceiling. Gangrose (2005) concludes from her studies of Chinese women in Singapore that the glass ceiling does not exist in a generalised form for all women, but is dependent on organisational type. These studies found more evidence of the glass ceiling in private companies, not in Singapore's state organisations. Only individual examples can be presented for China due to the small number of studies of women in management that have been carried out to date. In a research on women in China's hotel industry, Yun

(2011) concludes that the glass ceiling exists there. Women make up around 60% of all employees, but only a few of the top managers are female. Women rise up the ranks faster, but are less likely to reach GM level than men. According to Yun, the main reasons are the difficulty of combining family and career and stereotypes that present men as better suited to many roles. Another study concludes that women in SOEs in China encounter the glass ceiling more frequently than in other segments (Zhang, 2012). Another study looks at prospects for women in science and engineering in China (Guo Congbin, 2009). Although more women study mathematics and chemistry and achieve better results than men in these subjects, they have lower starting salaries than men and lower employment prospects over-all. In another study (Frank, 2001), 72 Chinese students attested to the existence of a glass ceiling in relation to the question of whether men and women are equally accepted. According to the study, women are less accepted the higher they rise in management. Korabik (1993) notes that although women's employment is higher in China than in the USA, "Chinese women managers ... appear to confront a glass ceiling similar to that encountered by their sisters in other parts of the world".

Female Chinese executives' view regarding the existence a glass ceiling

As described before, the glass ceiling concept describes an invisible, insurmount-able obstacle faced by women trying to reach senior management (Eagly and Carli, 2007). In the literature, the glass ceiling is only described for women and is hence gender-specific (Ragins, 1998). The research participants were asked whether they have experienced a glass ceiling for women in management in their environment, and if so to what extent. Their answers can be categorised into three groups. Group 1 does not believe a glass ceiling exists in China. Group 2 does believe there is a glass ceiling, but defines the phenomenon as dependent on nationality rather than gender. They believe the glass ceiling applies to all Chinese at multinational com-panies, regardless of gender. Group 3 concedes that there is a glass ceiling for women but believe that it only applies to the very highest position in a company (CEO, President), not to all other senior management roles.

Group 1 – there is no glass ceiling for women

Ten of the interviewees deny the existence of a glass ceiling for women in top management at all three types of company – state-owned, private and multinational – though their opinions on how difficult it is to attain a GM post in the different types of company differ. Having high career ambitions and a well-organised family life were mentioned as preconditions for reaching the top position at a company.

J., GM: "The glass ceiling does not exist. Even though there are always discussions about female being emotional and having family duties in my experience I do not see a glass ceiling. Most female CEO perform better. And they give up their families."

Z., IT director: "I do not believe in a glass ceiling – everything is possible – for men and women."

A., VP: "The glass ceiling is still highly linked with the risk-taking spirit and your career aspiration. I don't think there's a glass ceiling. It depends on how much aspiration a woman has. In multinational companies it is more difficult compared to local Chinese companies. For the level below CEO there is no glass ceiling."

J., Sales Director: "I do not think it exists. It depends on if the women really want to go to a top level and how she organizes her family life. I know some CEO women in the government-backed companies. There it is easier than in the multinationals or private companies."

Group 2 – there is a glass ceiling, but it applies to all Chinese

Eleven of the women defined the concept of a glass ceiling as not being restricted to women, but as applying to all Chinese at multinational companies regardless of gender. They noted that CEO and GM positions are still reserved for people of other nationalities and are not filled by Chinese. Hence, the glass ceiling phenomenon is understood in cultural terms rather than as depending on gender. The interviewees do not believe this culturally defined glass ceiling exists at Chinese private companies or state-owned enterprises.

C., HRD: "The glass ceiling is for Chinese – not male and female. In state-owned and private companies it does not exist."

K., HRD: "It is there for Chinese people in multinational companies. The percentage of Chinese people that have been send to Europe is still small compared to the number of foreigners coming into China. Chinese people are more introvert and foreigners like to present themselves. Intercultural prejudgements are also one reason for the glass ceiling for Chinese."

Group 3 – the glass ceiling exists for CEO roles

Fourteen of the interviewees believe there is a glass ceiling for women in China, but in their view it is only to be found directly beneath the CEO role, that is to say the highest position in a company. The majority of interviewees do not believe there is a glass ceiling in China for any other hierarchical level, such as other C-level functions, management team, director or vice-president roles.

> *T., GM: "In our company we talk a lot about the glass ceiling. Here women are many on the level below CEO. There are in general not enough role models at CEO level. So women decide to be comfortable on the second level."*

> *M. M., President: "Yes, it exists in all companies. The problem is only for CEO level. Most women do not want it. And some do not have the required skills – like strategic planning. Some women like to be in a lower function because they can give responsibility away."*

> *M., CFO: "I had no experience with that but I think it is existing starting from GM level. Perhaps there is a psychological difference in male and female when it comes to obtaining GM levels."*

The women identified four main reasons for the existence of a glass ceiling. Firstly, the family-related challenges faced by mothers are incompatible with the requirements of a CEO or GM role. The main example given of this difficulty was the travel that such roles inevitably involve. Mothers thus rule out the possibility of being able to meet the requirements of this role from the outset.

> *J., HRD: "Traditional family burden are the main reasons why there is a glass ceiling for the CEO level for women in China. It is not because people have a bias; it is because naturally men and women are different."*

> *M., HRD: "I think female in many cases do not want to go up there but male want it. I do not want to deal with all the hurdles and have no time for my family."*

A second reason that was mentioned is women's lack of ambition compared with men. According to the interviewees, many women feel comfortable at the second executive level and do not strive to become CEOs. This reason is again seen as related to the challenge women face in balancing their professional and private lives.

> *Z., CFO: "I think it exists. Men have bigger ambitions. And it is more difficult for women to balance their private life."*

> *A., HRD: "The glass ceiling exists in multinational companies because women do not want to move further up – they feel good on the second level."*

A third factor mentioned by one participant is the different retirement ages for men and women. She remarked that since women retire five years earlier on average, they have less time to dedicate to reaching the highest level in a company. Another factor behind the glass ceiling that was also only mentioned by one woman is prejudices about female leadership styles. According to this interviewee, women are stereotyped as being overly focused on small details and more emotional, which has a negative influence on perceptions of their suitability to be CEOs.

In the literature presented earlier, the glass ceiling phenomenon is normally described in connection with the issue of gender. Nationality tends not to play any role in this context. So a definition of a gender-neutral glass ceiling for Chinese represents a new and different aspect to the phenomenon. Moreover, in some studies and interpretations it is unclear at what precise hierarchical level the glass ceiling that is being described kicks in. Some of the studies relate to the CEO role, while others start further down the scale and include department heads and directors.

In summary, although a majority of the group believe there is a glass ceiling in China; only 14 of the 35 participants think it relates specifically to women. This means that the studies by Korabik (1993), Frank (2001), Yun (2011) and Zhang (2012) are neither clearly confirmed nor refuted. In the view of the interviewees, the glass ceiling primarily applies to all Chinese at multinational companies, and is exclusively restricted to CEO roles rather than to the second executive level that is generally also classified as senior management. The interviewees believe that in their environment, all other senior executive level roles are just as accessible for Chinese women as for men.

Influence of social origin and family situation on careers

Social origin and female careers

As well as the question of the extent to which Chinese executives' careers are influenced by their own family structures, there is also the question of the role played by the executives' social origin and family of origin. This section addresses the latter question. The literature contains various researches on the question of whether and to what extent a person's social origin affects their career path. The findings of these studies are closely bound up with the overarching cultural and social conditions in the countries where they were conducted. Social origin generally refers to family structure variables such as parental occupation and socioeconomic status. Family of origin refers to one's natural family or the family into which one was born or adopted. A broader definition is the family in which one was raised and spent one's formative years, and this might include grandparents, aunts and uncles, nannies and others who have played an active role.

Pierre Bourdieu offers a theory of how parents' social milieu can impact on their children's careers. In a highly simplified form, his theory is that we possess social, cultural and economic capital, at least a portion of which we inherit from our parents (Bourdieu, 1977, 1982). According to Bourdieu, social origin influences people's lifestyles in early adolescence, which in turn influences their subsequent lifestyles and creates the "fine differences „that can contribute to coarse differences in career success. A glance at more recent career theory shows that many academic publications have adopted the theory of individualisation. In fact, career theory narrowly construed has engaged relatively little with the topic of social origin. This may be due to the significant influence of US literature on this field, which often puts forward the image of a free individual who is responsible for their own professional development. However, research in the fields of gender and ethnic studies shows how strongly individuals can be influenced or held back by social structures. So although the connection between social origin and educational prospects has been repeatedly demonstrated, the connection between social origin and career paths has been largely ignored. One of the few studies to deal with this topic, by German sociologist Michael Hartmann, presented findings that diverge somewhat from the picture of the modern, open-ended, "boundaryless" career. His research shows that the chances of achieving an executive position are 50% higher for individuals with a service class I background and 100% higher for individuals with an upper-class background in contrast to individuals with a working or middle-class background. Therefore, the functionalist view can be regarded as incorrect; in fact, Hartmann holds that social origin has a strong direct effect on the social selection of elites. His study shows, for example, that the German business elite (that is, the top managers at major German companies) has remained socially exclusive to the same degree for decades. More than 80% of these (almost always) men come from the upper or upper-middle classes (Hartmann and Kopp, 2001).

According to Fietze, only 8.6 percent of the inequality of career opportunities can be explained by reference to differences in personality. However, differences in job choices and career paths are more influenced by social origin (Fietze, Holst, and Tobsch, 2011; Rescht, 2014). In their review of literature on the influence of the family of origin on career development, Whiston and Keller (2004) conclude that family does influence individuals' career development in specific ways. According to this research children seem to strongly identify with their parents' occupations. They also found some indications that mothers' employment seems to influence the occupational choices of daughters. Mothers seem to have more influence than fathers on career decisions. For women, the most important influence variable was the fostering of autonomy by their parents. The interaction of family factors (for example, mother-daughter relations) appears to have a particularly strong influence on certain career outcomes for women.

European researchers have observed that economic scientists in countries such as Austria and Germany tend to come from the "better classes": that is, classes whose members work in higher-level professions and have a higher level of education. For men, there is a more direct positive correlation between parental education and average annual income: the higher the father's education, the more the son earns. For women, there is a negative correlation between parental education and the women's satisfaction with their own professional development: the more educated a woman's father is, the less satisfied she will be with her professional develop-ment, and the more painful she will find it to encounter the "glass ceiling" and to experience the incompatibility of career and family.

Little is known from research about the influence of the family of origin, family structure and process variables on careers in China. Riley (1994) writes that in China, parents' *guanxi* networks are often far more important than the family's wealth. *Guanxi* is defined as a system which is used to exchange favours or a way of achieving private goals (Yang, 1986). These favours are equal exchanges and do not infringe upon any rules or regulations. In China, *guanxi* is one of the few re-sources that parents can pass to their children. Children will naturally tie into and use the *guanxi* networks of their parents. Examples of the use of *guanxi* in relation with careers might be access to quality education or having contacts with the right people in relation to a job opening or career information. Accordingly, parents might use their *guanxi* relations to help children get into a university or to make decisions regarding a good job. Hence, the influence that traditional *guanxi* bonds have on careers in China may be greater than that of wealth or membership of a particular class, though this connection has not been adequately studied. Riley (1994) conjectures that the level of exchanges might be different for different classes in China, but it is not clear whether the intensity or number of exchanges vary among different social groups. The section on networking will explore the importance of *guanxi* networking in greater depth. A research by Wong investi-gated parental influence on career choices. He identified three parental influence factors: "perceived parental support for a specific industry", "perceived parental career concerns about welfare and prestige" and "perceived parental barriers to ca-reer choice" (Chak-Keung Wong and Jing Liu, 2010). This also leads to the ques-tion of parental influence on the careers of female executives. In China, many chil-dren aged under six are mainly raised by their grandparents, which suggests that grandparents may be a key influence on children. Mothers are also role models for women in general. It can be assumed that both mothers and grandmothers represent the main role models for their (grand) daughters.

Evans (2007) studied mother-daughter relationships in China and how mothers influence their daughters' development. According to her findings, mothers were clearly crucial figures in explaining their daughter's capacity to become "independent", educated and high-achieving women. She also describes the connection between political phases in China and women's socialisation by their mothers and grandmothers. Mothers of daughters who grew up in China in the 1950s and 1960s regarded gender equality as synonymous with "going to work". The daughters who grew up in the 1980s were guided by more flexible models of gender practices, which included both work and the home. Certain specific features that resulted from China's political development are noted in the study. Examples of the specific situation include women who were separated from their parents for several years in their early childhood during the Cultural Revolution. "Socialist androgyny" or "supposedly gender-neutral representation" have been discussed by researchers in connection with China's "Red Guards" period. The effects of these specific environmental influences on careers have not been directly studied.

What has been studied, however, is the more general influence of maternal employment on children's development. Schellhorn (2014) describes how children of working mothers quickly become flexible, independent and self-reliant. With regard to families who own businesses, it is important to note the collectivist significance of family in China. Each family member does their part to secure the family's economic status. Chinese society is characterised by a significant cultural emphasis on collective family interest over individual interest. To give one example of this principle of collective interest: while it is generally the case that the oldest sons will inherit management of a family business, studies show that there is no reason why a daughter cannot be the successor, provided she has prospects for success. This means that family origins can also have an influence on the careers of women in family-owned companies in China.

Influence of the Chinese women's families of origin

The limited literature that exists on the relationship between social origin and career success, as presented before, primarily investigates the education and wealth of parents, parents' expectations for their children and, specifically for women, the influence of mothers or maternal role models. The women in the study were asked to talk freely about their childhood and the people they were closest to. In the following, the picture that emerges from the study group's responses regarding the aspects described above is presented.

Answers regarding the family of origin were obtained from 25 of the 35 interviewees. The majority of the women come from Shanghai. Only a small portion come from other Chinese cities, including Beijing, Guangzhou, Hunan and Xian. This means that many of them come from families that have been living in Shanghai, which has long been an international megacity, for generations. One woman explained what difference she thought being a true "Shanghainese" made. According to her, there are clear differences between the language and traditions of the city's original inhabitants and those of the newcomers. Some of the women come from the region immediately surrounding Shanghai, which now belongs to the city. They reported the differences that existed at the time of their childhood between living in the rural areas around the city and living in the centre of the city itself. Most of the women were, thus, socialised in an urban environment, but some of them grew up in completely rural environments.

Although parental occupations were not recorded for all women, answers that were collected show that in every case bar one both the women's parents worked. The most common occupation among the women's mothers was teaching. Two of the mothers were professors. In second place were bank workers, factory workers and farmers, which were tied with the same number of mentions. Other maternal occupations received a single mention each: gynaecologist, military employee, working in the family business. Only one of the mothers was a housewife. Hence, the housewife role model is very much the exception in this study group. The most common occupation among the women's fathers was engineer, with five mentions. If occupations such as working for the government, police, army or Communist Party are combined, they also add up to five mentions. There were two mentions each for teacher, accountant and farmer.

In six families, the parents had identical occupations. Looking at the parents' occupations overall, it is striking that they include both academic, medical, political and entrepreneurial occupations on the one hand and factory and agricultural workers on the other. However, occupations that require a higher level of education predominate. Hence, the majority of the women come from highly educated families, but there are also women from families with very simple backgrounds. So although there is a slight tendency for more women from highly educated families, the results do not confirm the conclusions of western researchers such as Mayrhofer et al. (2005) that there is a positive correlation between social origin in more educated classes and career success. If government officials, police officers and teachers are combined, they make up the largest single group. The women were not asked about how close their parents were to the government or about their *guanxi* ties and the influence these might have had on the start of the women's careers, so this study cannot present any conclusions on these matters. As explained in greater depth in chapter 2, Riley (1994) describes the importance of parents' *guanxi* networks for their children's careers. According to Riley, in China these networks have a greater influence on career paths than other factors that play a role in Western cultures, such as wealth. However, a connection could be posited as a working hypothesis. Specifically, one of the women described how the ties are especially crucial for careers in state-owned enterprises.

Table 5: Occupations of mothers and fathers

Participant	Occupation mother	Occupation father
1	**trading company**	**trading company**
2	Farmer	*no information*
3	factory worker	*no information*
4	Teacher	Army
5	**Farmer**	**Farmer**
6	**family business**	**family business**
7	Manager	Accountant
8	Teacher	government officer
9	**Teacher**	**Teacher**
10	**Farmer**	**Farmer**
11	Teacher	Police
12	teacher (dance)	Surveyor
13	*no information*	member communist party
14	engineer factory	government officer
15	Housewife	Stockbroker
16	**factory worker**	**factory worker**
17	*no information*	engineer trainer
18	work in bank	Engineer
19	professor (maths)	manager (state-owned company)
20	**Accountant**	**Accountant**
21	Accountant	Engineer
22	national defence	*no information*
23	Gynaecologist	Engineer
24	*no information*	engineer (state-owned company)
25	Professor	research institute
26–35	*no information*	*no information*

Some of the women grew up in larger families, since the one-child policy did not yet exist at the time of their childhoods. Grandparents, aunts and cousins were mentioned alongside parents as other close figures. It is known that 12 of the women in the study have siblings. Most of them have a single sibling. Three women have two siblings, one woman has three and another woman has five. Most of the women have older siblings; only four women reported having young siblings. The distribution of brothers and sisters is uniform. The incomplete figures on siblings that are available do not allow any reliable conclusions to be drawn. It is only possible to observe that, according to the women's accounts, some of them were socialised in families with multiple children and that women without siblings reported the importance of other family members, meaning that they were embedded in large family structures. Neighbours were very important for some of the women, since they took on childcare responsibilities if the women's grandparents did not live locally.[4] The women described their childhoods as marked by their experiences of having two working parents who were often absent. Where the grandparents were unable to do so, aunts took on childcare responsibilities in their place. Grandmothers and mothers had key roles in the women's socialisation. Only a few of the women also described how they followed their fathers' example. Many of the women were raised by their grandparents until the age of five or during their primary school years. These women lived at their grandparents' homes away from their parents, who they only saw at the weekends. The interviewees characterised this arrangement is very typical in China, where it is traditional for both parents to work and for grandparents to raise younger children in their families. This results in close ties between children and their grandparents – particularly, in this study, the grandmothers.

Several of the women described their mothers as very strong personalities who had a profound influence on them. The women described their mothers as having leadership qualities and achievement motivation. For many of the women, their mothers' goal of achieving a better future for their daughters played a key role in their upbringing. According to the women's accounts, the mothers repeatedly pointed out that it is only possible to achieve a better life through hard work, education and lots of discipline. These values were imparted to the interviewed women from an early age. Moreover, many of the women's mothers had highly qualified occupa-

---

[4]   Thus women reported that they used to do their homework together with the neighbours' children
       until their parents came home from work. One woman described the system of neighbourly relations
       that existed in Shanghai during her childhood as supportive and protective. This woman openly de-
       plored that links between neighbours in today's Shanghai are far less close.

tions that earned them a lot of respect and acceptance in their social environment. Hence, all but one of the women have as role models mothers who were employed and professionally successful. Chinese women do not have the image of mothers as housewives that predominates in parts of the West. Their grandmothers had also had careers before taking on childcare responsibilities post-retirement.

> *A., VP: "My father is accountant and my mother was a leader of a company. Very active. She was used to be the head of factory or a company. She's always active as women leader. She's very active. My father is not that ambitious."*

> *L., HRD: "Although my mother she was not very well educated, she actually is very aggressive on the target, on the result. What I mean is ... she wants to achieve the best. No matter on herself or on her kids ... she will not be satisfied. She will say, next time you need to get number one. Something like that. She always gave me a stretch target. She always inspired me to move out of this island because she already spends her half-life in the island."*

> *J., COA: "I was living with my family in the courtyard ... there were a lot of neighbours there. Basically my mom is ... the one with the highest title. They always call her in a nice way. Professor Wu. It's a little bit like joking because normally in Chinese culture you don't call somebody with the title but in a good way. I feel really nice. I also feel benefit from my mom's background, she is professor, she always have a lot of students in the same age like us. I call them big sister, big brother ... my mom always understands how the young people are thinking. It's not really like normal parents who say you have to do this or that. Her students somehow like us."*

The women mentioned their fathers less often. Individual accounts described them either as strict disciplinarians or as frequently absent. In one case, a woman mentioned a demanding parenting style in which she had to "barter" with her father for privileges. She attributes her own highly money-motivated character to this experience. On the other hand, there is also the image of less ambitious fathers who progress less far in their careers than the mothers.

> *L., HRD: "My father he is very commercial. Even the relationship between kids is very commercial. He will measure how much he invested in me. Seriously. Like if I ask for I want to enrol in some piano learning class. It is about like 2000 RMB, he would say 'Okay I will give you the cash but next time when you can do something in return for me, what can you do for me?' Always. He always travels outside. I always spend most of my time with my mother. Give me a strong feeling that father is always very busy and my par-*

ents always have some disagreement, argue. My childhood was full of their arguments and their stretch target to me."

The studies by Whiston and Keller (2004) and Evans (2007) indicate that mothers' role model function has a crucial influence on their daughters' career decisions. Women who grew up in China in the 1960s in particular came to regard gender equality as synonymous with "mothers who work". The interviewed women's socialisation corresponds to research findings showing that working mothers influence their daughters' future career success through their role model function.

Other aspects of socialisation were brought out by descriptions of the values that the parents imparted or of special events during the women's youth that influenced their personality development. One of the women, who grew up in the country in a farming family with lots of children, described her parents as very hard-working people whose aim was to enable the best possible education for all five children. The thought of a better future away from farming life defined this woman's youth. Boys and girls were treated the same, and the parents made up for their lack of wealth with lots of love. In this account, it is notable that the boys and girls were treated equally by their father even though the family in question came from the rural north, where it is generally said that the genders are treated differently.

> *M., HRD: "I think my parents just motivate us to be self-motivated. Self-manage our studies. Told us, that they don't have much money. But they can ensure us that we will have enough tuition as long as we can continue our study. So we manage our self. If we don't study harder then I will we farmer. We will be farmer. This is their own way to educate us. They told us, you do not need to worry about money. You do not need to worry about tuition. You just worry about your study. This is your task. Our task is make money for you. Your task is manage you own study.*
>
> *My parents work two times harder than other farmers at their age because there are so many kids to feed. And so many kids which go to school. It's unusual. It's unusual so many kids in one family go to school. Normally one only sends the son to school. Because my father is very open. He thinks son and daughter are the same so he treat us the same."*

The oldest study participant described how she was separated from her parents, both senior government officials, during the Cultural Revolution and worked as an agricultural worker for ten years. She described how she was marked by these years and became exceptionally strong, which she interpreted as a factor that helped her to rise to the top of a German company in her future career. Even back in the agricultural workers' group she became group leader within a year. She also described how she learned from both parents how to exercise power: before the Cultural Revolution they had kept company with very powerful people, and as a little girl she had been able to observe how powerful people behaved.

> *M. M., President: "....Yes, in the countryside. I was born in Beijing and my parents belonged to the government, the central government, but during the Cultural Revolution it was made equal to the ground and we kids had to go on the countryside. I was sent far in the north and had to stay there for ten years. In the beginning I needed to work as a farmer, a normal farmer...Most of us girls were in middle school and had been send to the countryside. We were many girls together. I was 15 years old and worked around 10 years on the farm. One was hurt sometimes and I grew into the situation and became strong...Yes, it was difficult. All who worked on the farm had parents in higher previous government functions. All girls. We were 12 girls all together, each day some girl cried. My nature is that I knew that crying will not help. Instead one has to see how to survive. My parents were send to prison during these times. After one year I was the boss of that group of girls." (Translated from German)*

Several other women described how they became independent at a very early age, either because they lived alone (so that they could attend a faraway school or look after younger siblings) or because they were raised by their grandparents in the country, where they learned to become independent more quickly than in the city. One woman reported how she became independent at a very early age living with her grandparents in the country and how her parents had big problems with her independence when she returned to the city.

> *C., HRD: "When I was very young I have to take up my family myself ... Because my father actually he works, he came home very late because the place he worked is very far away. He used to take buses. Long time buses from where he worked. He still came back home every day but he very late. And my mother was sick in hospital for quite a long time. So it's just only me and my brother. I, as a bigger sister, I have to take care of my younger brother and also cook for the family, do laundry for the family. I think compared to people my age; I took the role to take care of a family much earlier."*

Describing their own personalities as children, several of the women said that they were naughty and possessed traits normally associated with boys. Hence, they themselves do not regard themselves as stereotypically "girly". One woman described how her wildness was redirected, especially by her mother, towards learning and the motivation to be the best. The women very frequently described how particular events in their youth helped make them even stronger. Others described how they asserted their own ideas about their lives and careers over those of their parents. It remains an open question whether they were at an advantage or disadvantage as girls compared with boys in this respect. None of the women mentioned that they had experienced their upbringing differing from that of boys, nor did they perceive any discrimination. However, it is striking that several of them described how their behaviour as children was perceived as more masculine.

> *J., Sales Director: "I was an attention seeker and also rebellion at that age. In China my dad in particular it's a very humble person but when I get very naughty he disciplined me quite severe. In China at that time it was quite normal. I was more of a boy's characteristic I would say. When I was in high school I brought up the very strong will again to my parents saying 'I want to go abroad'. At the time we were talking about Germany but actually knew somebody in the neighbourhood that went to the UK and adjusted quite well. We talked about it and my parents finally said ok if that's what you want to do that's fine."*

The following overall picture emerges from the study participants' accounts of their families of origin: most of the women grew up in families where both parents worked. Both highly educated professions and labourers are represented among mothers and fathers alike. Although a greater number were in highly educated professions, the results do not support the findings in the literature that women from families with a higher social status are more likely to pursue careers. It is also not possible to establish the connection between a high level of paternal education and dissatisfaction with women's own careers that was found by Mayrhofer in the German-speaking world. The women primarily described their mothers as role models. This corresponds to the studies by Evans (2007) and Schellhorn (2014) on working mothers' influence on their daughters' socialisation. Fathers were mentioned as role models less often. Some of the fathers were less career-oriented by tendency.

The women described how they learned certain traits and capacities, such as discipline, industriousness, assertiveness and how to handle power or money, in their families of origin. In the women's view, being separated from their parents at an early age either intermittently or for an extended period, which as already mentioned above is described as typical for China in other studies, led to them acquiring additional traits at an early age, such as a sense of responsibility, independence and perseverance. According to the research of Bourdieu (1982), there is a connection between parents' lifestyles and their children's career success. In this study group, most of the traits and capacities described resulted from the parents' social environment but also from experiences of separation. The women regard these capacities as relevant to their career success.

Based on the available material, it is only possible to draw limited conclusions regarding the influence that social class has on careers in China. However, it is clear that the issue cannot be measured against the Western standards of comparison found in existing studies. Given that there are very few results in the literature even for Western countries, the connection between social origin and women's careers in management roles in China is a topic that requires further in-depth study.

Influence of women's own family situations on their career

Roles and identities of career women

In order to describe the influence of family and motherhood on women's careers in general, it is important to precisely define the meaning of family and the different familial structures that women live in. The factors of marital status, parenthood and partners' employment status yield various combinations of what can be meant by "family". As well as the classical family with one or more children where one or both parents work, there are also single mothers, wives whose husbands do not work and women without children. There are also women who are widowed, re-married or divorced (Powell, 2011). The social stereotypes associated with a particular familial situation influence the perception of women and their performance as executives in the workplace. Hence, career women with a family have various sub identities or roles: they are wives and mothers as well as career women. How they integrate these sub identities and switch between the roles is one of the key factors determining the career success of women in this family situation (Law, Meijers, and Wijers, 2002). Hall (1976) presents a theory conceptualising the way in which people engage in various social roles and develop a variety of sub identities. According to Hall's theory, career success is only truly achievable if managers invest in and prioritise their career role. Women face more challenges combining different roles than men. Family support and the organisation of childcare are of central importance.

According to western research it is generally expected in companies that women will become mothers when they reach "child-bearing" age and that they will, at least temporarily, leave their companies, be less mobile and have more family-related absences. The consequence is that employers often favour men over women right from the outset when making recruitment or promotion decisions, seeing women only as potential mothers (Henn, 2012). Family and parenthood consequently seem to have opposite effects on the careers of men and women. In general, the more successful a man, the more likely it is that he will be married with children (Hewlett, 2006; Cheung and Halpern, 2010). The effect seems to be more the other way round for women. Career women with children need to respond to social norms regarding how much time a good mother needs to spend with her children. These norms differ between cultures. Studies from the West show that in general mothers equate raising a child well with selflessness and emotional exhaustion on the part of mothers (Eagly and Carli, 2007). Moreover, work and family tend to compete for women's time. Overtime is regarded as time that has been taken away from women's families. In addition, in many studies career mothers have reported feelings of guilt about their children and their work. In collectivist societies such as China, family and career are regarded as more than just interdependent domains. Against the background of a collectivist society, a commitment to one's career is regarded positively as a sacrifice for the financial security of the family. As such, the work-family boundary is more permeable in Chinese society (Yan and Chen, 2000).

Pursuing a career with and without children

It has been observed in western research that women in senior management roles are more likely to remain single and childless in order to avoid the dual demands of family and career. In a 2013 study from Germany, it was found that 20% of female managers were single, while 71% of women in the study were childless (Holst, Busch-Heizmann, and Wieber, 2013). In one Swiss study, the proportion of single female managers was as high as one in three. This phenomenon has recently become a topic of discussion in China, where it is common to speak of "leftover women". This term refers to more career-focused women who subordinate their life to work and do not, as is the norm, marry at a young age and become mothers by the age of 25 or so.

Studies that compare the careers of unmarried, childless women and married women show that married women do more housework than single women (Powell, 2012). Moreover, several studies show that mothers are viewed as less competent and are worse paid than women without children. This has resulted in career women being practically forced to "choose either a baby or a briefcase" (Cheung and Halpern, 2010). After controlling for differences in experience, education, working hours and other factors, mothers still earn less than childless women, a phenomenon labelled "the motherhood penalty" (Budig, Misra, and Boeckmann, 2012). A significant portion of the motherhood penalty results from reduced labour force participation, yet the penalty remains even after adjustments for mothers' greater forgone work experience, pre-empted education and training, and reduced work hours. This penalty is an important source of inequality among women, and between women and men, that is well documented and appears to vary significantly cross-nationally (Budig and England, 2001). Research by Budig 2012 shows significant motherhood pay gaps in most countries. Mothers earn less than childless women in 60 percent of the 22 countries involved in the study. Absences due to maternity leave have a particularly strong impact. 70% of participants in one study by Thompson reported that maternity leave had damaged their career, and 30% said that they had consequently not taken the full amount of time that they were entitled to (Thompson, Bauvais, and Lyne, 1999).

A research from various major Chinese cities regarding current ideals of women, which was mentioned in an earlier section, may serve as a counter to these findings. According to that study, the high-flying professional who was also a successful mother was the ideal of 940 of the men and women who were surveyed (China Daily, 2001).

In summary: according to various Western studies, mothers will be disadvantaged compared with single women and men if they do not develop strategies for combining the demands of motherhood with their role as an executive. On the other hand, as a career woman with children they correspond to the ideal held by many people in major Chinese cities.

Advantages and disadvantages of combining work and family

Western research describes that women in management roles have to constantly strike a balance between the demands of work and family. These "trade-offs" seems to hit women harder than men. The main trade-offs are long working hours, business travel and absences when children are sick (Eagly, 2007). For many married partners, the conflict between family and career is a cause of stress. In China too, women are subject to higher expectations and demands in relation to their families. Nonetheless, some studies on the topic indicate no difference in men's and women's perceptions of their workloads (Choi and Chen, 2006).

Fulfilling family responsibilities can decrease the amount of time that women invest in their careers. Birth and motherhood often lead to women taking career breaks. This frequently results in negative prejudices about women among employers, who expect these absences from career women right from the outset and judge them negatively (Rothbath, 2001). Investigating the working hours that women invest in their careers reveals the following general picture: the more children that women have and the more highly educated their partner, the fewer working hours that they invest in their careers. For women, the question of independence also often depends on their family situation (Powell, 2011). Men's career decisions are less influenced by household duties or childcare responsibilities than women's.

Paid work at a company and unpaid work in the family have a reciprocal effect. Conflicts generally occur when women have no choice but to do both at once. Emotional and psychological stress results from competing requirements, combined with constant feelings of guilt at not being able to fully live up to the demands of both roles. However, being caught between the different roles can also have positive effects, for example a greater ability to handle complex issues, stronger social support or a healthier mental state (Mennino and Brayfield, 2002). Friedmann and Greenhaus (2000) found that when work and family were integrated, the two roles complemented each other. A cross-national comparative study (Spector, Cooper, Poelsmas et al., 2004) showed that for both Chinese and Latin American managers, being married and having children were associated with higher job satisfaction and psychological well-being. Aryee, Field, and Luk (1999) showed in their research that work and family involvement *per se* did not lead to work-family conflict. A somewhat different picture emerges in the work of Kim et al. (2010). In their study on work preferences, they describe the traditional image of the ideal woman, which proclaims her role to be that of a wife and mother (*xianqi liangmu*, 贤妻良母). In their view, many women continue to identify strongly with this image, while their husbands primarily identify with their work. Accordingly, women choose flexible jobs in order to be able to fulfil their familial responsibilities. Many women also place great emphasis on job security when making their choice.

Consequently, it can be observed that motherhood not only has negative spill over's but also offers advantages for women's careers; however, these advantages depend significantly on familial support, women's self-conception and strategies for integrating both sets of demands.

Results from the Shanghai Women's Career Lab – motherhood has an influence on female careers

The above findings (both from Western research and from a Chinese perspective) describe the influence of motherhood and the challenge of combining different roles on women's careers. During the interviews, the women were asked to explain either what effect being a mother has had on their careers or, for women without children, what effects they perceive motherhood as having on women who are mothers.

Most of the women in the group are married (89%) and live with their partner and have children (74%). Nineteen of the women have one child and seven have two children. This means the proportion of mothers in this group of executives is higher than in other studies from the West.[5] For around 70% of the women with children, the women's parents or parents-in-law live in the same household or in the immediate vicinity. 26% of the study group are childless. Three of the childless women specifically expressed a desire to have children and are planning to do so. Only four of the 35 women are single, live alone and do not have any children. At 11%, the proportion of single women in this study is lower than that described in many international studies of women in executive roles.[6]

Both women with and without children described their perspective on motherhood and its effects on careers. One of the key questions regarding career success is how women are able to integrate their different roles as career women and mothers. Hall (1976) writes that career success is only really possible for managers who prioritise this role. For women, this means they have to focus more than men on combining the two roles. The attitudes in the Shanghai Women's Career Lab towards their own role as mothers are ambivalent. The women mainly said that they regard work as their core task, and do not have to constantly be there for their children. This contrasts with a study by Kim et al. (2010) which found that many women identify more with the role of mother. On the other hand, some women said that their strong career orientation and frequent absences have caused their bond with their children to suffer. As a result of their socialisation and political influences, for the female executives in this group it is the norm for women to work, pursue ca-

---

[5]   75% of respondents in a study of female business executives in Germany by Henn (2012) had no children. This value confirms other studies that give the proportion of childless female executives in Germany as 71 % (Holst, Busch-Heizmann, and Wieber, 2013).

[6]   In Germany, the proportion of single women among female executives is given as 20% and in Switzerland as 33% (Holst, Busch-Heizmann, and Wieber, 2013).

reers and primarily identify with their occupation. It is also the norm for these women to frequently spend time away from home, including for extended periods. According to the women, in Chinese families childcare is not just the mother's responsibility; especially in the classic one-child family, childcare is the collective duty of the family system. Society recognises work and careers as having a high value that benefits the entire family system (which is more extended than in the West). According to the women's accounts, there is no expectation that mothers have to primarily take care of the household and childcare themselves. While they work, the family support system comes into play, backed up by external helpers.

L., HRD: "I like to work rather than take care of everything at home. And I am also aware that my kid is not just my kid. It belongs to the whole a family. Everybody owned her and she belong to everybody. It's not myself assets ... So I start to empower my family. I start to not take care of something and let my family handle it. Slowly, slowly until today basically I don't need to take care of everything. My parents-in-law take care of almost everything of my kids, on her daily life. Even school."

A., HRD: "Yea and I am travelling a lot. I'm not the person that can be at home every day on time. And accompany my daughter to study. It's not my life. But if I look at work-life balance, I think I'm balanced. I don't feel unbalance. But I don't spend like everyday 4 hours with my kids. But I think I'm balanced in my kid, also view, she understands. I think I m a good example for her because if I work something, I work very hard and dedicated on something. So she actually is pretty self-independent study. I feel good on that as well. She never complains, she never says that I'm not spending time with her. She is happy with this as well. Of course my husband helps her on the academic side because he is better than me on that. And my mom helps on the logistics. So like eating and all this. I think I'm lucky to have the family support. It's like everybody have their own job at the family. I never feel I'm not work-life balance."

K., HRD: "I think for myself I'm not like traditional or those big population of Chinese moms. I'm more independent and I want to be that ... They combine their kid's success with them. For me I definitely expect my son to be the most excellent one but on the other side if he cannot do it I will not regard it as a failure of me. Myself is myself. My son is my son. My success is my success. My son's success I expect that but I will not pin too much hope. Some Chinese parents think if their son is not excellent, their whole life is not worth. I don't think that."

According to the study group, there are two fundamental tendencies regarding the influence of motherhood on careers: motherhood changes one's priorities, and motherhood often delays career progression. Only three of the women expressly remarked that they do not believe motherhood has imposed any restrictions on their careers.

M., CFO: "I think it is more or less the same. Not too much change. I feel kids were never a barrier for me to do stuff."

The women pointed out that as a mother and career woman you yourself are responsible for achieving your own individual balance between the two areas. In their view, this necessarily involves sacrifices or trade-offs, since it is impossible to strike a perfect balance that accommodates everything. The women noted that they often observe that women who become mothers weigh their priorities differently: children become the focus of many women's lives after giving birth. Some of the women view this new priority positively while concluding that the balance that mothers strike may be at the expense of career decisions that are difficult to combine with motherhood. In particular, the long absences from home that some roles involve are seen as major challenges. On this point, the women's accounts correspond to the findings of Eagly (2007), who describes long working hours and business travel as "trade-offs". Many of the women focused on career development in their own careers, and accepted the trade-off that they were often away from home. The section on challenges that arise during women's careers returns to this point in greater depth.

M., HRD: "I don't think it impacted my career. It just impacted my priority. Its more by nature that I find my daughter is more important than anything else. Of course when I make a decision I will choose some job that's not so busy."

Some of the women reflected on the consequences that their strong career orientation has had on their relationships with their children. Some of the children have developed stronger relationships with their grandparents or fathers.

K., HRD: "My husband actually spends more time with my son. Because I need to be away 2 weeks that's why my son had to sleep with my ayi. He got more used to the ayi before he was three because I could not guarantee every night he will be home ... Frankly speaking my husband, because the nature of his job, spend more time with my son. My son is more close to my husband."

Other women described positive effects of motherhood, such as the personal growth resulting from the experience. According to the women, their experiences as mothers helped them to cultivate positive strengths such as patience, empathy and the ability to deal with conflict. Cultivating these strengths has had a positive effect on the women's leadership styles.

> *Z., CFO: "It has not changed my career actually. It changed my personality ... when I had the baby, I got the feedback from my peers and colleagues who told me that I became very much patient than before ... Changed me a lot. And also when you have a baby it becomes one of your priorities. You take less part to other things like people conflict, like something that makes you unhappy. Forget it."*

They also reported that in organisations mothers receive a very positive response and lots of respect for their dual roles, and that they are supported by their colleagues. This does not correspond to the picture that emerges from the literature, according to which mothers are regarded as less competent and receive less support (Cheung and Halpern, 2010).

Most of the interviewed women described motherhood as slowing their career progression. The interviewees spontaneously reported that it is easier for single women to pursue careers, since they are more flexible, can travel frequently and are able to move around the world without shirking childcare responsibilities. This suggests that the phenomenon known as the "motherhood penalty" also occurs in this group (Budig, Misra, and Boeckmann, 2012). However, in these women's experience, the impact that this penalty has on women's careers has a clearly limited duration. The women certainly did not describe it as a career stopper. They spoke of career "delays" that were subsequently followed by further career development. The family support network plays a key role. If women receive strong support from their families, especially with respect to caring for young children, this reduces the supposed disadvantages, since the women are quickly able to concentrate fully on their careers again.

> *H., VP: "Like on the highway, I put my foot on the brake, little slower, but now I am back."*

> *C., HRD: "It will slow a little bit down. Cannot say affect, because, I always like to observe other people, I think a lot of successful women have a very good family and take care of their children and I believe, that at some stage of their career they will slow down, because they are giving birth to one child or to the second child. So, I am pretty comfortable with this slowing down part."*

The women gave the following examples of ways in which motherhood delayed their career development:

- Took longer to advance to the next stage of their career
- Colleagues were chosen for promotions over them while they were pregnant
- Too many business trips; in some cases, this led to the women quitting or changing jobs
- Loss of mobility, due for example to children's schools or dependence on family support based in a particular area
- Having to give up an overseas post

Interestingly, the descriptions gradually moved away from the women's own experiences and expanded to cover women as an overall group, with the women reporting from their perspectives as supervisors or HR managers. The interviewees think that absence during maternity leave has a particularly negative impact, since it is used to deny women promotions. In China, women are entitled to four months of maternity leave, followed by six months of parental leave. There is a legally protected breastfeeding period of one year. The women reported that it would be a significant hindrance to a woman's career to take a whole year off after giving birth. None of the interviewed women reported that they had taken the full leave they were entitled to. However, even shorter periods of maternity leave can apparently bring disadvantages with them.

> L., HRD: "That's because I had a very great company and great boss. She supported me. She said family first. This is the most time you need family. But in most cases, the boss just treats people like workforce. If you take long maternity leave they will give them lots of pressure and when they come back they might lose their position."

For young or recently married women who do not yet have children, merely the prospect that they might take time off often has a restrictive effect on their careers, according to the women. They remarked that employers often discuss the possibility of pregnancy as a criterion when making recruitment or promotion decisions. Observations on this point were particularly common among interviewees who work as HRDs, since they deal with female staff in this situation every day. According to these women, how well pregnancy can be integrated into women's careers depends significantly on the company culture and bosses. The group gave both positive and negative examples, though ultimately most of the women reported a "delay". Isolated comments such as "I could have progressed further without children" were made by the women with two children. Raising two chil-

dren was described as an additional stress factor that has an impact on career development. In one case, a woman chose to temporarily go part-time after giving
birth to her second child. By contrast, one of the interviewed executives who already had a young child was promoted to an even more senior executive role while
pregnant. Although most of the top managers who were interviewed have children
and rose up the career ladder as mothers, pregnancy is generally viewed as a disadvantage for women at multinational companies. A few women reported that pregnancy was viewed less critically before China's economic reforms and at state-
owned enterprises.

In summary, the women (with only a few exceptions) believe that motherhood
slows down women's career progression. They have observed female employees
being disadvantaged simply because they were of "child-bearing age". Some of the
women described having experienced disadvantages themselves, but ones that "delayed" rather than "limited" their careers. Many of the women believe that motherhood does have real consequences and remarked that they had to actively strike a
balance themselves. Following a delay, all the women's careers subsequently continued to progress again. The women regard their personal attitudes towards integrating the roles, their active engagement with reality on the ground and the way
they organised childcare as key factors behind their career success.

Childcare models of Chinese female executives

Different cultures have different approaches towards the balancing act of combining multiple roles. In China, grandparents play a key role in looking after children.
Given the high women's employment rate in China combined with the absence of
part-time working models, grandparents are the most important link in the childcare chain. This reflects not just the strong bonds between parents and children, but
also a strong cultural focus that values the family over the individual (Chen, Liu,
and Mair, 2010). Childcare by the grandparents can be interpreted as a familial adaptation strategy that aims to bolster the well-being of the whole family by reducing the burden on the mother, who then in turn supports the family financially.
Grandparents either live at the home of the working parents or close by. This support is based on the grandparents being financially dependent on their grown-up
children and on their taking the key role in the support system. One result of
China's "floating population", who move from the country to the cities for work, is
that grandparents are often temporarily the main guardians for their grandchildren,
since parents leave their children behind with the grandparents. A 2004 study
found that 45% of grandparents live in a single household with their grandchildren.

This phenomenon also demonstrates the social acceptance of working mothers who live apart from their children for extended periods of time (Liang and Zhondong Ma, 2004). Unlike in the past, it is no longer just the parents of the husband who play a key role in caring for young children. Rapid socioeconomic changes have transformed cultural traditions. According to several authors, maternal grandparents can be just as involved as paternal ones (Cong and Silverstein, 2008; Whyte and Xu, 2003).

Studies on intergenerational conflicts show that although there are more perceived conflicts of this kind in China than in other countries, conversely there is also more perceived support from grandparents (Ling and Powell, 2001). However, there are insufficient studies to be able to measure the precise extent of support. In conclusion, it remains unclear to what extent, on the one hand, career women's workloads are relieved by grandparents and to what extent, on the other, career women have to carry out certain everyday duties for their families (including the grandparents) (Budig and England, 2001).

Another source of support for top female managers is the widespread practice of hiring housekeepers (*ayi*, literally "aunt"), who are a sizeable presence on the labour market in China's major cities. Despite increased wages, it is still possible for families on middle to high incomes to employ full-time *ayis,* who in big cities can earn an average monthly income of 700 to 900 Euros for a six-day week with fixed hours.[7] The *ayis* do all the housework, cook meals and generally look after young children. In addition, home teachers are often hired to supervise older children, or children are sent to an after-school tutor.[8] All-day schools and boarding schools are the third key factor that makes it possible for Chinese mothers to work full-time. However, although there are other possibilities, the involvement of the grandparents is the classic model of childcare in China. Unlike in the West, where grandparents often look after their grandchildren as a favour, in China it is a matter of familial traditions and interdependences and is instead regarded as (so to speak) a post-retirement "vocation" for grandparents that is firmly anchored in society.

There are different perspectives about the link between work and family roles in the Shanghai Women's Career Lab. According to an optimistic view, people benefit from juggling their work and family roles. The more pessimistic view points out that women suffer when they try to combine both roles (Powell, 2011). According

---

[7]   Average salary 2016, based on the author's own personal experience of living in Shanghai.
[8]   Author's personal knowledge based on living in Shanghai and numerous conversations with local inhabitants from various income levels, 2012–2016.

to Powell, national culture influences the extent to which women experience work-family conflicts. When asked how they organise childcare for their own children or how they used to do so, the women made clear that career-oriented Chinese women enjoy strong support on this front due to China's national culture. According to the women, when career women are successful in China this is regarded as a success for the whole family. Families hence support women's career orientation and make sure they are able to concentrate fully on their careers.

> *Angel, VP: "Female have more equality than male – especially at home."*

Some of the women are supported by an entire family system. "Family system" refers here to the core family, comprising the children, parents and both sets of grandparents, as well as aunts and uncles. Traditionally, parents-in-law often live in the married couple's home or nearby. Moreover, the parents of the wife in particular have a fixed role in the support system, due above all to the one-child policy. Especially in Shanghai, the wife's parents often have a more central role, contra the tradition described in the literature where it is the husband's parents who play this role. The grandparents help the family with housekeeping and childcare, and are often financially supported by their children in return. Generally, the wife will hand over her baby to the care of her mother or mother-in-law and return to work after a short break. Since the retirement age for women is 50 or 55, many mothers-in-law or mothers seamlessly assume this second role after they stop working.

Accordingly, for most of the study participants it is not just their husbands who play a role in their family units, but also both sets of parents.

> *Lily, HRD: "She's 58. She's very diligent woman. She takes care of me, my husband and my kid. She can organize everything. Sometimes I feel that I need to do something so I will buy something which maybe they don't have time. They never ask me for anything."*

The women's parents-in-law and parents assume regular duties supporting the women and their husbands. These duties include household management and childcare. Grandparents play an integral role in childcare for young children in particular, and are often the primary caregivers. All the interviewed women with one or two children described their family environments as highly supportive. The women are able to draw on a network of familial and external support to help with housekeeping and childcare. All the women reported that they have a full-time housekeeper (*ayi*) to help with their household. The *ayis* do the housework, cooking and shopping, and provide support to the grandparents. The women's parents and parents-in-law assume full responsibility for looking after young children and oversee the *ayis'* housekeeping tasks. There are special night *ayis* who look after the babies of working mothers from the evening to the early morning so that the mothers can sleep. Some of the women also reported childcare facilities at former employers in the state sector, which were fully tailored to the women's working hours.

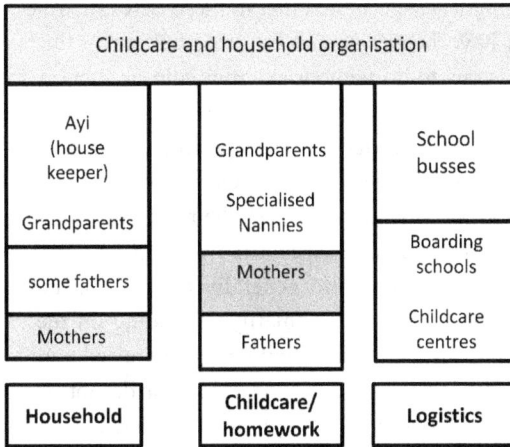

Figure 6: The pillars of the Chinese participants' childcare organisation (developed by author)

Several of the women with just one child reported that they feel completely liberated from housework. However, they are required to help older children with their homework, and believe this places more demands on working women than in other countries. One woman who previously lived in Germany, for example, reported how much more time it takes to help children with their homework in China.

M., CFO: "I don't do big things in my family. I just come back to home and I'm playing or discussing or reading with my son. I do nothing for the home.....If I want I have a lot of freedom, I have a full-time nanny, and I have one cleaning lady. And I have my mom on a daily basis, and you know the Chinese grandmas, they are just unbelievable. They just stick to the baby. My partner, generally speaking, he is a nice man, so on the weekends I like to read books and drink coffee, so if we are together he is playing with the baby, so I drink my coffee and read my books. So theoretically speaking, if I want I can completely free myself from the whole thing, but I do not want. The reason I have my baby is I want to give my love to him. When I come home from work,

I like everyone to go, so I can take care of the baby by myself, changing dia-
pers, feeding him, put him to sleep, I insist he sleeps in my room, rather than
by the nanny. I am emotionally attached to him, so I am willing to do this, but
if I want, I am free. For the job I need to travel, yes."

It is striking that culturally mixed married couples and Chinese parents who have
lived abroad for extended periods make less use of external assistance, and that
women in such couples take on a lot of household chores and childcare duties
themselves. It might be speculated that in these cases the role models for mothers'
responsibilities have been changed by other cultural influences. The women reported that decisions to do without external help or support from grandparents as
far as possible had been made jointly. Three of the women previously lived in
Germany, and one is married to an American. Attitudes differed in particular
among women who previously lived in Germany. They regard themselves or the
fathers as having more central roles in their children's upbringing. The woman
who was married to an American and the women who had previously spent extended periods living abroad also generally believe that mothers should care for
children themselves rather than primarily depending on the child's grandparents.
Many also see drawbacks to young children being raised purely by poorly educated
ayis. They also think that some women cannot or do not want to delegate the su-
pervision of children's homework, which is regarded as women's primary parental
responsibility for children of school age. This was reported by women whose children attend a multilingual school. They said that they spend a lot of time helping
their children with their homework in the evenings before then responding to their
business emails after 9 or 10 at night. Some other women choose not to delegate
primary responsibility for their children's upbringing to their parents or housekeepers. They justified this decision based on their observation that children who
are not primarily raised by their parents develop less well. One woman described
how her elderly parents struggled to cope with her son and that he had problems
with language development, since his grandparents spoke different Chinese dialects.

Z., IT Director: "...And I also see the difference of kids who have been raised
by grandparents or by their parents. The kids are different. I would say the
kids who have been raised by parents are better educated."

G., Customer Service Director: "I don't think my parents-in-law can properly
educate the kids. They take very good care of the kids as a Chinese old person.
They feed him well, clean, you know, all this kind of things, but I feel like the
kid is isolated because I live in the eighth floor of a building and we don't

*have the lifts, because it's an old building. So my mother-in-law said, it's im-
possible for her to bring my son down to interact with other kids. So my son is
very isolated, very timid, afraid of a lot of things. Even the ants he feels afraid
of. And he cannot speak. We have a few different dialects at home that also
brings him more problems ... So there are a few different languages happen-
ing at home and my son just decides not to say at all. So I feel worried and
then because my husband works in a state-owned company and they have a
company-owned kindergarten, which took young kids right after one year's
age, so we decide to bring him in there."*

All the mothers in the Shanghai Women's Career Lab placed great emphasis on the
importance of organising childcare. The group can be split into two categories.
Women who previously lived in Germany or have foreign husbands were particularly likely to have a different conception of their role in their children's upbringing, and regard themselves as having more obligations. Women with two children
also face challenges. They described problems combining the roles and increased
stress. The other women mostly reported not experiencing any problems with
childcare or housekeeping, since these responsibilities are almost entirely handled
by their parents and *ayis*. They feel they receive enough support in these areas that
they can concentrate fully on their careers.

Chinese husbands' attitudes to the senior executive careers of their wives

Another very important aspect that can have a positive or negative impact on career success is partners' attitudes towards their wives' careers. A study by Kawa-
hara, Esnil, and Hsu (2007) shows how much emphasis Asian women in management roles put on relating to others and creating a harmonious environment, both
of which are reflective of collectivistic values. Family and partner support were
recognised as playing an important role in these women's achievements. Studies of
marital relationships show that one of the biggest problems for working women is
a lack of support from their partners (Gilbert, 1993). Many Western studies describe how career men tend to seek out women who are hierarchically beneath
them. A wife who is more successful than her husband would encroach on his traditional role. Moreover, women's careers and career success only appear to moderately affect the distribution of household chores and childcare between partners.
Powell (2011) writes that the proportion of family income that women bring home
typically has little effect on how much work their partners do around the house.

Married couples in China traditionally choose their jobs together in accordance
with their role as "one family, two systems". The husbands are able to be more

flexible and take more risks in their choice of job, in accordance with their abilities (Lin, 2000). One study found that younger participants do not see any gender-specific differences in relation to factors such as career and development opportunities or quality of work. However, women continued to show a preference for the factor of security. Hence, they preferred positions at state-owned enterprises, which offer a combination of security and opportunities for progression, over ones at private companies. A research by Halpern and Cheung (2008) shows how Chinese career women describe their husbands. Against the background of patriarchal norms, it was assumed that women's success would represent a threat to their husbands. However, in this study the women described their husbands as their biggest fans, coaches and mentors. According to the women's descriptions, their husbands took on a lot of housework, gave emotional support and encouragement to their wives, were confident and self-assured, and saw both partners as equals. They did not feel threatened by their wives' careers, as is often described in other accounts, and were happy to accord their wife the "higher status". In these marriages, the partners grew together and negotiated a lot in a spirit of give and take. In several studies, women expressed gratitude for their husbands' support. According to their accounts, this support was essential for the long-term survival of their marriages.

Familial support is one of the most important success factors for women attempting to progress into top management. Having collective identities that emphasise family loyalty, women also fall back on their families for support. In many studies, a combination of extended families, hired help and supportive husbands is described as a key foundation for women's career success. Especially in collectivist societies such as China, close relationships with the extended family are the primary support system.

Result from the Shanghai Women's Career Lab:
husbands provide emotional support to their wives

According to Gilbert (1988), one of the biggest problems for working women is a lack of support from their partners. This refers to practical help with household chores and raising children as well as emotional support. Before presenting the women's answers regarding their partners' role in relation to their careers, it is important to understand the types of couple that exist among the women in the group. There are four groups of married couples:

1. The husband has a senior executive position himself: 7 (university professor, GM, president, company owner)

2. The husband has a job with regular working hours and no business travel: 21
3. The husband works part-time or as a freelancer: 3 (consultant, architect)
4. The husband was not working at the time of the interview: 4

Five of the husbands have foreign nationality and five are Chinese men who have spent a lot of time abroad.

According to Halpern et al. (2008), against the background of patriarchal norms it might be supposed that Chinese husbands would be less likely to support their wives or would feel threatened by their wives' careers. But just like in the Halpern study, this proved not to be the case for this group of women. Rather, the opposite was described: a large majority of the study participants said that their husbands are very supportive of their careers. The term "supportive" was mentioned in many of the answers.

The following positive descriptions were given of support for their careers that the women receive from their husbands:

- Supportive (9)
- Follows my wishes in a conflict (2)
- Encourages me/gives advice (6)
- Understands my stress
- Does not want me to compromise
- Wants to see me happy

> A., Legal Director: "He actually encourages me to work. It's not like some other cases; some husbands will say I need you to have full attention to the family, to the kids. He really thinks I need to get more connected. We have more common language. I would discuss with him some of the challenges I have and he would give advices. That's very helpful. We have more issues to talk about."

Two different types of husband were described: ones who are strongly career-oriented themselves and ones who are family-focused rather than ambitious about their careers. The latter are in the majority in this study. The husbands who are not career-oriented take on a portion of household organisation, often with the support of housekeepers and grandparents. The less ambitious partners take a particularly strong role in their children's upbringing. This group of husbands was described by the women as follows:

- Contributes to housework/has bigger part in housework
- Stays home to care for kids
- Helps with kids
- Family-centric

A., VP: "Actually my husband is very supportive. He's not the career ambitious person actually. He likes more freestyle. He works as like a finance consultant. Takes care of children. He did not like have my job full-time. He had a lot of free time. I think he does more than me. Before we had an ayi. 5 years ago my sister left us, than I have ayi but a few months ago she left. And we decided not immediately backfill. My husband does the cooking, buys vegetable, shopping and a lot. He drives. It's easier for him. He does a lot of house things. He's very supportive to my career – always when I talk to him, should I go to Hong Kong, should I go global. Basic decision of course we discuss but he's always supportive."

J., GM: "I have talked to my husband (laughing). And he stayed much longer at home than me. Yes, he has stayed 3 years at home. (Laughing) Yes. When I had the offer from company XY we discussed this, because one had to stay home for the child. In China it would be common to bring the child to the grandparents, but his parents are dead. My parents take care of my nice already. And I did not want to bring our son to my parents and hire another Ayi (housekeeper). Therefore I said one of us must do it."

The wives with husbands who are not career-oriented expressed regret at their husbands' lack of career ambitions. They described how it was only in the course of their marriages, and in particular after giving birth, that they also saw advantages in this distribution of roles. Common descriptions of husbands in this regard included "no ambition", "lazy" or "I need to push him". The female executives themselves appear to have stereotypical ideas and hopes regarding their husbands' careers.

L., HRD: "He is a person who never thinks about future. He thinks about today. Even today is not planned. He's a very peaceful person. Not aggressive. His job is very normal. What I mean he is an operational personal. He manages the plant. Do the productions. All the things actually have been scheduled. He starts work at 8:30. Arrive home at 5:30 every day. Almost same unless he has some trip."

J., HRD: "My husband is just opposite but I pushed him. I say 'see I don't want you to be so successful but you have to be the same as what I'm doing. We have to be equal.'"

Lin (2000) describes how couples in China choose their jobs together in accordance with their role as "one family, two systems", with greater scope for flexibility attributed to the husbands. This does not appear to be the case in this study group. Only a few women in this group are married to men who are also career-oriented. Career-oriented husbands also support their wives' career activities emotionally and provide advice and encouragement. The men with their own careers take on parental duties that are more associated with men, such as supervising sporting activities. Most of them do not do any of the housework, since that is taken care of by the *ayis* or grandparents or coordinated by their wives.[9] Most of the women in the Shanghai Women's Career Lab earn more than their husbands. However, this was never spontaneously brought up by the women in the interviews. They only made very brief remarks on this topic when directly asked. The women did not describe how their partners felt about the pay gap, but they did express their regret at their husbands' lack of ambition. There were no indications that the women specifically sought out partners who are not career-oriented. When asked about this, the women said that they were more or less on equal footing to begin with and the role distribution came later. One woman with a foreign husband who works as a freelancer replied that it was more of a side issue when choosing a partner. However, the fact that he is a freelancer makes their family very flexible and is the factor that has made her own career possible. At the time of the interview, this woman was pregnant with her second child. She was promoted during her maternity leave.

It is striking that in the Shanghai Women's Career Lab, there were no negative reports of husbands who are critical of or obstruct their partners' careers. Only in two cases were there repeated mentions of conflicts about the distribution of responsibilities for their children's upbringing. The husbands in question work as CEOs or senior executives themselves. Their wives described them as less family-oriented: less involved in their children's upbringing and household management.

> *A., Legal Director: "That's something I've been struggling to be honest. He has busy job and he travels a lot. It's hard for him to get more attention to the kids although in a weekend I think there was something to do with Chinese men and their role in the family. In a weekend sometimes he would play golf, again half day is gone. Kids already are used to calling mom whenever something happens and I am not happy with that. I'm trying to doing adjustments but he will discuss with me the weekend arrangements etc... I would try to keep him at home or to go to kids' activities."*

---

[9] Cf. footnote 8.

One woman's foreign, career-oriented husband persuaded her to go part-time after the birth of her second child. She said that she had not originally regarded that as an option for her, but ultimately came to see her husband's intervention as positive, caring behaviour with the aim of protecting her from overwork.

> *H., VP: "That's an interesting question. I think the decision to go part-time he pushed me definitely. I think if not for him, I don't know if I would come to the decision so quickly. I think I always had some thoughts about it, but he was understandable very concerned that my workload was very heavy. But I think we got a line on this very quickly. I don't think he pushed me into something I didn't want. But I think he probably pushed me to make the decision faster."*

Conflict generally arises over travel, which frequently takes the interviewees away from home. But here, too, the women's accounts suggest their husbands have a high tolerance threshold, given the frequency of the absences described.

> *M., CFO: "You can get men to cook for you in this country. You don't get that very often in Germany."*

In summary, the role of the husbands in the Shanghai Women's Career Lab can be seen as a largely positive factor, but conflicts over childcare and the time that their wives spend away due to work play a role here too, and these conflicts are not entirely alleviated by the strong support networks. This factor was primarily mentioned by interviewees who have two children in their household or a partner who is pursuing his own career. In this study group, two factors are associated with increased pressure on women if they occur together: firstly, having more than one child; and secondly, having conceptions of childcare that differ from the traditional Chinese system and assign more familial responsibilities to women. Such conceptions exist among women who previously lived abroad in the West (especially in Germany, in this study) or are married to a foreign spouse.

It seems that the women found a way to live their family concepts with partners supporting them in their careers. The concept of partnership that Professor Gesine Schwan[10] described as her vision for the German society with equal shares of both partners in family duties though is not the family model of this group. It seems that most couples here in a way changed roles and most husbands step back when it comes to career building. Husbands' positive attitudes towards their partners' careers is a constant in this study. This results in those husbands who are not career-oriented being willing to take on more or most of the familial responsibilities.

---

[10]   In her presentation at the German Consulate, Salon Yongfu Lu, in October 2014.

Those husbands are in majority supported by grandparents and housekeepers. Husbands with their own careers focus on providing emotional support to their partners. They do not assist with household responsibilities and only occasionally with childcare responsibilities. These results are consonant with the research of Halpern et al. (2008), who also found that female Chinese executives described the support they received from their husbands in positive terms. They are also consonant with western research where female executives described how their partners give emotional support to their career development but very little practical help with household tasks (Henn, 2012).[11]

The role of mentoring and networking on female careers

Mentoring as opportunity for Chinese women

Various researchers have asked the question of the importance of mentoring for female careers (Burke & McKeen (1990), Morehead, Maurer & Schipiani (2012), O'Brien, Biga, Kessler et al. (2008). Against a background in which women remain a minority in management and encounter gender-specific challenges, mentoring and networking are highly promising career development strategies (Rastetter and Cornils, 2012). In a review of literature on mentoring, Ragins (1989, 1997) also attributes particular importance to mentoring for women: "Mentoring relationships, while important for men, may be essential for women".

The term mentor dates back to ancient Greek literature and describes a relationship between a younger adult and an older, more experienced one who helps the former to navigate the world (Allen, Eby, Poteet et al., 2004). According to Kram and Lynn (1985), a mentor is an experienced, productive manager who relates well to a less experienced employee and facilitates his or her personal development for the benefit of the organisation as well as that of the individual. The mentor is often higher in rank and older than the protégé. The relationship can be initiated by either party, is generally long-term and is characterised by substantial emotional commitment from both parties (Ragins, 1989; Noe, 1988). The mentor can be part of the same organisation or external to it. According to Levinson (1978), the relationship with a mentor is often described as the most important experience in the

---

[11] In a study of 56 German female executives by Henn (2012), the majority of women describe receiving support from their partners. Only 18% of responses mentioned little support. Only seven comments suggested the support received was more practical help with household tasks. The results of the present study also suggest women receive relatively little practical assistance compared to strong emotional support from their husbands.

early years of a person's career. Mentors are not just an important source of learning for their protégé, but also play a central role in helping them to develop self-confidence and identify with their work. Although there are many different definitions of mentoring, there is consensus that mentoring consists of two central key constructs: career development and psychosocial support. These two core functions, which are mentioned in almost all scholarly works, go back to the work of Kram (1985). According to Kram, the career development function of mentoring comprises sponsoring, coaching, protection, exposure, visibility and challenging work assignments. The psychosocial support comprises encouragement, friendship, advice and feedback, as well as help to build up the mentee's expertise, self-confidence and effectiveness. The benefits of mentoring fall into two categories: objective career successes, such as promotions and salary, and subjective career outcomes. The second category includes more affective, "softer" criteria such as career satisfaction, career commitment and job satisfaction.

Formal mentoring can be distinguished from informal, traditional mentoring. The former is less widespread, but has recently become more common at many companies. In informal, traditional mentoring, a mentor selects a protégé, usually in order to foster their individual talents, because they stand out due to their exceptional achievements. The aim of formal mentoring programmes, which are initiated and coordinated by companies, is to foster the talents of new employees, university graduates or specific groups, which can include women in management. These formal programmes generally have more structured timeframes and content, and the mentor and mentee are often placed together by the organisation (Ehrich, 2008). Underhill (2005) indicated in a meta-analysis that mentoring improves career outcomes in general while informal mentoring produced larger and more significant effects on career outcomes than did formal mentoring. The newest form of mentoring is known as e-mentoring, which largely takes place via email and reduces organisational and geographical boundaries, enabling women in particular to access a variety of mentors (Headlam-Wells, Gosland, and Craig, 2005; Leck, Elliott, and Rockewell, 2012). Due to the barriers faced by women in management, mentoring is regarded as a particularly crucial factor for women's career development. In this connection, scholars working on the topic of gender difference and mentoring point to gender discrimination, male hierarchies and a lack of informal networks to support women's careers (Tharenou, 2007). Several studies have looked at gender differences in relation to mentoring. If the two relevant categories of career support and psychosocial support are not separated, a mixed picture emerges. Some results show no gender-specific difference, while others actually show negative effects in women as a group (but not men). Other studies (Young, Cady and Foxon, 2006) show more positive outcomes for women. Kimberley, Eddelston, Baldrige et al (2004) describe how mentoring positively influenced women's sense of marketability and exposure to powerful networks. Overall, studies investigating the effects of mentors on women's careers in comparison with men show that in the category of career support women tend to gain more benefits for their career development from mentors than men. This category has more positive effects in relation to women's careers than mentoring's psychological function. There are even indications that the effect of psychological support may tend to have a negative impact on women's career development (Lyness and Thompson, 2000).

Shanghai Women's Career Lab: Accounts of the individual benefits of mentoring

As described earlier, there are contradictory findings in the literature on the effects of mentoring on women's career development. While the effects appear to be mainly positive for men, women experience negative as well as positive effects. These disadvantages relate to the psychological support aspect of mentoring (Lyness et al., 2000). When asked about the influence of mentoring on their own careers, the women described different types of person: sometimes, they described mentors who were formally appointed by their companies, while in other cases they described informal mentors. Formal mentoring programmes are special programmes, often aimed specifically at women that are being established at an increasing number of companies. However, only a minority in the study group (three women) mentioned formal mentoring relationships.

> *T., GM: "Our company encouraged the culture of mentorship so ... I told them is better to (have a mentor from) ... overseas because I need some global connection and also global mentoring. And then the HR assigned this person to me because they see it very relevant so I connected with this person. We have been working together for about a year and it was good and he recently left the company and started his own business."*

Twenty-four of the women mentioned informal mentoring relationships that came about without any formal programmes. Some of these mentors were working at the same companies as the women, while others were based externally. Eleven of the women spontaneously described multiple individuals who had acted as mentors to them. These women had actively and deliberately initiated the mentoring relationships. Personal chemistry, the potential mentor's comparative expertise and hierarchical considerations were key criteria when it came to choosing a mentor.

H., VP: "Informal I have a few people that I have from the past companies that I stayed friends with and sometimes when I would discuss with them o things or things I'm not sure about or even when I'm thinking of new job opportunity I would talk to them but it is not a formal mentorship. I think generally if you have people like that. It could be your friends. It could be your previous colleagues I think it is great to have just a few people. And my husband is a great person. I think it's nice to have a few people you have in your life that can do that."

The women also mentioned the term "sponsor". Ideally, a sponsor should come from the company's headquarters and be as high-ranking as possible. The terms "sponsor" and "mentor" were used synonymously at several points.

A., VP: "... When I am joining this company I had four rounds of interviews. The final interview is the CEO of Asia Pacific. A 60-year-old French. 35 years in the company. He's among the top 5 decision-makers global. After interviewing he liked me. He says let's choose a lady that will be the right fit for China. In the past 4 years in every talent discussion he is the decision-maker for all Asia Pacific talent. He would say A. is good talent, let's invest in her. ... He didn't give me a call of mentor but in the key decisions he always sponsors me."

Since only a minority of the women had formal mentoring relationships, the question arises of how actively they looked for a mentor or whether a mentoring relationship was instead offered to them. The women in the study group are aware of the benefits that properly functioning mentoring and sponsoring relationships can have for their careers. They described how they actively considered who should be their mentor, how to find a mentor and the positive effects this relationship could have on their future careers.

A., VP: "I think one thing is clear in my mind is I need to have a mentor. A mentor, who is in Paris. A person that would know there is a China Angel and even everybody says good (things) about her ... I decided to have a coach woman because currently my boss is a female. I want to look for the opportunities for woman because I'm a woman. Sometimes we have different language, how we think. I think they help me out a lot ..."

Table 6: Responses to the question "Who was your mentor?"

Who was mentor	answers
Boss	11
Female	3
From overseas	2
From Senior Management	2
HRD, Asia HRD	2
Coach	1
Specialist in the company	1
Friends, previous colleges	4
Husband	1
Clients	1
Headhunter and training providers	2

Formal mentoring relationships are mainly viewed critically, since in the women's experience the success of support depends on how good the personal relationship with the mentor is. These experiences are in line with the research on satisfaction with mentor relationships of Ortiz-Walters, Eddleston and Simione (2010).Three women described formal mentoring relationships and the benefits that they experienced, but these relationships were shorter in duration and were only regarded as having a limited impact on their careers. Phrases such as "not effective" and "only a formality" were used. The women all agree that informal mentoring relationships have had more benefits for their careers. "Support", "understanding" and "encouragement" are the main factors that were spontaneously mentioned when the women were asked about the benefits of mentoring. They reported how mentoring had helped them to cope with very difficult times at their companies or to persevere in positions that they did not particularly enjoy and then nonetheless advance in their careers. Other perceived benefits of mentoring included trying out new approaches or stepping out of their comfort zone.

> *V., GM: "I think they can give you very important advice to let you avoid unnecessary concerns or worries ... If you will be with something that is not important they can tell you what is really important. And also when you in big pressure with challenges, mentoring encourages since they can look much further away from your view, they can say 'It's not a big deal...you can conquer that.' You will deal much better and become stronger."*

> *K., HRD: "... always when you look back you will find those 'wow moments' from them. From your conversation with them and from the information they share with me ... When I do the reflections with them ... and I mention what I did and what is such challenge and how I come up with it. They also share*

with me their similar experiences and we come up with learning from each other from all these different experiences."

The interviewees also regard mentors as playing a key role in teaching about cultural differences (for example, the art of debating at French companies). The interviewees repeatedly emphasised how mentors help to explain other ways of communicating. Another important contribution made by the mentors was helping the executives to understand the corporate system. This is regarded as particularly helpful at early career stages. The women regard mentors who act as career coaches and supervise the women for a long period of time, even after switching companies, as highly beneficial. There were reports of specific support that resulted in career advancement, such as rising to a GM role. Several of the interviewed women thought it important to emphasise that mentoring is equally beneficial for men and women. The point that mentoring can benefit all staff at a company, not just women, was made on multiple occasions.

H., VP: "I have a pretty strong view – I hear a lot of women – and even if you read books about women leadership I think many people are saying that women need to do more in mentoring and networking. I think for me mentoring and networking is equally important for men and women. I'm having a hard time understanding why this is particularly important for women. For anyone if you want to go up in the corporate world you need to network. You need to find people to be your networks. I don't see the particular importance for women?"

One possible risk ascribed to mentoring is that mentees become dependent on their mentors' reputation at the company. A few women reported being disadvantaged by their mentor relationships when their mentor's position at the company became weakened.

What was most clearly emphasised in the answers is the connection between sponsoring and career success. The higher up the company hierarchy the sponsor is and the better and longer-lasting their relationship, the more beneficial the women described it as being. According to the women, the difficulty with sponsorship is finding a sponsor at the company's head office when one is based far away from it. They said that this is only possible after reaching a certain level in the hierarchy or if one's work requires frequent travel to the head office. One participant from a large American company described the difficulty that she faces making contact with possible sponsors simply in virtue of being a Chinese woman. She does not believe this obstacle exists at private or state-owned Chinese companies; the disadvantage she describes is thus one that is connected, *inter alia*, with not working at the head office.

Mutually beneficial alliances

The group most frequently mentioned in connection with mentoring is the women's bosses. More than half the women mentioned female bosses who supported them. The interviewed women attributed a central role to their bosses in their career development. They compared their relationships with their bosses to those with their parents, describing these mentoring relationships as ones that, due to Chinese values, are not challenged or questioned. Trust and longstanding loyalty were integral to the interviewees' relationships with their bosses, who then in turn helped them to advance in their careers. They described long-lasting bonds that continued even when the bosses returned to Europe or the USA. They regularly reconnect with their bosses during business trips and maintain these relationships over the long term. Their bosses' success is often closely related to their own success. The women described how certain CEOs/GMs of multinational companies in Shanghai have or had particular prestige both within and, especially, outside the companies. According to the women, these leaders attract employees who want to work at their companies simply because of the bosses' personalities.

> *K., HRD: "She was Chinese. That was my first Chinese boss. She was my first Chinese boss. Previously all my bosses were foreigners. She said don't regret just go. Don't hesitate just go. After 2 months ... I got a notice that she resigned. She had proposed to our headquarter ... that I was successor candidate. So became her successor.*
>
> *She is also top 10 global. Of the most influential women leaders in the world. I think she sees a lot of opportunities. And she's the one that is taking actions very quickly. And she's also empathetic towards the local situations. She's very brave. She has the guts to make tough decisions."*
>
> *A., VP: "The boss, she was a French lady. Very, very smeary. She brought the brand to China in 1994. Very, very successful ... during the Olympic. I would say I grew the company. Recruit people. Build organization. Build HR function and brought company to be top employer of China market ... When we talk about the leaders of this generation in the market, these people all remember me and they are all very, very successful. They are all company manager levels. CEO levels. And I feel that's really rewarding ... they are all the key players in the market now."*

Trust is central to the women's relationships with their bosses. Chinese women are shown more trust than men by foreign or female bosses. As a result, they are given high levels of discretion and responsibility, even at early stages of their careers.

> *J., GM: "I was his assistant. When he was away I was the GM of the whole factory, looked after purchasing department, operational, even selling."*

Unlike traditional mentoring relationships described in the literature, the mentoring relationships in this study were characterised by mutual dependence. The foreign GMs, were dependent on trusted Chinese subordinates with local market knowledge, local connections and networks and language skills, and preferred women to men because they trusted them more. The female executives needed the foreign mentors to rise up the corporate ladder and to gain access to the head office, the centre of power in multinational companies, to further build their own career progression. A term that describes this mentoring relation best is "mutually beneficial alliance."The women's bosses' influence on their careers covers three areas: promotions within the company, taking the women with them to another company and supporting their career there, and imparting certain skills that were important for their career advancement. Examples of promotions included positions in the head office, taking over from the boss themselves or general promotions to a higher-ranking position. The interviewees' decisions to switch companies were also often closely linked to their bosses. In this connection, the women described how their bosses had the female executives follow when they switched companies themselves and specifically enticed them away. The women also mentioned agreements between the heads of multinationals over appointments to executive roles: the bosses of companies are very closely connected in certain industries in Shanghai and negotiate with each other over how to fill key positions. One woman even reported taking a pay cut to follow her boss to another company.

> *A., VP: "The reason I left actually is again my boss ... I worked for her for 9 years. She is a real respected leader with me. Very smart. Then she resigned first. (Company name) is her baby, however this is not her company, so her dream was to create something of her own ... They invited my boss to be the chairman of that big project. It was very exciting. Then my boss talked to me and said: Angel, are you interested to join that company?"*

The women reported receiving particular support in exceptional situations. One study participant's foreign boss gave her a sabbatical to care for her terminally ill husband and supported her promotion despite this absence. Many of the interviewees described their bosses as their role models and explained how they helped them to develop crucial career skills that enabled their subsequent progression. An additional important factor of the mentor relationship was acquiring intercultural skills through working with a number of foreign bosses. One participant from the HR sector had worked closely with general managers of six different nationalities over the course of time. The majority of the women have worked with bosses of four different nationalities on average.

> *X., BU-Head: "I started at (company name) and I have to be honest I was very lucky because I have a good manager. My first sales manager was a lady. She was a very good coach and taught me a lot of things like selling skills, how to become a good sales person. I became the top sales person in (company name) after two years for three products."*

> *M., CFO: "I had a very good role model who was previous, previous CFO for (Company name) in Greater China. She is from Singapore. A very tiny, tiny lady. I know her now from my Hong Kong time. More than ten years. She is now the (Company name) CFO for Greater China. She was a pretty good role model for me. She said: '... you do not really need to be stronger in whatever than men. You really can use different strategies to be still powerful.'"*

The women's experiences show that formal mentoring relationships were not especially important for their career development. Most of the women have benefited from informal mentoring relationships, usually with bosses at GM/CEO level and often with female superiors. These relationships were characterised by trust and loyalty. The mentors supported the women in earlier career stages with advice on western management skills. In return the women supported the mentors with local market knowledge and acted as their spoke person inside and outside the company. Most commonly, however, the women reported being given promotions within their companies or higher positions at other companies if their mentors switched companies. None of the women reported any gender-specific barriers in relation to mentoring like those described by Tharenou (2007). By contrast, being a woman at a multinational company in China appears to be a key advantage for building trust between mentees and male mentors from other countries. It is also important that many of the mentors in this group were also women.

Networking and guanxi relations

Networking refers to developing contacts with other relevant individuals both inside and outside an organisation. It includes various tactics for forming alliances in order to achieve personal objectives. Networking is also described as a micro political power tactic (Weber, 1972; Reiners, 2008) through which members of organisations attempt to strategically shape and draw on the network of relationships that surrounds them so as to promote their own interests. Depending on the definition, mentoring and sponsoring can be described as intermediate forms of networking in which a temporary, asymmetric relationship is established where both parties enter into binding obligations that can be either inclusive or exclusive. Mentoring can provide additional career support that complements networking, and networking can make it easier to find a mentor (Rastetter and Cornils, 2012). Networking can be useful at all stages of a person's career, whereas mentoring is more helpful for women at early stages of their careers. The relationships developed through networking are of long-term importance and are not affected by hierarchical differences. Mutual give and take is a central aspect of networking. Networks can vary in terms of how close-knit, large and heterogeneous they are. A very close-knit network offers solidarity and help. Large networks offer more resources than small ones, but can become unwieldy and encourage competing subgroups. Heterogeneous networks offer highly varied resources but can involve potential conflicts due to the different cultures and attitudes of their members. Opportunities opened up by networking include access to information, the mutual solidarity of network members and a certain degree of regulation, since the rules and role expectations are defined and offer security and protection. The risks lie in the investment costs, mainly in terms of time, and the unclear, uncertain and unenforceable return on this investment. There might also be conflicting objectives that undermine the opportunities created by the group. For example, conflicts might arise between solidarity and over integration, or between heterogeneity and homogeneity. Networking is based on socialisation practices and processes of social inclusion and exclusion. In keeping with the findings of gender studies, many professional networks are still dominated by men. This is particularly evident in management. Male networks are traditionally rooted in the military or in university fraternities, and are often based around all-male communal activities such as drinking or sports that exclude women from the networks. Studies from the 1970s show that women had fewer opportunities to access male-dominated networks (Kanter, 1977). Being excluded from the "inner circle" of top management is a significant obstacle to women's advancement.

In the cultural context of China, *guanxi* networks play a key role. Numerous studies have been conducted on the issue of *guanxi*, meaning intricate and pervasive networks of social relationships (Yeung and Tung, 1996; Li and Wright, 2000). *Guanxi* connections are a culturally distinct form of social capital, which has been variously defined as "special relationships" between two or more people (Harrison,

Scott, Hussain, and Millman, 2014). These connections, which form part of Confucian tradition, lead to a reciprocal exchange of favours and mutual obligations. In China, success in business often depends on making the right use of complex networks, with family networks playing a key role. *Guanxi* can be thought of as a system used to exchange favours or a way of attaining private goals (Yang, 1986). These favours are equal exchanges and do not necessarily follow any clear rules or regulations, and are as such not corrupt in the narrow definition of the term (Oi, 1989). *Guanxi* usually does not involve a patron-client relationship. Because traditionally people lacked things in all aspects of life, connections with people at all levels were useful and necessary. Those who have power in one sphere can offer help in that area in exchange for similar help in an area to which they otherwise have no access. Some *guanxi* ties are strictly instrumental and some are very much tied to personal feelings. Most *guanxi* ties are a mixture of both (Pye, 1985).

Some researchers believe that *guanxi* stems from the five cardinal role relations (*wu-lun*) of Confucianism. Other researchers have suggested it may have more to do with transactional governance structures and institutional uncertainty (Boisot and Child, 1988). As a means of overcoming structural barriers, *guanxi* is very significant. The Chinese are very conscious of the role of *guanxi* in constructing relationships, consolidating interpersonal bonds and building personal dependence (Leung, 2000). It is considered an important substitute for formal structural support and used as a form of protection in the absence of structural alternatives: "It exercises power over one's career and has significant impact on the accomplishment of personal goals" (Leung, 2002, p. 606). *Guanxi* is seen as very important in Chinese society; it has been suggested that most Chinese individuals and organisations cultivate these relationships (Peng, 1997). Although men and women both ascribe the same strong influence to *guanxi*, they see it as having different benefits for their careers. According to studies, men are in a stronger position to develop *guanxi* relationships. *Guanxi* is associated with "face", the public self-image that a person strives to present. "Guanxi only helps (your career) if you have strong motives for competing", according to one interviewee in a study by Leung (2000). The reason why women make less use of *guanxi* in their careers is mainly attributed to the fact that traditionally a woman's reputation can suffer in Chinese society if she forms overly strong bonds with men in order to advance in her career. Another reason are business rituals that exclude women (Zhu, 2015). Harrison et al. (2014) have studied how much benefit female Chinese company founders can gain from *guanxi* networks. The authors identify familial solidarity, as an element of *guanxi*, as a positive factor that can support women who are founding a company. By contrast, women tend to use *guanxi* less than men to generate capital. The study also described how the possible sexualisation of close contact with male *guanxi* network members can present an obstacle. Harrison et al. conclude that, alongside *guanxi*, other factors such as experience, training, education and finance are also key success factors for female Chinese company founders. In multinational companies Guanxi relations seems to have clear limitations and even can lead to draw backs because of overlapping guanxi networks (Tam, 2016).

Use of networks for career development in the Shanghai Women's Career Lab

The women were asked what kind of networking they do and how they think it has affected their careers. They regard networking as important for their careers and described different networks that they cultivate both within and outside their companies. As well as the social side of networking, they regard the following five factors as the most important: (1) learning; (2) discussing career challenges; (3) platform for finding a mentor or sponsor; (4) marketing oneself and career development; (5) source of information about career progression opportunities. These five points encapsulate the interviewees' answers regarding the goals of networking.

In the following the networks described by the women are presented. These were mentioned in relation to the Western definition of networking. It is notable that they gave extensive and detailed accounts even though some participants described their networking activities as insufficient. It became clear that all the women consider networking extremely important.

1. The head office

The head office is seen as essential to career development at multinational companies, since key personnel decisions are made there. If a woman's position allows her to travel to the head office frequently or regularly, she has an opportunity to directly influence her own career development from within the company's system. All the women are aware of this factor, and trips to the head office were accordingly mentioned as an integral part of networking. Joint social events with the movers and shakers at the head office are actively used to cultivate contacts. Only a handful of women in the group do not make regular trips to the head office and described their networking opportunities in this area as limited.

> *M. M., President: "I have contact, even if not so frequently. Three years ago the whole family[12] visited China, therefore I know them. Because I belong to*

---

[12]   The board member and his family, from Germany.

the Worldwide Senior Board Management Club I join regular meetings. Every
two years my husband and I make a tour, with all board members and their
families. Like hiking or so ... " (Translated from German)

2. Senior management

This refers to networking with CEOs or other members of the head management
team. For women who are themselves the CEO in China, it refers to networking
with their immediate superior at head office. Some (but not all) of the women find
accessibility can be a problem with male CEOs of foreign nationality. They described the challenge of how best to cultivate relationships with men from other
countries. The women did not describe this problem arising with female or Chinese
managers. Hence, findings from the literature showing that women find it more
difficult to develop relationships with male superiors through, for example, social
activities (Leung, 2000; Harrison et al., 2014) also apply to parts of this group. The
women did not mention the possibility of negative social reactions to overly close
relationships between women and male decision-makers.

3. Professional development groups and training providers

The women mentioned several MBA groups, for example at CEIBS, and professional qualification programmes. The training groups are used as long-term networks outside their own companies. They act as sources of knowledge and inspiration. The women also draw on them when planning to change jobs. The women
systematically and intensively cultivate new contacts and friendships among the
training participants. Joint learning and development are also a primary focal point.
It is normal to create WeChat groups in the very first break at a seminar. These
groups are maintained for years after the training itself is over and symbolise close-
knit bonds.[13]

> J., GM: "For example in the CEIBS-Group we were 60 General Manager.
> And we had worked out a very ambitious plan that we all will meet each year
> in the next 3–5 years. We had already one meeting where all were present,
> and we visited companies, analyse them and show them advantages and dis-
> advantages, challenges and give them tips. This networking is good for me."
> (Translated from German)

The women identified training providers as good network contacts, since they have
extensive market contacts. As recognised authorities, seminar leaders are also in-

---

[13]   This is also confirmed by the author's own experience as a provider of training for over 40 professional development groups in China between 2011 and 2016.

cluded in networks. According to the women's accounts, once you are an accepted member of a study group you can draw on your contacts in the group time and again.

4. Expert circles

These groups are specific to particular fields: for example, Shanghai has a CFO group with around 100 members and several specialist HR groups. They provide platforms for people to promote themselves as experts in their own market and increase their own market value.

> S., CFO: "For example I know all the CFOs for the group. I am in a club organized by our company including quite a lot CFO or financial people of the companies of Shanghai. Then I always use my network with XY (Consulting Company, former employee)."

5. Old friends (including school friends) and colleagues

Old friends and colleagues play an essential role in networks. School and university ties are maintained, providing a firm basis for the women's own networks. Friendships are maintained with former colleagues, and these contacts are drawn upon if required.

6. Chambers of commerce

The chamber of commerce that a multinational is affiliated to represents a gateway to the rest of the industry and to international employees at the company. Examples of how the women use chambers of commerce included regularly attending events, giving talks and professional networking.

> M. M., President: "They have invited me as speaker for a project. Because I would be the speaker I had to prepare the topics. I have learned during two months during my free time. What is leadership, what can one do to influence better. This has helped me like a self mentoring, because I needed those skills. I have delivered 2 workshops. On leadership...." (Translated from German)

7. Digital media: WeChat

WeChat is a Chinese instant messaging platform that can be used to exchange private messages between individuals and groups and also has an open area where information can be shared publically. The women use this messaging app several times a day to maintain constant contact with their networks. The focus is on exchanging information and knowledge. Many of the women also actively use

WeChat to position themselves as experts by regularly posting topical reports and news for public consumption.

8. Headhunters

"Headhunter" friends are actively used when changing jobs. Some women reported having longstanding friendships with headhunters and actively seeking their advice. These headhunters were often also described as mentors.

In reply to the question of how much time she invests in her own network, one respondent said that she feels she only invests a little. In detail, she reported that she calls "old friends" every two days or so, goes to an event once a week and has several events with university friends and their families each month. The women communicate on the platform WeChat constantly. Women with children reported a decrease in the frequency of contact since becoming mothers. None of the women said that they do not have a network.[14] There were a few remarks such as "I need to do more" or "I'm not really that good at it" or women who described seeing other people developing networks at their company more quickly and proactively. This refers primarily to networking with people from other countries in their companies. In this connection, they reported how difficult it is for Chinese to cultivate relationships in this important group that go beyond purely professional contacts. The women did not mention gender-specific problems, but they did mention cultural barriers that could make it more difficult to establish contacts among high-ranking international staff at their companies.

The women did not explicitly mention *guanxi* in connection with networking. However, since *guanxi* is firmly anchored in Chinese society (Peng, 1977) it seems likely that the women use and cultivate *guanxi* networks. On the other hand, some studies (e.g. Tam, 2016) have reported *guanxi* having specific limitations in multinational companies due to overlapping, and therefore conflicting, *guanxi* networks. It remains unclear what role traditional *guanxi* plays in relation to careers at senior executive level in multinational companies in China. The women described the relationships that they maintain with old school and university friends, training participants, headhunters and training providers as particularly close and personal. A connection could be seen between parental *guanxi* connections and career entry for women who started their careers in China in jobs assigned by the state. Around

---

[14]   In Henn's study (2012), 9% of the female German business executives interviewed said either that they had no network or that they did not want one. 23% said that women do not use networks or are bad at networking.

80% of these women mentioned their extended families' *guanxi* connections when asked how they got their first job at a state-owned company or institution. In relation to the future course of their careers, table 5 summarises the number of times that particular sources of support were mentioned when the women were asked who provided assistance when changing jobs. Headhunters have a clear lead, ahead of bosses, colleagues, friends and family. The women's accounts of their relationships with headhunters suggest that in some cases intense and longstanding personal bonds were established.

Table 7: Support with getting a job

Who or what supported	Answers
Headhunter	15
Former GM, Colleague, HR director	9
Overseas connection	1
Friends and family	9
Newspaper, Internet, Amcham directory	7
Spontaneous job application	1

In conclusion, it is not possible to precisely ascertain how big a role *guanxi* networks in the traditional Chinese sense have played in these women's careers. Since the women operate in a culturally mixed environment and the people who decide on appointments to senior management roles are or were usually foreigners, it can be assumed that although *guanxi* networks play a role they may not necessarily be applicable to decision-makers at the international head office or bosses with foreign nationality, since the tradition, understanding and mutual acceptance of this kind of relationship networks bounded by rights and obligations is specific to China. These findings are in line with Tam (2016) and Zhu (2015). What is certain from the interviews is that all the women in this research have specifically invested time in developing varied, complex networks in order to promote their careers. Some of these networks are situated within the women's companies, but some cut across different companies or into their personal lives.

Summary: How environmental factors influence the careers of female Chinese executives

In accordance with the Female Career Model, the interviews addressed topics such as cultural influences, the gender situation, social origin and family, and mentoring and networking.

The results concerning the influence of Confucian traditions suggest that the portion of traditions assigning women an inferior role to men has been superseded by gender equality laws and policies. The women who were interviewed do not feel that their career development had been negatively influenced by Confucian role models. They take a largely positive view concerning the benefits of traditional values for their management styles and personal lifestyles. These results contradict most gender-based theoretical accounts.

The interviewees rated the prestige of women in executive roles in China highly. Their career success is seen as a success for the whole family and is socially recognised. Hence, the women rate their image in society as predominantly positive.

They believe their opportunities are equal to, or even better than, those of men, and also that the glass ceiling at multinational companies is gender-neutral and applies to all Chinese, though only at organisations' most senior level. Only a few women think there is a specific glass ceiling for women, and again only in connection with the CEO role.

The women feel strongly supported by their families. As mothers they are able to draw on a large support network that offers them more support overall than women in comparable positions in the West typically receive. Husbands mostly take a positive attitude towards their wives' careers and primarily provide emotional support.

Motherhood (or the perceived possibility of motherhood) and the periods of absence associated with it were described by most women as factors that slow down their career progression. Women with two children were particularly likely to describe having experienced disadvantages. Women with foreign partners or who have lived abroad for an extended period have different attitudes regarding the role of mothers and the aspects of children's upbringing that they believe women themselves should be responsible for. A minority of women in the Shanghai Women's Career Lab (generally women with two children and career-oriented husbands) believe that family and motherhood has a stronger negative impact on women's careers.

All the women reported informal mentoring relationships, particularly with bosses who supported their careers. The mentors were often female and/or foreigners from the company head office. The key to successful mentoring was trust. The interviewees believe that female Chinese executives have an advantage over men, since foreign CEOs trust them more than male executives. These mentor relations, by contrast with how mentoring is normally understood, can be described as "mutually beneficial alliances" in which not only the mentee but also the mentor strongly benefits from the local cultural and business knowledge of their mentee. All the women cultivate networks, which include diverse groups of networking partners. The influence of *guanxi* networks at the start of their careers was explicitly mentioned. The women described the great importance of networking in the subsequent stages of their careers. It remains open how much of this networking is based on *guanxi* principles that differ from the networking activities of Western executives.

6. Individual factors supporting Chinese women to rise to top management

Education and qualifications – Competencies of female Chinese executives – Personality analysis – Leadership motivation – Working behaviour – Assertiveness, self-confidence and the ability to handle conflict – Initial impression on others – Chinese women's leadership style

Education and female careers

Personal investment in education and professional experience is one of the factors with the strongest impact on career success, though it has less effect on satisfaction (Tharenou, Latimer, and Conroy, 1994; Judge, Cable, Boudreau, and Bretz, 1995). In general, a good education has a positive effect on career development, since it represents the basis for knowledge, skills and credibility for performance in senior management roles. A high level of education also improves access to other training (whether offered by others or undertaken on one's own initiative), since decision-makers have greater confidence that training will be successful if participants are already well educated. Professional experience, which includes factors such as the number of years spent in a company or continuity, are consistently associated with career progression by researchers.

The connection between academic success at school or university and subsequent professional success remains highly relevant in practice. When making recruitment decisions, recruiters have information about the candidates' educational records. This information might help companies to make better selections, but only if there is a proven connection between the two factors. The arguments for and against such a connection are clear. On the one hand, it seems plausible that individuals with strong attainment at school and university would also perform well later on in their professional life. Underlying this idea is an assumption of "universalism", which is also formulated in similar form in management theory: someone who achieves strongly in education will also do so in other situations. This assumption is generally justified on the basis of a person's general traits, such as achievement motivation, intelligence or social skills. These are taken to be significant in all situations. Strong attainment in formalised educational processes is a reflection of such features, meaning that early attainment at school and university could be a relatively good predictor of subsequent attainment in a person's professional life.

On the other hand, there are also powerful arguments against the idea that academic achievement and career success are connected. These arguments are primarily based on the view that the acquisition of formal qualifications only has a limited influence on professional attainment, which is highly situation-dependent and not at all stable over time. Qualities that have no effect in a particular job or company due to specific situational factors such as peculiarities of the role or relationships with colleagues may result in great success in a similar role at another company, even though nothing has changed in the person's academic attainment. Moreover, a person's professional and, in particular, personal situation can change over the course of time. This can have a crucial influence on their career path and success regardless of academic attainments (Mayrhofer et al., 2005). Almost all studies find a positive correlation between school/university attainment and various success criteria in subsequent professional life. However, the correlations are normally fairly weak (Reilly and Chao, 1982). A metastudy on people in highly qualified occupations, such as architects, technical specialists and scientists, concluded that academic attainment has no particular relevance for subsequent professional attainment, whether measured in terms of publications or appraisals, or for exceptional creative attainment. However, certain personality factors are clearly associated with outstanding creativity (Kraiger and Ford, 1985). Academic success is not a simple, objective measure. Grades or duration of study are just one aspect: other activities that a person engages in during their studies are also relevant, such as spending time abroad, working alongside their degree or acquiring additional qualifications. The reputation of the chosen institution is also key factors. Different educational institutions vary in terms of educational quality and social prestige, meaning that graduates of universities with a very high reputation may do better in their professional life than ones who went to a "bad" university.

There are less robust findings on the impact of studying abroad while at university on future career success. It is often assumed that spending a semester abroad or completing a similar overseas project looks good on one's CV and increases the chances of a successful application, especially at large multinational corporations. There are also indications that studying abroad while at university results in stronger interest in working abroad in the student's future career. However, little research has been done on the correlation with subsequent career success variables. Another factor relevant to subsequent professional success that goes beyond academic achievement *per se* is the prestige of the university that a person attends. A

North American study shows that the projected earnings of graduates of especially prestigious universities over 20 years of working life are over half a million Euros more than those of graduates who received the same quality of education at equally good but less prestigious universities (Judge et al., 1995).

Tharenou et al. (1994) found that education and experience have more impact on men's career success than women's. This also confirms the general picture that, overall, female managers earn less than male ones. Women's career success is often attributed to factors such as luck or external support (Kirchmeyer, 1998). However, almost all studies show that a good track record of successful accomplishments is one facilitator of career advantage (Ragins, 1998). A good track record may be more important for female than for male managers because research has shown that gender stereotypes may be overcome when job-relevant information is available to the decision-makers (Lyness and Thompson, 2000). Turner (2007) describes that women in post-reform China have been educationally disadvantaged compared to men. According to this research from 1994 until 2004 Chinese women were seeking opportunities in international higher education to overcome domestic prejudices.

The interviewees' education and qualifications

As described above, a large number of researchers have investigated the connection between education and career success (Tharenou, Latimer, and Conroy, 1994; Judge, Cable, Boudreau, and Bretz, 1995). Lyness et al. (2000) describe the importance of a good track record, especially for women. The researchers believe that gender stereotypes may be overcome by women with high educational attainment. A good track record is one of the facilitators of career advancement. Accordingly, it was important to ask the women in the Shanghai Women's Career Lab about their level of education when they started out in their careers and the qualifications they have acquired during their careers. The women of the Shanghai Women's Career Lab are highly educated and motivated to learn. Many of them have acquired additional qualifications in the course of their careers. All 35 women who participated in the study went to university. Most of the women have a BA as their first degree. As well as languages degrees in English (eight women) and French (two women), there was a broad range of BA degrees in subjects such as electronics, computer science, biology, chemistry and law.

144 Individual factors supporting Chinese women to rise to top management

Table 8: Academic education – first degree

First degree	Number
Bachelor in English	8
Bachelor in French	2
Medical Doctor	1
Computer Science	1
Degree in Electronics	1
Bachelor in Biology	1
Bachelor in Chemistry	1
Degree in Arts	1
Degree in Chinese	1
Degree in Law	1

But only 22% of the group reported that their highest (and only) university degree is a BA. Twenty seven of the research participants hold an MA or equivalent qualifications; 19 of them have MBAs and four have MAs in science, law, history or physics. Four of the women hold a German MBA equivalent, including *Diplomkauffrau*, *Diplomökonomin* and *Diplom in Maschinenbau*.

Table 9: Academic education – highest degree

Highest degree	Number
MBA	23
Diplomkauffrau (Business)*	3
Diplom in Maschinenbau (Engineering)*	1
Bachelor Degree	8

* German Diplom is MBA equivalent

The MBA schools that the women mentioned attending include world-famous institutions such as Harvard, ESSEC, Stanford and the Shanghai-based business school CEIBS. Five of the women have two or even three MA qualifications. There have been various studies on the connection between the prestige and reputation of the university that someone attends and their subsequent career success. Several studies measured the connection by reference to impact on salary development. (Judge, Cable, Boudreau, and Bretz, 1995). Although participants in the present study were not asked about this connection, it can be noted that the women hold some highly respected qualifications and attended many highly prestigious universities.

C, President: "I think that it is Harvard just to be honest. I think that HBS had a stronger brand globally. INSEAD may have a very good brand in Europe but then globally HBS has a better brand, so I go with the better brand."

The women regard the reputation of local universities and business schools and the global reputation of MBA providers as important, and they described how they actively focused on obtaining their qualifications from one of the best institutions. One participant chose between INSEAD and Harvard based on the institutions' global reputations. Twelve of the study participants studied abroad. One woman even studied in two countries outside China and obtained qualifications in both. Germany was the most popular choice of location to study abroad, ahead of the UK, France and Singapore. 7% of the women chose to study in the USA, Hong Kong or Australia. Twenty-four of the women obtained their degrees exclusively from Chinese institutions. There is little research in the literature on the connection between studying abroad and career success. It is assumed that studying abroad increases the odds of successful applications to multinational companies. However, relatively little research has been done on the connection with future career success variables (Mayrhofer, Meyer, Steyrer et al 2005). It is conceivable that it might be an advantage for career development at a multinational company in China to have studied in the country where the company is based. Studying in the country where the company's head office is located signals a greater cultural and linguistic understanding of that country, and hence could be taken as an indicator not just of linguistic skills but also of intercultural competencies. One factor that speaks against this assumption is that the majority of women studied exclusively in China. This aspect is addressed in greater depth in the section on career paths.

Table 10: Overseas study locations

Country	Number
Australia	1
UK	2
Germany	5
Singapore	2
France	2
US	1
HK	1

When asked how they chose which country to study in, the women who chose Germany explained that it was because it was the least expensive country due to there being no tuition fees. France was selected on the basis of romantic ideas about the country and lifestyle. Other reasons for choosing a particular country included having friends or relatives living there who were on hand to provide assistance. These friends and relatives were generally parental connections. One woman studied in Australia because her husband's work took him there.

Language skills are very important for executives at multinational companies in China. All the interviewed women speak English to a high standard and use it on a daily basis in their working environments. Many of them studied English for their BA degree and are completely fluent in both written and spoken English. Fifteen of the women do not speak any foreign languages besides English. Another fifteen are proficient in a second language, and five women in a third. The second most common language in this group is German (nine women) followed by French (four women). Seven of the women have passive knowledge of Japanese as a third language. Italian, Korean and Spanish were also mentioned. Due to the women's high level of English, the interviews could be conducted in English without any comprehension problems. Four of the participants preferred to carry out the interviews in German, which attests to their strong proficiency.

Table 11: Foreign languages

Language	Number
English	35
German	9
Japanese	7
French	4
Spanish	2
Italian	1
Korean	1

It is striking that most of the women who work at German or French multinationals are proficient in the language of the head office. Only one of the nine women who work for a German company does not speak any German. Four of the nine women who work for French companies are fluent in French. According to the interviewees, particularly at the time of China's economic reforms language skills were an enormous advantage for potential executives, since they made up for the fact that most foreign executives could not speak any Chinese. The women's proficiency in multiple languages gives them an advantage over foreign executives. Purely in virtue of being able to speak other languages, they are able to carve out greater scope for decision-making and make use of the power vacuum resulting from the foreigners' linguistic dependency. The women believe that this advantage was greater at the start of their careers, when proportionally fewer applicants spoke English or other languages and almost no foreigners were proficient enough to conduct negotiations in Chinese. This point is addressed in greater depth in the section on career paths, including in relation to work experience abroad.

There are some contradictory findings in the literature on the connection between education and career success in comparison with men (Tharenou et al., 1994; Kirchmeyer, 2002). However, it appears relatively clear that a high level of education is a facilitator of career advancement (Ragins, 1998; Lyness, 2000). With 27 MBA-equivalent qualifications and 12 degrees obtained abroad, this group is highly educated. A large number of renowned universities, both local and international, appear on their CVs. The women also exhibit a high level of multilingualism. All women in the Shanghai Women's Career Lab reported placing an emphasis on ongoing learning, and had obtained several business and leadership qualifications in the form of courses and certificates during the course of their careers. One example is coaching certification, which many of the women in the Shanghai Women's Career Lab possess.

Competencies and female careers – Specification of a good leader

A search through the literature for the competencies that executives need to be successful yields various different specifications. Executives need to fulfil the role of leaders if they want to pursue a career in management. They are expected both to display leadership competencies within a group and to represent the group within the organisation. In addition, executives need to live up to their role in the overall system of internal and external stakeholders. Competency theory builds upon earlier research on skills, abilities and cognitive intelligence, and anticipates later work on emotional and social intelligence. A competency is defined as a capability or ability (Boyatzis, 2011; McClelland and Boyatzis, 1982). It is a set of related but distinct behaviours organised around an underlying construct called "intent". Many researches on leadership competencies generate a sample of outstanding or superior performers. Because the studies derive the competencies from performance inductively, they reflect effective job performance. There are three clusters of competencies that distinguish outstanding from average performers in many countries of the world: cognitive competencies, emotional intelligence and social intelligence.

There is no universally valid profile of specifications for a good leader. In order to live up to a demanding leadership role in a changing world, managers need to meet additional requirements. These requirements are exacting and multifaceted, and vary according to field, company size and position (Henn, 2012). Regnet (2014) formulated specifications for executives based on the results of the IBM Human Capital Study, which surveyed 400 companies worldwide. These specifications, which are listed below, are intended to provide a specification profile for the competencies required by executives. This profile will be used throughout the remainder of the study. Personality factors are then discussed in the next section.

Capacity for motivation: This refers to the executive's capacity to persuade others and how well they are able to use this capacity to enthuse employees and unite them behind certain goals and activities.

Ability and willingness to learn, employability: This refers to the executive's continuous independent learning, with the goal of always keeping their knowledge up to date. Employability refers to a person's ability to participate in professional life. It includes all personal, professional, social and methodological competencies and their individual capacity for work.

Teamwork: Executives need to be able to work together with employees across the whole company and to bring together individuals and groups that are separated by organisational barriers, time zones and cultures. In doing so, they need to master the balancing act between intra team competition that stimulates performance and competition that undermines solidarity.

Management of diversity: This refers to an executive's capacity to make use of employees' variety and diversity and to support the opportunities resulting from them. This includes not only forming teams in line with diversity principles, but also helping employees to achieve results together despite different approaches, ways of working and perspectives.

Communication skills and conflict management: The executive needs to motivate and enthuse people through their communication skills and role model function. This includes using specialist feedback techniques and being able to keep tensions at an optimum level that harnesses conflict's potential for innovation and transformation.

Change management: Continuous change is necessary in order to be able to respond quickly to dynamic markets and new requirements. Executives need to be able to supervise change processes by motivating, supporting and involving employees. They also need to suggest new opportunities to people who lose out from change processes. *Innovation management* and *creativity* are other specifications that can also be categorised under this heading.

Systematic, holistic thinking: This refers to the capacity to structure poorly defined problems and assess consequences for the company as a whole, which requires a holistic way of thinking. This competency includes the ability to deal with uncertainty and complexity, possessing the necessary flexibility and having information management, evaluation and decision-making skills that are adapted to changing circumstances.

Health and ability to work under pressure: This can include the executive's own ability to work under pressure. But it also refers to "healthy leadership" in the sense of acting in a way that values employees and helps to reduce or prevent pressure, stress and burnout.

Conveying meaning and vision: This refers to meaning-based leadership in accordance with the concept developed by Hinterhuber (1977). The key pillars of this concept are "being visionary", "being a role model" and "creating value". The development of a shared vision is also a component of the learning organisation concept presented by Senge (1996).

Intercultural leadership skills: This competency is described here in some depth, since it is of great relevance to the results. Intercultural leadership ability refers to a person's sensitivity to foreign cultures and ways of behaving and to the flexibility to adjust one's own behaviour and communication accordingly. The intercultural ability is not limited to language learning and is not necessarily something that is developed simply by spending time abroad. Intercultural communication competency is not confined to knowledge of the culture and language, but also includes affective and behavioural skills such as empathy, human warmth, charisma and the ability to manage anxiety and uncertainty (Spiess, 1998). Two other concepts that are used in this context are global leadership and global mindset. A definition of global leadership competencies is given by Jokinen (2005). According to this definition, global leadership competencies are those universal qualities that enable individuals to perform their jobs outside their own national and organisational culture, no matter what their educational or ethnic background is, what function they have according to their job description or what organisation they come from. In this context various researchers bring up the concept of global mindset (Jeannet, J.-P., 2000, Ranker, G., McLeod, M., 2017). A global mindset is the ability to understand, connect and integrate different cultures. Tucker, Bonial, Vanhove and Kedharnath (2014) describe executives with intercultural competency in other words as "leaders who have the ability to move easily between different cultures". Rosinski (2003) developed a five-step ethno relative approach for establishing a person's level of intercultural competence. The first step is to acknowledge that your worldview is not central to everyone's reality. The second and third steps are to recognise differences and accept them. The next step is about integrating these differences. This step occurs when one is able to hold different frames of reference in one's mind at any given time. Integration is therefore an advanced form of cultural development. It is about understanding that culture is a process and that there is more than one reality. The final step is adaptation: the willingness and ability to accept differences, without feeling that your integrity is threatened. Chin, Gu, and Tubbs (2001) developed a similar pyramid of global competencies. At the lower level are deficiencies such as ignorance. The pyramid builds up to awareness, understanding, acceptance and transformation. At this stage, globalisation becomes a way of life. Instead of fear of things that are new and different, there is interest in trying new and different things and an eagerness to solve problems collaboratively. Black and Morrison (2014) offer a broader concept with their definition of global leadership. According to this concept, global leadership requires executives to be consistently competent in four areas: inquisitiveness, perspective, character and savvy. In their definition, perspective refers to the ability to embrace uncertainties and balance tension; inquisitiveness refers to curiosity about new international markets; savvy refers to broad-ranging international business and organisational knowledge; and character refers to integrity and the ability to connect emotionally. Black and Morrison argue that every global leader must have this set of global capabilities. Their approach is broader than defining intercultural abilities as one part of the skill set of an executive. Instead, all capabilities, interpersonal abilities and skills of an executive are measured and judged from the global leadership perspective. The authors suggest that global leaders' capabilities are a matter of both nature and nurture.

Traditional specifications: Finally, Regnet lists factors such as intelligence, analytical skills, exceptional commitment, loyalty, capacity for enthusiasm, exam grades and specialist professional knowledge.

Other specifications for executives concern their effectiveness. The key here is developing the capacity to present oneself effectively in order to be perceived in a certain way. This factor is regarded as an indicator of flexibility and the ability to handle different social situations. Strong self-monitoring skills result in greater opportunities for advancement, though women perform worse in this area than men (Korabik, 1992). Women are modest about their own achievements, which has an effect on their career development. Researchers look for the causes in female executives' self-esteem and self-conception. A person's self-conception, which comprises the sum of their self-referential experiences, combined with their evaluation of this knowledge is defined as self-esteem (Henn, 2012). Another factor that is crucial to an executive's success is their competitiveness. Experimental comparisons have shown that women enjoy competition less on average and tend to shy away from it. Men and women have different competitive strategies. Bischof-Köhler (1993) distinguishes the female prestige hierarchy from the male dominance hierarchy. According to this distinction, women have just as much of a need for admiration as men but are less prepared to slot into a hierarchy, and ranking structures are less clear. When both genders compete, the male strategies beat the female ones. One factor here is that women appraise their odds of winning more realistically, which in combination with an underestimation of their own ability becomes a disadvantage. Finally, there are frequent references in the literature to what are termed "social skills": "Managers identified social and interpersonal skills as important characteristics of the 'effective manager'" (Kanter, 1977). Social skills can be defined as behaviours that help a person to achieve their personal goals in a socially acceptable way in a particular situation (Kanning, 2005). They therefore correspond to various other definitions from the literature of many of the skills described above that a person can use to help them achieve their goals, taking into consideration their own values, those of other people in their environment and the consequences of their actions.

Competencies of Chinese female executives for rising to senior management

As described before, there is no universally valid profile of specifications for a good leader. Successful managers generally have to meet exacting standards covering a wide range of different areas (Boyatzis et al., 1982; Henn, 2012). The women were asked to describe from their own perspectives which of the competencies they possess have been most helpful for their careers. Their answers were summarised and categorised according to the profile of specifications for executives developed by Regnet (2014) that was presented above. Personality factors are looked at separately in the next section.

One noteworthy feature of the women's answers is that they were very readily able to state their own strengths, skills and competencies. They reported extensively on this point, with descriptions coming thick and fast. None of the women appeared reserved, modest or shy when they were asked about their own strengths. It was not unusual for them to use superlatives in their descriptions.

VP-HR: "I am the best HRD in China."

Table 12 presents an overview of the competencies that the women spontaneously described. It lists their chosen terms and how frequently they were used.

Table 12: Competencies and strengths, self-image of participants

Influencing and communication skills (27)	Understanding the system (15)
persuasiveness/convincing decision makers *good communications/rhetorical competence* *strong network with top management* *presentation skills/story telling*	*understanding of company system* *actively use structures and hierarchy* *understanding of interests of all stake-* *holders* *understand needs of subordinates* *strategically chose staff and successors*
Expert knowledge (24)	**Visionary/Innovator (12)**
knowledge of many industries/companies *long experience/deep knowledge of context/expert knowledge* *lifelong learning* *Management knowledge*	*many ideas, creative/ find new solutions* *set visions/inspire with new ideas* *work on ideas for next 5 years* *see the whole picture/bring up the big topics* *smell the changes coming*
Intercultural Skills (37)	**Analytical Skills (12)**
be Chinese amongst foreigners/China expert *global view and local understanding* *good understanding of foreigners/high adaptability* *use language to build trust* *language skills/influence through translation*	*logical thinking/fast analysis/ strategic thinking* *understanding of complex issues* *good with numbers*

Understanding of the system and analytical skills as building blocks of careers

The women's descriptions make clear that their main advantage over others is their in-depth understanding of local and global hierarchical structures and ways of working at companies. They described an understanding of global structures and a familiarity with the ways of thinking and distribution of tasks prevalent at the head office as a clear strength both of their own and of women in general. One woman noted that although it took years, her understanding of the system is now fully developed. This also includes understanding different internal and external stakeholders. The women also emphasised the importance of quickly coming to understand all company functions, especially when changing companies and starting in a new position. The women ascribed the capacity to do this to themselves. Another key ability they described themselves as possessing is the capacity to make the right strategic selection of staff and successors in order to secure their network in the corporate system of their company. Strategic thinking, the ability to quickly understand complex issues and a good head for numbers were described as core competencies by women with leadership roles in the management team, marketing, controlling and finance, and sales in particular. However, HR directors and women in other roles also confirmed that they had demonstrated above-average analytical skills compared with other staff over the course of their careers.

Expert knowledge in more than one world

Most of the answers can be assigned to this category. They can be broken down into two subcategories. Firstly, in-depth understanding and knowledge of specialist issues and topics. Secondly, broad knowledge of many different industries or very different companies. Both types of expert knowledge were described as core competencies and strengths, either singly or in combination. One major advantage that all the women emphasised is the many years' experience that they now possess. All the women described having an in-depth understanding of business in China as an employee of a multinational company as a clear competitive advantage over other executives and over international colleagues and bosses. This understanding includes proficiency in multiple languages, with English and Chinese considered of equal importance. At German and French companies, being able to speak the language of the head office represents a big advantage for the women. Another strength that was repeatedly mentioned is the ability and desire to constantly learn about new things. Lifelong learning was a theme that ran through all the interviews; the women perceive it as one of their core competencies.

Communication and motivational skills – culturally rooted and female strengths

The women emphasised that they have a persuasive communication style and can vary and adapt this ability depending on the culture of the people they are addressing. This involves being able to present information, persuade others and tell compelling stories in Chinese, English and possibly other languages. According to the women, the aim is to motivate employees and influence superiors. The women described the ability to influence decision-makers as one of their personal strengths. One of the things this involves is constant contact with higher-ranking groups or networks of decision-makers, as discussed in the section on networking. Some of the women described a persuasive executive presence when engaging with local and international target groups as one of their strengths.

Visionary thinking and innovation – to be further developed

Generally, the women rated themselves highly in this category. However, the two aspects were intermingled in their answers. Lack of vision in particular tended to be regarded as a weakness of women in general. The aspect of innovation was more in the participants' comfort zone. This may be because some of the women are responsible for innovation strategy at their company or were previously responsible for innovation in marketing or HR at earlier stages of their careers. There were some mentions of visionary thinking, but they were less frequent than mentions of other capacities. A separate question was asked to explore this topic in more depth. Some women described "the ability to see the big picture" as one of their strengths. They also described this ability as the capacity to anticipate changes before other people and to prepare for or take advantage of them. One participant gave the following example of her visionary thinking:

> V., GM: "My capability to know where the business is going, to anticipate it, link my actions to the same direction ... Smelling the changes coming."

The women described how they use business schools' MBA networks to network with local CEOs and investors and develop their own visionary thinking. Another woman sees her role in this connection as adapting American-centred visions to the specific features of the Chinese market.

Women critically observed that they have to subjugate their own visions to the systems of multinational companies. Several of the women expressed dissatisfaction and frustration in relation to the topic of vision. The women described how in general all multinational companies have the same or similar messages as their visions, which are drilled into new staff in particular. Many of the women have greater admiration for local private business owners, who they believe have greater flexibility to follow their own visions. Many of the comments on vision suggest that the women have the capacity for visionary thinking but are limited at their companies to imparting established visions to employees and are often unable to develop their own visions.

On the topic of innovation, the women gave many specific examples where they were able to exert an influence on the development of strategies and products at their companies. Innovation as an independent area of responsibility and the introduction of new processes and rules were frequently given as examples of a capacity for visionary thinking.

M. M., President: "OK, after five years I knew how much I did, but also that I can do more. And then I presented my idea to the company. We also produced paper on the country side, but also in Germany. Why shouldn't we sell paper from Germany in Asia? And I proposed to have an office in Hong Kong, which I would lead beside the joint venture. So that not only our Chinese products but also German products would sell in Asia." (Translated from German)

M., CFO: "Innovation is not really an important thing, but at least visionary is important. People need to have a bigger picture, envisioning what your next 5 or 10 years are supposed to be. Not only on your career path but other things you do your daily job. In the company, not stick to the small area."

Only some of the women described the ability to inspire others, which is closely linked to the capacity to communicate persuasively, as one of their strengths.

Intercultural skills – key USP of Chinese female executives

When asked about cultural differences and their importance for their careers, the participants' answers were varied and detailed. A very large number of descriptions corresponded to this category, with the majority of the women describing intercultural skills as one of their strengths. Most of the women have worked with several foreign cultures during their careers, with many of them reporting in detail about their experiences with multiple cultural circles. Most of these experiences related to encounters with foreign superiors, colleagues and the head office in China. Many of the women reported an in-depth understanding of the ways of working and cultural differences of two other nationalities (in some cases up to five) that they had worked with very closely and over extended periods of time. This distinguishes the Chinese female executives of this group from executives who have never worked with intercultural teams, have done so only occasionally or for short periods, or have only worked with colleagues from a single foreign culture.

The women share a very open-minded, positive and curious attitude towards other cultures as well as the desire to learn about and understand them in depth. They are open to adapt and integrate the foreign cultures depending on the context.

"[My] *initial idea of working with foreigners was the idea of freedom*" was how one participant described her original expectations of the values of multinational companies. All the women started out with great curiosity mixed with very positive assumptions and expectations regarding foreigners in general and their ways of working and management styles in particular. The participants frequently formulated goals involving working with foreigners. The most frequently mentioned goals were to be able to work well with people of different nationalities and to be able to lead them effectively. Another goal that was mentioned was the desire to learn from people from other countries by focusing on their strengths. These descriptions tally with the accounts of a "global view" and "global-mindedness" found in the literature, which are described *inter alia* as essential elements of intercultural competency. Researchers also describe a "commitment to global learning" as a precondition for developing high intercultural competency (Tucker, Bonial, Vanhove, and Kedharnath, 2014). All the women see themselves as possessing an exceptional capacity to adapt to the different cultures of foreign superiors and colleagues or the culture of the head office. However, being able to "move" and operate between cultures, and to strategically use this advantage to one's own benefit, is regarded as the most important factor for the women's career paths. The literature speaks in this connection of "flexibility when working with other cultures". Chin, Gu, and Tubbs (2001) note that leaders are only effective in relation to a particular context – as the context changes, so too must the leaders' behaviour. Being able to consider and acknowledge new ideas and to take multiple problem-solving approaches is necessary for effective global leadership. The ability to "move easily between cultures" described by Tucker et al. (2014) is an important skill that is common to all members of the study group and is prominent in their descriptions.

The women also presented detailed descriptions of different leadership styles from a cultural perspective and, drawing on their many years' experience, were able to describe, compare and evaluate strengths and weaknesses. This is what constitutes their intercultural strength. Rosinski (2003) describes his ethno relative approach that proceeds through several stages, starting with acknowledgement and recognition of differences and ending with adaptation. Using different terminology but following the same approach, Chin et al. (2001) describe this stage as transformation: "At this stage globalization becomes a way of life. It is internalized to the degree that it is out of one's own volition. The process having become more or less completed, one's behaviour almost becomes effortless, subconscious, and second nature. Appropriate words to describe this level are competent, fluent, balanced, broadminded, and international. One can truly be himself or herself at this level. The use of empathy or frame of reference has shifted. There is no longer fear of things that are new and different. On the contrary, there is obvious interest in trying new and different things. There is an eagerness to solve problems in cooperation." (Chen, Gu, and Tubbs, 2001). The Chinese women's self-evaluations correlate with these definitions.

The women precisely described many and varied cultural differences that they have experienced and learned about during their careers. Table 12 summarises the women's observations. Their detailed observations about the culturally specific working styles, communication and values of different nationalities are presented. These precise observations were made possible by the women's high level of cultural sensitivity and keen perception.

M., CFO: "Chinese say 70, German say 100, US say 120 – for 100."

The observations concern management and work styles, communication and personal values. The answers are, of course, subjective, but are based on many years of lived experience and observations. The women reflected on their own management styles and similarities and differences compared with another nationality; many of the women made comparisons with multiple nationalities. They described skills and ways of thinking that represent particular strengths of people from other countries compared with their own culture, and reflected on strengths and weaknesses of Chinese culture. The consistently positive and also humorous way in which the women describe cultural peculiarities is worthy of note.

Chin, Gu, Tubbs et al. (2001) summarise typical Chinese leadership practices as follows: leaders should instil in followers a sense of security and peace of mind and need to be able to identify a person's talent. They should establish themselves by promoting the success of their followers and enrich followers by extending to them opportunities to develop their careers. At the centre of traditional Chinese leadership is harmony, which should be achieved without compromising one's integrity. Some of the terms used to describe typical Chinese behaviours included in the summary above are along similar lines. This is the original context in which the women are embedded. They are able to apprehend differences in great detail and adapt themselves. Hence, their greatest skill (and something they take pleasure in) is to be able to "move" between the worlds of Chinese and foreign cultures and to make use of the positive strengths of the other cultures. This explains what Rosinski (2003) means by leveraging differences. It is a proactive attitude, looking for gems in your culture and mining for treasures in other cultures. Trust was repeatedly mentioned in this context, especially among women who work at German companies. Specifically, some participants observed that German executives are more likely to trust Germans, especially when it comes to CEO appointments. Hence, their own nationality is a competitive disadvantage with respect to trust. However, this disadvantage is more pronounced for men and probably only affects women at CEO level. In their experience, as women they have clear advantages

Table 13: Description of experienced cultural differences

Executives	Chinese	German	French	US	Hong Kong
Communication	Indirect reserved, do not speak up "face" is most important	Direct do not talk much never give best ratings strict, never give good ratings	nice language	speak up/talk much/loud	direct
			prefer French Debate high toughing	provocative/attacking direct feedback positive, but without meaning	aggressive
Work style	Unorganised some are lazy some do not answer mails	Accurate Disciplined	Actors Relax	Motivating high targets	pushing harsh
	doer – start first later think more risk taker	strict reporting	too many ideas	Dominant	very detailed
		slow processes conservative decision making plan each step, all follow the rules	make rules to break them	result oriented	
Leadership	sensitive about relation engaged with people's heart	strict/very assertive	give freedom	give freedom to act	
		Calm lack ambition no risk taking, no innovation do not care about "face"	do not respect rules trust relationship detailed with figures	influencing, pushy high rewards Visionary	
	subjective judgements				
Values	Learning respect strengths of foreigners	gender issue/discrimination of women	similar to Chinese	open minded	
	Hospitality stereotype "greedy for material things" Warm-hearted	trust issue reliable/honest	value networking Arrogant	can hide insecurity well no understanding for Chinese	
	unlimited love of parents	weaker in networking high quality high balance of private versus work life	Superior Romantic	values/families more technical less heart	

over their male Chinese counterparts, since they are trusted more. Hence, several of the women described building up trust as another key intercultural skill. In the view of the interviewed women, "being a Chinese woman among foreigners" is one of the biggest advantages they have when it comes to advancing in their careers at multinational companies in China. This refers to a capacity to not just understand but adapt to the culture of the head office or foreign decision-makers at their companies that goes far beyond simply understanding the language and being able to communicate in multiple languages at company management level.

> *A., VP: "You need to unlock the culture of origin in a multinational, understand it ..."*

Some participants noted cultural differences in how female executives are treated. In this study, these observations were made exclusively by women who work at German companies. According to these women, at these companies intercultural competency involves being able, as a Chinese woman, to develop successful strategies for responding to German executives' different ways of treating women.

> *M., CFO: "At the beginning it was a little bit shocking, I mean the cultural shock was there at the beginning when I arrived in Germany, I still remember when I went to Germany being a young woman, nobody took me seriously, because in Germany generally speaking because up to the age of 25 you guys are still in the university. And as a lady most of them are working as a secretary. They simply don't take you seriously. That was not very nice, that's why I really had to work very hard to establish myself there ... I think in Germany you really have to prove or establish yourself. Especially in a company and at least show yourself not as a woman in order to be in a certain position. In China I don't need to be specially to dress very formally, to be a female leader. I saw in Germany the women really have to make themselves as men in order to gain such acceptance at the job. Which for me is an advantage, because I am a foreigner. And I don't need to necessarily follow the same rules. And I still got a little bit of acceptance even though I do not dress and look like men."*

The descriptions suggest the women possess strong empathy for cultural peculiarities. They also have a strong understanding of their own market and are able to build bridges with people from other countries. However, ultimately it is the adaptation (or, as Chen et al. define it, transformation) of the women in this group that constitutes their particular strength: their ability to adapt to different cultures as and when necessary.

Summary: Competencies of the Chinese female executives

In summary, the women reported on their own skills and competencies with great self-confidence as well as critical self-reflection. Most of the skills and competencies that they mentioned can be assigned to the category of expert knowledge, followed by intercultural competency. The latter category elicited the most detailed and numerous descriptions. All the women exhibited a high level of intercultural competency in the defined sense. They seethes competency, in combination with their language skills, their many years' experience of the market and their ability as Chinese women to build up trust with foreign decision-makers, as the main competitive advantage they have enjoyed in their careers. They feel this combination gives them a clear edge over their male counterparts.

The findings here are in line with Rosinski's definition of intercultural leadership competency. The women are not merely able to recognise and accept fine-grained intercultural differences, but also view such differences in a very positive light and find it fulfilling to work in a professional environment characterised by cultural diversity. They possess the ability to switch between different worlds. The findings also suggest that the Chinese women have global mindsets, i.e. the ability to understand, connect and integrate different cultures. In terms of the broader interpretation of global leadership offered by Black and Morrison (2014), it can be concluded that the Chinese women possess savvy in the form of strong knowledge not just of their local market but also of international business and on an organisational level. They also have what Black and Morrison term inquisitiveness, meaning extremely high curiosity about and interest in foreign cultures, international business and foreign leadership styles. The women in the Shanghai Women's Career Lab also possess the other two central traits of this definition of global leadership, namely perspective and character. These traits are discussed further in the next section, which looks at personality in relation to careers.

The strongest differences within the group concerning leadership competencies can be observed in relation to visionary thinking. Only some of the women consider themselves to be visionary. Others feel their capacity for visionary thinking is limited by the rules of international companies. A far greater number of specific examples were given of capacity for innovation.

Personality and women's careers

Theory shows that personality impacts on careers

Scholars use the term "personality" to refer to the individual mixture of certain mostly settled traits, attitudes and values with which a person responds to their environment (Mayrhofer, 2005). The number of different personality factors studied varies depending on the research approach. Some theories distinguish up to 16 factors (Catell, 1986), but many other researchers believe that five are sufficient (Catell, 1986; Digman, 1990; Judge et al., 2002). The "Big Five" personality theory considers five dimensions: neuroticism, extraversion, conscientiousness, agreeableness and openness to experience. The model is also known as FFM ("Five Factor Personality Model"). The development of the Big Five theory began in the 1930s and it is now internationally regarded as the universal standard model in personality research. It has been used in over 3,000 academic studies in the past 20 years. Openness to experience describes an individual's interest in and degree of engagement with new experiences and impressions. Conscientiousness primarily describes a person's level of self-control, precision and determination. Extraversion describes activity and interpersonal conduct. It is sometimes also referred to as surgency. Like extraversion, agreeableness primarily describes interpersonal conduct (Rothmann and Coetzer, 2003). Neuroticism describes individual differences in experiences of negative emotions. Some authors also refer to it as emotional lability. Its opposite is referred to as emotional stability, contentment or ego strength. Research shows differences between men and women in relation to these factors. Women tend to achieve lower values in the self-confidence aspect of extraversion but higher values on dimensions related to human warmth and positive emotions (Ayman and Korabik, 2010).

The leadership motive pattern (LMP) model was developed on the basis of longitudinal surveys ranging in length from eight to sixteen years. The LMP model helps to predict successful future career development. McClelland and Bovatzis (1982) describe the following three needs, which they studied in relation to advancement in management: need for achievement, need for power and need for affiliation. The need for achievement is defined as the drive to excel, achieve and succeed in relation to a set of standards. The need for power is defined as the need to make others behave in a way they would not have behaved otherwise. The need for affiliation is defined as the desire for close, friendly interpersonal relationships. McClelland studied the connection between these three factors and success in management. He concluded that a medium to high need for power is advantageous for managers to reach senior hierarchical levels in an organisation. The need for achievement is more important for smaller organisations or entrepreneurs, so individuals with a high achievement motivation are disproportionally likely to be successful independent entrepreneurs. According to McClelland, a high achievement motivation does not lead to a successful career in management. He found that successful managers only had moderate levels of achievement motivation. However, affiliation need tended to be low among top executives, since individuals with a strong need for affiliation invest a lot of time in interpersonal relationships and place greater priority on being liked and accepted when making decisions.

Another approach to studying executives' motivations is Miner's role motivation theory. Role motivation theories deal with the relationships among organisation types, role requirements for key performers that follow from these organisational forms and motivation patterns that fit these roles. They are theories which tie together the macro-organisational and micro-individual level of organisational theory (Miner, 1993). Anything of a motivational nature that fits or matches the role requirement is included in the pattern. The theories specify a set of informal role requirements that derive from the form of organisation and the relation of the key performer to that organisation. A matching set of motive patterns is specified, one for each role requirement. Miner (1978, 1993) and Miner, Chen, and Yu (1991) have shown in several studies that managerial success and managerial motivation are related. Hierarchical levels correlate with the motivation to manage, and so can be predicted on this basis. According to this theory, some role requirements are common to many different management roles. In order to achieve success as an executive, people need to have the desire and motivation to fulfil this role. According to Miner, there are six role requirements and corresponding managerial motive patterns.

A number of researchers have studied the motivation of female managers and international differences in relation to China on the basis of Miner's results. Accordingly, his studies represent a good theoretical basis for the purposes of the present research of female Chinese executives. Chen, Yu, and Miner (1991) investigated managerial motivation and its relationship to managerial success in a study of female executives at Chinese state-owned enterprises. In this connection, the question arises of whether managerial motivation theory is compatible with Chinese cultural norms and whether the model is applicable for women given that it was developed on the basis of male executives. Hofstede (1996, 1998, 2005) classifies China as a nation with high power distance: that is, a high level of inequality between managers and employees. China is also an extremely collectivist country where organisations' goals have priority over those of individuals. Hence, it could be argued that collectivism is not in keeping with certain dimensions of the motivation to manage, such as the desire to compete or stand out in a group. However, Chen, Yu, and Miner (1997) present several reasons why the dimensions are also applicable to Chinese managers. They argue that collectivism and competitiveness are not necessarily exclusive. The fiercely competitive nature of university applications is one example that supports this view. The authors also argue that cross-cultural differences do not necessarily manifest in intracultural variations. In direct comparison with American managers, Chinese managers may be less willing to be distinctive and stand out from the group. But this does not mean that within China managers will necessarily be less willing to stand out than non-managers. Instead, the opposite can be assumed, since the role of an executive makes it necessary *per se* to stand out. Ebrahimi and Miner (1991) found differences with respect to the motivation to manage in a comparison of managers and non-managers in China. The group of Chinese managers exhibited higher levels of motivation, competitiveness, assertiveness and desire to impose their wishes. Powell and Mainiero (1993) studied the second aspect: namely, the extent to which managerial motivational theories can be applied to women given that they are mainly based on studies with men. They too looked at the effect of cultural and economic differences between individual countries on the applicability of theories that were originally developed in the West. In his review of a number of different studies, Powell comes to the conclusion that there is no difference between the genders with respect to the motivation to manage. Miner's findings were confirmed both for men and women. Earlier differences in the US studies disappear in later studies from the 1980s.

There are only a few studies on the motivation of female managers in China. There are some views arguing that Chinese women have a strong managerial motivation, and others arguing they have a weak one (Korabik, 1994). According to a review by Korabik, one factor that might speak in favour of the view that Chinese women have a lower motivation to manage is the cultural feudal traditions and interpretations of Confucian values according to which women should take subordinate roles. If these stereotypes are internalised by women, this would decrease their motivation. In their study of managers in Hong Kong, Dolecheck and Dolecheck (1987) conclude that women probably have a lower managerial motivation due to their familial orientation. The idea that men and women have the same level of motivation is supported by the view that Mao's equality policies helped to loosen the grip of Confucian interpretations of the role of women. Factors such as the high proportion of women in employment and management and the strong level of success by women shown in the country's educational statistics lend further support to this view. Another factor is the influence that the Cultural Revolution had on many women in their youth, which contributed to a new, less male-focused image of women. The one-child policy could also be mentioned in favour of the view that women have the same managerial motivation, on the basis that Chinese women are less occupied with raising children and have more energy to concentrate on their careers. Korabik's review concludes that women in China can no longer be stereotyped as being subordinate and lacking the motivation for senior executive roles. Three well-known studies by Chen, Yu, and Miner (1997) and Ebrahimi (1991, 1997) confirm that there is no difference between Chinese men's and women's motivation to manage. The empirical study of 82 managers in Hong Kong by Hau-Siu Chow (1995) also concludes that there is no justification for the view that Chinese women have less drive and motivation for management responsibilities.

Personality dimensions that influence careers

The Business-Focused Inventory of Personality (BIP) developed by Hossiep and Paschen (2003) is the leading method used to categorise personalities in the German-speaking business world. "Personality" refers here to the structure of all a person's behavioural dispositions, including motivational structures and values.

The BIP measures the following constructs. The definition that each construct is based on is given in abbreviated form.

- Achievement motivation (motivation to continuously improve one's own performance)
- Power motivation (motivation to change something that is incorrect, readiness to influence things and to transform structures)
- Leadership motivation (motivation to exert influence in a social context, perception of oneself as an authority figure)
- Conscientiousness (carefulness, trustworthiness, perfectionism, attention to detail)
- Flexibility (readiness to take on unexpected situations, acceptance of change)
- Action orientation (willingness to rapidly transform a decision into a goal-oriented activity)
- Social sensitivity (capacity for empathy)

- Openness to contact (initiating contact with people, both familiar and unfamiliar, maintenance of relationships)
- Sociability (friendliness and respect)
- Team orientation
- Assertiveness (persistence in striving to achieve goals even against resistance)
- Emotional stability (degree to which emotional reactions are balanced and not volatile; capacity to recover from defeat and failure)
- Working under pressure
- Self-confidence (emotional independence from the judgement of others)

According to the literature, there are a total of nine personality dimensions that can be expected to contribute to career success. These dimensions are of critical importance to analyse the personalities of the women in the Shanghai Women's Career Lab.

Conscientiousness and achievement motivation

Individuals who are highly conscientious describe themselves as determined, hardworking, persistent, strong-willed, disciplined, reliable, punctual, orderly, precise and meticulous. Many studies attest to the positive side of this dimension. However, conscientiousness is very broad in scope and covers a wide range of personality features that impact strongly on many different areas of life. Achievement motivation, an element of conscientiousness that is narrower in scope, is even more relevant in the career context. The notion of achievement motivation stems from the study by McClelland (McClelland and Bovatzis 1982) mentioned above. It refers to a willingness to measure oneself against a high benchmark. It has been shown that a high level of achievement motivation leads individuals to make above-average efforts and attain above-average achievements in their professional life. Accordingly, both conscientiousness and achievement motivation are associated with progression in management careers. One aspect that is described under the heading of achievement motivation is the desire to compete with others, which Miner makes a dimension in its own right. People with a high achievement motivation constantly measure their own achievements and compare themselves with others, with the aim of improving their own performance (Hossiep, Paschen, and Mühlhaus, 2000).

Leadership motivation

In order to take on leadership tasks, one also needs to have leadership motivation. This dimension essentially refers to a person's power orientation. This personality dimension involves directly exerting influence on other people and social situations and being aware of one's air of authority or status as a role model for others. McClelland and Bovatzis (1982) showed that people with a high leadership motivation have an exceptional will to exert power and influence other people. They also have a relatively low need for affiliation with other people. A study by Gough (1990) identifies leadership motivation and the striving for power as key features that may be the only ones that distinguish leaders and non-leaders. The connection is especially evident in women. Women with high leadership motivation achieve leadership roles more quickly and easily than other women (Tokar, Fischer, and Subich, 1998).

Openness to contact, extraversion and team orientation

In the Big Five theory, extraversion refers to a person's openness to other people. The dimension of openness to contact is more relevant in relation to professional performance. It primarily measures the development of interpersonal relationships and networking. Team orientation refers to the willingness to sacrifice one's own interests for the sake of working as a team. It also involves taking responsibility for helping a collaborative project to move forward and being prepared to share in and support team decisions. A study of over a thousand employees showed that openness to contact and team orientation were the best predictors of professional achievements and advancement (Markman and Baron, 2003).

Emotional stability

Emotional stability, which refers to emotional reactions that are balanced rather than volatile and the capacity to recover quickly from failures, has also been shown to be related to career progression, though less strongly than achievement motivation and conscientiousness. In this connection, neuroticism refers to the opposite: emotional lability. This refers to people who have less control over their needs and desires. Conversely, control over one's needs and desires is a key aspect of emotional stability (Borkenau and Ostendorf, 1993). Individuals with low emotional stability tend to constantly view their professional position in a negative light. They are more prone to stress and burnout. Emotional stability, by contrast, not only helps to prevent stress but is associated with more resilient health.

Flexibility

In the Big Five theory, this dimension is classed as "openness to experience". However, the latter notion is more broadly construed than is necessary for the present, career-related context. As used here, the scope of the term "flexibility" is limited to changes in one's professional life. It refers to the capacity to adapt to frequent changes in working conditions. However, the relation between flexibility and career success is not uniform. Studies show that exceptionally flexible people tend to earn less and advance less far. However, the opposite is true for women. They see flexibility as a tool for career development. The more independent women are, the higher they rise (Tokar et al., 1998).

Capacity for self-presentation

This dimension refers to the deliberate, conscious strategies that individuals use in social situations to create as positive an impression of themselves as possible and the ability to influence the picture that other people have of them. It is based on the theory of "self-monitoring" developed by Snyders (1974). According to this theory, individuals who adopt these strategies deliberately do not share their true opinions or feelings. Social interaction requires the capacity to regulate one's verbal and non-verbal presentation of oneself so as to make a positive impression on others. There appear to be indications that both an extreme capacity for self-presentation and a complete absence of this capacity can have a positive impact in professional life (Williams 1997). People without this capacity are perceived as being more honest. Executives who have this capacity and present their achievements positively receive support from employees. This means that both aspects can have a positive influence on careers. The capacity for self-presentation is important right from the earliest stages of a career. Managers who have a strong capacity for self-presentation are regarded as particularly effective leaders by others. However, there might be doubts about their competence. For this research these Dimensions which are included in the BIP-dimensions are used as base in order to describe the personalities of the female Chinese executives.

In summary: many studies show a connection between personality and professional achievements. However, most of the findings are reported individually and combinations of dimensions are not considered. Certain features that seem to help women are apparently not necessary for men, or at least not to the same degree. In a study on women's capacity for career advancement, Henn concludes that women in management roles are primarily characterised by high flexibility and team orientation (Henn, 2012). The same study found that the factors of assertiveness and the ability to work under pressure distinguished men from women. Furthermore, when analysing personality it is important to note that every person has a unique mix of the different dimensions. This leaves open the question of what effect this specific mixture will have and what dimensions need to be maximised in order to rise right up the ranks (Mayrhofer et al, 2005). Furthermore, it has not yet been clarified whether different personality dimensions or combinations thereof are relevant to different aspects of career success.

Analysis of the personalities of the Chinese female executives

Overview of the self-descriptions

The previous section presented several theories of personality factors and how these factors relate to careers. Below, there now follows a summary of the women's descriptions of personality features that were relevant to their advance-ment to, and success in, senior management. The analysis is also based on the women's self-descriptions as given in the interviews. No personality tests were carried out. Answers that allow conclusions to be drawn regarding individual ele-ments of the women's personalities primarily occurred in response to questions about their strengths and career motivation and associated sub questions. These answers were varied and wide-ranging. They were assigned to different personality dimensions in order to generate interpretations and conclusions regarding personal-ity factors relevant to the careers of the female executives who participated in the study. The analysis was informed by the theoretical approaches presented before. It was primarily based on the dimensions of the BIP, which combines many different theories. It also drew on the results of Miner et al. (1995) and the Managerial Mo-tive Pattern model that they developed. Table 13 shows the main results produced by summarising and counting the terms used by the women. In the following sub-sections, these results are described and analysed in context. Supplementary expla-nations of other personality dimensions that could be identified in the study group are presented in the subsections.

Table 14: Results regarding relevant selected personality dimensions*(self-descriptions)

(* Based on the BIP dimensions developed by Hossiep et al., 2003)

Professional Orientation
Performance motivation (49)
be the best/do my best (12)
ambitious/stand out/move up/ be successful/achieve (11)
self-motivated/take charge
high-clear targets/high standards/result-target driven (8)
push things through
decision making
do something special/meaningful
looking for challenges (8)
initiative/pro-active/be driver
Leadership motivation (25)
influence others/set expectation for my team
delegation/Coaching/support
interest in people/believe in others
motivate others/award others
be a role model
can build a team
strong sense of responsibility
power orientation
wanted bigger responsibility/active looking for power/knowing power from early on
not following rules/orders
Motivation to shape/influence processes (11)
find new procedures, processes/find solution for challenges
knowing how to use resources

Working behaviour
Conscientiousness (20)
disciplined/hard working/persistent (7)
planning/structured/organisational skills/organise well/priority setting/detail oriented
committed/committed to work ethics
Flexibility (33)
flexible/ embracing change, welcoming change (4)
welcome risk/courage/more courage than others/courage for decision, no fear (10)
look for variety, change/not be bored/fun/excitement (9)
optimistic/ positive/enthusiastic (8)
mobile/fast

Social Competencies
Team orientation (36)
support others, bring value, contribute (9)
have good relationships/team player/people oriented

build trust (honest, trust worthy, loyal/ respectful/looking for respect from others) (10)
emphatic, caring, interpersonal skills (5)
looking for recognition from others (8)
Assertiveness (15)
aggressive, hard (4)
can do the hard things (layoffs)/can do attitude
strong willed/push things through/determined
manage conflict

This summary presents a quantitative weighting of certain dimensions. It also makes clear the precise terms that the women used in their self-descriptions, which have been assigned here to different dimensions. The frequency of mentions must be understood in the context of the method that was used, which only permits conclusions about tendencies to be made. Generalisable conclusions that go beyond this would require quantitative methods and the use of personality tests. In terms of frequency, most of the women's coded self-descriptions could be assigned to the categories of achievement motivation and team orientation, followed by flexibility and leadership motivation. According to Eagly et al. (2007) and Henn (2012), women in leadership roles are primarily characterised by their high team orientation and flexibility. The answers as categorised above confirm these findings for this research group too. Below, the individual results are described and analysed in greater detail. The key category of team orientation is not discussed here but in the section on leadership styles.

Achievement motivation and attitude towards competition –
being the first from early on

In terms of frequency, most of the women's descriptions could be assigned to the category of achievement motivation, which studies very clearly show is associated with progressing further in management. Achievement motivation refers to a willingness to measure oneself against a high benchmark, to constantly measure one's own achievements, to compare oneself with others and if necessary to improve one's own performance (McClelland et al., 1982). Achievement motivation can be understood as an element of conscientiousness that is focused on the context of everyday work, which researchers subsume under the term "working behaviour". Numerous studies show that a high level of achievement motivation leads individuals to make above-average efforts and attain above-average achievements in their professional life. The women in the study group described themselves as ambitious. They set themselves high personal goals and benchmarks, and are very focused on success. One woman summarised this high goal motivation as follows:

> *J., HRD: "Ambition. I should say I'm a very ambitious person. I want to be somebody because in (company name) I worked with many smart people. I want to be my boss. That's always what I think. I want to be my boss at the end of the day."*

The goals "be the best" and "be outstanding" were frequently mentioned as career drivers. The women believe this originated in their childhoods and upbringing. The women were raised with the goal of being top of the class at school. They were identified as exceptionally gifted, and their teachers and parents gave them further encouragement to excel.

> *A., VP: "That's very interesting. When I was young I think I was always a top good student in the teacher's eye. ... Always on the top. Maybe in my teacher's eyes I should be in this way. I don't know. Everything I do should be outstanding. That's maybe in the beginning, in childhood. Feels like I should be a role model. Probably that's kind of influencing me – in everything I do I should be role model."*

> *M., CFO: "Yes, I remember very well when I was 8, I told everybody I wanted to be like Marie Curie, I think it was like the lady who won the Nobel Prize for physics, the lady who was in the quantum physics together with her husband. I really wanted to be a scientist, I wanted to be a physicist to make a lot of research, find out the rules of the universe. That or be a professor one day, that was my original dream, and I was very good in abstract thinking, so I read a lot of physics study, like Einstein, when I was young."*

The women regard it as important to have a challenge. They formulated this wish in very active terms, and said that they constantly look for challenges. Others said that they want to do something special and meaningful in their work.

> *J., GM: "First, I always wanted to do something special. The reason why I wanted to go to Germany was my fear to foresee with at the age of 20 the routine of my next 20 years of life. Like my parents – school, study job. A relaxed job, high reputation, not well paid, not so that we had to suffer from hunger, but enough to live. This is not what I wanted. I wanted to do something valuable, something different."*

Based on the content and frequency of their self-descriptions, all the women in this study group can be considered to have high to very high levels of achievement motivation. According to research findings, this is a precondition for advancement to senior management roles.

Achievement motivation is connected to attitude towards competition. Individuals with high achievement motivation like to measure themselves against others. Miner et al. (1978, 1993) summarise this personality factor under the heading desire to compete, and regard a positive attitude towards competition as one of the essential preconditions for success in senior management.

Table 15: Handling Competition (self-description, multiple)

Positive attitude with competition (17)
excited/ source of inspiration
like it/ looking for it/feel great with it/ happy to compete
want to win from early on
easy for me
keep my competitiveness by learning
develop from strengths of competitor/ develop through competition
Necessary
Not relevant for me any more (15)
do not think about it/ignore it
compete with myself/focus on myself
I care for others as I am most senior
Dislike of competitive situations (9)
not good for company
do not like it/avoid
feel a bit uneasy with it

The women's answers concerning their attitude towards competition with others can be divided into three groups: very positive, neutral and dislike. Most of the interviewees reported that they see competition as a motivating factor for their careers. It is notable that competition is generally regarded very positively. Descriptions that can be assigned to the category "desire to compete" from the Managerial Motive Pattern model were very frequent. The women described competition as a source of inspiration, strength and learning. Many used the phrase "excited about a fair game" or interpreted competition as competition with themselves with the goal of improving. They described competition as making them stronger, more assertive and tougher.

> *V., GM: "Competition? Sometimes competition can make you stronger ... the competitor maybe somehow has some strength which you don't have. You should very frankly observe yourself and him and what things he does better and you should learn from him. I think the only way to face the competition is to make you stronger. So competition for me I think its okay. If you are stronger, really stronger, you should take the higher position ..."*

They once again traced their positive handling of competition back to their sociali-sation, and presented examples from school and university. Even back then, the women already wanted to be "number one". They see winning as something very positive and valuable. Many of them described how they could not bear to lose children's games such as card games or table tennis, or mentioned dreams such as "wanting to become world table tennis champion". For many of the women, their parents (alongside factors such as school and other groups of children) had a strong impact on their positive attitude towards competition. A desire for success and the goal of becoming more influential were mentioned as motivations for competing. Another motivation is the feeling of happiness that they experience when they win. The women with a positive attitude towards competition seek it out. One executive described how she specifically wanted to move to Germany to work because she believed she would find more competition for herself there than in China. Again, self-improvement, learning and development are central to this conception of com-petition.

> C., HRD: "This is funny story but it help explain my competitive side. When I was small my mother, as boys and girls, would play cards. We would play a game. If I feel I am not going to win in this game I would quit. I would not join in. I would find reasons to say that I'm sick today. I'm tired. I feel like if I am going to win a game I am very active in participating ... Later on in work I always want to be the best. I always want to have the highest score. Be the best to get recognized. That also was part of problem when I became a leader. I probably was not able to appreciate the people who are different from me. I would encourage people to take on challenges and to be aggressive ... I probably was not able to appreciate in full those more introverted styles ... Later on of course I learned about that. By nature I'm actually competitive ... Later on I learned to better manage that side of me. I actually feel excited when I have a chance to compete. But I have to use that in a good way."

> H., VP: "What drives me is that I am a very competitive person. Perhaps it's also linked to the way I was brought up. My parents' expectation in me. I wanted to succeed. I wanted to have more influence. I wanted to apply my knowledge whatever capabilities."

> B., V-GM: "Yes, that is the reason I would like to return to Germany...I want to face more competition. My profile here is quite unique, because there is no-body who has exactly this profile...And so I do not have much competition, I have to say, my position is unchallenged. Also I feel competent, so I see noth-ing that would tell me that I am challenged here. Yes, competition would help

my own development. Perhaps emotionally not so easy to cope, but I would like to measure myself more on others." (Translated from German)

The interviewees attributed more competitiveness to women than men. One example given was preparations for important presentations, which according to the group women always invest more time in. One executive from sales, who is responsible for over 1,000 staff, described her experiences with Chinese men and women in competitive situations. In her view, the women had been three times as strong as the men, always wanted to win and did not fear losing face. She said that women were more aggressive overall; they observed their competitors more closely and then targeted their weaknesses. She remarked that she herself finds it very easy to deal with competition in her job.

X., GM: "... for men I believe they are more afraid to lose face so you have to be more careful because they are men. But for women, for some RMs, my observation is they are tough. They are aggressive. Otherwise they will not in that position. They are very competitive. Very, very competitive. They don't realize they are very competitive. They are not afraid to lose face because they are so competitive and so aggressive. They fight back and the want to win. They want to win always. If one is woman and the man in the same position normally the woman is three times stronger than the man. This is the comment from my boss 10 years ago. When I look at this female, managing in my team now, I will remind them they are so competitive and their peers may not be so comfortable to deal with that. I will remind them."

Another group of interviewees explained that they focus on their own skills and actions, since they are so senior that they no longer need to deal with competition. They also noted that they have recruited all their staff themselves and so are no longer in competition with them. The Chinese principle of respect for age and rank may underlie these answers. Around 15 of the answers were along these lines. Competition is no longer of any real relevance to these women, since they hold a senior management role. This group regards handling competition as something they did at earlier stages of their careers, when they were still rising up the ranks.

M., CFO: "But when I grow older, I don't feel the competition is that obvious any more. You don't compete with anybody for any specific thing. So I am more focusing on myself. In other words, I am competing with myself every day, whether I can be better than before ... It is also the maturity of age. Seriously, you don't compete with anybody. That is why my first question was to compete with whom?"

When asked about the drawbacks of competition, a few women answered that competition is only meaningful if it is good and fair, generating good results and achievements for the company. The interviewees reject unfair competition. According to the women, winners or stronger performers deserve respect and their advancement is not resented.

> *Q., GM: "For me it is more about source of inspiration because I always thought*
>
> *that I learn things from those types of situations ... I think then it depends on how the game is played. Most of the time I feel excited, if it's a fair play that the person is playing ... if not then I will feel kind of, I may lost my interest. Feel a bit frustrated if it's not the same way I expected. Like for example if I argue with reason and the other person is rather more emotional then I lose interest."*

A total of nine of the interviewed women view competition with others unfavourably. Typical explanations for this were that they find it unpleasant or that their company does not have a competitive culture. One of the nine women said she simply does not like it. She only gets involved in competitive situations in exceptional cases where she is absolutely certain and convinced of something. The women presented examples of situations where they were promoted and other people avoided them or left the company as a result.

This more reticent attitude towards competition in a minority of the group could be due to cultural background factors that, according to Hofstede (1996, 1998, 2005), derive from China's collectivist orientation. According to this theory, the desire to compete runs counter to this traditional group-focused orientation. In this connection, the question also arises of the women's ability to deal with conflict, since several interviewees see conflict as closely linked to competition and therefore think that they should only compete when it is worthwhile, not over trivial matters, since competition can lead to conflict. Results regarding the ability to deal with conflict are considered in greater depth in the discussion on assertiveness.

In summary, most of the group has a generally positive attitude towards competition. This corresponds to the results of Chen et al. (1997) and Miner et al. (1991), who found that managers in China are more willing to compete and stand out in a group than non-managers. The findings of the Shanghai Women's Career Lab also correspond to Powell et al. (1993) who confirmed that the findings of Miner et al. also held for women.

Financial considerations – a strong motivator in early career stages

The women mentioned both intrinsic and extrinsic career motivations. In this connection, several interviews touched on the financial incentive of rising to senior positions. This factor was very openly described as one of their key motivating factors, especially at the start of their careers. The women noted their strong negotiating skills and financially focused goals. According to the women's descriptions, financial motivations for careers appear to be socially accepted. All the women addressed the topic openly and directly. Key goals that the women aim to achieve by advancing to a position with a higher salary at their company included providing support and security for their families, becoming financially independent (especially from their husbands) and strengthening their own position within their families.

> *J., Asia HRD: "If I look at all the steps I had in the past, I think from intuition point of view there is something in my body that I really like money I should say that.*
>
> *Because why I say that is if you look at all the things I've done I'm always very self-independent. I didn't ask my mother or my parents for any financial support. I also want earn my little penny to support myself. Why I say that? Because when I was in the university I had plenty of two part-time jobs. One is to be a teacher for a small child. That earn me in that sense I can earn some money to support myself. I wanted to be financially free."*
>
> *L., HRD: "I think freedom. What I mean is the control of my life. It's also a motivation for me. I'm talking about money. Actually, my earning is much higher than my husband. And my husband his earning can almost manage my family livings. So basically my money earned money doesn't have any use for my family unless we want to invest in something. But we are not really plan so well the investment. I have a freedom to manage my money. I enjoy this kind of situation that nobody controls me. When I was very small my parents let me go, let me free, whatever you do, you just do what you want to so I enjoy this kind of thing. For family or myself I don't want anyone control me. That's my work motivation number 1. I earn the money. I earn the freedom for myself."*
>
> *M. M., President: "...Yes, what do you want, what we pay you is enough for a Chinese (they said)...I said yes but the company earns a lot of money because of this position. The position is paid, no matter woman or man, German or Chinese...At the end they agreed. I negotiated a fixed salary plus a bonus. If the result gets better, I get more bonus, if not it goes down. This has to do with performance. At the end I renounced a bit as the result was so good, we had not thought that." (Translated from German)*

J., Sales Director: "Both quantitatively and qualitatively I would say in terms of salary package, which XY (company name) had higher, and benefits as well. Secondly recognition is very important to me I think. I'm one of those persons who believes if I spend enough effort and contribution I will deserve what I need to deserve."

In line with China's rapid economic growth from the 1990s to the present day, the women reported rapid increases in their incomes compared with the low starting salaries when China's economic reforms were just beginning. Some women reported a 16-fold increase over their starting salary; others reported ten – and then five-fold increases in their salary within a short period of time. They described how China's 1970s generation, which most of the women belong to, was not affluent, and that consequently women needed to earn an income in order to start families and safeguard or improve living standards. In their view, the 1990s generation has a different relationship to money and generally has higher expectations. They also observed that the 1970s generation did not have to fight much for more money: pay increases came about pretty much as a matter of course, provided their performance was good. In general, the women described their generation as being motivated both by achievement and money. However, they said that the financial motivation becomes less important the further up the hierarchy one rises, and is replaced by other intrinsic factors.

S., HRD: "Respect. Also money. Because you have senior position, you earn a lot. You earn more than others. Now ... my motivation is self-satisfaction."

Only a small portion of the group reported that money is not particularly important to them. However, this answer was relativised by reference to the fact that they have already risen to a high level and are financially comfortable. Two women reported deliberately taking pay cuts for the sake of career moves that they knew would mean a lower salary.

The women were also asked about what role status plays for them personally in connection with their career motivation. For the interviewees, status primarily represents success and recognition from their families. The women said that, for them, status means their parents and children being proud of their success.

Another definition of status in this group concerns being recognised as an expert in their companies, in their networks and among their colleagues. Many of them equate status with a good reputation in the market.

They also regard working at a company with a good reputation as an aspect of status, as this in turn increases the recognition from their family. Accordingly, women described how, for them, status means working at a top 500 company that attracts admiration in their social environment. The women only demand externally visible status symbols from their companies if this is justified by the company's success and is in keeping with the company culture. In this connection, they described their own titles as a means of getting things done more easily at their companies.

> *M. M., President: "That was important to me, I would say. But only through my hard work. Company XY asked me if I wanted a bigger office. I said no, first we have to earn money, than we will make that bigger. At the first joint venture I got a Mercedes as bonus, but at the beginning I had an old car. I do not need it, but if the company earns well than I want it. If we build a swimming pool for the staff than I want one for myself." (Translated from German)*

> *M., HRD: "I was very proud when I leaved (company name) my north Asia president asked my boss to offer a farewell party for me and a very precise gift. It's a crystal something and very expensive. About 3000 Rmb as a gift for me. And our greater China HR department went to Hangzhou and stayed in five-star hotel for my party. That's a special award the north Asia president offer for my farewell. That's really amazing. I got a lot of recognition."*

The female executives furnish their offices in simple style, with no recognisable status symbols. The offices of CEOs and vice-presidents differ from those of directors only in terms of size. All the interviewed women have a personal assistant and an office with a window, but none of them have a traditional anteroom. The women's assistants are based in open-plan offices near their bosses' offices, and their role is not immediately identifiable to visitors. An assistant was only involved in preparations for one of the interviews. Hence, for the women in this group status primarily means social recognition and recognition within the company. There was no sign of external status symbols.

Leadership motivation and need for power

In order to be given leadership responsibilities, one needs leadership motivation and the power orientation associated with it. Leadership motivation is a key career determinant. According to studies, people with leadership motivation are more likely to rise to senior management levels. A strong correlation between leadership motivation and obtaining leadership positions is also observable among women: it is easier for them to achieve leadership positions if they have higher leadership motivation (Tokar, Fischer, and Subich, 1998).Leadership orientation essentially also describes people's power orientation, which incorporates two dimensions: firstly, directly exerting influence on other people and social situations, and secondly, factors that do not necessarily relate to power motivation itself but to how people with a high power orientation see themselves, such as an awareness of their status as a role model for others. Leadership motivation is based on the "Leadership Motive Pattern" concept developed by McClelland et al. (1982). The factors at the core of the model are a need for achievement, a need for power and a need for affiliation with other people. According to this model, people with high leadership motivation have a high desire for power but low need for affiliation (for example, low interest in forming friendships).The women's answers show a need and desire to serve a role model function at their companies and in the market. In addition, they are motivated to influence and support others in equal measure. The women's descriptions of leadership motivation primarily centre on the desire to be a role model, on the willingness to assume responsibility, and on influencing other people. The women frequently described achieving a respected role model function as their main motivation.

> *S., HRD: "I think I want to be a person that my colleagues see me as very professional, that I can support them, they can learn from me to be successful. This kind of recognition is not just achievement. You are the person that can really help them to be successful and very professional."*

Strong and genuine interest in their employees also plays an important part here. The women see themselves as responsible for motivating employees and supporting them so they can develop. Chin et al. (2001) describe traditional Chinese leadership principles that might underlie these descriptions of their motivations. According to their research, Chinese leaders establish themselves by promoting the success of their followers and enrich these followers by extending to them opportunities to develop their careers. This matches the descriptions of the women, who want to support others. In order to achieve this goal, the women delegate tasks, issue clear instructions or provide coaching, according to the specific situation. The answers regarding the women's own relationship with power and the role this relationship has played in their careers reveal that the women engage with the issue in a nuanced manner. Many of the women believe that female executives in China are very good at exercise power, and better than their male counterparts. Once again, they trace their strong, positive relationship to power back to their own upbringing and early experiences. According to these accounts, parents in positions of power teach their children from a very young age how to exercise power in later life. These accounts suggest that it is important not to be afraid of power.

> *M. M., President: "That comes from the Cultural Revolution. My parents came from the government, my father had power and my mother had power. I have always seen how powerful they were…I always saw people in high position and heard that these are normal people. I had no fear of the big boss, because I was used from early on being around them. All are the same for me. Sometimes it disturbs people in big meetings that I say what I think…most important, no fear. My company says, this woman has no fear, she is too courageous…no fear. I have no fear." (Translated from German)*

In this connection, the women emphasised the responsibility that goes with power. Some of them said they believe they have less power than outsiders and company employees assume in virtue of their position, since the corporate system and its rules generally limits the exercise of power within the system. On the other hand, examples such as the power to dismiss or hire staff demonstrate the great power wielded by HRDs, CEOs or similar. The women said their personal goal is to use power with sensitivity, rather than exploiting it. They think that power should be used fairly and transparently. The women distinguished between hierarchical power in virtue of position and power arising from communication skills and assertiveness. They use hierarchical power, which they described as more straightforward, but would not want to use it as their main tool. Rather, they use it when quick decisions are needed. Many of them only like to use hierarchical power very rarely, "only when there's no longer any other alternative". Excessive use of hierarchical power was equated with "immature leadership". One interviewee defined power as peace and quiet. Elaborating on this point, she explained that having power also means having the complete trust of her boss, the foreign general manager. Another woman commented that she generally regards the term "power" as negative. She prefers to speak of "setting a direction". Only one of the interviewees explicitly explained that she has a negative emotional reaction to exercising hierarchical power. The answers show that power in the form of persuasiveness and assertiveness is used frequently and is emotionally preferable. It is not possible to reach a clear conclusion for the group as a whole concerning the low need for affiliation attributed to successful executives by the Leadership Motive Pattern model. The women described how important they consider recognition from their team and generally good relationships in their everyday work. Against the background of traditional Chinese management principles, a high priority is given to maintaining good interpersonal relationships with the goal of achieving harmony

(Li, 2013). This would suggest that the women do have a need for affiliation. However, many of them said that their actions are generally not dependent on other people's opinions. This point is addressed again in more detail in the team orientation section.

Working behavior – determined and flexible

One personality dimension that is especially important for professional achievement is conscientiousness. Individuals who are highly conscientious describe themselves as determined, ambitious, hard-working, persistent, disciplined, systematic, punctual, reliable, orderly, meticulous and precise (Mayrhofer et al., 2005). The career benefits of conscientiousness appear obvious and have been demonstrated in many studies (Barrick, 2001). A large number of answers describing the women's commitment to their careers and their high levels of discipline and perseverance could be assigned to the category of conscientiousness. Miner considers this aspect under a heading that is defined slightly differently, namely the "desire to perform routine administrative responsibilities". Around 20 individual descriptions provided by the women in the group could be assigned to this factor. The terms discipline, persistence and hard-working were especially prevalent. They were associated with high career commitment. One woman who works in purchasing specifically linked commitment to professional ethics. She was primarily thinking here of the compliance issues entrusted to her. Some of the women also described having an organised, structured working style. Purely in quantitative terms, there were far more descriptions that could be assigned to the category of achievement motivation, which could also be considered a subset of conscientiousness that is more relevant to the career context.

In the Big Five theory, flexibility is classed as "openness to experience". In relation to career development, the aspect of flexibility that concerns openness to changes in one's professional life is of interest. This involves the capacity to adapt flexibly to frequent changes in working conditions. High acceptance of change and openness to new perspectives and methods fall under this category. For women in particular, it has been shown that there is a link between flexibility (understood as a tool for independent career development) and the executive level that they reach (Henn, 2012; Tokar et al., 1998). The descriptions provided by the women in the Shanghai Women's Career Lab that could be assigned to the category of flexibility are highly varied. They repeatedly described themselves as flexible and as welcoming change. Some of them described how they are constantly looking for new challenges and variety. Boredom triggered by overly monotonous work and professional environments is one of the main demotivators for these women. The most common phrases that occurred in their descriptions of their career paths, which will be considered in greater depth in a later chapter, included "to be exposed to many industries, experience different businesses, see different ways of managing, experience different roles in different departments". This suggests a high degree of flexibility concerning different types of work.

> K., HRD: "I think that was for me key challenge is to getting to know the different market of other countries. I don't know I was put on the spot I remember to Malaysia. At that time we do not have an HR. the whole team was gone before I took it over. That was very challenging because that period exactly is our budgeting period (inaudible) year. I have no idea how the salary is calculated. What are the package we are talking about? What are the benefits? Package that we need to include in this budget? I have totally no idea and what are the government compliance regulatory and monetary requirement. I totally have no idea but I need to do this in 3 days. I really slept like 3 hours maximum per day. I go there and spend my whole weekend in the hotel. I searched the website of their government policies. Study one by one. And consulting my external HR consultant in Malaysia and ask her to provide me guidance suggestions. I gave her call during weekend, I apologized but I have to until I come up with a very accurate budgeting plan on my own."

> C. President: "I think at that point I did not know which industry or which particular company would be interesting. I interviewed with XY Company and the consultant role sounded very challenging, very interesting to me so I joined XY. I think it was come to think of it; it was good thing because I got to be exposed to a lot of different industries. A lot of different business issues.

> ... I think it was different of course and you got to work in one company, work in one industry instead of different industries. I think one good thing about YZ (Company name) is we have multiple business units with more than one. It still gives me a little bit of different sectors to look into. So it is not that boring and so that was good. The fact that YZ has given me different roles and keep me challenged I think that was also good ..."

> L., HRD: "I wanted to join relatively small company but I want to join a consumer or rented company. I told him very clearly my background and my personality ... I talk to headhunter and luckily they got this opportunity. ... I'm looking for not looking for balance. I'm looking for some stretch and challenge. I want to really step from supporting role, nice role to a very business impact role. Impact again. This is my first role in YZ (Company name). It's an HR business partner role. Its (inaudible) builder so when I joined in 2012 it's

an individual contributor. It's an HR partner. My key work is really about re-design the company and support the company to do the change management, the layoff. All the tough things ... "

The women's descriptions of their career paths reveal that the women in this group are very flexible not just with regard to their work, roles and experiences, but also with regard to geographical mobility: both intra-organisationally and when switching companies. Examples of this included relocating, living away from their families and commuting. The women accept frequently being away from their family and, if necessary, having to travel between family and work, sometimes over thousands of kilometres. Examples that were given of this flexibility were linked to the expansion of multinational companies: for instance, opening new factories or offices in China, or acquiring new sales regions. Many of the women's career development phase coincided with the period of Chinese expansion following the economic reforms. The women offered a number of accounts of how they took the chances that were available. This required acceptance of change, both mental and geographical, and the flexibility to reorganise their families in the face of the new challenges. A number of examples demonstrated a high degree of flexibility in order to meet companies' requirements and develop their careers even in difficult personal situations such as a partner falling sick or needing to arrange childcare for two young children in their home city.

C., HRD: "I always chose work first. That's why I think in 2007, I worked in Shanghai for about 10 months. I travel back every week to Beijing because my son, my husband were still in Beijing. Just I came here just to temporarily replace a colleague who had to be off for 8 or 9 months. So I take her job and kept my job as well. Two jobs and then travel every week to Beijing. "

The women described themselves as being more courageous and more willing to take risks than other colleagues. In this connection, they also frequently mentioned the courage to take decisions, noting that it was important that they are not afraid of certain risks. Qualities described in this context included optimism, a capacity for enthusiasm and a positive attitude to change.

M. M., President: "I have always worked as an executive in China, I knew that getting recognition would be difficult in Germany, but I thought, it will come one day. The third company was a company in Rheinland-Pfalz (part of Germany) that started a joint venture in Yunnan province. The newspaper 'Welt' had made an article about my career, you can have that. They wanted a joint venture but Yunnan was not cultivated, but a poor place to be. This company was small, they needed someone. For a joint venture a strong Chinese partner is important." (Translated from German)

The women described seeking out challenges, developing themselves and avoiding boredom as the main motivations behind flexibility. The vast majority of the women seek out and welcome change. As explained in the section on intercultural competencies, this is strongly linked to the ability to embrace uncertainties. These descriptions confirm the "perspective" dimension from Black and Morrison's (2014) definition of global leadership.

Assertiveness, self-confidence and the ability to handle conflicts

In the Big Five theory, a person's openness to other people is measured by the dimension of extraversion. The dimension of openness to contact is an even more useful measure in relation to professional performance. Developing and maintaining interpersonal relationships are very relevant aspects of extraversion in the context of careers (Judge et al., 2002; Digman, 1990). The interviewer was able to subjectively assess the dimensions of extraversion and openness to contact on the basis of her observations of the 35 women during the interviews. All but two of the women went into the interviews in a spirit of openness and very quickly bonded with the interviewer within the short period of time allotted. As shown by the length of the transcribed interviews, all the women spoke profusely. The detail in which they described their personal strengths was striking. They also discussed their personal weaknesses openly and self-assuredly. Overall, the women were quickly willing to report on personal issues such as the role of their husbands in their careers. In general, despite the artificial interview situation it was very easy to establish a bond because of the women's openness to contact. In only two cases did the women speak significantly less, as reflected in the correspondingly short length of the transcriptions. These women could be subjectively described from the perspective of external observation as more introverted or less open to contact. Openness to contact can also be assessed by reference to the women's answers regarding networking. If it is assumed that more introverted and contact-averse executives are less interested in networking or at least find it difficult, then the majority of women in this group should be considered more extraverted.

In the BIP, assertiveness refers to an individual's tendency to dominate social situations. Assertiveness consists in persistence in striving to achieve one's goals even against resistance and a strong ability to deal with conflict (Hossiep et al. 2003). The main question in this context could be "How persistently do executives pursue their goals compared with others?"

Several of the women noted that persuasive communication is one of their personal strengths.

> *J., GM: "I think my strengths is communication, empathy. In a joint venture communication is essential. It is not like company XY has the say in all, it is all about persuasion of your partner, I think I have an advantage with my language skills and my convincing skills. It is not working like you just say 'it is like this and you must accept it', but convincing is important."*

> *M. M., President: "...difficult to say. As a female I can communicate, convince well. I am not good at logical talk, but I can convince with some good examples. The disadvantage is that they did not take women seriously (compared to German men). In the board meetings for example, when I had ideas, at the beginning they do not take it seriously. This is crazy as many innovative ideas are difficult to accept in the beginning. I had to prepare better. But here in China I am always accepted right from the beginning."*

> *B., V-GM: "Yes it is my strengths – I am target oriented and have no fear of obstacles. And I am not afraid of the change and I look for the change. I want to learn new things and I believe it is also my strengths that I can see the whole picture."*

(All three quotes translated from German)

Most of the women described their attitudes and responses to conflict against the background of their socialisation and upbringing, which primarily focused on avoiding conflict. In Chinese culture, a high value is placed on respect and friendliness. This corresponds to the studies by Chin, Gu, and Tubbs (2001) and Li (2013), who found that *he* (harmony) is central to classical Chinese management. The key traditional values of Chinese managers are maintaining good personal relationships and respecting face even in cases of conflict. According to one woman, bosses from other countries sometimes fail to respect these values out of ignorance, which can often have drastic consequences – even to the extent of Chinese managers quitting.

> *C., HRD: "I'm not really good at that. For example if I have an argument, I never really have an experience of having an argument with a male people. At XY (Company name) especially no because we are too gentle with each other. We don't argue a lot with each other. But at YZ (company name) yes I had a really bad experience. Someone came from US and we had an argument and he made me like a fool in front of a group of people. I didn't handle it very. I*

was silent here. And I hide my emotions although I was very hurt here inside. That's one of the thing I decided to leave. There's no longer a place for me.

... Like my subordinated? Here I don't think they're fighting in front me. They don't do that. But if they do I would not take sides. I would not say who's right who wrong. I would not say that even if I think one part is right and one apart is wrong. But I would do that. Make sure no one lose face here."

However, some of the women welcome conflict and believe this means they are closer to the directly confrontational American style. From their descriptions, it does not appear that these women adopted this more direct response to conflict as a way of overcoming intercultural challenges; rather, they present it as part of their personalities. Many of them described how they deliberately bring conflict to the surface so they can look for solutions. In this connection, the women often used the terms "aggressive" and "hard". The women described themselves as capable of making unpleasant decisions. A number of women gave the example of dismissing staff. Several women explicitly mentioned their own strength at dealing with conflict.

The term "tenacity" also occurred very frequently: the ability to keep going when times are tough and to take difficult decisions.

M. M., President: "This came with age. At the beginning with the joint venture I was young and I fought until the bitter end and achieved it all. Now I am better, more compromising. Little things I will let go, peanuts. With small things I am easy now, but with important things I fight until the end. No matter, fought all the way up to the CEO, everywhere I will go. They say I am assertive." (Translated from German)

Examples of typical conflict situations

- Dismissals
- Competition for a better position
- Disagreeing with the boss
- Overtime
- Jealousy
- Departments or external partners with different interests
- Situations with individual members of staff
- Poor performance by staff, laziness
- Conflicts with partners due to business travel

Many of the women pay great attention to the emotional aspects of conflict. According to the women, the first step in dealing with conflict is to bring emotions under control; feelings need to be brought out into the open and calmed down. When conflicts arise among their staff, the women want to be authentic, like a friend. The most commonly mentioned values in this context were kindness and honesty. The women expressed a desire to coach their employees, find out what the problem is and listen to both sides impartially.

> C., President: "I think that I try to get the emotions out of the topic first. Because the conflicts for example we had a recent so-called conflict. I think that first of all do not get overwhelmed by the emotions and because the emotions may burn you and make you so you first of all understand that the emotions are there but do not let those emotions burden you or consume you. You take them aside and look at the issue. The issue you will find you usually have to accept it or you can do something about it. If you need to accept it you will just have to accept it. You will have to help yourself and help your team to accept it. And if there is something you can do differently about it whether to change it or do something then you can work on it. If you let the emotions consume you and you argue not over the facts but over the emotions that's probably not very meaningful I found. Sometimes we argue over emotions. There is no right or wrong over emotions. Something happened and how I feel about is very different from how you feel about it. There's no point in arguing if your emotions are correct or not. There is no right or working. I have different emotions, you have different emotions, somebody else has different emotions. So there's no point to argue over emotions. If you take that aside and only look at the issue sometimes I also accept that things are not going to be always to my liking. It's not going to work out. Every time not going to work out the way that I want them to work out every single time and if they don't work out like the way I want them to work out either I can still do something about it or I have to accept it and I if have to accept it then I will not."

Other women described a more rational approach towards finding solutions. In cases of conflict, they like to stick to the facts and concentrate on the concrete issues. These women frequently spoke of not getting "too excited".

> M., CFO: "Conflicts normally come when you have different opinions to certain things. And on a job you normally always have conflicts. How do I handle them? I am usually a very rational person. I state a lot of facts, I stick to the facts either until the other people convince me, then I give in or I still stick to it. But I don't normally get too excited. Even when I get excited I try to calm down a little bit, for example when I write an email, I don't send an email

right away, I just hold it for some days until I take out all those emotions. And then send the things out. I am not so good in front of a person, when you start a very hot discussion, then it may be appearing on my face, then my emotion is a little bit less controlled. Then I start to get a little bit hot. This is still something I need to work on in general. "

Z., Director: *"You have to watch the other person first and find out what each of you controls. How the person reacts to you. I mean to observe the opponent very carefully. This is very, very important. There is a clear strategy that fits for each person. Number 1, observe the opponent, what is important for him, what not. And when it is very important for him, try to not tough that point, but go around. But some cases compete aggressively, they want to win all. That you must know. In that case I say, ok, I give you this and I get that, find a compromise. But there are persons, once you made a compromise, who always want you to give in. With such persons you need to stay tough. Perhaps not always, but for the important things, stay firm and strong. " (Translated from German)*

The older women in particular described gradually learning to not only fight for their own solutions but also to avoid taking conflicts too personally and to put themselves in other people's shoes. They described their ideal strategy as making a case based on solid facts and remaining rational and calm. Other interviewees made clear that competing and fighting for their own solutions generally remains their primary strategy in cases of conflict. They mainly illustrated these points using examples from their personal lives. Some participants explained how they become very emotional and allow themselves to express their individual emotions in this sphere. They described their behaviour as "loud" and combative. In their private lives, they give their emotions free rein and their primary strategy is to assert their own interests against their partners. Compromising or cooperating were mentioned as alternative approaches. Some of the women described how they have become more willing to compromise in cases of conflict. The oldest women in the study in particular noted that they listen and wait when conflicts arise, and have found this strategy to be the most successful. Another frequently mentioned strategy is to give way on small things. On this point, one of the older interviewees described how as a young woman she always fought her corner in cases of conflict but is now more often willing to compromise, depending on the situation.

In summary, the women see themselves as assertive. A very small minority of the women tend to avoid conflict, something that should be viewed against the background of their socialisation. Others described themselves as being good at dealing with conflict and very combative. Their strategies for dealing with conflict change as they get older, from constant competition to more compromises and coopera- tion. For many women, saving face plays a role in their dealings with employees.

Dealing with criticism and mistakes against the backdrop of cultural norms

The way the women in the Shanghai Women's Career Lab deal with mistakes and criticism must also be viewed against the background of cultural values. According to Li (2013) "saving face" is one of the core values that translate into management practice. Traditionally, direct criticism was seen as damaging to relationships and hence avoided. Overall, the women are very ambivalent about this whole area, in- cluding the way they deal with criticism and mistakes themselves.

> *S., HRD: "I don't feel lose face if I make a mistake. Because if I made a mis- take I will say, Oh I'm sorry. This is my mistake. I need to correct it... If I communicate my work failure I will say ok. For what is the reason? But I will not blame the team. If they have done wrong then I will ask few questions, let them think if this way and that way. For example the sales revenue go down and then in the sales meeting I have to let them think what we can be im- proved."*

Taking a rational view, the women try to see criticism positively as an opportunity for improvement. Emotionally, criticism is rejected as shameful and unpleasant. This can be assessed against the cultural background of "saving face", which led to Chinese managers traditionally taking a more indirect communication style that preferred to avoid conflict. This management style, which derives from Confucian tradition, was already discussed in greater detail in chapter 2. However, according to the interviewees, losing face (something that is universally feared in China) is easier for women to bear than men, since they can count on more empathy when they are criticised, especially from foreign bosses.

> *S., HRD: "First of all, there's no big mistake in my career because I am very careful. Each time when I make a decision or make a judgment I do a lot of re- search. Of course I have little mistake. I just confess. I'm sorry."*

> *T., GM: "Woman and failure. Well, I think for women, women are very persis- tent and also in fact I saw a woman stronger than men in times of failure. So when woman fail they come back and they do it again and they fail and they do it again and again. And then for men if they fail it may take longer time for them to reenergize. For woman it may take one day to reenergize. Typical ex- ample will be when, when, when my female colleague broke up with a male friend. I mean broke up with boyfriend they recover so soon but for male it's*

difficult ... and then women are not afraid of failure I think men are more ar-
rogant and also men sees failure losing face. But women see failure as a natu-
ral so something like that and then they come back."

The women described one of their strengths as the ability to take criticism more calmly than men. On the other hand, they also noted that women are more critical, since they think everything through more than men. The women frequently said that they have learned to accept criticism, though not personal or subjectively base-less criticisms, which they said could quickly trigger aggressive responses. The study participants described China as a country without a culture of mistakes. Making mistakes entails shame, reproach and the dreaded "loss of face". Again, they claimed that men are more afraid of losing face and react to mistakes in a very hostile and arrogant manner, whereas women find it easier to deal with mistakes since they have greater perseverance and, as one participant put it, are "able to get back on their feet again more quickly" after being criticised. According to the in-terviewees, it is easier for women than for men to relieve their feelings of tension when they make mistakes, for example by crying. Afterwards, they are quickly able to deal with the situation again.

> *C., HRD: "I guess being viewed as a failure is really hard. It's really hard for*
> *me. And that would give me a lot of pressure. I would try to work very hard to*
> *avoid that ... Avoid being perceived as a failure. Later on I learned to accept*
> *failures more and more but when I was younger it was very bad ... In my case*
> *not really. In general people would not care so much. But I think if there is a*
> *career failure it is easier for women to accept it than men in our culture. But*
> *personal life, no. It's still bad for both sexes."*

However, the overall tendency in the group is to avoid making mistakes. "I had to learn to deal with mistakes" was the most common response. "As a young woman, I couldn't forgive myself for making mistakes" and "I chose the 'safe road' so as not to make any mistakes" were typical answers. The women described finding it easier to permit themselves, admit to, reflect on and find solutions to mistakes now they are more experienced. A handful of women emphatically said that they no longer fear losing face and that mistakes simply have to be rectified. The overall picture resembles the findings of Henn's 2012 study on women in executive roles in Germany, where most women admitted to finding it difficult to deal with mis-takes and failures. However, some differences emerge in comparison with male executives: in the German study, some women there considered men to be better at dealing with failures (though this point was only mentioned a few times). The Chi-nese women see themselves as being better at dealing with failure than Chinese men, even though the tendency to avoid mistakes remains culturally embedded for them too.

Women with high self-confidence

Self-confidence refers to independence from the judgements of others and a high level of confidence in one's own abilities and performance. A high level of self-confidence is associated with high self-efficacy (Henn, 2012).The women in the Shanghai Women's Career Lab generally regard themselves as self-confident or very self-confident. Twenty-two of the women classed themselves as self-confident, ten said they are very self-confident and only four said that they generally lack self-confidence. These answers match the interviewer's perceptions of the women and their detailed accounts of their personal strengths. Only four of the women do not consider themselves to be truly self-confident or think they would be more successful if they had more self-confidence. They all consider a high level of self-confidence to be a critical career determinant. They regard it as a significant advantage to be self-confident, especially in relation to being assertive towards colleagues and superiors. Self-confidence was often equated with courage. When asked how self-confidence manifests itself, the women said it could be seen in a person's bearing, eyes and way of talking. Many of the women believe it is an ability people are born with. They reported that even as children they had leading roles: for example, they would speak in front of groups. Key phrases included "natural leader" and "from early on". According to one participant, her high level of self-confidence derives from her strengths as a woman: good intuition, persuasive communication style and the ability to sense things that other people cannot yet see.

M. M., President: "Good question. They said, we already have a chief representative. I was General Manager at that time, I can lead big topics, I know both markets, I speak both languages. I do not need a boss here in China. No chance. When I go, I will be chief representative. The CEO said, that will be difficult. The board has to decide, I cannot decide alone. So I said, you do not need I go to the board. Two months later they had a board meeting and called me in. I flew to Germany. At the meeting during lunch I talked to all...they said Ms. Ming is no engineer, she is Chinese, she is a woman. This company has 80.000 people and 80% engineers with a technical background. This woman has none of this, why should we take her. I convinced them as follows: you have so many engineers, you do not need more, you need people with other skills. To sell your technology. A woman and so many men, that means the woman makes it extra good. Where I work now all others are men and I

am the only boss, as female. And I make it better and I can do it better for you. And Chinese? And what? You want to do business in China and since seven years your boss has been from Austria....Self-confidence from my good feeling as a female. I think I have a good intuition. This convinced in many situations, there for I know this is my strengths. Many people cannot see something while I already feel it....I also learn easier and quicker (laughing). Every new environment, new topic, I gather it quickly. I believe this makes me a bit stronger."
(Translated from German)

Several of the women noted that female Chinese executives are generally very self-confident. This claim came up in all the interviews. The participants said that self-confidence and assertiveness are key characteristics of Chinese women, especially women in Shanghai. They reported that all their female colleagues are very self-confident. Some of them equated high self-confidence with "not caring much about other people" and focusing on oneself. The women described it as follows: "I can't waste any time on the feelings of other people." This expresses the idea of being independent from the judgements of others and corresponds to the Leadership Motive Pattern model, according to which successful executives have a low need for affiliation (McClelland et al., 1982). However, these sorts of answers were few in number and cannot be considered representative of the group as a whole. In relation to team orientation (which is covered in greater depth in the section on leadership styles), the women clearly expressed a desire for friendly and close interpersonal relationships. One woman reported that she had to specially build up her self-confidence from scratch when she came into an international environment. A phase of learning and adaptation was necessary until she felt she had reached her usual level of self-confidence in the intercultural environment (which was still new to her at the start of her career). Another woman reported how attending a German school, an experience that she found difficult, helped her to develop her high level of self-confidence.

Capacity for self-presentation of the Chinese women

Various authors describe the capacity for self-presentation as a career-relevant personality dimension. The concept is based on the theory of "self-monitoring" developed by Snyder (1974). According to Snyder, individuals influence the picture that other people have of them in order to make the most positive impression possible. To do so, they develop deliberate strategies and adapt their opinions and utterances to this goal. In accordance with the studies previously mentioned, both an extreme capacity for self-presentation and an almost complete absence of this capacity can have a positive impact on career success.

The interviewees' most common response regarding their self-presentation was "I am not good at it". This perception of themselves was justified by reference to cultural differences between them and people from other countries at their companies. According to the women, marketing oneself is not part of Chinese culture, which instead requires people to be "humble". Shyness was given as the reason why, in their own view, the women do not use strategies for marketing themselves. Other women described how they go beyond what is asked of them at work and trust that this will lead to them being perceived positively by those around them. They think that other people's good opinion of them ought to be based on the strength of their performance and conduct, and that this is more important than strategic self-presentation.

> C., HRD: "By nature I'm still quite humble. That sounds weird. From time to time I'm still quite confused and I think that self-confidence piece still got shattered from time to time and I don't know if I'm making the right impact or not. Self-marketing? I guess as a Chinese we usually would not say a lot of good about ourselves."

> G. Customer Relation Director: "Well, I have to say I'm doing 'natural marketing'. I say what I believe and I do what I say. And I always want to be true to people and want to be true to myself. So that is the marketing, the self-marketing that I want to build. I hope I'm walking my talk. So that's generally my self-marketing. I didn't purposely doing a lot of making-ups, show-off things. Not a lot."

Examples that were given of successful self-presentation included public appearances such as giving talks outside the company. They were approached to make these appearances on the basis of their accomplishments so that they could share their expert knowledge. Some of them received awards for their talks. They did not actively instigate these appearances, but were invited by others to make them. Hence, here again the guiding principle is to achieve something first before talking about it.

> M., VP-HR: "I didn't do it before but now I do a little more ... the reason that I started to do that, last year a HR company invited me to do a presentation to tell the HR professionals about projects I have done. When I go there, there are over 200 HR professionals in Shanghai. I make my presentation and introduce what I have done in this company to those people. And afterward a lot of calls and emails and questions more about what I have done. Some people even copied what I have done here with their companies and it was successful. Interesting. My one presentation made so big contribution to other companies

other HR professional. Last year I was invited twice, once in Shanghai and once in Beijing. Because the best three go to Beijing to do the second delivery. I say okay that's a good thing."

Even the women who regard themselves as having strong self-presentation skills said that self-marketing should be preceded by exceptional performance that they could talk about. Presentations outside the women's companies are used to market themselves effectively to the outside world. A few women also remarked that they always talk about the results they have achieved so as to make other people aware of them.

S., HRD: "Self-marketing. I will show people that Stella is a very easygoing person and knowledgeable and professional and also has a lot of vision to share with you. And I'm powerful."

J., Asia HRD: "I only put in the LinkedIn my things. I have more than 500 connections. I seldom do self-marketing because I think I don't have time ... That is maybe one of the weaknesses so that I cannot be Obama."

Hence, this group predominantly believes that they are not especially good at marketing themselves. According to Snyder (1974), this factor can promote career advancement if executives without a strong capacity for self-presentation are perceived as being more honest. Henn (2012) also found that over 50% of the female executives in Germany who participated in the study think they market themselves too little. However, around 41% thought they were moderately strong in this area. Again, 14% of participants explicitly said they wanted to be judged purely on the basis of good performance and so chose not to market themselves. The results of the Shanghai Women's Career Lab are similar. This might indicate that women tend to promote themselves purely on the basis of the results they have actually achieved.

Initial impression on others

When asked what initial impression they think they make on others and how they are spontaneously perceived by others, the Chinese female executives gave very thoughtful answers. The responses indicate they are very conscious of the impression they make on other people and how this affects their image as an executive. They talked very openly about the ways in which initial impressions can help or hinder them in their role. The descriptions they gave of the impressions they make on others can be classified into four main categories: assertiveness, loyalty, accessibility and competence. Women who think they are primarily perceived as asser-

tive described themselves as tough, strong, determined, target-oriented and demanding. They also described themselves as coming across as less tolerant, strict
and distant on first impression. The women are well aware that these impressions
are not entirely positive, but do not regard this as a problem. Some of them described themselves as making a dominant and aggressive impression. They regard
this image as positive and helpful for their career success.

> *J., Asia HRD: "I recall one of my male university classmates. I used to be the
> monitor in the University for my class. He told me, my dean, sent him to my
> group because I was a leader, to lead those in the university who had to go to
> manufacturing plants to do the kind of real working practice. So I was the
> small leader of organizing these kinds of activity. This young gentleman was
> in my group and he had a very open discussion with me. ... That was the re-
> flection of what is my image to others. He told me that I was really very de-
> manding and what word did he use ... He made me think that I'm a little bit a
> kind of monarch ... that every time I want to try to use my power. This is what
> he described. Then I always remember this because I don't want to give this
> kind of image. But in XY (company name) you have to because you have to
> show your own confidence. You have to show you are a decision-maker and
> very decisive or otherwise you cannot win. I'm a naturally this kind of person.
> That's the reason I can be hired by XY. Their hiring philosophy is they want to
> hire people with similar values. Mindset and values otherwise XY don't think
> this person can survive in the company culture."*

> *M., CFO: "What my impression on other people is, as I told you already, I
> look very dominant, determined, strong lady. Very tough ... Less tolerance,
> not so patient because, I talk normally very fast."*

Several women described themselves as projecting an initial impression of loyalty
and a strong focus on compliance. Against the backdrop of significant problems
with compliance at many Chinese companies, this initial impression is more than a
general attribute; it embodies a leadership value and a particular attitude towards
corporate ethics. This attitude is characterised by loyalty, trust and strict adherence
to company regulations. Women who said they came across this way on first impression described themselves as strict and distant. They regard it as important to
reinforce and resolutely embody this initial impression. Hence, once again they
took a positive view of the characteristics that they described. A second group of
women emphasised accessibility to staff as the initial impression they make on
others. They used terms such as easy to approach, accessible, open, friendly and
caring. Attributes such as nice, gentle, calm and humble correspond to conven-

tional, traditional role models for women. They were mentioned multiple times, by HRDs in particular. The third group described themselves as conveying an air of competence on first impression. These women described their image using terms such as knowledgeable, very professional, intelligent and competent. Other features of this group include being disciplined and the ability to deliver well. The handful of women in the study who come across as more introverted are very focused on the initial impressions they make. These women reported that they seem shy, quiet and calm on first impression, and consider this to be a disadvantage – one that they are focused on overcoming. Many of the women stressed that they are very competent and self-assured despite how they come across.

In summary, all the women in the Shanghai Women's Career Lab have reflected on the impression they make on others. They are aware of how they come across and of how their image helps and hinders their success. The women make use of this awareness by reinforcing and cultivating certain aspects and deliberately compensating for others.

Appearance – professional and not "too beautiful"

The Chinese female executives were unanimous about the importance of appearance and presentation for careers in senior management. In their view, Chinese women at executive level should look professional but not beautiful. Or, as one woman put it, "pretty is good, but not too much, because people will feel distant". Younger women see both advantages and limitations to beauty and good looks for their careers. They think a little is an advantage, but being too attractive is a disadvantage for rising up the career ladder. According to the women, it creates distance, causes women to be misjudged and engenders reactions such as "not very professional". They do not think beauty is important for leadership roles in China. The group was unanimous on this point.

> *V., GM: "I saw some quite not good-looking women leader they take very senior level … very smart, very sharp and also very political."*

On this point, the participants in this group differ from German female executives, 37% of whom think that attractive women find it easier to progress up the career ladder (Henn, 2012). It is notable that in their answers, several women described themselves as not being conventionally beautiful and listed with aplomb the advantages this brings with it.

> *Q., GM: "I mean I was never told I am pretty … I think I give overall people the impression of being smart and rather friendly. So that helps a bit. So I say*

if I combine everything together I say I'm average. And physically I'm quite
small and quite petite so that is not so helpful in creating the presence. Be-
cause physically I do not have such a big presence. "

Older women formulated matters in more drastic terms, and see good looks as having clear drawbacks for women's careers. They regard good looks as irrelevant.
According to the women, a female Chinese executive should ideally look professional, capable, confident and smart. All the women consider professional appearance important, as emphasised by their deliberate choice of clothing. They all identified formal clothing and a smart, presentable look as important for being seen as
an executive.

In the view of the interviewer, all the women in the study group share the following features. They wear markedly little make-up, no (or only colourless) lipstick
and not much jewellery. Their clothing style is less formal than in countries such
as Germany. They do not wear trouser suits and only a few wear blazers. The style
could be described as business casual and in a few exceptional cases as feminine
formal. Nothing about their clothing style indicates their position at their companies.

The topic of age was mainly raised by the younger women. They said that "grey
hair" (referring to ages 45+) is a plus for management roles in HR. In certain industries (for example, the fashion industry) a youthful look is, by contrast, considered an advantage. The younger study participants reflected on the issue of age and
careers. Some of the women have reached senior management positions while still
in their early to mid-30s. They think that their youthful appearance can detract
from their image as an executive. In particular, male German bosses were given as
examples to illustrate this concern; some of the German bosses have even expressed these reservations explicitly. Several of the women who previously worked
in Germany at German companies.

Chinese women's leadership style

There are many different definitions of leadership. Common to all the definitions is
the ability to persuade others to set aside for a period of time their individual concerns and pursue a common goal that is important for the responsibilities and welfare of a group (Hogan, Curphy, and Hogan, 1994). What counts as good leadership depends on context. There is no single correct leadership style. Instead, a
leadership style will be successful when its approach is suited to the particular
situation at hand. Good leadership is generally associated with a focus on the fu-

ture, the capacity to secure commitment from others and the ability to contribute creatively to the success of organisations. Women are often deemed incapable of leadership *per se*, even though it has been shown that they are sometimes more effective and possess the right combinations of leadership skills. Respondents to a Gallup study from across the globe consistently expressed a preference for a male boss. Among women who stated a preference in this study, 40% favoured a male boss, compared with 34% of men who favoured a male boss. Female managers face greater obstacles to acceptance by colleagues and employees (Friedel-Howe, 1990). Researchers have described the following leadership styles, which tend to vary between men and women.

There are two distinct types of behaviour that managers may use to influence the actions of their subordinates. The first type, a task-oriented style, refers to the extent to which a leader initiates and organises work effectively and is associated with the masculine stereotype. The second type, a people-oriented or interpersonal style, refers to the extent to which the manager engages in activities that tend to people's moral needs or welfare and is associated with a feminine stereotype. Both approaches are associated with leadership effectiveness.

Managers may also exhibit different decision-making styles. Researchers distinguish between democratic and autocratic styles of decision-making. Democratic decision-making allows subordinates to participate and is associated with a feminine stereotype, whereas autocratic decision-making discourages participation and is more associated with a masculine stereotype (Powell, 2011). According to the analysis of Eagly and Carli (2003), it makes sense for women to avoid a highly autocratic leadership style because of the potential for harsh reactions. The distinction between transformational, transactional and laissez-faire leadership has played a key role in theory for many years (Barbuto, 2005). Transformational leadership theory assumes that a leader who is perceived as behaving in a transformational manner inspires subordinates to high level of efforts (Ayman, Korabik, 1993). Transformational leaders motivate subordinates to transcend their own self-interest for the good of the group. This style is described in terms of four features: charisma, inspirational motivation, intellectual stimulation and individualised consideration (Judge and Piccolo, 2004). The style is characterised by hard work and personal contact. Charisma means that leaders display attributes that induce followers to view them as role models and behaviours that communicate a sense of value and purpose. Inspirational motivation is achieved through exuding optimism and excitement about the mission. Intellectual stimulation consists in encouraging followers to question basic assumptions and consider new perspectives. Individualised consideration focuses on the development and mentoring of followers and attending to their specific needs. Transactional leaders focus on clarifying the responsibilities of subordinates. They make use of the power and authority associated with their position, and alternate between reward and punishment. Laissez-faire leaders avoid taking responsibility for leadership altogether.

Transformational leadership is generally ascribed to women, whereas men tend to have transactional leadership styles (Rosner, 1990). An analysis of 45 studies showed that women tend to have a transformational leadership style, with a central focus on individual consideration in the sense of supportive and encouraging treatment of subordinates. Women were also more transactional with respect to rewards. However, the overall differences between men and women were small (Eagly, 2007). Different studies come to different conclusions about the extent of differences between the genders with regard to leadership styles. Many of the studies do not claim any clear-cut differences between the genders. Since the same roles at companies demand the same styles, the expectation is that women and men will have the same leadership style. However, for women there is a conflict between different roles that they are expected to fulfil – the role of a woman *per se*, who is supposed to be caring and nice, and that of an executive, who is supposed to conform to the male stereotype. According to Ayman and Korabik (2010), leadership is not a gender-neutral phenomenon. Women who adopt more male leadership behaviours tend to be judged negatively. However, women who are intelligent and androgynous are more likely to become executives. Ayman and Korabik regard androgynous styles as a way for female executives to be successful. Androgynous managers often have a transformational style that combines task-focused and person-focused elements. This is associated with higher leadership effectiveness. Situational leadership theory suggests that leaders should be successively masculine, androgynous, feminine and finally undifferentiated as subordinates increase in maturity. Tannenbaum and Schmidt's leadership theory recommends that leaders behave in an increasingly feminine manner as their subordinates develop greater independence, responsibility and the ability to work well as a team (Tannenbaum and Schmidt, 1973). Rosner (1990) describes an interactive style as typical for female leaders. According to Rosner's research, female leaders encourage participation, try to instil group identity and facilitate inclusion and involvement. Studies that directly measure leader effectiveness, however, rate women as being neither more nor less effective than men (Powell, 2011). In summary, however, following gender studies research it can be concluded that women have a more interpersonal style than men. They rank higher in dimensions of transformational leadership and the reward dimension of transactional leadership. They make greater use of a democratic decision-making style. And they rank higher in dimensions of behaviour that contribute to leader effectiveness, such as charisma, inspirational motivation, intellectual stimulation, individualised consideration and contingent rewards.

Chinese women's descriptions of own leadership style – democratic vs. autocratic

The previous section explained different categories of leadership and differences between Western and Chinese leadership models identified in the literature (King and Wei 2014). It was shown that more transformational leadership styles and democratic decision-making are attributed to women (Eagly et al., 2007; Powell, 2011). Most of the women in the Shanghai Women's Career Lab spontaneously described their own leadership style as "democratic", and distanced themselves from hierarchical styles. By democratic leadership styles, they mean ones that are open, encouraging and involve everyone.

> S., CFO: "Before a problem I think we should discuss. Perhaps my manager has her solution and I have mine we should put all together on the table and discuss to find the better solution. I don't like the hierarchy. I think everyone is equal and someone is more competent than the other with more experience or something like that. But everyone should really take down his or her own opinion then we decided together."

The aim of a democratic style is to be approachable to employees, minimise hierarchy and give staff autonomy. Table 15 summarises the descriptions that were given for this category. The terms categorised as "democratic" were mentioned multiple times and by the majority of participants. By contrast, just under a quarter of the women described themselves as having leadership styles closer to ones referred to in the literature as "autocratic". They used terms such as dominant, task-driven, telling people what to do and strict. One woman compared her style, which she described as strict and prescriptive, to the German style.

> M. M., President: "My leadership style. I am a strong character. Most people say dominant. It shows quickly that I am a dominant character. I became like this through my work. I am not like this naturally. I am positive and open. I like to sing, to dance and make sports. I laugh a lot with others. I like to sew and I am good at designing. Making many beautiful things, that is my nature. Originally I wanted to be an artist. But with the culture revolution we had no choice. I came to Germany and then saw that there is a chance with that job in Yunnan as nobody wanted to go there. So I went. The people in the factory

have to be lead strongly. This was my leadership style." (Translated from German)

The younger women described themselves as strongly convinced of the benefits of this more autocratic style. The older women reflected on times when this style is more advantageous.

Table 16: Description of own leadership style

Democratic
minimise sense of hierarchy, approachable, give autonomy *democratic, engaging in decision, open minded,* *freedom of decision making, involve everyone* *encourage to express opinions, empowering, ask for collective wisdom*
role model
leading by example
Stimulation
inspiring, give ideas, motivate
Develop others
delegation to develop others *develop others, identify talents, feedback, develop their careers*
Considering
high people agility, people person *combine western and Chinese way of leading – share emotions* *care for feelings* *care, like a Chinese mother, like a parent, like a family, respect and trust*
Team oriented
support others, bring value, contribute *have good relationships/team player/people oriented*
Build mutual trust and respect
honest, trust worthy, loyal/ respectful/looking for respect from others
Autocratic (one fourth of participants)
dominant, demanding, strong leadership, task-driven, tell, result driven *push, German style, strict, give clear instructions, high expectations*

The terms team development and team leadership occurred very frequently. The participants said that they lead teams in a way that maximises performance, and once again mentioned the "democratic" style described above. "Team performance is my performance" said one participant, who described seeing herself as part of a group. Team orientation is important for success as a manager and career advancement. It refers to a desire and willingness to sacrifice one's own interests for the sake of working as a team. It also involves taking responsibility for collaboration and being prepared to share in team decisions. Descriptions relating to high team orientation and ability to work in a team were the second most common personality dimension category in this group after descriptions concerning achieve-ment motivation (see table 13). The women described building up trust as one of the highest values for their careers. They want to develop honest and trustworthy relationships, and want other people who work with them to see them as a person with these qualities. They frequently mentioned supporting other people and con-tributing to their success as personal strengths and intrinsic motivations, and de-scribed themselves as team players with a high people orientation. Empathy and caring for others were repeatedly emphasised as social competencies. At the same time, receiving recognition from others is an important aspect of collaboration. Recognition from the team is very important for all the women; they want to be seen as role models.

A majority of women in the group gave descriptions that could be categorised as examples of a transformational leadership style. Transformational leaders motivate subordinates to transcend their own self-interest for the good of the group (Judge et al., 2004). According to the literature, this style comprises four features: charisma, inspirational motivation, intellectual stimulation and individualised consideration. The women gave descriptions of all four features. There were multiple mentions of the charismatic role model element. The women want to lead by good example and present a model for others to follow.

> *S., HRD: "I think I want to be a person that my colleagues see as very profes-sional, can support them, they can learn from to be successful. This kind of recognition does not just come through achievement. You are seen as the per-son that can help them to be successful and very professional."*

One focal point of the women's descriptions was staff development. In table 13, the descriptions that fall into this category are summarised under "develop others" and "considerate".

This category could be understood in terms of the "individualised consideration" element of the transformational style, which concerns development and mentoring of followers and attention to their specific needs. Many of the women mentioned delegation and employee coaching as personal strengths in conjunction with a style that recognises, motivates and supports others. They described this style using terms such as engaging, empowering and encouraging, with a focus on employee motivation and a desire to minimise the sense of hierarchy. Approachability and developing trust are regarded as especially important. Being approachable, involv-ing others and listening were other frequent descriptions. Accordingly, the main aim of their leadership is to develop and support other people.

Three of the interviewees used the metaphor "like parent and child" and a comparison with a typical Chinese mother ("like a Chinese mother, a dominant Chinese mother") to describe their leadership style. By this they meant, firstly, being 100% behind employees and giving them their full support, and, secondly, combining everyone's goals and giving employees flexibility in how to implement these goals. The aim is to give them the freedom to make their own decisions while setting clear targets. Staff development is particularly important to the women. As executives, they see themselves as having a role model function. The term "caring" occurred frequently, relating both to employees' feelings and enabling work-life balance. There were slightly fewer descriptions that could be categorised according to the "intellectual stimulation" component of a transformational leadership style. The women said that they are exceptionally able to "bring up the big topics". They described themselves as inspiring, motivating and a source of ideas. At several points, they specifically noted that they are willing to subordinate their own views to better ideas that come from employees and that they view it as their primary task to create a climate in which everyone can contribute. However, some of them feel that their staff are too inexperienced and so need clear instructions. Some women described their style as a mixture of Western and Chinese leadership cultures. They noted that they share their emotions with their employees and develop high levels of trust and respect. They classify this as part of the more Chinese-influenced aspect of their leadership style.

The intercultural aspect of leadership is regarded as especially important by women in functions with responsibility for Asia. Again, these women consider good listening and emotional understanding to be important.

> *J., Sales Director: "I think I have a natural advantage, which is being educated and lived in the UK. I think I learned how to managing people in the westernized way. And being Chinese myself I think I do share the emotions with Chinese colleagues and friends. I guess I combine the two, which made me quite smoothly in terms of managing people ... I do give them the autonomy to do what they think they can achieve. I am very result-driven style ... two of my managers, very senior said to me when I just join the company we are very experienced manager within the industry. I don't need someone to be the mommy... I said fully understood. I am very result-driven as well. As long as you deliver I will not interfere with the way you manage. As long as you are not coming out of the standards frame. They were very clear if they don't reach the results I expected I would interfere for sure. So far it has worked well."*

J., Asia Director Purchasing: "Maybe this is from my female part. Currently I'm leading a team of five people. Three in China, one in Malaysia, one in Korea. A Korean guy. So I'm leading a multicultural people. I think ... they will say quite good boss. Why good? They will say I try to understand. I try to talk to them ... I think I take care of their feelings in the work. I spend little time with my family but I make sure they spend time with their family. Although some travel in weekend I say is it necessary. Please don't worry if you fly out on Monday and spend one night more or later. I try to reduce them to spend private time for the business. If they have some issue at home, I say go there."

In summary, most of the women in this group described their leadership style as democratic and transformational. Around a quarter of them class themselves as having a more autocratic style. Among the descriptions that could be assigned to a transformational style, quantitatively speaking the largest number concerned the feature "individualised consideration". This is consonant with the findings of King et al. (2014), according to which Chinese executives emphasise people orientation over results or tactical considerations.

Table 17: Results on female Chinese leadership in comparison with existing research (developed by the author)

Western female leadership[15]	Chinese female leadership
Transformational	Transformational
Democratic decision-making	*Democratic but also autocratic*
Visionary	*Acting as role model*
Facilitation of communication	*Ask for collective wisdom*
Involvement of employees in team building	Team development and team performance
Reward power	*Developing others, care, consider emotions*
Inspiring and motivating	Inspiring and motivating
Fostering mutual trust and respect	Mutual trust and respect

If the results of the Shanghai Women's Career Lab concerning the women's own leadership styles are compared with the model of women's leadership developed by Stanford et al. (1995), which was based on a similar data collection method, they have four elements in common: women involve employees in teambuilding; prefer rewarding power; inspire and motivate; and foster mutual trust and respect. Visionary thinking and facilitating communication were mentioned less or not at all. Unlike in Stanford's study, the women's conception of their own leadership styles involved being a role model and developing others. Moreover, a quarter of interviewees described having a personal decision-making style that is more auto-

---

[15]   Based on Stanford et al., 1995; Eagly et al., 2007; Powell, 2011.

cratic. This corresponds to the findings of King et al. (2014), according to which more authoritarian leadership is still accepted in China.

Chinese women's leadership styles compared with men's

The Chinese women were also asked about their views on differences between men's and women's leadership styles in general, separately from the question concerning their own leadership style. The women often spontaneously began by saying that men and women are generally equal in China and at their companies. In general, the respondents believe that women's leadership styles are more empathetic and sensitive than men's and that they care more for their staff overall. They also think that women are better listeners and communicators, and that women are in principle not able to act the same way as men. The respondents think that women are sometimes judged differently for the same behaviour and that there is a general social expectation that women should be nicer than men. Hence, they believe that women in leadership positions should focus on their strengths rather than attempting to copy men. In their view, women's strengths lie in interpersonal relationships, including caring for employees. Only one participant generally considers women to be less sensitive towards employees.

> *T., GM: "I think about one is the female leader cannot act as a man. I think this was given to me as a reminder by a lot of friends. She has to know she's a woman and then as a woman she knows she's, she may be sometimes she may being perceived as less stronger or less strong than males so she has to know all these things and to visualize these constraints in her company so this is number one. I think number two is as a female leader the advantage is female are more sentimental so people likes female to remember all the details like the birthday or celebrate the success. All these things females are more tedious at working it out. So expand it and strengthen it to make people realize only this female leader can do it. The male will forget because they are not very tedious. So and I think number three will be networking with both female and male because as a female climbs up the ladder including myself I always remember I have to network with the big males in order to make myself in the circle but it's not true. A lot of the time I forget we should build a female supporting team and to get some emotions out because in the male they don't talk about emotions and it's very difficult for me just to talk about logical things. So female supporting group even though it's outside of the company is very important."*

In the view of HRDs, female executives are less strong than men at more internally focused leadership tasks such as HR or finance. There were also individual mentions of micromanagement and excessive focus on details as weaknesses of women's management styles. Some of the participants said that some women are too focused on their own appearance due to societal expectations. This is seen as an impediment.

> *M., Senior HRD: "I think female leaders need to be, one think I think we need to speak out. ... some female leaders maybe they are not as good as the male leader on the business argument side. I think that if we can pay a lot of attention on the business side we really can talk with others from the business perspective it will make us even stronger."*

> *Q., GM: "I don't know if it's just my perception or just by chance. I find that certain common issues with the female manager that I worked with. They were less, overall less confident, as a result do more micromanagement. Tend to do more micromanagement. Put more attention to details. And also in terms of social and kind of social ability they are less, I feel it's less relaxing to work with them. It seems to be they are more sensitive and as a result they are sometimes sensitive and delicate to deal with them. And overall they are less generous."*

According to the female executives, women have twice as much responsibility as men in the same roles and are burdened with more demands, since they also have responsibility for their families alongside their careers. Consequently, they are believed to be more likely to burn out. The interviewees believe that families expect more from women than men, and so work-life balance is of greater importance to women in executive positions. This once again picks up the theme of different role expectations for women. In the view of the study participants, women are dependent on a corporate culture that takes account of their family lives.

> *H., VP: "There are many important factors for women to succeed, to take leadership positions. Number one is in the social connect that women still have a significant role to play in families. Even when the whole Chinese society is encouraging of women to work. There's still a lot of ... women still have to care for the family even if you have two nannies, three drivers, there's still something's that people cannot do on your behalf. To replace a mother, a wife in a family. I think two important factors are to figure out – and every family is different, dynamics is different – for women to figure out what that balance is. Every family is different. For the family to come to an agreement. I think that's the most important."*

The question regarding the women's observations of other women's leadership styles or women in general did not yield any further findings on leadership styles.

This once again expresses the "individualised consideration" aspect of a transformational leadership style, though here more in terms of empathy and sensitivity to employees' feelings rather than in terms of supporting employees. There were also individual descriptions of stereotypes and role expectations, as previously discussed in the section on equality.

Summary: the impact of education, competencies and personality on careers of Chinese women

The group of female Chinese executives is characterised by a high level of education (with some of them holding multiple MA qualifications) and mastery of foreign languages. A third of the women have studied abroad.

The women's own competencies were analysed on the basis of the specification profile for executives developed by Regnet (2014). The competencies the women ascribed to themselves most often are expert knowledge and strong intercultural and communication competencies. They appear to have a stronger capacity for innovation than for visionary thinking, which only some of the group described as one of their particular strengths.

The descriptions suggest a strong capacity for empathising with cultural peculiarities, which in combination with good knowledge of local business and management culture lead to adaptation and transformation or the ability to "move between cultures" as a key competency. They possess global mindset by exhibiting a strong understanding of different cultures and by integrating them. The women see themselves as having an advantage over male counterparts in this regard, especially at multinational companies. In terms of the broader concept of global leadership developed by Black and Morrison (2014), findings suggest that these women are consistently competent in all four of the areas defined above – inquisitiveness, perspective, character and savvy. They are curious about cultural differences and flexible about embracing change, have high levels of integrity and therefore gain trust from others, and possess exceptional expertise concerning their industries and organisational requirements.

The women exhibit exceptional achievement motivation and a positive attitude towards competition. This is in keeping with the results of Chen et al. (1997) and Powell et al. (1993), who found that Chinese executives and also female Chinese executives actively compete and stand out from the group despite a collectivist cultural background. The women spoke openly about financial motivations. These are an important factor for many of them but have receded into the background as their careers progress. Their descriptions of leadership motivation primarily centre on the desire to be a role model, a high willingness to assume responsibility and influencing other people. The majority of the group have a positive attitude towards exercising power. However, they only make use of hierarchical power in exceptional cases. They prefer to get their way by using their powers of communication and persuasion. The women's attitudes towards conflict can be explained against the background of their cultural values, in particular "striving for harmony" and "saving face". Some of the women deal with conflicts in a very direct way, others described themselves as taking a highly rational approach and a small minority tend to avoid conflict. The women are exceptionally flexible: not just with regard to their work, roles and experiences, but also with regard to geographical mobility. Many described themselves as seeking out and welcoming change. They are demonstrably willing to take on career challenges even if they are very difficult to combine with family life. At several points in the accounts, the women noted that female Chinese executives are seen as very self-confident. The interviewed women confirmed this perception in their own cases. The picture is different when it comes to self-presentation: most of the women do not regard themselves as being very strong on this front.

The women's descriptions of their own leadership styles can mostly be classified as democratic and transformational. A detailed analysis reveals elements in common with the study of women's leadership carried out by Stanford et al. (1995). However, a quarter of the group emphatically categorised themselves as having a more autocratic style. According to King et al. (2014), more authoritarian leadership is still accepted in China, unlike in Western countries. A high number of the descriptions given by the women can be assigned to the "intellectual stimulation" aspect of transformational leadership styles. Some women described their style as a mixture of Western and Chinese leadership, with the more emotionally caring aspect ascribed to the Chinese side. All the women in the Shanghai Women's Career Lab described having a high level of team orientation, with developing trusting interpersonal relationships, supporting others and serving a role model function seen as central elements of leadership.

7. How Chinese women rise: Analysis of career paths and pattern

Women's career patterns: traditional versus alternative paths – The significance of careers in the Shanghai Female Career Lab – Starting positions – Effect of choice of company type on careers – Moving up: analysis of career steps – Geographic mobility – Reasons for changing companies – Alternatives to actual career choices – Career strategies of female Chinese executives – Planned and unplanned career decisions – Downsides and challenges of careers – Future career goals

Women's career patterns – traditional versus alternative paths

Several researchers have addressed questions concerning career patterns and paths (Lepine, 1992; Lyness and Thompson, 2000; O'Neil et al., 2008) in order to describe women's career patterns more precisely. A career path is generally defined as a trajectory of work-related experiences in which an individual has engaged over the course of their life. It describes how a person progresses from their first job to their current one. A career pattern can be defined as a consistent and recurring characteristic or trait that helps to characterise a career, and serves as an indicator or model for predicting future career behaviour. The two concepts are often used interchangeably in the literature. Vinkenburg and Weber (2012) analysed managerial career patterns in a review of empirical studies. They state that the existing empirical evidence on managerial career patterns is rather limited and that upward mobility is still the norm, even when contrasted with "new" careers. Familiar, traditional paths are typified by strong upwards mobility and leave little space for sideways moves or frequent changes of organisation. These paths demand advancement-oriented executives who strive for a vertical career. Lehnert (1996) describes "serpentine" careers, where employees rise up the ranks by switching between organisations. This career form still follows a fixed path that remains relatively similar to the traditional career path. However, the possibility of changing job requirements is integral to this new career type.

O'Neil et al. (2008) found that women's career paths exhibit a wider range and variety of patterns than those of men. Studies suggest that women's careers are uniquely different from men's and exhibit a broader range and variety of paths (Hurley and Sonnenfeld, 1997; Lepine, 1992). Patterns range from traditional, hierarchical advancement and corporate ladders (Lyness and Thompson, 2000), to "snake-like" patterns (Richardson, 1996) and "zigzag patterns" (Gersick and Kram, 2002). Gersick and Kram followed Levinson's 1996 study, *The Seasons of a Woman's Life*, to explore life stages and their connection to career phases. Research participants described their career paths as zigzag-like. The findings suggest that women experience transitional periods pegged to the turn of each decade of their lives, involving shifts in the content and priority of one or more elements of their life structure. These periods are reflected in their career development and differ in various ways from those of men. Lepine (1992), who identified a variety of career patterns for women managers, is frequently cited in connection with female career path analysis. Half of the women in the present study are employed in a traditional upwardly mobile career and the other half in patterns that can be categorised as downward, lateral, transitory or static. A somewhat divergent but fundamentally similar account is offered by Huang and Sverke (2007), who describe women's occupational paths as diverse, exhibiting patterns such as upward mobility, stability, downward mobility and fluctuation. Hurley and Sonnenfeld (1997), meanwhile, investigated the question of whether the tournament model of career as a series of wins and losses in a race to the top is applicable to women's careers. They concluded that the model is not valid for women to the same degree.

All these approaches address the distinctive features of women's careers and attempt to express these features in models that replace or expand traditional patterns. Like other recent concepts that are less gender-specific, such as "spiral", "nomad" or "post-corporate" careers (Reichel, Chudzikowski, Schiffinger, and Mayrhofer, 2010), these models are associated with dynamism, mobility, flexibility and employability to a greater or lesser extent. Career patterns are changing rapidly and becoming increasingly hard to predict and plan. New career forms can no longer simply be integrated into traditional career paths. Alternative concepts are needed to describe them. Various career pattern typologies attempt to describe these new paths. Some researchers specifically study women's career development, while others take a gender-neutral approach.

O'Neil et al. (2004) combined sociological factors, path and context, and psychological factors, choice and control, in their career model, and found that combinations of career pattern and career loci resulted in three distinct career types for women: achievers, navigators and accommodators. Patterns were characterised as a continuum between ordered (planned, organised) and emergent (serendipitous, circuitous).The ordered pattern can be characterised as being strategically planned and executed. An emergent career follows a reactive rather than a proactive path, with unexpected twists and turns and serendipitous events. It is designed to accommodate aspects of one's life other than traditional work. The "kaleidoscope career" exhibits aspects of an emergent career. Loci were characterised on a continuum between external and internal. An internal locus is manifested in the belief that one is responsible for one's own career and is in charge of creating and managing one's career by oneself. The "protean career" has an internal career locus. An external locus expresses the belief that the course that a career takes is caused by chance or other external interventions, such as networks or contacts from which career opportunities emanate. The career patterns developed with a view to women's careers that have been described above are of significance to the analysis of the finding of the Shanghai Women's Career Lab, since they can be used as a theoretical foundation and frame of reference. Both sociological and psychological career theory approaches are relevant. These aspects are supplemented by parameters that influence careers. In order to capture the specific situation of the women in their environment in China, a sociological analysis of external influencing parameters is here included. Psychological analysis is relevant in relation to the role played by personality aspects of the Chinese female executives and associated factors such as career motivation. The book does not include an institutional careers analysis. Reference to institutions is only made where choosing a particular type of company had an effect on the career development of these women. However, these references are made from the perspective of the interviewees and only where relevant to their individual career paths.

The significance of careers for the interviewees

As described at the start of the book, career success is a central dimension for describing careers, alongside what Arthur et al. (1996) termed "sequences of work experience over time". The women in this study were selected according to the objective career criterion of being in a senior executive role. A more subjective perspective on careers asks how people view their careers in the context of their lives as a whole. The significance of careers for the Chinese women is also essentially connected to their understanding of success and how satisfied they are with their achievements. In addition, questions surrounding work-life balance, which are of central importance to women's careers, are also relevant to an investigation of this topic. When asked about their personal definition of success, the Chinese women mentioned objective and subjective components in equal measure. Fulfilment, joy and personal satisfaction were the most common individual definitions of success. Objective components of success that can be clearly measured from an external

perspective were described using terms such as good results, efficiency and achieving high targets. Terms that can be categorised as relating to subjective career success included fulfilment, being happy, enjoyment, a sense of achievement and doing a job that you love. Supporting and standing up for other people were the third
most common terms mentioned in the women's definitions of success. Single
women in particular also mentioned giving something back to society. These answers were followed by far less frequent ones such as work-life balance and a good
family life. Hence, with respect to the four central concepts of career success – effectiveness, happiness, utility and satisfaction (Mayrhofer, Meyer, and Steyrer,
2005) – the women's definitions of career success placed just as much emphasis on
factors that could be categorised under the heading of effectiveness as on the more
subjective concepts of satisfaction and happiness.

Table 18: Responses when asked about the meaning of success

(Multiple answers)

Answers	Number
Fulfilment and joy	**19**
fulfilment/be happy/enjoy/feeling good	12
sense of achievement/achieve a dream	3
be satisfied with yourself	2
make a job that you love	2
results, targets and added value	**18**
good results/achieve what I planned	9
make organisation more efficient/add value	6
achieve high targets	3
Recognition	4
supporting others/see people improve	6
good family life/balance work-life	6
financial independence	2
learn, personal development	2

Melamed (1996) and Sturges (1999) describe how, due to their socialisation,
women tend to define career success by reference to obstacles that stand in their
way rather than in terms of the external corporate criteria favoured by men. This
conclusion could not be verified in this group; all that can be said is that the Chinese women mentioned external and subjective evaluations of success equally often. In response to the slightly modified question concerning the personal rewards
they have derived from their careers, the top answers were fulfilment and recognition followed by financial freedom and personal development. Recognition refers
to acknowledgement from their team and the respect the women have earned. Fi-

nancial independence, lifelong learning and the opportunity for social contact were other aspects that were mentioned.

When asked how they would define private versus professional success, most of the women drew the following distinction: private success is defined as a happy family, usually including children, while professional success means respect, recognition and advancement. The group was evenly divided between women who clearly prioritise professional success and ones who strive for a balance between professional and private success. Only one woman said that she clearly prioritises private success. These answers are in keeping with other studies of female executives, such as Henn (2012), though in this study there tended to be less of an exclusive focus on private success than in, for example, studies with German female executives. White (1995) describes that the majority of successful women included in her research displayed high career centrality. The portion of the women who regard professional success as more important described their attitude as follows: "home is no option, want to work, chose work always first, important for independence". These interviewees tend to measure success in purely professional terms.

> *C., President: "I think that I will for me it's more professional success rather than private. My private life is very simple. I don't have a family of my own. I have my mother and my brother and so I don't spend a lot of time worrying about them although sometimes. I have a very simple family and my private life I think you can call it my church life and my surface those are also relatively simple and I try to have the balance but because that side is relatively simple, so I will more think of the professional success."*

Many of the women who favour balance described how they focused exclusively on professional success in the early stages of their careers. According to these women, it was only as they got older and rose up the ranks that they became aware that private success also mattered to them. These women's strongly career-oriented definitions of success only changed with age and the attainment of a high degree of professional success; only then did they redefine success to include life outside work.

> *C., HRD: "I think that is the problem for most Chinese people, we just combine our professional and our personal life. Actually last week I attended a training that one colleague shared that she once thought that if she leave XY (company name), that's all who she is and she doesn't have the answer for what comes after that. I may have the same problem (laughter!!) So I think I didn't have my definition of private success, I always think maybe career is what I can do more. But I think from last year, I did some change, small*

changes about myself, which make me feel more content with my private life. I picked up one hobby, the Chinese calligraphy. So that makes me feel better for me as a person, because I don't have a hobby before. Which I think is very strange for foreigners. Because the way we are raised, parents just ask you to focus on your studies. So, a very small step, but a big meaning for myself, that I have something to identify myself. So for private life, I think I will think about it further and define what success means to me. First I think just separated professional and private, now I think about it."

This is interesting given that most of the women in the Shanghai Women's Career Lab who have not previously lived abroad became mothers at a relatively young age by modern Western standards (23–25 on average). Hence, becoming a mother at a young age did not change the women's attitudes to their careers. The women described themselves as being primarily focused on their careers as young women until around their early 40s, regardless of their role as mothers. According to the Kaleidoscope Career theory developed by Mainiero and Sullivan (2005), women are typically simultaneously focused on career and family, but this only holds true for some of the women in this group. Many of the interviewees displayed attitudes that according to the kaleidoscope career model are more common in men. The women focused on their careers for much of their lives independent from the fact of becoming mothers and only came to accord a greater status to their private lives at a later stage. The answers are in line with a study on values and social status involving 1,550 Chinese women from Taipei, Hong Kong and Shanghai that was published in *Reader's Digest* in 2001 (Reader's Digest, Chinese Edition, in: Gangrose, 2005, p.86). 81% of the women from Shanghai in that study described careers as very important, ahead of women from Taipei (66%) and Hong Kong (61%). However, family is a very important and undisputed value for all the women in the present study.

X., BU-Head: "To be honest in the past 20 years, I wanted be very professional manager in multinational company to have skills, different kind of skills ... Just more recently I said I want to have good family. I start balance the work and my family. And think about should I go to UK or US? My husband went to US for several years."

A., VP: "I enjoy my career very much. Really, very much. That's why I still feel I'm very energetic everyday coming here to work. I also enjoy my personal life a lot. I, without my personal life I probably do not have the energy. This is more and more important. One day I remember I was in a leadership training and the Indian master of meditation asked all of us a question. Can you think about five years, ten years later how your office looks like? Interesting I found when I deep think about five minutes later, in the past my office in XY (company name), I almost have no family photos. All XY different Olympic photos, XY trophies, XY things, it's all XY souvenirs everywhere. They were right. Now when I move from XY (Company name) today you will see more and more I put family photos. Small big family photos. My sons' small notes sometimes and also my different peers in global write small notes to me. And my training partners send Christmas card and I keep each one. These are the thing is keep more and more in my office. I still have one or two XY trophy, XY trophy that reminds me of my career. This is part of my blood but it's not all company things. "

Those women who said that they strive to achieve a balance between professional and private success equate private success with the amount of time they can spend with their children. This point is especially important for the women with two children. "You cannot have it all" was how one woman described the conflict between spending time with children and being committed to one's work. It is striking that reflections on the role of mothers and what constitutes successful mothering brought up dilemmas of conscience more frequently for women in the study who had previously lived in Germany for extended periods or have a foreign partner.

J., GM: "Privately I would describe myself not as so successful, because I do not have enough time for my child. I try to spend as much time as possible for my parents, they are both over seventy. I take them to vacations. I have bought an apartment for them. I always take them with us, we have been together to Hawaii. I pay all of the holidays for them. I try to make it possible as much as I can. My son calls me still a successful mother. Because I do not go in the office on week-ends and I do not bring my laptop home. I try to spend as much time as I can with him. A typical Chinese mother does not allow so much freedom. I am discussing topics with him, because he already has his own ideas with his seven years. "

H., VP: "Private success I think for me is very easy. For me is to be there for my kids. Again, I have very strong minds about not delegate even my kids now. I coach their homework. I don't hire tutors to do that. For me if you miss out on that you miss out. "

M., CFO: "I think professional success is according to the work. Did you deliver the result? Did you motivate people? People work here, work hard and also work happy because sometimes if you do not work happy there is no meaning. It's all meaningless. I want to work hard and work happy. As long as you get result you enjoy the process. Sometimes the process is painful once you get the result you feel happy. I feel that professional result you get your salary. You get your pay so you can contribute back to the family. For the family success I feel first of all it is the entire family's happiness. Including the husband, the kids, even the parents in law. We enjoy live together. Especially I would say most of the time I feel my happiness come from my kids instead of myself. When I see they are happy I am happy. And also I try to understand what they need and try to get what they need."

Another aspect that came up again and again, though here it was not the most frequent answer, was recognition from others. Some of the women's personal definitions of career success make direct reference to respect from employees and superiors.

S., HRD: "Private I think is you have happy family. Have family members that rely on you. You feel ok you have a responsibility I think is good. Professional life I think is maybe the position. You get higher position. You can show your success. Second is that you are you really recognize by the many people. Even you are not in the higher position but you are well accepted and well respected by the boss by the top management. By the peers. By the people. I think that will be success."

When asked how they rate their satisfaction with their career success, the interviewees sounded a positive, grateful note with respect to their achievements. They placed their satisfaction in the 80–100% range. Bar a few exceptions, overall they are satisfied with what they have achieved. However, many of them wish to achieve even more. They gave examples such as getting to the next step up the ladder, learning even more, pushing through improvements at their companies or generating higher sales. One woman reflected that she wants to do the things she has not yet managed to implement.

C., President: "If you call it I'm very grateful for what I have done and I think that I am also very lucky and I'm very grateful. From that perspective I'm very satisfied yes but I'm also from the perspective that ok if I want to do more I want to do more and contribute in bigger ways."

Work is viewed as a crucial factor behind satisfaction and happiness. With the exception of one interviewee who did not become mother herself and regrets this, none of the women in the study regard it as sufficient to have lives that revolve solely around children. The interviewees' self-worth is closely tied up with their career success. Answers in this connection included *"work is more important than they would like"* and *"I tasted blood"*.

Z., IT-Director: "Because the main target is work and the main target of my life is work. I have a 'road map' in my head and it makes me happy to conquer it day by day. I do not have so many private targets. I do not have many private hobbies either. Beside making sports and travelling I have no private stories." (Translated from German)

The mothers rate family as a slightly more important factor for happiness and satisfaction than the single women in the group, but all the women in the study tend to attribute considerable importance to their careers, regarding them as an essential component of self-worth.

Evaluation of own work-life balance

When asked how satisfied they have been with their work-life balance over the course of their careers, the answers tended to be very similar. All the women concentrated almost exclusively on their work at the start of their careers and invested many hours in their careers. Today, many of the interviewees see their lives as more balanced, with more space given to their personal lives. This must be understood in the context of the fact that most of the women became mothers at a young age but did not as a result reduce the amount of time they devoted to their careers.

The women said that they currently work between eight hours a day at the lower end of the scale and up to sixteen hours at peak times. All the women reported that there have repeatedly been times in their careers when they have worked extremely long hours, including regularly working 12–16 hours per day in the early stages of their careers. One woman reported that over long periods of time she left home at 7 in the morning and returned at 11 at night. All the women said that they spent far longer at the office or travelling on business at the start of their careers than they do now.

T., GM: "In the first ten years I would say a lot of the time because I know what I want to get and I know I have to invest extra so I would say 90% of my time is on the job. Particularly when I moved to Shanghai I have no friends, I have nothing to do to start with so I invest a lot of the time even Saturday and Sunday too to work. And this is almost like my leisure time and I like because I also like it. Like, most of the entrepreneur like yourself. We work long hours but we like it. And I really enjoyed it. but in the last maybe I would say in the last ten years so it's the second half of my company career, I had a very different perspective so I want to reach out to more people from my church and also from my personal connection and also I learn some more new skills like playing the piano or like nutrition etc. So I think after ten years with the com-

pany I know how to survive. I may not be reaching out to the division presi-
dent's job but I know I will not be fired so I'm more comfortable to do some-
thing on top of the career so I have my habits, I have my religion. I think my
life is a lot well more balanced over the last ten years and I'm happier with my
job and other interests."

Today, they work 11–12 hours on average, including travel to work. Only a few of the women reported working only 7–8 hours. Most of the women return home between 7.30 and 8 p.m., and the majority also work on their computers for another one to two hours each evening after returning home. Many of them travel a lot, with trips lasting days or entire weeks depending on the stage of their careers. The women have a positive attitude towards work-intensive phases that place great demands on their time and see themselves as responsible for restoring a work-life balance after such periods. Examples of phases where they have to work long hours include changes of position or field or special processes such as restructurings. They regard regularly recurring periods of intense work when they have very little free time, such as the end of the accounting year, as normal.

M., CFO: "In my case it didn't change much in terms of my own choice, but it
rather depends on whether there are things to do, there are some busy peri-
ods, there are sometimes not busy periods. But overall I am a person crazy at
work when I have work to do, I wouldn't be able to put it down. But I also
need entertainment; I always need a strong balance at both ends. I mentioned
the period of time when I was taking three jobs together – in Germany, here
and also study, that was a very exhausting period, because I slept two or three
mornings, then I also get up on the weekends and I still do a lot of partying
meeting friends. Now because the company is relatively in a stable stage and
my position I have been here already quite a long time, the challenging thing
is becoming less. Then you could say I don't work as much as in the past, it's
the normal working hour. But if anything comes and requires me to work as
much as in the past as I used to do, it depends on the need."

A., VP: "Of course there cannot always be work-life balance. There's always
peak and low season. Especially first years. The first-year work-life balance is
not good but the family will understand because you just choose a new job.
But in the second year I know I need to go to work-life balance. So in the first
year I make sure I achieve several things. One, I build a good team so that
team can later on be empowered to do things. Two, I build all of the trust with
my boss and peers. So they can trust me to do a lot of things they will not ask a
lot of things and I have to prepare answers for them. Three is I understand
business as quickly as possible so in future whatever small area happen some-

thing I know what is the course. Lastly the fourth thing is I view the relation-
ship with Paris and Asia pacific. They know China is doing the right track so
they do not question us and appreciate us. Actually I'm more and more our
client balance. I have regularly meeting to make sure my team is alright. I
have regular meeting with my boss to make sure one on one update with him.
Things are on track. I also have time to actually go out of my regular work.
Sometimes go to a seminar to share what works in China best practice. And I
design some best practice for Asia pacific. All of the other Asia 15 countries
learn a lot from China best practice to implement their country, which is
highly appreciated by Paris as well."

When asked about their work-life balance, the mothers with two children remarked
that they are constantly in a race against time. One of the small numbers of mothers with two children who participated in this study calculated that she spends one
to one-and-a-half hours a day with her children. Another mother said that she
spends an average of 30 minutes with her son on working days.

H., VP: "I think it's very stressful. I cannot say that I feel peaceful and bal-
anced every day. I think it's very difficult to balance. I'm a very practical per-
son so I look at every day. If I go through every day and being able to still do
my job and still be there for my kids. I think that's success already. I don't
have the illusion that there is a balance. I think depends on how you define
balance. For me you cannot have that perfect balance. It's just not possible. If
you have a big job and you have two kids and you don't want to delegate your
kids you're going to have to have a very stressful life. What I would rather
work on is how I can build energy for myself. I pay attention to what I eat. I
exercise a lot. I have to have the energy it requires for me to do all that."

J., Asia Purchasing Director: "My work hours are really long. I leave 7.30 my
home and arrive home 8 or 8.30 and I travel about 25% of my time outside. If
you are talking about work-life balance and the time I spend, I spend more
time in the work. This is definitely not balance. But I tell my friends I am look-
ing more about the qualities. How I keep the relationship with my family
members although I do not stay at home as long as the other moms. We try to
enjoy something together on the weekend or summer holiday or winter holi-
day. I make the time I spend with my family very good."

In summary, most of the Chinese female executives take a positive view of their
current work-life balance. All the women described having a very high workload
during the career progression phase, with long hours and frequent business travel.
Mothers with children tend to be the exceptions: they see themselves as constantly
having to balance their time between their careers and their children's needs.

Career paths analysis for the Shanghai Women's Career Lab

Earlier, a career path was defined as the trajectory of work-related experiences in which an individual has engaged over the course of their life. Hence, a career path analyses looks atman individual's progress from their first position to their current one. As described earlier, career theorists attempt to capture the complexity of career paths in a way that allows certain characteristics or features to be identified and predictions to be made about people's careers. Below, information from the interviews about the women's career paths is presented in conjunction with answers concerning their decision-making, alternatives that they weighed up, challenges they have faced during their careers and their planning processes.

The start of the women's careers

The women's starting positions can be viewed from different perspectives: according to the labour market context at that time and whether, as a result, their first job was assigned or freely chosen, according to place of residence and hence *hukou*, according to field, according to company type (state-owned or multinational) or according to the country where they began their careers. It is important to understand the start of these women's careers against the backdrop of China's political and economic development. The effects of developments in the labour market were described in section 3.It is clear from the distribution of ages in the study group, ranging from 32 to 63, that the points in time when the women started their careers span a wide spectrum, between 1973 and 2006. Section5 explained the different stages of political and economic development in China. In the light of this development, it is clear that very different conditions obtained on the Chinese labour market at the different times when the women started their careers.

The small number of older participants began their careers in the 70s or 80s, during or before the start of the gradual opening-up of China's economy. At that time, there were no or very few multinational companies in China, and career choices were made exclusively by the state – that is to say, jobs were assigned (Gangrose, 2005; Leung, 2002). The largest age group, aged 36–45, began their careers around the 90ies when a special zone was set up in Pudong, a district of Shanghai. It was something of a transition period: some jobs continued to be assigned by the state, but some of the women were able to freely choose their first jobs. However, nobody around them had any experience of planning their own careers, so they were unable to draw on such experience. Specifically, 17 of the women in this group said that their first job was assigned by the government. Another ten women were able to freely choose their first job in China, while eight started their careers abroad. The 1990s can be seen as a phase of adaptation to the new situation in which people were responsible for finding their own jobs and choosing their own careers. The transitions between the phases in table 25 were fluid. The three youngest members of the group, aged under 35, began their careers after China joined the WTO in 1999. When these women started their careers, the ability to choose one's career was already firmly established in China's economy and they were able to draw on the experiences of others.

Table 19: Time of career start

Labour Market Context	Participants
Initial reform phase 1980–1990	6
Expansion phase 1990–1999	26
After China joined WTO in 1999	3

77% of the women started their careers in China. This group is divided between those who chose their first job freely and those who had it allocated by the government. Of the 27 women who began their careers in China, 17 started in jobs assigned by the government in places allocated according to the *hukou* system.[16]

Table 20: Labour market context and location

Decision of first position	Country	Location
Free choice of first position: 18	8: overseas	in Germany, UK, Singapore, HK
	10: in China	Shanghai
First position placed by government: 17	China	Wuhan, Xiandu, Guanzhou, Nanchang, Beijing, Shanghai

M., HRD: "Because in China there's a hukou. Hukou means that you have your resident of that city. At that moment hukou is very important or was very important. Only in the state-owned company you can easily get the Guangzhou hukou. So I choose that state-owned company and I got a Guangzhou hukou."

Most of the women with Shanghai *hukous* started their careers in Shanghai. Other cities in China where women started their careers were Wuhan, Xiandu, Guangzhou, Nanchang and Beijing. During the early stages of these women's careers, it was only possible to change place of residence within China by being assigned to a state-owned company (Tagscherer, 1999). This was a critical limiting factor for the women who were not resident in Shanghai or another major city. Some of the

---

[16] For more information about the background to the *hukou* system, see section 2.2.2.2.

women reported that they specifically attempted to obtain certain state-assigned jobs so they could get *hukous* for a particular city. Hence, the women who came from the country had to make plans to move to a big city in the initial phases of their careers. Accordingly, *hukous* were the most important decision criterion for the women at this stage.

Almost all the women who began in state-assigned jobs started out as English teachers or translators, or in a role at a research institute. Only four of the women said that they started in the HR department at a state-owned company (as administrative staff or an importer).

> *J., Asia HR: "I was a teacher. I was assigned to Shanghai East Technology University as an English teacher for freshman ... Not English major. I spent almost 4.5 years over there because according to the government policy at that time as a graduate from normal university I can only work for a kind of university schools. We have a kind of concrete building. I had to work there for five years but after 4.5 years I paid something and I got the freedom. After that I went to my first multinational company."*

> *G., Director: "I graduated and then went to an import and export company, state-owned, after my graduation. And that was when China import and export is booming. So, really good time. I spent there, like, five years, working as an importer to my client in America, so I have some really good time."*

Depending on the time when they started their careers and how this point in time correlated to China's economic reforms or the restrictions imposed by the *hukou* system, the women spent between just three months (at the lower end of the scale) and eight years (at the upper end) in their state-assigned jobs. The specific answers regarding how long they spent in their first jobs were as follows: three months (1), one to one-and-a-half years (3), two years (1), four to five years (3) and eight years (1). The oldest interviewee worked at state-owned companies for approximately 14 years before moving to Germany in 1989 for political reasons. Two of the women who spent five and eight years respectively at state-assigned jobs in Guangzhou and Nanchang reported on the connection with the *hukou* system. Their ability to switch jobs depended on the political and economic context, and they could not freely plan the start of their careers themselves.

Table 21: Starting positions of participants

First Position	Participants
English teacher	6
Translator	1
GM assistant/executive Secretary	4
Research institute/Laboratory	2
Junior Editor	1
Importer	1
Administrative staff	3
Sales assistant	2
Consultant	2
Financial analyst/system specialist	2
Trainee program	3
Process Designer	1
Production Planner	1
Advertising Role	1
Marketing Role/product manager	1
Compensation Manager	1
HR Function	2
Legal department	1
	35

A little over half the women (18) chose their first job freely rather than having it assigned by the government. Of these eighteen women, ten began their careers in China and eight began them abroad. The proportion of women in this group who deliberately chose to start their careers abroad is very high, at 45% of those who were able to freely choose their first job. The ten women who were able to freely choose their first job in China started in roles such as personal assistants, sales assistants, consultants, financial analysts or administrative assistants. These women started out immediately at multinational or foreign-invested companies. One woman began in the finance department at a prestigious hotel. The executive assistants were also the GMs' translators and were involved in all key decisions at the companies. They had trusted, powerful positions, since GMs were dependent on their language skills and local knowledge. One of the women reported on starting her career at one of France's biggest companies in 1985, where she was at the GM's side right from the start. Another woman explained how she automatically took over the GM's responsibilities when he travelled to the head office. Women who started their careers at a later stage, when China's economy was already more liberalised, selected companies on the basis of their size and renown and on the extent to which the companies' image and the experience they expected to obtain in their first job would be likely to boost their subsequent careers.

H., VP: "I always felt that the first job, the point about the first job is that it is not something you'll stay for 20 years. For me it's almost irrelevant that it's a sales job, a marketing job. It's a first step in your career development. I wanted to join a good company. A big company where I could learn. I love sports and the culture of XY (American sport company name) and the focus in the sports company fits my personality. The competitiveness of the company. I liked the culture and after the interview I like them. For me it wasn't, I didn't feel I need to think long and hard for the first job."

K., HRD: "Actually after I graduate from my bachelor degree I joined an audit form actually. At that time we called Big 6. It's quite a lucky experience because I know for a lot of mature markets fresh graduates cannot go to the consultant for directly. Rather they will stay in an industry for a few years then get an MBA, then move to a consultant industry. But at that time XY, YZ (list of consulting companies) also have consulting business. They just entered into China market so they wanted to recruit some fresh blood to develop inside. I was lucky. At that year they recruited six fresh graduates from two universities. One is Jiao Tong; one is Fudan the most famous in Shanghai. So I joined the consulting business and then I stayed there for five years ... So during the five years actually I complete my MBA because MBA is a part time and I studied maybe one night and one meeting and one weekend. Kind of two-and-a-half years. At that time also I got pregnant. So I got my MBA diploma after because there is another semester I need to pass after I deliver my son. They said my son will receive quite a good education."

K., HRD: "Then I had this opportunity actually it was my first offer, that's by an executive search firm. Its US based and at the time it was rated #5 globally. I was very excited looking at the profiles of all the colleagues, the consultant. It's a very high profile and it's really a great group if I could join. It all looks like an elite in this market and I want to join in this group. So that's how I joined that company. Started to do executive search. At the time, it's really very early. I think it's a very new concept in China market for executive search. Nobody actually knows what it means. It may just translate as headhunter, but headhunter is very new concept in China market. I ever encounter to make a call to that person, that's showing him or her that I have a great opportunity and whether this person will be considering any external opportunities, or go forward and explore. The answer was usually 'I need to talk to my boss first.' That's how it works. That's really interesting. I think that also its kind of luck we need to make some further progress to educate the market to hook up the client company and the potential talent in the market. That was the fun part. I explored a lot different industries and even back to 2000, that

*was the .com years so the millionaires came up. Although there is a lot of
bubble in the market we also tried to dig out all of the potential talents."*

Eight of the women began their careers abroad: four in Germany, two in Hong
Kong, one in Singapore and one in the Kit is notable that four of the eight starting
positions abroad resulted from an internship or dissertation that the women completed while they were still studying. The four women who started their careers in
Germany made contact with their future companies while they were still students,
and both the women and the companies shared the same goal: namely, that the
women would in future take up posts in China. The other women went through
companies' conventional selection processes or used their universities' recruitment
forums, and hence started in their first job without having previously established
contact while still students. Two of the women specifically selected an overseas
management trainee programme. All the women who started their careers in Germany said that the German companies specifically hired them because they were
Chinese with the necessary qualifications. Hence, their competitive advantage at
the start of their careers was to be Chinese abroad. They were selected for a potential position in China at a future date. One woman reported that she chose not to
take her first job at a particular company in France that only wanted to hire her because she was Chinese. This woman deliberately accepted an alternative job in
France where she had the impression that the factor of being Chinese was less important, because she wanted to build up professional experience in the country over
an extended period rather than returning to China after a brief time.

> *Z., IT-Director: "I started as process designer… So I started with a big pro-
> ject of company XY. They wanted to build (AB big project in the aviation in-
> dustry) in China, which is finished now. My boss was in charge of all the IT
> projects and he wanted someone with Chinese background. This was a good
> chance and I got the job. As a process designer it was easy going in the first
> two-three years. I had no real responsibility, but worked for a college, who
> checked all I did. It was a lot of work, but relaxed as I had no real responsibil-
> ity on the outcomes. But one day they said, ok, you are incorporated now, you
> will be in charge of a system now. Since then I was project leader, it was not a
> big one like with 20, 30 or 50 people but a small one. Then they gave me re-
> sponsibility of the Chinese SAP and said you have a budget now and you are
> in charge of the functioning of this system and all the new developments. Since
> then I have a big responsibility. The step was a bit unpleasant first. Because
> the first two years I was controlled so much and now the message was 'this is
> your business.'" (Translated from German)*

In summary, the group of executives in the Shanghai Women's Career Lab was split in two based on differences in the labour market context that impacted on their freedom to choose. Almost half of the women had their first jobs chosen for them by the government and were unable to decide freely how to start their careers. A notable number of the women who were able to choose freely studied abroad and then took their first job abroad too. Women with Shanghai *hukous* had the best chances of quickly finding a good starting position at a multinational company in Shanghai. The point in time when the women started their careers was another key factor that determined how straightforward this proved to be.

Effect of choice of the company type on careers

The women described their original and current motivations for working at a foreign company and the advantages their choice of company type has had for their careers. They were also asked to compare multinationals with private Chinese companies and state-owned enterprises and what effect they think it would have had on their careers if they had mainly worked at those sorts of companies instead.

Most of the women either briefly worked at a state-owned enterprise at the start of their careers or are familiar with this type of company from their parents' work. A few women in this study group previously worked at state-owned enterprises for extended periods.

Only one interviewee worked at a private Chinese company for a relatively short period in the middle of her career before switching back to a multinational. None of the women have returned to a state-owned enterprise in their careers to date. One interviewee explained that even if she wanted to change to a state-owned enterprise, it is now too late. According to this woman, you have to build up your career at such companies right from the start and establish the necessary networks over a period of many years.

Many of the women's perspectives on the differences between the three main types of company have changed in the course of their careers, but they were able to very precisely describe their past motivations and their past and present perceptions of these differences.

According to the women, particularly in the time after China's economic reforms lots of career opportunities presented themselves at foreign multinationals. The women were able to choose between many different job openings. These openings were a great opportunity also for women who did not have any *guanxi* ties at state-owned enterprises.

All the women reported that they were curious to learn about people from other countries and foreign cultures and ways of working. The women expected to expand their knowledge and skills by working for foreign companies. Hence, learning and an interest in foreign cultures were in the foreground right at the outset when they chose to work at a multinational company. Learning about other cultures and ways of working in addition to their own local approaches was highly beneficial to their careers. Hence, choosing to work at a foreign company gave the women a competitive advantage.

They described the leadership style and corporate culture at multinational companies as more goal-focused and democratic. The interviewed women identify more with these values than with those they observe at state-owned or private companies.

Other incentives included higher salaries, better-equipped offices and the prestige of working for a big-name international company.

> Director: *"One reason is that when I graduated, working in a multinational company is the first choice versus currently the national company is the first choice. Personally, I think the multinational is more equal opportunity, meritocracy, culture, less political. And I think because my major is international business English. I like to have the opportunity to meet foreigners and to communicate."*

> Director: *"I think multinational give me a very good impression because they are very professional. Their offices are very beautiful. (Inaudible) Many things were impressive. The boss, the whole line manager they all seem very mature and professional. She taught a lot about the soft skills and communication skills, language skills. Also some computer skills. I can learn a lot. That's why I chose this."*

> Director: *"I think I am working in multinational because you can see my family doesn't have a very strong background. If you live in China long enough you know what that means. And my parents are only farmers. They don't have strong relations to put me in a state-owned company easily. And at that time when I looked for jobs, the multinational company is coming to China and there are more opportunities. I can find myself in the multinational companies. That's why."*

It is interesting that answers in which the women gave assessments of opportunities in state-owned companies were greater in number and length than the responses that discussed multinational companies. It appears that many of the women regard their clear preference to work at a multinational company as needing no explanation, since at the time when they started their careers there was a trend for working at the new companies, which were seen as more attractive employers. This trend contrasted with the experiences of the women's parents. Many of the women worked briefly at a state-owned enterprise or research institute for their first job. Most of them only stayed there for a short time, and moved away as soon as the opportunity arose. Others stayed there longer due to the *hukou* problem. Only the oldest woman in the study group was forced to stay at a state-owned enterprise until the age of 38, since she started her career long before China's economic reforms. State-owned enterprises represent stability, security and low risk. The women described SOEs as having a completely different, more relaxed way of working than multinationals. According to the women, the values system at SOEs is primarily focused on relationships and is very political. A cautious communication style, indirect rather than open, is critical for career success at such companies. The women described the management style as hierarchical, with orders from above to be obeyed without question. Good connections and a strong network were mentioned as the main factors essential for career progression.

> Director: *"The state-owned company has a lot of protocols, which is not exactly what I expected as a foreign language student. You have status, you have very strong sense of status among all the peers, who is junior, who is senior, who should do this, who should do that, there's a lot of hidden competition among the company and among the small peers. I felt like I was not interested in this kind of things. I hate doing some things below the surface. Something that is hidden, unspoken, but it is happening. And I don't like this."*

> VP: *"I never really seriously. But that's a good question because when I graduated from Nanjing University I had an opportunity to go in the government to work. I could go the Ministry of Foreign Affairs. I didn't. I just didn't feel the working environment attractive. Those jobs are not just about how competent you are but I also see it as a very political environment. It's probably more dependent on how many relationships, connections you had. It's just isn't the type. I think I would do better in a more straightforward business environment. And then the pragmatic reason is I was dating my current husband and he's not Chinese. If I go into the government job that would not be very good. That's just another consideration for me."*

Director: "I'm so open-minded. I'm straightforward. State-owned company might not welcome this kind of people. Because they are tend to be more political and you need to talk very cautiously and they are not inviting conflict in discussion. I don't think I can survive."

Director: "Now probably it's slightly better because we have banned corruption and everything. But government backed or state backed company its very seniority is very important, background is very important, your family background is very important, where you come from is very important. For example I have some friends who worked in big banks in China. They are all from very wealthy families in China or government background parents. That's why they can (inaudible) that position in Chinese government-owned banks. Very good positions but they are not externally hired. You have to have connections to be there to start with."

Director: "My view of working in government is always you can go higher or not based on your capability. It's many other reasons. Connections or other reasons. This is something I don't like. My parents tried to persuade me. They are government officials. I said no from the beginning. I want to be in a job that you can work hard based on your skill then you can up."

The women said that an individual's family background is of key importance for a career at a state-owned company. It is advantageous at such companies to come from a relatively prosperous and well-connected family, according to one woman who lacks this kind of family background and so ruled out pursuing a career at a state-owned enterprise. One woman who previously worked in the HR department at an SOE for five years described the benefits of working at such a company: retirees are looked after like family members and receive generous pensions; there is high job security with no layoffs; one's colleagues are like a family. She reported that she acquired her relationship skills at a state-owned company. According to the woman, only people with good connections can rise to the top in the state sector.

Director: "The time changed. Probably the state-owned company I worked at cannot be compared to state-owned today because they have lots of evolution since. Compared with state-owned company which I joined in the past few years the multinational company is more open and more employee oriented. More efficient."

In the view of this participant, one important advantage of state-owned companies is that Chinese do not face any linguistic barriers there and there is no glass ceiling preventing them from becoming GMs/CEOs. Hence, some of the women in the study group no longer view state-owned companies as critically as they did at the start of their careers.

They also discussed private Chinese companies as a career option. According to Cooke (2012) the number of private enterprises as a business ownership category has soared since the mid 1990s. Numbers of people employed in private Chinese enterprises went up from 4,8 million in 1995 to over 55 million in 2009. The interviewed women see these companies as the future, and as an option for their own future careers. From today's perspective, they mentioned significant financial benefits, such as stock options and high salaries, as key advantages. According to the women, private Chinese companies are still relatively new and in the process of establishing themselves, and need to bring expertise on board. The women believe this could give them a real competitive edge. They reported that success at private companies is closely linked to the owner. Apparently, one needs to share the owner's or boss's values in order to be successful; the chemistry must be right. The women said that, overall, there is more of a focus on relationships than on performance alone.

> GM: "I think definitely the private company will be the big segment. Even, it's hard to say when you say private and multinational. Because now with the globalization of investment and shareholding structures you cannot really very specially define the type of company and nationality of the company."

> GM: "I considered it seriously as all my study friends come from the private sector. The company owners have many ambitions, the spirit, get the spirit out of people, that is very attractive. One has a feeling of living the dream of the company owner with him. But in Western companies you just do a job. It is about a job, but not really about...I think, if I had such a chance...The disadvantage in Western companies is it is about the system. But in private-owned companies it is about the head of the owner. If the chemistry is not right, one can never come together." (Translated from German)

> Sales Director: "Very good and you have stock options. If it is privately owned, the owner is willing to hire people to develop his company because he knows he doesn't have what it takes to build the company ... The owners normally are from very simple backgrounds. They work very hard. They prove to themselves they are opportunistic. If they are coming from those backgrounds they're not very career driven. They don't develop people, as they should be. They invest in people, money terms but they don't develop people in a potential."

Some women reported that at a private company they could be part of a dream – namely, the owner's dream for the company's success – and could really have a stake in this success. At multinationals, by contrast, they said that things revolve more around the corporate system. Hence, in their view the main difference is that the most critical factor for careers at multinational companies is understanding the system, whereas at private companies it is chemistry with the company owner. The women believe that at their current career stage, private Chinese companies are the only viable alternative, since it is too late to pursue a career in the state-owned sector where it is necessary to establish oneself right from the start.

Moving up – analysis of career steps

Career steps: number of previous companies and positions

When asked how many companies they have previously worked at, the group's answers ranged from one to ten. Most of the women have worked at four or five different companies. One participant said that she has worked at ten companies, while two others said they have worked at seven. Most career theory literature proceeds on the basis of a dichotomy between bounded and boundaryless careers (Arthur et al., 2001; DeFillippi et al., 1994; Sullivan, 1999). These concepts were described in chapter 3. A simplified analysis of the study group, based purely on the number of companies they have worked at in the course of their careers, reveals the following picture: only four of the interviewed women have spent their entire careers to date at one and the same company. These four women can be described as having a bounded career path. It is notable that for three of the four women who have only ever worked at one company, the company in question is a German one and they started their career there in Germany. All the other women have had careers that were closer to the boundaryless pattern, since they are not tied to a single company but have pursued a career across multiple organisations. In this connection, the question arises of how much account the definition of boundaryless careers should take of the special labour market context in China. It could be argued that simply the step of moving to a multinational company from one of the usual state-assigned jobs is enough to satisfy certain criteria of a boundaryless career. In these cases, not only were career decisions influenced by individual goals rather than organisational ones, but, by taking the step from a state-assigned job to a multinational company during the early stages of China's economic reforms, the women were opting to make a pioneering move in defiance of prevailing norms on the labour market, which were closely interwoven with political factors. This decision involved more dimensions than simply switching companies in a liberal market economy. Accordingly, in this context a bounded career would be equivalent to remaining in one's first state-assigned position at a state-owned company or research institute. This perspective might be especially relevant for the early careers of four women who made the move to a multinational company in the early stages of China's economic reforms.

Table 22: Number of companies worked for

Number of companies	Participants
1	4
2	4
3	4
4	10
5	6
6	5
7	1
10	1

The women's answers in the interviews about their previous roles and positions were given from memory, so it is unclear whether all the women precisely remembered all the individual roles they have held during their careers. It can be assumed that there might be small gaps in their answers and so in some cases it is only possible to state the minimum number of positions they have held. The woman with the most different positions has held a total of 14. Most of the women could recall working in six to nine different positions. It became evident that none of the women in the group have worked in the same position throughout their careers; given the way the group was selected, this was to be expected. Hence, there were no "static" career paths (Lepine, 1992). The number of positions recalled by the women makes clear that the women have held many different positions.

Table 23: Number of positions the women could recall holding during their careers

Number of functions	Participants
<4	No
4	2
5	3
>5	2
6	4
>6	1
7	9
>7	1
8	5
>8	1
9	3
>9	1
11	2
14	1

An analysis of the industries chosen by the women shows that only six of the women (including the three who have never changed companies) have pursued their careers exclusively in one industry. Two of these women have worked exclusively in the pharmaceuticals industry, one woman in the automotive industry, one in the materials sector, one in the steel industry and one in the luxury goods industry. The vast majority (29 women) have changed industries at least once, and many of them have switched multiple times. Sixteen women have pursued careers in a single department type: HR (7), sales (1), finance (2), finance/controlling (5), legal (1). These women have remained true to their chosen fields and worked their way up to the highest ranks. Nineteen women, by contrast, have consistently switched between different roles and obtained qualifications that cut across different departments. Eleven of the women can be categorised as "lateral movers". As well as working in the corporate world, they have worked at agencies, service providers, consultancies or institutes, or been self-employed. This does not include work in state-assigned jobs. If these are included, eight other women would have to be categorised as "lateral movers" in accordance with the above definition, for a total of 19 women whose careers have not been confined to the corporate world. The women who have worked as consultants did so before starting at multinational companies. Many of the other career moves described took women away from multinational companies and then back again. These career paths resemble the patchwork careers described by Bloemer (2005). Patchworkers characteristically acquire different qualifications in different industries and switch between sectors.

Geographic mobility during the women's careers

In this section, mobility is defined as geographic career mobility, either within China or abroad. It does not refer to mobility between companies. In total, 26 of the interviewed women said that they have worked abroad in the course of their careers. Table 30 shows the different countries where the women have worked. Seven of the women started their careers in the countries where they studied. As mentioned in the section on education and training above, a total of 12 of the women studied abroad. Nineteen of the women worked abroad at later stages of their careers without having studied abroad.

Table 24: Countries where the study participants have worked

Country	Participants
US	4
Germany	8
HK	3
Singapore	2
France	2
Switzerland	2
South Africa	2
UK	1
Malaysia	1
Sweden	1

Four of the women followed their partners abroad: that is, their partners' careers rather than their own were the decisive factor behind the decision to move abroad. Only two of these women described this as having a negative impact on the start of their careers. These moves altered the direction of their subsequent career development. A specific problem faced by one woman, a lawyer, arose when her husband took a position in Hong Kong, where she could not automatically make use of her knowledge and qualifications. Another woman was unable to find a comparable management job in the USA and subsequently became self-employed there, just like another interviewee who first obtained her MBA in Australia and then founded an online business. In these cases, the husbands' careers resulted in a career break and temporary change of direction, but not in the end of the women's careers. The oldest woman in the group suffered a real setback in her career when she followed her husband to Germany at the time of the student demonstrations in China. She described how she practically had to give up her career and try out various low-qualified jobs, since language barriers prevented her obtaining a management position. Meanwhile, the lawyer mentioned earlier, reported that she feels she now lags behind others who started their careers at the same time but did not move abroad. Looking back, all the women believe that moving abroad, although it was primarily instigated by their partners, made sense for their own career development since (as they themselves described) it opened up new and completely different experiences that would not have been possible if they had stayed in China.

The women can be divided into subgroups with respect to mobility within China. One subgroup, which started out with Shanghai *hukous*, has generally worked continuously in Shanghai with intermittent assignments in other cities; the main examples given of these assignments were times when the multinational companies opened new factories, making it necessary for the women to relocate for longer or shorter periods of time. The other subgroup, which started out with non-Shanghai *hukous*, has a high level of geographic mobility within China. The women in this group mentioned working at the following cities in the course of their careers: Wuhan, Yunnan, Nanjing, Xiandu, Szechuan, Beijing (multiple mentions), Shenzhen, Tianjin, Guangzhou. Several of the women reported moves between Shanghai and Beijing.

For the sake of their careers, the women accepted relocations that in some cases meant having to travel long distances between work and family each weekend sometimes for periods of up to two years. Around 75% of the women in the Shanghai Women's Career Lab have high or very high geographic mobility.

Reasons for changing companies

When asked why they left their first job, the Chinese women mentioned a large number of points that can be viewed in the context of their original career motivations. The desire for personal development was most important at the start of their careers.

Table 25: Reasons for leaving first job

Reasons for leaving first job first job	Answers
was bored	5
needed challenges	5
wanted to learn more/do MBA	4
did not like kind of the job	3
wanted to use my foreign languages	3
followed my boss	2
industry declined/not stable	2
changed from state owned to multinational	1
was send to China	1
had a baby	4
	30

The most common spontaneous responses to the question of why they left their first company were: *"I was bored"* and *"I needed a challenge"*. Closely linked to these responses were answers that in turn reveal a strong motivation to learn and progress in their careers. This is in keeping with the findings in the section on personality dimensions. The women were unable to satisfy their desire to learn more in their first jobs. It was in this context that many of them decided to do an MBA. Other women said that they did not like the type of job they had. This once again indicates that they did not feel fulfilled.

> *C., HRD: "It was very nice, like a dream job for many people. But the job itself was not a lot of fun. I worked as a translator and then editor. But it was not very fun because in China the TV station is again part of the government office. A lot of rules. A lot of censorship. And not really a lot of fun. After one year I met my husband and he actually was working in Shenzhen, which is a city just to the south of Guangzhou. We got married then I moved to Shenzhen, I joined the Shenzhen TV station. Worked there as a translator and basically as translator. Then I also do some editing job for news program. Again it was not very fun. Not really made me freedom to work on the things that I'm interested. And not a lot of work at all. Three years later I feel like I got bored and I felt I could see myself in ten years. It was not fun."*

> *A., VP: "I became a university teacher. Teaching English. I taught for one year. I thought number one it was repeating work and boring. At that age I want to explore what is outside of school campus. I quitted an 'everybody respected job' – a university teacher, which could be likely three years later become a professor. I could have got a professor career road map and went into an industry and stuffy from the very beginning as an HR clock. Doing payroll, doing calculation, doing administration but it was on a fast track."*

The desire to switch from a state-owned company or institute to a multinational was given as one of the main reasons for leaving their first job by women who were unable to freely choose this job. This was linked to the desire to make more deliberate use of their personal language skills. However, early-career motivations to switch companies among women who started out directly at multinational companies were also always linked to a desire to progress rapidly rather than stagnating. Some of the women took pregnancy or the birth of their first or second child as an opportunity to quit their job and take a deliberate break between two stages of their careers. In these cases, pregnancy was a pretext rather than a reason for the change. Three of the four women who specifically reported on this point became mothers early in their careers and deliberately chose to take a break and make a change. All the women already had a firm desire for changing companies independently of becoming a mother.

Table 26: Reasons to change companies over time

Reasons for leaving	Job 1	Job 2	Job 3	Job 4	Job 5
Restructuring, downgraded, organisational changes		4	8	4	3
Was bored, needed challenges	10	2	4	1	
Wanted more/broader experience/to learn/to do MBA	4	3			
Wanted higher position/no chance for growth, frustrated with company, did not like the job	3	7	6		
Had a baby	4		1	3	
Followed husband, personal reasons		1			1
Health reasons			1		
Followed market trend, changed field, changed company type	3	1	1	1	
Followed boss	2				1
Conflicts with boss, internal conflicts, culture did not fit		6		2	1
Wanted to go to China, was sent to China, went overseas	1		2		
Political reasons		1			
Wanted to use my foreign languages	3				
Too much travel			2		
	30	25	25	11	6

Only some of the women's answers concerning reasons for change could be clearly assigned to particular career stages. So the findings about reasons for changing companies over the course of their careers are somewhat patchy. During the interviews, the women mentioned restructurings, conflicts with bosses and corporate culture as reasons for leaving companies. The women frequently described leaving companies and looking for higher positions at other companies at times of restructurings or organisational changes that would weaken their position. Many of the specific examples occurred during the Asian financial crisis, when many companies outsourced operations or set up Asian headquarters outside China that threatened to limit some of the women's roles. Hence, these women became less attached to their companies and pursued their personal career goals more strongly. Arthur et al. (1996) describe how "boundaryless careers" (a concept developed by Arthur) are influenced by individual career goals instead of organisational goals. Other features are frequent changes of organisation and temporary breaks. The model of the "protean career" developed by Hall et al. (2004) focuses instead on psychological components. According to this model, the main criteria pursued in protean careers tend to be subjective, for example psychological success, rather than objective, such as position or salary. It was not possible to identify an exclusive focus on subjective criteria among the women who explained their motivations for switching companies at times when restructurings were taking place. They mentioned both subjective and objective reasons. The aim of obtaining a higher position was a constant across all the answers.

The birth of a child was used as a pretext for implementing career decisions that had already been made, for example to switch companies or take a temporary break. None of the women described the fact of becoming a mother as the initial reason for changing companies. The group only mentioned other personal reasons for changing companies very occasionally.

The women's subsequent descriptions of their motivations for changing companies indicate highly strategic, long-term career planning that incorporated deliberate changes of industry and responses to market trends into their personal career development.

In summary, most of the women of the Shanghai Women's Career Lab described their motivation for leaving their first job as the desire for new challenges. They described proactively responding to change and conflict over the course of time, with changes of company motivated by both objective goals (such as attaining a higher position) and subjective ones (such as finding interesting work that would enable personal growth). The female executives regard these subjective and objective factors as intertwined.

Reasons for choosing a position

The women were further asked why they chose a particular position and what the decisive factors behind this decision were. Many of the female executives reported that it was not unusual to receive four or more job offers at the same time during China's boom period. Hence, the women's selection criteria reveal something about their career motivations and decision-making processes. There were three main motivations for choosing a position:

- Developing personal expertise and market value
- Interpersonal relationships
- Prestige

Table 27: Reasons for choosing a company and a new position

Reasons for choosing a new company/position	Answers
Broader responsibility, challenge, learn more, experience regional experience, work with many business units/departments	10
liked the industry, good for female	2
liked the people /liked the people in the interview employee care, respect for people	5
liked the GM, reputation of GM in market	5
good reputation of the company, German company multinational company, American company	5
Hukou for Shanghai/be near family	2
wanted to go to China	2
	31

The women who gave answers that primarily focused on developing their personal expertise spontaneously mentioned "gaining experience" as a reason. This was the most frequent response. Examples included positions that gave them responsibility for the whole Asia region or for multiple business units instead of just one, or ones that allowed them to work with several companies. The increase in their personal market value that these positions entailed was described in terms of "more influence in the market". One older interviewee said that she strategically chose a job in Hong Kong because there were positions there that did not exist in China at that time. She wanted to try them out so that she had an edge when she returned to mainland China.

C. President: "I think it was different of course and you got to work in one company, work in one industry instead of different industries. I think one good thing about XY (Company name) is we have multiple business units with more than one. It still gives me a little bit of different sectors to look into. So it is not that boring and so that was good. The fact that XY has given me different roles and keep me challenged I think that was also good. I would say I don't regret joining XY."

S., HRD: "I think at that moment maybe because actually I think its two reasons. One is because the situation at that time at XY (company name). Of course XY offer me another job opportunity. They want to move from the automotive group to the building business. This position is large, covers the whole China. But I didn't go. I refused because that is only for the commercial office. Is more service, business itself is not so interesting. There is no manufacturing. Only the offices in China. Compared with AB (company name) I think at that time more attractive to me is the people. Because of the interviewers. French. Then also HR and also the HR director. Then have the HR

director in France. He came to China to interview. All of them they show you
they really care about you. Respect you. Because this time I am busy. They're
also busy people and found a way to adapt the interview time and all the
things. They really respect you very much. I was even interviewed in the car
with the French people, the HR director from France and then after his busi-
ness trip he go to Pudong airport. On the way he picked me up and then the
car went to the airport. Then we have a time. We talk."

J., Asia Purchasing Director: "What attracted me is in (company name) it is
in Asia region. The scope is regional. I was still a manager although there is
no direct reporting line in that organization after I went there I realized eve-
ryone is called manager. I said fine. Sometimes title is not most important. It's
what you're doing in that position."

L., HRD: "I was not looking for balance. I was looking for some stretch and
challenge. I wanted to really step from supporting role, nice role to a very
business impact role. Impact again. This is my first role in (company name).
It's an HR business partner role ... when I joined in 2012. My key work was
really about redesigning the company and supporting the company to do the
change management, the layoff. All the tough things. Then I was promoted to
be the China HR head in 2013, April. At that time I start to own everything in-
cluding operation, strategic at partner level to today."

The most common interpersonal reason mentioned was the desire to work with a
friendly team. For these women, it was important that they could see right from the
interview stage that their potential future bosses showed their staff a lot of respect.
In these answers, personal bonds, relationships and networks were key decision
criteria.

C., HRD: "I still wanted to work in an American company and retail. And
(company name) was at that time, very, very good business. Stock price high
and reputation good. And actually I was kind of interviewing with different
companies. The people that I met at (company name) were very, very good. I
liked them very much and I thought it would be great if I could work with
them."

The women's accounts placed particular emphasis on GMs. Many of the women
considered it important to work with a boss who had a good reputation in the market and was very well known. As well as the prestige of the boss, interpersonal factors such as trust, respect and how well they treated their employees were especially important.

Z., CFO: "Then I was quite motivated to try it. Because the GM he has a very good reputation in the industry. He's an old guy. An old age. Very experience. Very good at the coaching part. My boss in (company name) worked with him for more than ten years. I was thinking I have the opportunity to work with (name of the GM) and he is kind of GM I admire a lot. So I have a quick decision. I say yes."

A third decision criterion for choosing a position was the type of company and its reputation in the market. The women also expressed preferences for particular industries and departments or for companies from particular countries. For example, two women specifically mentioned that they were determined to work at, respectively, a German or an American company. Other women selected companies *inter alia* because of the strong brand awareness of the companies' products, which they could identify with. They also hoped that working at such a well-known company would boost their own careers. Only one of the women mentioned personal reasons alongside these factors, namely a desire to move to a particular location so she could live with a relative. Hence, the woman wanted to switch positions in order to obtain one of the *hukou* permits that have previously been mentioned at several points. In China, these permits can only be acquired with proof of an employment contract at the new location.

Alternatives to actual career choices

When asked about possible alternatives to the career choices the Chinese female executives actually made, the most common answer was that they could have worked abroad instead. Seven women in particular repeatedly mentioned their desire to work abroad at different points of the interviews. This desire was connected to the belief that overseas experience could have allowed them to progress to an even higher position than they actually have. One example was the interviewee who said that at the time of the interviews, one condition for becoming a director at her company was overseas experience. In addition, the original motivation for working at a multinational company, namely to learn about foreign cultures and ways of working, was brought up again at this point. The women who mentioned wanting to work abroad did not pursue this alternative for family reasons. They described how they believed moving to another country would be problematic for their children, parents and partners. According to the women, their existing family system, which strongly supported their careers, could not be transferred abroad. Fischlmayr and Puschmüller (2006) examined the experiences of female combining global careers and frequent international business travel with family. They found that integrating family and long-term expatriation poses many challenges on women. A second alternative considered by several women was to work in similar or more senior positions at other companies, especially at well-known ones with "great products". Whether the alternative position was equal or higher depended on the stage of the women's individual career development. Generally, their goal was a higher position or better title. The third career alternative mentioned by some women was to work in a different department. In particular, the HRDs who had worked continuously in HR for many years wondered whether it would make sense to move to a different field. In addition to these three main alternatives, there were some alternatives that were only considered in individual cases. These cases are described below. One of the women who did an MBA in the course of her career described choosing between several well-known business schools, Harvard, Stanford and INSEAD, all of which had accepted her. She chose Harvard on the basis of its prestige and the prospects it gave her for attaining a senior position in future. Another woman who spent several years abroad reported on choosing between an American investment company (which would have meant staying in the USA for an extended period) and a German company (with a clear goal of a future position in China). In the same context, a more strategic role was mentioned as another alternative.

Table 28: Alternatives to career choices

Alternatives to choices	Answers
working overseas	7
work in another company same Industry, local law firm	6
work for another GM	1
stay in US instead going to Germany	1
chose other function/area	2
private company	2
open own hospital	1
stay in UK for my partner	1
chose money/higher salary/higher title	2
	23

One participant described how she specifically decided not to work for a brand manufacturer in France because she had the impression they only wanted to hire her on the basis of her nationality. She opted for a consultancy instead. Two other women had specific opportunities to switch to a private company. Above all, they see this alternative as promising faster career progression without the limitations they believe come with being Chinese at a multinational company. One woman from the pharmaceuticals market mentioned the alternative of founding her own company, specifically a hospital.

> *X., BU-Head: "I think yes, if I will have a work I can do volunteer. I think that's great. But I think in the multinational company, is impossible because. This is maybe I think I need to change the challenge another operation. I need to have some or we can see some places or change some jobs. We can do maybe you don't have the income but it is still a job. In the future you can have some people. To be honest I think about to run a hospital by myself. Maybe five years later because in China the industry has changed and the government have changed. The government is starting to think about open the door for the private hospital. But China most hospital are public hospital but in the future have private. We can try, right?"*

Another participant previously took a pay cut in order to get a foothold in a new market; the alternative would have been a higher salary. She opted for long-term career planning and future prospects in the luxury goods market, and consequently accepted a lower salary in the short term. However, other women reported a clear focus on salary. The alternatives that these women weighed up were between salary increases and longer-term career planning. Other alternatives described by the women would have amounted to prioritising their families and personal lives over their careers in cases where the two options were not compatible. One woman reported that she left a potential life partner in the UK for a position in China, putting career ahead of personal happiness. This decision also involved choosing between living in London and Shanghai. Another woman reported that she left her child with her mother in China for several years so she could start her career in Germany and then later experienced the same situation in reverse when her daughter stayed behind in Germany while she moved to China to take a position as a general manager. In these examples, the alternatives would have been to prioritise personal life instead of work.

The women's reflections on and responses to alternative paths and possibilities indicate that most of the women in this study group exhibit a high degree of self-reliance in their career planning. Moreover, it can also be seen that they make relatively little mention of influencing factors from the personal sphere. Only when it came to working abroad did some of the women make decisions that prioritised staying in China for their families.

Career strategies of female Chinese executives

The most immediately striking thing about the women's answers concerning planned and unplanned career steps is that there were far more about the former than the latter. In their descriptions, the women used terms such as *I chose to, planned to, asked for, raised my hand, applied for, initiated, voiced out* or *was determined to*, which suggest very active career planning and an autonomous approach. Several interviewees explained their motivations for their planned career steps. Answers such as "wanting to rise up higher", "expanding my responsibility" and "striving for a position with more influence" were very common in this group. Other factors linked to career planning included being visible in their companies and having variety in their daily work.

Table 29: Planned career decisions (multiple answers)

Planned career decisions	Answers
Asked for/looked for next step, voiced out, got people engaged	12
Rose higher, expanded scope, higher responsibility, more exposure, pursued a career, looked for challenges	7
Always planned, planned to be where I am now, knew what I wanted and what I did not want	7
Looked for companies who planned a joint venture in China, wrote my final thesis on joint venture with China	6
MBA, Harvard, top university	5
Went to production site and not headquarters, worked cross functional, chose HR, planned according to market trend, went to Australia to get Western experience	4
Went to Shanghai, went to the first special economic zone (Shenzhen), Went to where I could get the hukou that I wanted	5
Planned financial independence	1
Followed my husband	1

All the interviewed women knew from early on that they wanted to rise higher in their careers, take on a lot of responsibility and reach a high level in the hierarchical system. Hence, the women's goals were already clear in the early stages of their careers. This applies even to the older women, despite the fact that overarching external factors meant that some of them were only able to pursue these ambitions at a later point in time. The women described the plans they made to achieve these goals. From their descriptions, it is possible to identify a number of especially common career strategies:

1. Long-term career planning
2. Developing expertise and lifelong learning at a high level
3. Internationalisation of career and/or mobility within China
4. Making use of local potential
5. Strategic choice of industry, company and field
6. Putting work before personal life
7. Considering factors such as happiness and backwards steps
8. Seeking exposure and allies

Figure 7: Model of female Chinese executives' career strategies (developed by the author)

Most of the women planned their careers with a focus on the desired end point taking a long-term perspective. Some of the women said that they approached their careers strategically right from the outset, while others started long-term planning in the early years of their careers. Only one interviewee said that she experimented in a seemingly unplanned way for a relatively long time, but even she said that she had a definite goal, namely to obtain a high position or greater responsibility.

Several of the women described how planning is a fundamental part of their personalities. They remarked that even as children they always planned everything. Some of the answers suggest a basic structure that was continuously planned:

- *Even as a child I always planned everything, I have always planned things right from my earliest years*
- *I wanted to plan my career in advance, the next step*
- *I definitely wanted to pursue a career*
- *I have a plan for my career, everything is planned*
- *I know what I want and what I do not want*
- *No zigzagging*

The second strategy that all the women have pursued is to be the best in their field. This includes planning learning and training and precisely selecting positions that allow them to build up specific expertise. All the women have strived to maximise their level of qualification in order to stand out, including making plans for lifelong learning. The oldest participant only completed her MBA at a late stage in her career, when she was already a CEO. The women in the study who went to university abroad said that they planned this step very precisely; since they believed a qualification from abroad and experience in a foreign culture would enhance their future career prospects. Some of them chose very well-known universities such as Harvard, INSEAD or Stanford specifically in order to increase their chances of landing a management role in future. The women who studied in China attempted to get into the best Chinese universities. For some of them, choosing a top university was more important than which subject they studied.

> *M., CFO: "I realized it maybe when I was six or seven. I do a lot of planning when I was six, seven already, I showed my notebook to everybody, they were shocked, they did not think this came from a little girl who write this kind of mature stuff, but I was kind of premature when I was young."*

> *L., HRD: "Planned is about I'm I think the plan is where I want to be today. I want to. I was quite aggressive compared with others my age. Not a very clear timeline but at that time I told myself when I was 35, 36 or 40 I want to be the head. I want to be really #1 owner of sort of area. Maybe OD number one in China or HR head but I don't have a very clear concept about power. I don't care basically. But I want to really become competitive with a sort of competency in the same industry compared with my peers or compared with my friends. This was clear. But a no part I'm fine even join some big company. One thing is very clear I don't want to join big company. It's also clear and planned. Even today or the past few years any huge company approach me I always say no."*

> *M., HRD: "I think everything is planned or not planned to be honest. I think the result is not planned but the thing I want to do very important is planned. For example when I want to get into (Company name) actually at the beginning I knew nothing about the company. I knew nothing about because there is limited information at that time. When we start to learn, know how the careers progress and how we need to perform in the company basically it's actually my plan or what I want to do in the company. I want to do financial analysis. I want to do a better job. I want to learn more and get promoted. Eventually I never set a target that I want to get promoted in two years or three years. That was not planned. Every promotion is not planned. But I will plan that I want to do this job. I want to grow into this level. Eventually it comes, it's good."*

The women continuously built up their expertise from the start of their careers. One interviewee gave the following representative description. Positions and companies were selected accordingly.

> *A., HRD: "Actually it's a kind of funny to say ... So when I move I'm thinking and say, Ok if I look at my skill set as pie. I will see which areas I still lack of. I'm more like how I can build my resume internally or externally ... This is how I choose the position."*

A large group of the women systematically followed their plan of acquiring overseas experience and working abroad. Others opted for mobility within China and moved to cities where there were good career opportunities. Another woman described seeing an advert for a position in Hong Kong and doing all she could to get the job.

> *S., HRD: "This is interesting. I worked for an amazing company for several years. Multinational company for several years. And I'm original from Shanghai right? I think I need to find some life experience and go abroad. To see the Western style. To deeply understand the culture. Even for the food. Just have some different experience. At that time also I just have to plan it. I need to obtain my Master Degree. The Master Degree I just applied to Sydney University. They located in Sydney and that's why I choose Australia."*

All the women who studied abroad or worked there at the start of their careers did so with the deliberate intention to return to China for further career progression in future. When asked about their planned career steps, several of the women replied "I wanted to pursue a career in China". One participant who studied in Germany reported that she specifically looked for companies that had joint ventures in China. She then attempted to get internships at these companies so she could write her dissertation about one of them. Hence, her strategic plan was to prepare for career progression in China right from an early stage. One of the older women in the study described how she specifically looked for an executive job in a less desirable part of China because she only began her ascent up the career ladder at the age of almost 40. She described her plan as follows: "I wanted to go somewhere where they definitely needed me."

> *J., GM: "Yes, I started with a basic training and an expert training with company XY (automotive supply, Germany) and build a relationship to them and I saw the advertising at our mechanical engineering department at University, they were looking blabla. And I started researching and saw that they had started the first joint venture with China just recently. In the 90s many had started there. That is the reason why I started goal oriented with company XY during my thesis with the topic 'Construction of a joint venture in China'. We had already a joint venture there but wanted to install an assembly plant. I planned the whole concept taking into account the country specifics. We had worldwide high automation, without automation, little automation, so I worked on specific assembly concepts for Shanghai. Of course I got the chance later to implement them and be responsible." (Translated from German)*

Another strategy mentioned by several women in the group was to observe economic and market trends and plan their careers accordingly. Examples included

China's early economic development at the start of the reforms. One woman described how she specifically followed the growth in foreign investment across different regions from Shenzhen to Shanghai, and chose positions accordingly. Another described developments in her industry and how she deliberately looked for an executive role in the growing sector with the assistance of headhunters. Targeted choice of industries, companies and fields was another key focal point of planning. Examples given included selecting companies based on their size or country of origin or deliberately choosing to work on the service provider side. For all the women, the decision to work at a multinational company rather than another type of company was the result of deliberate planning.

> A., VP: "And then I feel my value or what I studied I used my English. It can be a commercial. After I find a job I talk to my school leaders and they say 'no you cannot'. No. You have to come back. But at that time I think the government in the country just started to allow that you can resign from a state-owned company and I feel I was the first person in my area, the first person resigned. It actually made a lot of noise. My education system people there they think 'how can she?' First of all nobody resigned at that time because teacher is still dream job for many people. You can teach and it's a state-owned company. You are guaranteed rights and decent jobs. Then you resign and you work in a remote city you do not know and it's called a capitalist. We were educated that capitalist always exploit the people ... My parents at that time my mother was very worried. She said, really you want to put yourself in the risk. I was struggling for about one month and I consult people and ask because in that company there are a lot of young people from different parts of the country. People like me have educated. Most of them resigned so I consult them but nobody give me the answer this is the right one. Nobody can guarantee. For me I say it's a risk taking but it's worth it to try. I write a resignation letter. In the end they have no way to prove. Then from there I just started take care of myself. Not the country. Take care of myself. That was 1990. That's my second start my career."

Many of the descriptions show that most of the women in this group have prioritised their careers over their personal lives in their decision-making. This once again confirms the findings in the section on the comparative importance of professional and private success. Examples of the women prioritising their careers included moving to places far away from where their families lived. Several women mentioned doing this; one described her decision to accept a more senior position in Beijing while her family stayed behind in Shanghai as something "which was totally against my family planning". Unlike in the Kaleidoscope Career Model developed by Mainiero et al. (2005), according to which women evaluate each action in the light of the impact a decision might have on their relationships, the women in this study are not swayed by personal factors when they make decisions about their career development.

> *E., VP: "After that there came a time that I requested by myself, to the holding CFO, that I need a change. I want to do something new. We discussed the different positions and finally also this was a hard decision to take over this real estate position, because it was never on my agenda list. And it was in Beijing again, which was totally against my family planning. Because at that time I already had family here in Shanghai. But we finally decided on a certain working model. And I took over that position. At that time it was in Beijing, later on came back to Shanghai."*

Another factor that became apparent in the women's descriptions of their planned career steps is how self-reliant they are in planning their careers. Although they attribute a role to factors such as chance and opportunity or being in the right place at the right time in determining the paths their careers have taken, what predominates in the women's descriptions is their own proactive action, initiative and planning: spotting opportunities and then seizing them. These descriptions suggest a more internal career locus, defined by O'Neil et al. (2004) as the belief that one is responsible for one's own career and in charge of managing it. There are some descriptions in the group that point towards a more external career locus, in which a career occurs as a result of chance or other external interventions from which the career opportunities emanate, but when the accounts are analysed as a whole such descriptions are always subordinated to the women's own goal-focused career planning and desire for career advancement.

> *E., VP: "I don't really say planned, in early ages you have certain desires and career steps and you want to plan it. There is definitely some luck being in the right place at the right time. My first assignment to Hong Kong it just happened, me standing there with my Asia face, at the time there was nobody there and they suddenly see me and say, Oh, she is doing the training and she knows it, maybe we should consider. A lot of people say this is luck, but if you really look back, but you also have to bring your own value."*

> *Q., VP: "It's difficult to say planned. Because it comes both ways. That means this new opportunity comes to the table and of course I took it. So in a way the opportunity, but also my choice. So if you say planned, the only think I can say planned is yea, I planned to progress more in terms of going to higher responsibilities and expand both the scope and both in terms of job and geography."*

So in a way that was the plan, but in a way the opportunities were always kind of given. So I was approached always by headhunter or referred by a friend. So I was approached even this moved within LVH group from Shanghai to Singapore was offered by the company. And I took it. Probably because I have expanded my scope beyond marketing it be involved in distribution, the overall brand management, and also having more experience in international organization. So it's clear for me that I want to have a bigger scope and have higher responsibility. And in terms of geography it's also, after seeing people being mobile across the market, and then I realized it's also a possibility for me."

The final factor mentioned in connection with career planning relates to exposure and looking for allies. The women specifically looked for and accepted positions that promised a high level of exposure in their companies. According to the women, exposure increases their chances of advancing further. Here once again, the women took the initiative and planned how they could maximise their visibility in their companies. They also involved key decision-makers in their career plans and continuously worked to win and retain their support. This point has already been discussed in the section on mentoring. What is relevant here is the women's individual planning and the ways in which they exerted influence on these connections. These factors also support the attribution of an internal career locus in keeping with the definition by O'Neil presented above.

T., GM: "I think a lot of things were planned. Planned in a sense when I started with my company I have a vision of working cross functions and then I always told my boss and maybe, the HR department and also my peers and also other functions had, that brought exposure. So and also in the American company you have to talk a lot about your career. You have to get people engaged and also connected of your career plan and then they could be able to provide me something. Maybe not the things I want but at least a door, more doors were opened. So the opportunities I had with (name of company unit) as well as the States I think I reach out to some senior people to get it and fortunately at that time, they want also to open my horizon and also get more exposure for me."

In summary, the women in the Shanghai Women's Career Lab described many different aspects of how they planned their careers. These can be described in terms of various strategies that the women have implemented in order to achieve their career goals. It appears that most of the women have more internal career loci, which means they themselves take responsibility for shaping their careers. This assessment is elaborated in greater detail in the section on typologies.

Unplanned career steps

There were far fewer mentions and reports of unplanned career steps. Many of the descriptions listed in the following were described by the participants as unplanned and so are presented here for the sake of completeness, but in the overall context are isolated occurrences that can ultimately be seen to be part of an overarching plan after all.

Table 30: Unplanned career steps

Unplanned career steps	Answers
company culture did not fit (private company)	1
husband moved to HK	1
downgrading after overseas assignment	1
headhunter offered me job	2
first job in state-owned	2
change into a multinational company	1
my start in HR	1
it just came to me/I did not plan	3
internal offer	1
Pregnancy	1
industry/company	3
luck helped me	1

Only three of the women described themselves as not having planned things, and that only in the very early years of their careers. According to these women, they tried out a lot of things at the start of their careers which in retrospect can be seen as unplanned. One woman said that she *"tried out everything like a little monkey"*. She said that she received no advice from her universities and that her parents were focused on job security. Since these descriptions were confined to the early years of the women's careers, they could also be viewed as evidence of a high level of flexibility at the start of their careers. Many of the women regard their first job at a state-owned company, which was generally assigned by the government, as unplanned, since they had little or no control over it. They also described some career steps at the start of their careers at multinational companies as unplanned. "I did not think too much", said one interviewee. However, most of them had a clear desire to pursue a career and rise up the ranks. Several of the women described their approach in the initial stages of their careers as being unplanned. A few women described offers that they received from headhunters in the course of their careers as unplanned, since they came from an external source without them having to initiate contact. Some interviewees also categorised offers within their companies as unplanned, which means that in these women's cases the initiative for an internal job change may have come from their companies or bosses rather than the women themselves. New positions, including more senior ones, were offered more or less by chance without the women having to apply.

> *C., President: "I didn't choose XY (company name). There was a head hunter that came to me and approached me and said XY is looking for someone and do you want to try? I think it was little bit of a coincidence. At that time I had already been ten years or so with AB (consulting company name) and I find that if I want to continue my consulting career my next hurdle was to become a partner at the consulting firm, which was more like required sales skills. You need to sells projects to clients and to be good at network. Good at client relationship ... I was not quite sure about continuing my career with consulting. Then at the same time XY was looking for someone and the headhunter asked me to interview and I did interview ... So I really did not choose XY it was maybe a little bit of a coincidence."*

> *M. M., President: "I knew I would look for another company. I found it by chance. I met them when we had an investment demand. We had old machines and needed new ones. So I went to Germany to company XY, because they make these machines....I went with 10 colleges – Chinese and German. We also went to another company in France. And in the end company XY said 'ok let's get this woman in our company'". (Translated from German)*

> *H., VP: "Why did I change? It wasn't really planned. I was almost an accident how I got into XY (agency name) because XY hired someone from my team. They were doing reference check with me about her. We had a very good chat. I had a very good chat with the headhunter that was working with XY. At end of the conversation she said it was such a good chat would you ever consider XY for yourself? It was one of those moments and I felt I was still quite young. I was 28. I just felt I was still at the beginning stage of my career I could still look around and see and experience different companies. Of course they offered one step higher in terms of title from manager to director. I didn't think so hard about it. I felt when I was so young it could only be positive for me to experience."*

"It comes both ways – opportunity and choice, always approached by headhunter" was how one interviewee summarised the issue of planned and unplanned career steps. Some women reported unplanned steps arising from their personal lives; one woman described becoming pregnant with her second child, while another followed her husband to Hong Kong when he took a position there and adapted her career to her husband's new place of work. Another woman described how she returned from abroad due to her elderly parents and accepted the negative impact that this decision brought with it. These descriptions of individual cases are in line with the findings of Mainiero et al. (2005), according to which women's careers always incorporate and take account of relationships.

A., Legal Director: "Most of the jobs I choose were my own decision. Other than moving to Hong Kong. That role was not really my move, my initiative. My husband decided to move there. I had no choice but to make that move. It was a very difficult move because I didn't think with my profession I could find another job in Hong Kong. I had to compromise. I have to compromise even though the job may not be what I really like I still took out. It turned out; I really have to look at the positive sides of a job. There's always something you can learn from and looking back I think I would still appreciate that part of the experience."

One factor that had a significant impact on most of the women's careers was economic developments. For example, the women reported that they had not anticipated the Asian financial crisis, which had tangible consequences for their careers; unplanned consequences for some of the interviewees included restructurings and downgrading. Many of the women chose to change jobs due to the effects of these unanticipated developments on the market. Again, this shows a proactive response to unplanned occurrences (see also the earlier section on reasons for changing jobs).

Another unplanned factor described by one woman was finding that the new corporate culture she encountered after switching from a multinational company to a private Chinese one was not to her liking. This woman described the unanticipated challenges that followed this risky career move, which eventually led to the unplanned step of changing jobs again.

The descriptions of unplanned career steps, which were few in number, often relate to the early stages of the women's careers, in which many women described themselves as experimenting. There were also unplanned career steps resulting from job offers that came from external sources. All the women described market developments such as the Asian financial crisis as unplanned occurrences. Other factors were only described in individual cases. The descriptions lend further support to the claim that, overall, the women have mainly internal career loci, since most of the women responded proactively to unplanned events with a clear focus on their individual career goals and modified their behaviour according to different situations.

Downsides and challenges of careers

The women were asked to describe downsides to careers. Overall, there were relatively few responses compared with the other questions.

Table 31: Downsides of career

Downsides of career
health concern, stress
fear of weakness, fear to disappoint, fear of being seen as incompetent
loneliness, not being liked by everybody
no second child, no family, gave up relationship overseas
little private time, little vacation, too much travelling, being forced to be always online
conflicting roles (childcare)
unfair company decisions on own career, move to headquarters (pay cut)

Their answers can be divided into several categories. Firstly, a few women described the impact on family life. Individual examples included deciding not to have a second child, being lonely as a single woman or choosing career over a particular partner. Only one woman mentioned conflicts between the role of mother and the role of career woman. She compared single women and men, and identified respects in which women are disadvantaged compared with men ("they can devote 100 percent to their careers"). It is interesting that this woman is married to a foreign husband who works full-time and has two young children; hence, her family situation is atypical for the women in this group.

> H., VP: "I think the down side again is you cannot be perfect on both fronts. What I tell myself is on the home front; sometimes I am definitely not as perfect as the other moms who can go to the schools. Cannot be on the school activities. Not go on school outings with them. I would love to be on that but I cannot. I cannot be as perfect as they are. At work I cannot compete with someone like – imagine there is something equally capable as I am but he or she can put in 50% more time to travel or network. I cannot do that and they deserve more opportunities than I am to get the next promotion. I am okay with that. I think that here are downsides on both fronts but for me this is the best outcome for me. The total outcome and I am very happy with that."

The second main category relates to health. Some of the women reported stress and pressure, and being worried about their health. According to these women, having a very high workload for many years can have consequences for one's health. There was a particular emphasis on the strain placed on them by frequent business trips. One woman remarked that men over 30 can pursue their careers aggressively for many years to come, while this tends not to be possible for women. This remark was made in connection with the strains that careers can place on women's health. Four women described feeling afraid. In particular, they are afraid of failing and being unable to live up to what is demanded of them. One woman was specifically afraid that she would never rise to CEO level. Other downsides that were described included the loneliness that goes with being in an executive position and the issue of how to deal with no longer being universally liked.

> *A., VP: "I feel sometimes there are some voices, concern is you would take more responsibility. Keep too much pressure for yourself. Just things like my health, maybe life. All these are things. Energy. I don't want to disappoint people but I don't want to over commit over myself. I just say I want to do something I can reasonably control. People sometimes have a middle age crisis. They don't know what the next one is. There is no ending. So I choose say is this really global, Asia Pacific role can bring me a lot of joy out of this? Probably a little bit but no. It's not truly what I really want."*

> *C., President: "I guess that of course you know with the role comes the stress and you just have to find ways to deal with the stress and sometimes of course you feel a little bit lonely because you ask me I'm the most senior person here. My boss is miles away and you also do not want to cry to your boss or complain to your boss although sometimes I do. You don't want to do that all the time or your boss will feel like you are just complaining. You have to do that. I think that you just have to handle stress. You just have to at least come across as professional especially the people who are younger and who are more junior. You do not want to come across as panicking or weak or don't know what to do. Because if you don't know what to do, how can they. I think that is really perhaps if you call it the downside. You just have to find a way to handle it."*

A few women criticised unfair decisions made by their companies that impacted on their careers. One woman described spending time abroad at the company headquarters, which she expected would have a positive impact on her career, as actually putting her at a disadvantage. She was not able to make full use of her capacities at the head office, and was downgraded when she returned since there were no suitable vacancies in senior roles at the company. Another downside experienced by some women is that companies function according to their own rules and some women were put in jobs that they did not like. Another woman reported downsides resulting from a poor fit between her personality and the corporate culture. She gave the example of the different national cultures and business styles at the head offices of US, EU and French companies, and how these differed from her own preferred style.

> *T., GM: "I won't say I regret. Because I, I think this is a very good question. I think for female versus male, male could be assertive, aggressive, over the period of 30, 40 years and then there's still for some of my male colleagues almost about same age they are still very aggressive. But for the female because we don't have more, we don't have a lot of females at this level anyway so I feel very lonely and also I feel if you are male you really want this type of career you might as well get it because you really need it for your self-actualization. I may not need it. I have a lot of things to do on my plate. So I think at certain level, certain age we certainly. I don't know. Because I don't have a family so don't have a lot of family burden. I certainly realize maybe that's good for me or I don't know if it's the peers or if it's the socialization I had in Hong Kong. . I, I might be a lot more aggressive to get more things but I chose not to."*

When the women were then asked about challenges they have faced in the course of their careers, many of them spontaneously replied that mistakes are probably necessary in order for an executive to really grow and become successful. The women reported the various challenges they have faced during their careers which represented the biggest obstacles for them personally. Their answers can be grouped into different areas, with most answers occurring in the categories cultural challenges and leadership. Table 32 shows the coded answers.

Table 32: Challenges during career

Cultural Challenges	*Politics at headquarters, not enough exposure to headquarters, not enough local power* *Intercultural misunderstandings, communication issues, intercultural leadership* *Adapting to new culture overseas, moving within EU during merger* *Relocating, finding good position on return to China* *Compliance issues*	15
Leadership	*Managing older staff, learning leadership, mistakes as a leader, leadership in high turnover culture* *Assertiveness(management at state-owned company, silo thinking of different departments,* *managing back office), Feeling powerless*	10
Influence of economy	*Economic crisis, restructuring, downgrading, had to make layoffs in huge waves*	4
Heteronomy	*Forced to do jobs that I did not like for an extended period*	4
Personal duties	*Small children, no sleep, second child, travel between two homes, family duties* *Having no children, caring for elderly parents, following husband to US with no job, feeling isolated*	5
Competing	*Competition*	2
Constant changes	*Constant need to learn, to be fast, to add value, constant change, feeling of pressure*	3
Influence of society	*Pressure from people around them and parents when leaving state-owned job*	1

Some women described the challenges of adapting to different cultures when they moved abroad. One participant recounted how isolated she felt in the USA; the challenge in her case was loneliness. Another woman found the experience of having to relocate several times within Germany and Switzerland due to a merger to be challenging, since she had no network there and felt alone. A problem that was also mentioned was the difficulty of gaining a foothold in cities such as London on a career-entry salary. Another woman described the early stages of her career in Singapore, where one of the women she was living with stole from one the others. The police became involved, and it was a big challenge for the young woman to deal with authorities in a foreign country in relation to a conflict of that kind. Meanwhile, one interviewee found the different way of working in her host country challenging.

> *J., COA (about time in Germany): "That was actually another challenge because although we brought XY (Company name), there are no AB (own company name) people. There are 5,000 XY colleagues and people move from (town in Germany) there and the entire AB people is less than 100 and I only know less than 10 or 20. So I need to find my way to survive in Berlin. I do in-*

terviewing with XY accounting people to find a new job basically. I still worked in the global controlling department but I changed a little bit their direction. In Wuppertal I started with the working capital management and added together integration with XY. I moved to XY basically they had everybody denied in this position but I am the one wanting to move. Not every German wants to move. So I changed the department to be controlling excellence ..."

C., HR (about working in France): "First I think the working, the way of working. The way of working is different. The understanding of collaboration is different as well. At very beginning I think the most difficult thing for me is you, every week, we had weekly meetings to oversee all our training courses and evaluations of (inaudible). Every training course. For some colleagues, when there some problem, they think it's your problem. They don't want to work for your problem. They just want to work for themselves. 'This is my course. Don't touch my course.' For others course nothing to do with me. So when I arrived I asked them to work together. To put everything on a big bulletin just like this to put every weekly thing and to share information together."

Hence, few examples in this category relate to challenges with first expatriations such as different ways of working and managing international employees abroad. These descriptions could be interpreted as running counter to the descriptions of intercultural skills given in the section on competencies. On this point, it should be noted that it was mainly a few of the women who have lived abroad for extended periods who reported challenges with expatriation. One explanation could be that the ability to move between worlds, which are highly advantageous for the executive women in China, was largely or completely irrelevant in the positions they held abroad. There it was less important to be able to move between Chinese and foreign cultures than it was to be able to adapt to the local culture alone. These descriptions reflect challenges that are also faced by many expats of other nationalities when they work abroad. For example, two women who returned to China from abroad (from Germany and France respectively) found that their overseas experience did not bring about promotions but, on the contrary, led to them having lower positions than before they went abroad.

J., COA (about returning from Germany): "Very unhappy. I shouted to my bosses, say how come. One of the reasons I came back to China was because of the family. My parents this year are 75 already. I want to move back to Beijing to be closer to them and take care more of them. This is also the difference Chinese and Western people. We are more family oriented. I'm moving back to China but not in Beijing but I also felt treated unfair because the other lady doesn't want to move to Shanghai. I have to. The boss says you don't move to Shanghai you can come back to Beijing. What position? He says I can give you projects. But it's not what I want. I want some real thing. Although I'm really unhappy I talk with my previous bosses, the German guys because we are really good friends. They are like my mentors. I decided ok I move to Shanghai. I take the one with real things. That's the reason I'm now in Shanghai."

C., HR (about returning from France): "It was planned for two years. From two to three years. And in China almost at the end of the two years my boss told me there's vacancy for staffing director, I want to come back? Every time when he came to Paris for meetings I always said boss don't forget me. I'm always willing to work with. So if there's any vacancy don't hesitate to tell me. Let me know. Because another reason, my husband doesn't speak English, neither French. He loves the living in Paris but it's the communication language problem. You can never really enjoy the time. So after two years I decided to come back to the new role ..."

However, in both these cases personal reasons were key factors behind the women's return to China and the resulting problems. These two women were unable to manage the balancing act between pursuing a career abroad and securing a promotion on their return, and hence ended up being downgraded instead. Cultural challenges were not just limited to differences between foreign cultures; there were also reports of such challenges arising from differences between corporate cultures within China. The issue of compliance was mentioned repeatedly. The main challenge in this regard was dealing with differences in values between companies when switching to a new employer. One woman described how, when it came to compliance, her superiors had values opposed to her own.

A., Legal Director: "XY (Company name) has actually very tough environment. The business environment is tough. XY's own business is tough. It's at a time of reforming. I have to pick up because of a lack of headcount I was asked to pick up some compliance job as well. It was really a good experience for me to know, to deal with people. Difficult people in their job to make difficult decisions. I cover employment law. I cover HR, so employment area. For a short period of time I covered companies. Just to give an example we had a case that had potential FCPA. Do you know FCPA? Foreign Corrupt Practices Act. FCPA issues. So we had to make difficult decisions to terminate a few of the employees. We receive strong resistance from the bases and at the end we still managed to do that. It was difficult ..."

Other examples of challenges arising from different business cultures included changing from a service provider role as an external consultant to an in-house corporate position or switching to a different consumer market, and the difficulty of adapting to the different environments, ways of working and mindsets that come with such changes.

H., VP: "I didn't have a very large team. I don't remember. I think I had five or six people. It was quite a challenge because I joined as the leader for the consumer practice. I quickly realized consumer is not for me. I think the challenge is the people on my team are really into consumer type of work. I think the challenging part is my heart is not on consumer. So I didn't, but then I quickly moved, they moved me to corporate practice and I felt the fit was better."

Several women mentioned leadership challenges. One executive who works in sales found asserting herself to be a particular challenge, for example when she had to manage older men in the sales department. Other women reported that they sometimes found it difficult to win their teams' trust and to learn how much to delegate. They regarded dismissals of team members as personal defeats. Examples were also given of managing multicultural teams abroad, which was seen as a particular challenge.

BU Head: "I think it was very challenging because my peers in 2000, my peers my directs are another 11 branch sales manager. The average their age is ten years older than me. There are only two ladies. And I'm one of it. I'm very young and lady so people look at me very different. And my direct reports some are ten years older than me so it's very challenging for me to manage the team. Some of them are very experienced and ten years older than me but because the two company merge some people left. For me half is existing colleague for three to four years but the rest is new hiring because some left the company. For the guys just joined us much easier because we can find people who have same value proposition with you. Some agree with you. But for me it was very challenging to manage the direct reports, ten years older than me. Also my peers were ten years older than me so it is challenging."

Only five of the 35 women reported on the challenge of combining a career at a large corporation (and the mobility this necessitates) with their duties as mothers. Some of them accepted living far away from their families for work and having to commute long distances to see their children. Other women described the challenge of combining their workload and working hours with their role as the mothers of two children. They reported dealing with emails at night for long periods of time. Once again, having two children appears to represent a particular challenge for the women in this study. One woman reported that she was forced to give up her job when she became pregnant with her second child, because her employer feared restrictions due to the one-child policy.

> HRD: *"It was a difficult decision to be honest.... I felt very happy working in that company...I enjoyed my life in Tianjin before. When this came to us actually we were seeking do we want to keep the baby or not. Because even the beginning both parents in law and my parents didn't support that decision. They feel you don't have to have a second baby. And you have such good job. Such good career in that company. Why do you want to give up? So I talk with my husband. Sometimes we want to keep sometime we want to give up. But my husband and I come to a consensus that we want to keep the baby because that's a life. It's a given. We didn't plan but since it's given. It's a life, it's something for us, so we decided to keep the baby. Then I talk with my boss and share with my family members that we want to keep the baby. Then they tell me the parents since we made the decision already we cannot change it. We help you anyway. If you decide we help you.*

> *Actually after I deliver the baby, after one or two months' rest I talk back to my old boss because actually we were kind of keep contact for a while and he said, yes, come back I have a job for you. I said actually because of family reason I want to stay in Shanghai. I delivered baby in Shanghai. Then he said okay let me find a Shanghai job for you and eventually he did find one for me in Shanghai and I was about to go back to the old company and we made an appointment with my boss and say tomorrow I'm going to come back, meet him. So we met in a restaurant and unfortunately he was very sad. Sorry, I have bad news for you, I cannot take you back. I talk to HR and legal and they didn't support this. They still feel there is a risk for the company even after the delivery of the baby. So I was shocked. Oh. Because even I made the decision before I left the company I feel I had support because my boss says he want to get me back. So I was pretty uncomfortable."*

Restructurings during the Asian financial crisis were mentioned as another challenge. In particular, four HRDs reported having to implement large waves of layoffs themselves. The conflict between, on the one hand, their own values and their fundamental desire to support employees and foster their development and, on the other, the necessity of reducing staff numbers was difficult for several of the women. They said that although they successfully mastered the challenge, the situation placed a great strain on them. Other factors mentioned in this connection included the pressure arising from the fast pace and constant changes and the difficulty of persevering with jobs they did not enjoy. The women see themselves as faced with the challenge of remaining constantly up to date and keeping pace with rapidly changing markets, for example retail or consulting. Persevering with certain less enjoyable phases at their companies was described as a challenge that was necessary for their career development. According to the women, they have learned that such phases are inevitable if one spends a long time at the same company.

One of the older women in the study described social norms and the pressure that can result as career challenges. Since she left the defined, state-assigned career path at a very early stage and proactively opted for the new, more autonomous career type that was still in its infancy, she felt judged by many people around her. In retrospect, she regards the risk of departing from safe, defined career paths and taking new, uncertain paths as a challenge.

> *A., VP: "But at that time I think the government in the country say, just initiative you can resign from a state-owned company and I feel I was the first person in my (inaudible Chinese name) county, which is in the education borough the first person who resigned. It's actually a lot of noise in that. My education system people there they think how can she? First of all nobody resigned at that time because as teacher is still dream job for many people. You can teach and it's a state-owned company. You are guaranteed rights and decent jobs. Then you resign and you work in a remote city you do not know and it's called a capitalist. We were educated that capitalist always exploit the people. Like this. My parents at that time my mother was very worried. She said, really you want to put yourself in the risk."*

In summary, the women's accounts of the challenges they have faced in their individual careers show how their flexibility (previously described in earlier sections) confronted them with various challenges for them. Most of these challenges concerned cultural factors or leadership. There were also many descriptions of situations specific to individual cases. In this context, the women's capacity to embrace and deal with challenges was critical. In particular, there were examples of individual cases where women were temporarily unable to make the desired progress in their careers after they returned from working abroad. How the women deal with setbacks and their strength at doing so were described earlier in section 4.2.3.

Future career goals – higher up and abroad

Descriptions of the women's hopes and ideas for their own future careers were recorded for 32 of the 35 women. Seventeen of the women described a clear goal of career progression, specifying desired positions such as CEO/GM, VP, regional director or board member. All of these women equate further progress in their careers with hierarchical advancement. Ten women responded with descriptions of self-development and learning. The women also often mentioned values connected to the image they wish to present, such as "having a good reputation as respectable advisor to others". Three women specifically mentioned that they believe a job abroad could provide the opportunity for self-development that they crave. Two of the women envisioned an independent future outside the corporate world. One imagined being a freelancer while the other saw herself running her own hospital. The former revealed that she wants to work as a freelance coach and trainer in order to have a better work-life balance and a greater sense of purpose. The woman who wishes to open her own hospital said that she comes from a family of independent means and regards the idea as an act of social philanthropy. It is notable that these two women are both widows who lost their first partners to severe illnesses.

Three of the women have "no clear dream" or have goals that are more personal in nature. All three appeared to be uncertain or frustrated about their next career step. One woman said that she has clearly come up against the glass ceiling in her company; the next step would be the GM position, which has previously been reserved for foreigners and is hence (she believes) more or less unattainable for her. This means that a total of five women do not wish to continue along the corporate career ladder. Two of them have a specific, credible alternative to corporate careers. The other three currently appear to be aimless or resigned. Four of the women mentioned more personal factors in relation to their career goals. This is consistent with the group as a whole, whose weighting of private and professional goals has been constant across different sections of the survey. Most of the women did not mention issues from their personal lives in response to this question. Hence, two tendencies can be identified in this group with regard to future career plans: hierarchical advancement and professional development. Only five of the thirty-five women expressed a desire to leave the corporate world or did not have any specific goals, which once again indicates that the group has a high career orientation, including with respect to the future.

Future prospects: Views on China's economic development in the coming years and the impact this will have on female executives

When the women were asked about their views on China's future development, a large majority of the answers predicted a very positive situation for female executives in China in future. Only three of the women expressed pessimistic views and two predicted that conditions would become more difficult for men and women alike. Only one of the thirty-five interviewees believed that it would be difficult for women to reach GM level in future. And only one other woman expressed the view that more women will stay home to look after their children, a matter that is the topic of ongoing debate in China.

Table 33: Future development of China and situation of female Chinese executives

	Answers	
Positive for China	11	*Growth, new industries, optimistic Opportunities*
Positive for women	15	*Independent, better educated, more women leaders, industries dominated by women, more open-minded globally* *More innovative, driver of economy, more female CEOs* *Many opportunities for women due to small talent pool*
Positive for men and women	1	
More difficult for China	6	*Phase of quality is starting, slowing down, mature, fewer jobs*
More difficult for men and women	2	
More difficult for women	3	*Question of CEO level for women remains (1)* *More difficult in IT industry than before* *More women might stay home one year to look after children (1)*

The women's views on private companies as a possible option for their own future careers were already mentioned in the section on the effect of choice of company type. Table 34 summarises the coded opinions about the option of working at a private Chinese company. It is evident that Chinese private companies are seen as a major potential future sector. As well as financial benefits, many of the women see a large number of opportunities for themselves, since they believe these companies need more global management expertise and so will want to hire qualified and experienced executives in the future. More critical voices regarded this option as risky for their own careers, since problems of cultural adaptation could become challenges.

Table 34: Opinions on option of future career at a private Chinese company

Private companies will be the segment of the future, they will become private Chinese multinationals
It is a possible future option for me (7)
Owners are visionary and inspiring
They invest highly in people, high financial rewards (3)
It was a very interesting experience for me (2)
They are very new and will need expertise
Not my choice (2)
Big cultural change, all depends on owner (1)
Risk, family businesses are relationship-based (not based on performance) (1)

Three different tendencies can be identified in the closing statements, for which the women were asked to complete the sentence "In the future, female Chinese executives ..." Most of the answers emphasised the advantages enjoyed by female executives, their equality in China and the good opportunities that exist for women in senior management compared with other countries due to factors such as better familial support. Other answers focused on future opportunities that would require the women to undertake further personal development first. A minority of only four answers related to the compatibility of career and family. This once again confirms the picture of the situation of female Chinese executives presented in this study. Unlike in prevailing discussions in the West, most of the interviewees in this study do not regard the compatibility of different roles as a central factor in descriptions of women's management careers in China.

8. Five pattern to senior management:
Career typology of female Chinese executives

Bounded global – Unbounded global – Stop and go – Flexible hoppers – Lean on and move up

There are various typologies of women's careers in existing career theory literature. Some examples, such as the theories of Lepine (1992), O'Neil (2008) and other researchers, have already been presented before. Many typologies are based on two criteria; for instance, O'Neil's typology is based on the factors career loci and career patterns, while Forrier's and Verbruggen's (2005) typology is based on the dimensions of career path and career aspiration. The first criterion for developing the typology for this research was the women's career paths. In addition, determinants that have a particularly high impact on the career paths were selected from the determinants described in the first part of the research. This enabled a very precise description of the different types. The women's personalities and motivations were criteria that could be derived from the individual determinants. The first step was to assess whether the paths were "bounded" (to a single company) and followed a traditional linear or ladder-like structure, or were "boundaryless" (as per DeFillippi and Arthur, 1994), with no ties or only weak ones to particular companies. Boundaryless careers were defined as "sequences of job opportunities that go beyond the boundaries of a single employment setting". Traditional bounded or "organizational careers", on the other hand, evolve within the context of a single company (Arthur and Rousseau, 2001).

In addition, in accordance with the definitions of O'Neil et al. (2004), it was also assessed whether the careers were ordered or emergent. According to O'Neil, an ordered career pattern is characterised "in terms of linear, sequential or ladder-like career advancement, choiceful learning opportunities and strategic planning and execution". An ordered career path involves purposive career enhancement behaviours. An emergent career pattern, by contrast, is a reactive rather than a proactive path, marked by unexpected twists and turns and serendipitous events, that is designed to accommodate aspects of one's life other than traditional work. It is a career path that involves responsiveness, fluid movement in and out of organisations and accommodation of non-work-related priorities. Alongside these criteria, the typology also incorporated the factor of geographic mobility, since this was of great importance in most of the career paths included in this study. A distinction is drawn between international mobility, local mobility within China and career paths that were confined to Shanghai. The career determinants that had a particular impact on different subgroups were taken from among the external and individual factors described earlier in this study. It was assessed which factors were described as having a stronger or weaker impact on the women's career paths. The classification of impact as strong or weak was based on the women's descriptions and, in line with the qualitative character of the study as a whole, is not quantified on a scale. The classification is hence subjective and unsuitable for quantitative comparisons.

The factors of internal and external career loci, as per O'Neil et al. (2004), lend themselves to assessing career motivation and orientation. According to O'Neil, an internal locus is reflected in a belief that one is responsible for one's own career success and in charge of creating and managing one's future career. Guan, Wang and Dong et al. (2012) examined the concept of career locus amongst Chinese employees and showed a positive relation of an internal career locus to objective and subjective career success. Hall's (2004) notion of a protean career as "based on self-direction in the pursuit of psychological success in one's work" reflects an internal career locus. An external career locus, on the other hand, reflects the belief that one's career direction and career success occur due to chance (being in the right place at the right time) or as a result of some other external intervention such as a network of contacts from which career opportunities emanate (cf. e.g. Allen et al., 2000) or institutionally determined structures. In a second, separate stage, all the women's career paths were restructured and grouped according to these criteria. Table 43 shows an overview of the five career patterns that resulted from the analysis of the career paths. How strongly the determinants influenced the careers was defined as follows: "(very) high" refers to factors that are highly and continuously relevant for the career paths of all the women in a particular subgroup; "medium" refers to career determinants that were described a few times some of the women in this group; "low" refers to factors that were described as being of little or no relevance, were not mentioned at all or were mentioned by less than 10% of the women in the group. The main characteristics of the different types are described in detail below. The descriptions incorporate the earlier findings from the qualitative content analysis of the group as a whole.

Table 35: Overview of the Career Pattern Typology of Female Chinese Executives (Career Typology-FCE) at multinational companies (Al-Sadik-Lowinski, 2017)

(* Total of 34 women, one exceptional case)

	Bounded global	Unbounded Global	Stop and go	Flexible hop-pers	Lean on and move up
Career path	Bounded	Unbounded			
Mobility	Global	Global	Local/global	Local	Local
Pattern	Ordered ladder	Ordered linear	Emergent	Ordered serpentine	Emergent/ordered
Determinant					
Intercultural	Very high Specific	Very high Broad	High	High	High
Mentoring	High	Medium	Low	Medium (various)	Very high
Family	Low	Low	Very high	Low	Medium
Personality/ Motivation	*Organisational Loyalty*	*Achievement orientation* *Assertiveness*	*Balance roles*	*Looking for challenge and variety* *Assertiveness, curiosity*	*Building trust and loyalty to mentor* *Developing others*
Career locus	Internal	Internal	Internal	Internal	External
Number in this study	3	10	8	10	3

1.   Bounded global

The three women classified in this group all began their careers in Germany working for a German company after having first studied there. Hence, the first phase of their careers took place in Germany; however, they were already firmly planning to return to China to pursue their careers. Two of the women work at German DAX companies and one woman works at a medium-sized German automotive parts supplier. All three have only worked at a single company: there has been no inter-company mobility, and their careers can be described as bounded and upwards linear or ladder-like. They all moved from staff jobs at the outset of their careers to line jobs fairly rapidly, within one-and-a-half, three and four years respectively, after they moved from Germany to China.

All the women have reached GM or V-GM level, and have responsibility for the whole company or major units at national level. They have previously held a diverse range of positions at their companies, and hence have wide-ranging experience within these companies.

All the women lived in Germany for an extended period and so are very familiar with the culture and language. All three made contact with their future companies while still at university, either through internships or their dissertation project. One of the women was sent to Sweden and South Africa for short projects as a trainee while she was still a student. The women described how their companies carefully prepared them for a career in China and that the fact that they were Chinese was the most important selection criterion for their hiring. Conversely, they themselves had specifically selected the companies in order to be able to pursue a career in China. Apart from the time they spent in Germany, international mobility at the start of their careers included one woman spending time in Hong Kong and another woman going to Sweden and South Africa for short projects. Two of the women have worked for their companies in other Chinese cities besides Shanghai, and so have also exhibited mobility within China over the course of their careers. The women's descriptions reveal the main determinant of their careers to be their specialised intercultural competence. They possess in-depth knowledge and an equally strong understanding of German and Chinese cultures and ways of working, including strong language skills. This intercultural competence was necessary in order to establish trust in their performance and loyalty among German bosses. All the women have a strong network at their companies' German headquarters, and are able to move relatively effortlessly between Chinese and German management cultures. The longer the women spent in Germany, the more they reflected on differences between German and Chinese ways of working and responses to leadership. It appears that the women tend more towards the German way of working, which may *inter alia* be due to the fact that they worked hard to adapt while still at university. Over the course of their careers, they have demonstrated a high degree of flexibility in responding to their companies' requirements, as is evident in their assuming responsibility for various areas in various places in China. In doing so, they have developed their knowledge and experience strategically, which is characteristic of ordered career paths (O'Neil et al., 2004).

> *One example for the "Bounded Global" group is E., GM who works for a German company. She started as a trainee (an internal company program for young people without University degree) in a large Multinational in Germany. In her first career step she was offered a position in Hong Kong as Assistant Manager. With support of the company she returned to Germany to finish a University Diploma. She explained that being Chinese in a German company was her competitive advantage and that the company developed her for a career in China. Two different bosses in that company supported her as informal Mentors. After university she returned to the same company as a financial*

controller. In a next step she took a financial controller position in China. She moved consequently up the ladder with taking CFO and Holding-CFO positions before finally becoming GM in her most recent career step. E. is married to a Chinese and has two children. She was commuting between Beijing and Shanghai, where her family lived, for longer periods. During the interview she never mentioned the wish of changing companies.

These women's career paths are typified by a strong bond with their companies. This is typical of traditional, ladder-like career paths, which according to career theory were common in the past and still remain so today in many cases, especially at large companies (Rump, 2003). What is distinctive about their career paths is the determinant of intercultural competence, which constitutes these women's major competitive advantage. None of the women described their career path as depending on the local labour market context. This means that the women were not affected by the restructurings triggered by the Asian financial crisis. However, one of the women deviated from the seamless, conventional career path at one point, when she resigned and took a year-long break after working in a role with a high level of responsibility where she restructured the company's entire Asian division. However, she subsequently returned to the company and continued her career progression. She said the reasons she resigned were the enormous challenges involved in the restructuring and a temporary dissatisfaction with her own role. She had a child during the break, though this was not the reason for her resignation but something that happened subsequently. Afterwards, she decided to return to the same employer in a new role works manager. She then became VP strategy and finally general manager for China. Hence, in this case internal structural changes were the reason for a short-term career break. It can be considered atypical for someone to be able to seamlessly resume their career at a German company after resigning. Family has not been a major influencing factor for this group. Two of the women have children (one woman has one child, the other has two) and are married to Chinese husbands who are less ambitious about their careers. The third woman is still single at the age of 32. She rose up the ranks at a very young age and at the time of the interview was planning to start a family. The woman with two children exhibits a particularly high level of local geographic mobility; she travels long distances between work in Beijing and her family in Shanghai.

All three women have more internal career loci and plan their careers strategically. Both choosing to study in Germany and to work for a German company in China were actively planned steps. All three associate career success with hierarchical advancement. This advancement came very quickly for the youngest participant in the study group. For the next step in her career, she is now looking for a challenge (in her own words, "more competition") at the German head office. This group is similar in some respects to the fast track group in Lepine (1992). The women in Lepine's study also quickly reached line jobs, had low employer mobility and worked at large companies. They were also similar in respect to family life, though the women in Lepine's study planned to have children either very early in their careers or at a later stage, which was not something mentioned by the women in this group. The women in Lepine's study were aware of gender constraints, and these guided their choice of company: they selected ones where they believed women's career opportunities would be less restricted. The women in this group did not select their companies on this basis. However, they did report that German men in particular often have a critical attitude towards women in senior management roles. In this regard, they have the advantage of being Chinese women with expert knowledge of Germany, which appears to have been more decisive for their career development than the discriminatory beliefs about women held by many male decision-makers in Germany.

The exceptional case

There is only one woman in the overall group whose career can be categorised as bounded and local. Since she is an exceptional case, she has not been categorised in her own subgroup. This woman has pursued a career in HR at a single large American company for her entire career to date after completing a rotation programme there and did not relocate overseas at any point. She is now HRD at the company's local research centre. However, she did spend four years in charge of a global project and spent 60% of her time travelling to other locations, such as Europe and India.

She is also an exception in the group in that she is flexible and has an achievement-oriented personality only to a certain extent, which is insufficient for her to advance further in her career. She has a mainly negative perception of her own prospects, with a focus on obstacles that limit her career. She has an external career locus and attributes responsibility for the path her career has taken to external circumstances or other people.

She is one of the locally based women in the study who expressed real regret about the fact that she has not been able to secure a position overseas. She also explained that she lacks a foreign sponsor to help her advance further in her career and that she does not know how she could initiate contact with one. She reported disadvantages that Chinese have at multinational companies compared with people from other countries. She believes one option would be to work at a state-owned company where Chinese are not disadvantaged in this way, but said that she would have no chance at such a company due to her lack of *guanxi* ties and that it is too late to make the change, since careers at state-owned companies need to be built up right from the outset. Her account, which presents external factors and circumstances as responsible for the course her career has taken, shows her external locus.

Due to the combination of a bounded local career path, external career locus and lack of international mobility, this woman cannot be assigned to any subgroup and is categorised as an exceptional case. The description of her case has been placed in this section because, like the bounded global group, she has only worked at a single company. However, she differs from the women in this subgroup on all other criteria.

2. Unbounded global

The ten women who were assigned to this subgroup have all spent time abroad in several countries outside China on one or more occasions. All but two of them studied abroad, and all have worked abroad on one or more occasions. Like the bounded global group, all the women were determined right from the outset to pursue careers in China. The women work in different industries and at companies from all three of the countries included in this study (Germany, France and the USA). The number of companies the women have worked at ranges from three (three woman), four (three women) and five (three women) to six (one women). Hence, there has been some intercompany mobility, and their careers can be described as boundaryless and upwards linear or ladder-like. The overseas experience of the women in this group differs from that of the bounded global group insofar as many of them began their careers in China and only worked abroad at a later stage. Some of the women gained experience in the USA or UK before pursuing careers at German or French companies. This means that their overseas experience is broad and not limited to their companies' countries of origin. These women have worked in two to four different countries outside China. One woman reported that when a merger took place during her time abroad, she adapted flexibly and relocated twice within Germany and once to Switzerland for her company. The women again mentioned that the fact that they were Chinese was the most important selection criterion for their hiring. They too specifically selected companies and positions with the aim of pursuing a career in China. The women in this group have reached the full range of senior levels classed as selection criteria for this study (as described earlier). The two highest-ranking women, with the title of president, are in this group, as well as two CFOs, one VP level and two senior directors. Some have experience in a broad range of different departments; others have worked exclusively in finance or sales. It is notable that five of the ten women started their careers in the consulting, headhunting or agency sectors. Another woman started out in the hotel industry. These phases of their careers varied in length from three to twelve years. This gave them various advantages, such as being able to judge complex issues from different points of view, to adopt a broad perspective on many different markets and companies and to develop large extra-organisational networks. Like the bounded global group, the main career determinant that can be identified for them is their intercultural competence, though this competence is not necessarily restricted to the nationality of their companies' head office. They also have wider-ranging global mobility than the bounded global group.

> *An example for the "Unbounded Global Group" is M., CFO at a German Company. She is highly educated with three top level degrees, two of which are international degrees, and has studied in the US. She describes herself as someone with a strong assertiveness and desire to succeed from early age. After working in Xiandu and Sechuan she took positions in Singapore, Germany, Hong Kong and Shanghai. She has changed companies five times and experienced functions in marketing and finance. She has one child and describes herself "free from home obligations". Her mother, a nanny and a housekeeper are supporting her. Her husband encourages her continued career growth and is active in child support. She sees China as more advanced in gender matters compared to Germany.*

These women's career paths are typified by a flexible choice of companies, especially at the start of their careers. This flexibility extends to the nationality of the companies' head office, inter-firm mobility and place of work. Some of the women previously worked in the USA and Germany, while others worked in the UK and then in China for Spanish and French companies. One woman relocated within Germany twice and then moved to Switzerland before going to Shanghai, though that was not where she had started out before moving abroad. Some of the women have worked in other Chinese cities besides Shanghai, and so have also exhibited mobility within China in the course of their careers. The oldest participant described how she strategically moved to Yunnan, a place where she believed there would not be many competitors with her level of qualification for the positions she was interested in. The women's intercompany mobility mostly tended to decrease later in their careers as they attained senior roles. These women also have internal career loci, with highly strategic global career planning. The oldest woman in the study group described how she went to Yunnan, somewhere nobody else wanted to go, so she could make full use of her competitive advantage and start directly at GM level. The women place emphasis on actively reflecting on their personal career ambitions and goals. The women are very flexible, both in terms of geographic mobility and accepting new responsibilities, and use challenges as an opportunity for advancement. They have strategically planned their own careers, and changes of location do not represent barriers; rather, they are firmly integrated into their plans and goals. All the women associate career success with hierarchical advancement. The women in this group are typified by very high achievement orientation coupled with strong assertiveness. Some of the women described how they were supported by mentors they chose themselves. However, this factor is only a moderately strong determinant of this group's career development. Family has not been a major influencing factor for this group either. This group's family situations differed from those of the majority of the overall group. Five women in this group are childless (out of a total of nine in the study group as a whole) and three are single (out of a total of four in the group as a whole). One woman only became a mother in her late 30s, a relatively late age by Chinese standards. Several of these women described how they prioritised their careers over the demands of familial roles. For instance, one interviewee lived away from her child on other continents for several years. Another woman left behind a potential life partner in the UK to take up a position in China. Only one of the women has two children and is married to a freelancer, who she described as not being career-oriented. When asked whether this influenced her choice of partner, she replied that it had certainly made her career planning easier.

3.   Stop and go

Eight women from the overall group whose career paths can be categorised as boundaryless were assigned to this subgroup. The frequency of company changes in this group is highly varied. Some women have changed companies twice, most have changed four times and one has worked at ten different companies. Again, these women cover the full spectrum of senior management roles. At the time of the interviews, they were GMs, VPs or senior directors. Four of the women were pursuing careers in HR. Other careers were centred on marketing, communications, finance and legal affairs. Four of the women attained line jobs after an average of five years, while it took two other women ten years to do so. Their career paths are characterised by an alternation of upward and lateral moves with varying frequency. They correspond to Richardson's (1996) account of snake-like careers or what Gersick et al. (2002) calls zigzag patterns. Many of the women have had career breaks when they went part-time, took time off or temporarily ran their own businesses. Some of them were even temporarily downgraded to more junior roles. However, the overall trajectory of all their careers is in the direction of continued hierarchical advancement. The main career determinants for these women are family and relationships. Their career paths are strongly emergent and, in line with O'Neil's et al. (2008) definition, involve responsiveness, fluid movement in and out of organisations and accommodation of non-work-related priorities. All but one of the women in this group have children. Three of the women have two children; all three have career-oriented husbands and one has a foreign husband. In total, six women in this group are married to men who are also career-oriented. This differs from the norm in the overall group, where the women typically have one child and a non-career-oriented husband. The women with two children in particular find themselves constantly trying to balance two different roles, career woman and mother. They receive emotional support from their husbands but little in the way of practical help that alleviates some of the demands placed on them. However, all the women also have housekeepers. It is notable that these women do not want to delegate certain aspects of their children's upbringing, such as helping their children with their homework. When asked if they have considered delegating some of these tasks, they rejected the possibility. They see it as one of their core duties to help their children with their homework themselves.

> One example for the "Stop and Go" group is A., legal director at an American company, married to a General Manager; two children. Her career path in four different companies is upwards oriented but shows breaks and lateral phases. She followed her husband to Hong Kong where she had to re-adjust her career into a new direction. After returning to China she took a six-month break to organize her family. Breaking from Chinese tradition, she parents without support from her or her spouses parents. Conflicts about sharing child education come up during the interview due to the dual career situation. She describes that without familial responsibilities her career advancement would have been faster. However, she also acknowledges that her Hong Kong experience that provided her with certain challenges was beneficial for her overall professional experiences. In her role orientation she wants to have a strong career but also take a stronger position in the education of her two children.

Over the course of their careers, the women in this group have at times made decisions that prioritised family over career. Examples include going part-time after the birth of their second child, something that is unusual in China, or a woman who quit her job for the sake of her son and his school when her company relocated. One woman switched to another company because her husband was also pursuing his career at the company where she had originally worked. Another returned home from abroad after a relatively short time, even though she knew this would prevent further career progression, because her Chinese husband could not adapt to life in France. One special case in the group is a woman who was dismissed when she had a second daughter, since the multinational company feared restrictions as a result of the one-child policy. Three of the women gave up their jobs in China and followed their husbands abroad when the latter took up overseas positions for the sake of their own careers. Their career progression differed from conventional corporate career paths; for example, they did an MBA, started their own business or (in one case) took up a post at a consultancy instead of continuing in a role at a company's legal department. In each of these cases, it was not possible for the women to seamlessly continue their careers in the other country, and so they adapted their plans accordingly. None of the women remained unemployed for long. Due to unconventional career steps that led them outside the corporate world, the women have accumulated a greater breadth of experience than the women in the other subgroups. Examples of the women's forays into independence and new experiences outside the corporate world included running an online service for Chinese export, providing consulting services for American companies who wanted to set up subsidiaries in China and running an internal university for a big-name American food company as a freelancer working from a remote home office. These women's career loci can be described as internal, since – despite a focus on their roles within their families at certain stages – they manage their careers autonomously and creatively, continuously building up their expertise. Nonetheless, when asked whether they think they could have progressed further in their careers if, say, they had not had children, the women were relatively unanimous that they have accepted compromises in their career progression. Although Lepine's lateral plus career group is not identical to the stop and go group, some elements of Lepine's typology are also applicable to this group. Some of the women in the Chinese group took short-term career breaks to have children, or used the birth of a child as a pretext to take a break and change companies. There are also women who followed their partners abroad. However, none of the women relocated within China for the sake of their partners' careers. Women who took a break when they gave birth or who relocated abroad because of their partner did not have less inter-firm mobility. Moreover, the upward mobility at later stages of life that Lepine identified in the lateral plus career group was not evident in the women in this study. The stop and go women correspond to Mainiero's et al. (2005) Kaleidoscope Career Model, which emphasises that women make holistic choices that take relationships, constraints and opportunities into consideration. The women in this group also shift the patterns of their careers by rotating different aspects of their lives so as to arrange their relationships and roles in new ways. Over 40% of the women who participated in Mainiero's study made career changes due to family demands or followed their husbands to a different city or country. The key parameters of "balance" (between the roles), professional "challenge" and situational, context-dependent "shifting" outlined in the model are also observable in the careers of the stop and go women (Mainiero et al., 2005).

4.   Flexible hoppers

Nine women who pursued their careers exclusively in China without spending time abroad were categorised in this group. The women have worked at four to nine different companies to date and exhibit an inter-firm mobility typical of a boundaryless career path. It is characteristic of these women's career paths that they deliberately choose hierarchical advancement without being bound to any particular company long-term. They go wherever the next career opportunity, and the next higher position, waits. Hence, their career paths can be categorised as boundaryless and linear. They closely correspond to the serpentine careers described by Lehnert (1996), where individuals rise up the ranks by switching between employers. Lehnert notes that this career form still follows a path that is relatively similar to the traditional career path. It is striking that six of the women have pursued their careers in HR, and only one in purchasing. Two of the women have broader-ranging experience in multiple department types. The women have reached GM, VP and national director levels. Only three of the women have worked in other Chinese cities besides Shanghai, something that was determined by their *hukous* in the earlier stages of their careers. These three women have exhibited mobility within China in the course of their careers. The others have worked exclusively in Shanghai. Hence, this group's geographic mobility is confined to mobility within China, and in most cases confined to Shanghai. The main determinants of these women's careers are individual personality factors. They all have a strong achievement orientation, are highly assertive and curious, crave challenges and variety in their careers and want to learn a lot as quickly as possible. These factors are also present among the other women in the overall group, but based on the women's descriptions are especially pronounced among the flexible hoppers. They are also exceptionally focused on objective career success in the form of hierarchical advancement. The flexible hoppers have internal career loci: they plan and act in accordance with their individual career goals. They are also interested in continuous further development, and incorporate this into their decisions and plans. The women possess high intercultural competence, which they have mainly acquired through working with various foreign GMs. Again, their curiosity and strong desire to learn were driving factors that led to their exceptional capacity to identify, understand and adapt to cultural differences in management styles. The women in this group have benefited from possessing vital local market knowledge (especially of the HR sector) that their foreign bosses lacked.

Of the five subgroups, the flexible hoppers have been the group most affected by changes in labour market conditions. They frequently reported restructurings following the major Asian financial crisis. As HRDs, some of the women had to implement mass waves of layoffs. Conversely, they also reported being responsible for initiating large-scale training programmes for new employees during boom periods. In the context of describing such programmes at a large American chain, one woman said that her company "is like a monster". Three women reported personal burnouts as a result of the strains these situations placed them under, which led to them taking career breaks and changing companies.

> *One example for the "Flexible Hopper" group is L., HRD at an American company in the fashion industry. She left her first government assigned job as a teacher after only three months to work for multinational companies. She specialises in HR and changed companies six times until she reached the level of Human Resources Director China. She reports about mergers and market decline as challenging factors during her career building. Typical for the "Flexible Hopper", her entire career takes place in China and specifically in Shanghai. Her daughter is cared for by her 58 years old mother in law. She describes her role in the family as "being free from all duties at home". L. is very assertive, has a strong orientation to be "first among equals" from early on and welcomes competition and change.*

A few women in this group also described the unanticipated negative effects, insecurity and risks that can come with changing companies. In four cases, the women described how changing companies did not lead to the next career step that they had hoped for. Changing companies led to lateral phases or even situations where the women quickly changed companies again, for example because the new corporate culture was not a good match for their personal value system in the way they had hoped. One example of this was a woman who, when she moved to a role at a new company, found herself at the centre of an intra-company conflict between the US and EU headquarters, which had very different management styles and cultures. She left the position after just a year for a management role in a different industry. The flexible hoppers benefited from China's boom, since they were able to choose between a wide range of different job openings. This group of women take the potential risks of changing companies into account when planning their careers or are able to rapidly react to unanticipated situations, if necessary by quickly changing companies again. Family has not been a key career determinant in this group, but three women reported career decisions involving their husbands. In two cases, the women's husbands were working at the same company as them, which (alongside other reasons) forced them to change companies. One woman declined to take a particular career move at her company because, due to her husband and their two families, she did not want to leave Shanghai. However, for all the women these decisions led to further advancement rather than having a negative impact on their careers. All the women in the group are married, with one woman having remarried after the death of her first husband. All but two of them have children. Based on their accounts, the women in this group have not experienced conflicts in combining their roles as career women and mothers. The women are primarily career-oriented, and almost completely liberated from domestic chores and duties by their families and housekeepers. For example, one of the women described how her mother-in-law manages the household and oversees her child's upbringing, so that she can be relieved of all duties within the family if she wishes. Another woman described how she was frequently away on business travel even soon after the birth of her son. As a baby, he was looked after by a night *ayi* so that the woman herself could get the sleep she needed to be able to do her work.

5.   Lean on and move up

Three women who have worked in five or six companies to date were categorised in this group. They have national mobility within China but no overseas experience.

All three of the women have careers in HR and are currently national HR directors or VP-HR. Two of the women obtained line jobs after four and five years respectively, whereas the third, one of the older interviewees in the group, only obtained a line job after around 14 years. This is a result of her career being divided into two different phases, one before and one after China's economic reforms. After eight years working in a state-assigned job as a teacher, she left this safe, defined path (against the advice of her parents and all her friends) and moved from Nanchang to Shenzhen, where she worked at a travel agency. The second phase of her career began in Shanghai in 1995 at the instigation of the general manager under whom she had started as an assistant. From that point forward, her plan was to pursue a career in HR. The careers of the women in this group are boundaryless and can be described as linear with some unexpected twists. Since these twists have only been occasional and the women's careers have nonetheless been strategically planned, their career paths are categorised between ordered and emergent. The more reactive components typical of an emergent career path can be described by reference to the dominant determinant of this subgroup's careers: mentoring.

The factor of mentoring has been more important over the course of these women's careers than in the rest of the group. Relationships with one or more mentors have had a profound impact on the women's careers. The lean on and move up type is typified by a strong focus on the career steps recommended by their mentors. One of the women followed her general manager to a new company on three occasions, while another changed companies at her GM's prompting on two occasions. The older woman mentioned above reported two changes of company that she undertook on the advice of mentors (a different one in each case). The women's relationships with the mentors, most of whom were general managers from abroad, were marked by strong mutual trust and exceptional loyalty on the part of the women. Both parties benefited from the relationships. The women benefited because they could be sure of support; the mentors benefited from the women's local knowledge and from having an "extended reach" in their companies through the women. Most of the mentors were women, but some were men. These women's career paths could almost be termed "mentor-bounded", since they followed their mentors to new companies on multiple occasions. Their careers are bound to particular general managers rather than particular companies. The women explained that they have always regarded their success as HRDs as closely linked to the strength of their relationships with these general managers. At various points in the interviews, the women noted that having a close, trusting relationship with one's general manager is extremely important for career progression in an HR department at a multinational company. By working closely together with their general managers from an early stage in their careers, the women were able to become intimately acquainted with a variety of senior management styles. Their observations benefited their own career development.

Their own careers were closely linked to the reputation and success of their general managers. Two examples showed that this strategy also entails risks if the GM suffers a setback. One woman followed a female GM to a newly founded private company that collapsed after a short time. Hence, these women have more external career loci, since their own career success is linked to a mentor from whom career opportunities emanate.

These women find their work in HR fulfilling and their primary motivation is a desire to help others to develop. This is combined with a desire to advance in their careers and be given greater responsibility and wider decision-making scope. It is also noteworthy that these women are motivated to achieve as good a reputation in their field as possible, both within their companies and in Shanghai, and potentially across China as a whole. During her interview, one of them said *"I am the best HRD in China"*. Hence, subjective success criteria are particularly pronounced.

Discussion of the career pattern typology

For this typology of career paths, five types were developed based on the criterion of career paths, certain other sub criteria and a subset of the determinants described earlier in the study that enabled relevant distinctions to be drawn. Most of the career paths could be assigned to one of three larger subgroups: boundaryless global, flexible hoppers and stop and go. These career paths are all boundaryless as defined above and have internal career loci. Differences arise with respect to mobility and the impact of the determinants (as measured on the previously described basis).

Four of the five types, and 89% of the interviewed women, represent boundaryless career paths. Only four women described a traditional, bounded, ladder-like career path; three of these women work at German multinationals. All five types are characterised by geographic mobility, though there are clear differences concerning whether this mobility is international or local in scope (two subgroups tend towards international mobility, while two tend more towards local mobility). All the subgroups represent an upward managerial track. Differences with respect to how much account is taken of aspects of life other than traditional work arise in one subgroup in particular, namely the stop and go group.

The typology developed here is not identical to any of the existing typologies of women's careers found in the literature. Lepine (1992) described seven career types based on her research with 49 female Canadian managers from Quebec. In this group of female Chinese executives, there were no women with a static, transitory, downward or lateral career as defined in Lepine's typology. This may be due in part to the way participants were selected using a theoretical sampling method, as a result of which the study group consisted exclusively of women in senior management roles. Lepine's "static pattern" group describes women who stay in one and the same job after graduation, whereas the "transitory pattern" group is characterised by women who choose a series of unrelated jobs. Meanwhile, a "downwards career" path is typified by regressive job shifts and a "lateral career" path classifies women whose careers consist of a sequence of jobs that mostly involves moves between similar levels and functions. None of the other three career types described by Lepine ("fast track", "lateral plus" and "linear" careers) are a 100% match either. They are only partially comparable to the types described here. The stop and go group has some similarities with Lepine's lateral plus group. However, the groups differ in terms of job mobility, which is limited in Lepine's group. Moreover, unlike Lepine's lateral plus group, the chronological structure of the Chinese stop and go women's careers is not determined by the births of children. The "stop and go" group also comes closest to Mainiero's et al. (2005) Kaleidoscope theory. However, overall the career paths and determinants of the different types are not comparable. The bounded global group comes closest to traditional bounded career patterns, but is distinguished by a specialised intercultural competence centred on the ability to move between German and Chinese management cultures, which was one of a number of key parameters in this group. The women in the unbounded global group have international careers of a type that, according to the literature, are mostly the preserve of men. Adler (1999) writes that "few women have, as yet, had the opportunity to use all of their strengths consistently in the service of senior-level global positions". The women in the group have had experience in multiple expatriate positions, making them part of a group of women that is still very small worldwide. According to various studies, only 10–12 percent of expats from Western organisations are women (Caligiuri and Cascio, 1998). The boundaryless global group are flexible in various respects, for example concerning the nationality of the companies they choose or with regard to changes of company, location or industry. Family is not an especially important determinant in this group: half of the women are married but childless, and three of the four single women in the overall group can be found in this subgroup. This distinguishes them from traditional male expats, who are typically assumed to have wives and children.

Flexible hoppers differ sharply from traditional bounded career patterns. Unlike other studies of women, family factors are of very little importance for this group. The women pursue their careers without making compromises for the sake of their families. According to various studies, this is more typical for men. Mainiero et al. (2005) concluded that the men in her study "tended to examine career decisions from the perspective of goal orientation and independent action – acting first for the benefit of career". Men in the Mainiero study tended to keep their work and non-work lives separate and were often supported by their spouses, who relieved them of demands on their time. Like the men described by Mainiero, the flexible hoppers strategically look for opportunities for development and hierarchical advancement. They are supported by their families, are largely unburdened by familial duties and make decisions with a focus on their careers. Mainiero et al. (2005) also notes that the women in her study were "more interested in creating a career their way, through lateral but challenging assignments, opportunities that fit their lives, entrepreneurial activities or flexible scheduling, rather than focusing on advancement for the sake of advancement". One conclusion of this study, which feeds into the kaleidoscope model, is that although women are focused on career advancement, they place greater emphasis on making their careers fit their lives. Many of the descriptions from Mainiero's research fit the "stop and go" group, who strive for balance between family and career. In order to do so, they alternate between lateral and upward career steps. These women opt for career breaks and changes of company or direction in order to balance their careers with other aspects of their lives. Nonetheless, they all have a firm goal of career advancement.

Mentoring relationships are of particular importance in the lean on and move up group. However, these relationships differ from, or go beyond, other mentoring relationships, in which a mentor generally selects and supports a mentee (Kram, 1985; Levinson, 1978; Ehlich, 2008). The mentoring relationships in this group are described as having a distinctive, mutually beneficial dynamic: the mentee enjoys career support, while the mentor benefits from the mentee's local market knowledge and language skills. The relationship is based on high levels of loyalty and trust from both sides. It is worthy of note that the women followed their mentors to different companies on multiple occasions as a result of these mentoring relationships. Rather than being bound to particular companies and organisations, the women showed loyalty and trust to specific individuals. In these cases, the career function of mentoring extends across different companies.

Due to the unique combinations of career paths and determinants resulting from the context of this thesis, the career types in the overall group of Chinese women selected for this study are not identical to other published career path analyses. Further studies would need to be conducted to determine whether these types can be applied to female senior executives in other countries and markets. Moreover, the scope of this career path typology is confined to the specific population of senior female executives from multinational companies defined by the theoretical sampling process and to the general line of inquiry pursued in this study. Hence, it cannot necessarily be applied to all female executives in China. Again, in order to assess the situation of other female Chinese executives further studies would be required that also look at state-owned and private companies.

9. How Chinese female executives conquer senior management – Learning and implications

Seven conclusions about Chinese women's careers in top management – Implications for women planning their careers in top management – HR strategies for increasing women's participation in senior management – Supportive environments for career women (and their children)

Figures from various sources show that in international comparison, China has one of the highest proportions of women in senior management. Accordingly, female Chinese executives represent an interesting "test lab" for investigating women's careers. The findings of the Shanghai Women's Career Lab are of value for both career theory and real-world practice because they come from a group of women who have attained very senior positions in companies and thus lend themselves perfectly as role models. This book has attempted to paint a holistic picture of the career paths and patterns of female Chinese senior executives at multinational companies in China that takes account of both external determinants and individual influences on careers. Accordingly, external and individual determinants relevant to the career paths of female managers, especially Chinese ones, were included in the theory-based analysis.

Due in part to the challenges involved in conducting studies in China, there has been very little previous research on Chinese women in management roles and the related question of the factors behind the high proportion of women in senior management positions in China. The few studies that do exist revolve around two poles: on the one hand, Mao Zedong's famous words "Women can hold half the sky" and, on the other, De Mente's claim that "Women are the moon reflecting the sunlight". Which of these better reflects female Chinese executives' experiences? The majority of previous studies, some of them now quite old, have tended towards the latter view. Chinese women are more often seen as being in a situation that impedes career progression rather than a position of strength from which they can attain the highest level in companies. Various researchers have called for studies focusing on the career experiences of Chinese women (Liu, 2013; Aaltio, 2007; Tatli et al., 2013). Scarcely any previous studies have attempted to look at Chinese women's career development and career influences holistically. This may be due to

the complex nature of holistic explanations (Tharenou et al., 1994) and the difficulty of gaining access to target groups in China (Korabik, 1993). The author has
gained insight on this from 35 fascinating female top executives for a unique research project, the "Shanghai Women's Career Lab". The core of this project was
to analyse successful mechanisms and women's well-planned career paths, which
are characterised by stringent advances and the strategic development of employee
positions in multinational corporations in China. Women can use the results from
this research to make their own career planning more successful. The project also
presents findings that are relevant to HRM management both inside and outside
China with respect to future diversification strategies aimed at getting more women
into management positions. Hence, the findings are of relevance both for career
theory and for actual HR practice when it comes to increasing the proportion of
women in senior management roles, whether in China or elsewhere in the world.
The specific Chinese context, as expressed in external determinants rooted in the
cultural, political and social environment, reflects a truly unique combination that
feeds into the findings. The findings about the environmental influences on
women's careers could provide international policy experts who want to increase
the proportion of women in management with inspiration from outside their own
national context.

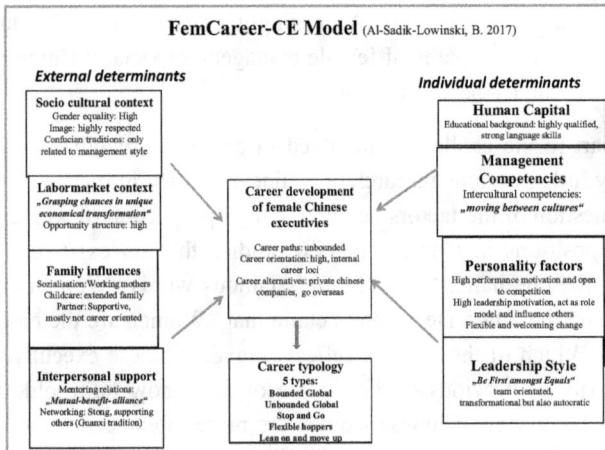

Figure 8: Overview of research findings: Female Chinese Executive Career Model (FemCa-
reer CE Model, Al-Sadik-Lowinski, 2017))

These findings need to be interpreted within the overall context of the research. Given the qualitative nature of the research design, the findings are particular rather than general and further quantitative studies would be required to verify them. However, due to the relatively high number of participants it was possible within the scope of this qualitative study to quantify the number of times that certain descriptions were given and to generate findings about the distribution of such descriptions within the group.

The women of the Shanghai Women's Career Lab feel equal to men in the context of their companies, and reported the advantages that women have over men. The women's observations correspond to published figures showing the high proportion of women in executive positions in China. However, regional differences are ascribed to northern China. Opinions in the group diverge regarding equality at the most senior executive level in companies (e.g. President or CEO). Many of the women believe there are differences but see them as related to nationality rather than gender. This contradicts various publications (Cooke, 2001; Xi, 1985; Korabik, 1993) in which the authors describe progress in equality between the sexes but ultimately paint a more negative picture of China on this front, but is in line with Stockmann (1995), who believes that in international comparison the situation of Chinese women is better than that of, say, American women.

Confucian traditions concerning gender relations have been replaced by a culture of equality. According to the results nowadays, women have an advantage over men when pursuing careers at multinational companies in China. Confucian traditions have a positive effect on the women's management styles.

Historically, very narrow interpretations of Confucian doctrines resulted in seeing women being subordinated to men across large swathes of Chinese society. Traditional Confucian conceptions of gender roles have not negatively affected these women's career development and are largely deemed to no longer be relevant today. As a result of China's movement towards equality, the interviewed female executives believe they are now equal to male managers. However, this does not apply to northern China, where the women believe that discriminatory interpretations of old traditions still hold sway. Many of the interviewees regard Confucian values as having a positive effect on their personal management styles. Hence, the results from this group of women run counter to many findings in the literature, according to which Confucian traditions generally have negative effects on gender equality (Frank, 2001; Liu, 2013; Korabik, 1993; Yun, 2011). However, they are consonant with other accounts that investigate the influence of Confucian values on management practices (Hall, 1976; Arthur et al., 2001). The women believe these values have a positive effect on their leadership styles, especially with respect to managing teams and supporting employees.

Female managers, especially those who are also mothers, enjoy a respected image in companies and in Chinese society as a whole. Women are regarded as just as good as or better than men at management tasks and for leadership roles.

These women have experienced the image of career women in Chinese society as mainly positive. This is expressed in the respect shown for their professional success by their families and those around them. They also enjoy a strong image in their companies. The lack of confidence in women's management abilities described by several researchers (Frank, 2001; Korabik, 1993; Rajerison, 1996) was not reflected in the interviewees' descriptions. Only a minority of participants mentioned critical views about the image of career women in Chinese society, and these were confined to judgements about their roles as mothers rather than their roles as managers.

The female Chinese executives are capable and flexible enough to recognise the potential for success inherent in given situations and exploit this for their own careers. They pro-actively seized opportunities in multinational companies that arose as a result of the opening and transformation of the economy in China. By choosing multinational companies rather than state-owned companies, they expected to achieve closeness to other cultures, financial advancement and a higher status, as well as gain the opportunity to learn from foreign management practices and leadership.

The transformation of the Chinese economy from a socialist planned system to a market system with numerous multinational companies entering the Chinese market and long phases of growth offered a vast range of opportunities for women and their careers in management. This applies particularly in the metropolis of Shanghai, one of China's largest economic centres. This transformation also meant a shift away from jobs that were secure but offered little autonomy and from the career rules that had applied to their parents and relatives in the old economic system and that most women them had experienced themselves in their first jobs. The interviewees used the transformation to move swiftly away from government-determined functions and adapt successfully to the new world of multinational companies. They proved highly flexible in adapting to and succeeding in a corporate system that was very different from what they had originally experienced and seen in their parents' cases. The search for a challenge, the desire for freedom and curiosity about foreign cultures and management practices determined their original choice to build a career in the multinational sector. Furthermore, the women were characterised by a high willingness to take risks and a positive attitude to change. The women were highly flexible, quickly adapting their career building both to the big changes in the economy as a whole with all the opportunities these entailed, as well as to later phases of market crisis, changing demands and company restructuring.

One could debate the extent to which this new economic environment in China and the many opportunities it offers is the real key factor enabling senior management careers in multinational companies for women. One might assume that it is easier for women to have careers in places where there is high demand. It would be possible to draw parallels to post-war Europe, where women were needed and there was a lack of men. However, this is not a valid comparison, as both women and men have had equal opportunities to build management careers in multinational companies since the opening up of the Chinese economy. There was and still is a lack of highly qualified Chinese managerial staff with intercultural skills and grounded knowledge of the Chinese market and management. From the interviewees' point of view, gender plays only a subordinate role. It would also be interesting to discuss whether any parallels to the opening of former East Germany can be observed; in the GDR, women were socialised in a comparable manner and were widely accepted in all functions. Across Germany as a whole, however, this has not lead to a high proportion of women in senior management; instead, the country continues to be one of the nations with the lowest percentage of female managers in international comparison. These reflections call for a more profound investigation of the dominant social and economic systems. Women's careers must thus always be seen within the larger context of social, political and economic conditions, and the various external determinants that influence women's careers need to be understood as complex, interwoven elements.

Female Chinese senior executives at multinational companies in China pursue management careers alongside being mothers. They are socialised to work full-time. Their families provide strong support that allows them to focus almost exclusively on their careers.

The high proportion of mothers (74%) in this group of Chinese executives is worthy of note. This figure is far higher than the proportion in Western studies (Holst et al., 2001). Moreover, there are fewer single women in this group than in comparable studies of senior female managers from other western countries. This shows that the women in this group have started families alongside pursuing their senior management careers. According to the study findings, this is due to factors such as good family support networks, in which grandparents assume primary responsibility for childcare and household management. The interviewed women's husbands also support their partners' career ambitions.

Nonetheless, some of the women, especially those with two children, regard being a mother as a factor that has tended to have a delaying impact on their careers. The group is not unanimous on this point and the degree to which individual women regard motherhood as a burden depends on the importance they attach to traditional roles in which mothers spend a lot of time with their children. Unlike in many Western countries, where it is often socially acceptable for women to be full-time or part-time housewives, all but one of the women in this study were socialised in families where both parents worked full-time. The women's mothers and grandmothers, their main role models, pursued their own careers. According to the interviewees, in China it is a socially accepted norm for women to accord a high status to their careers and for mothers to frequently prioritise their work or spend time away on business travel. It was the women who have two children or have adopted more Western conceptions of the role of mothers in addition to their Chinese socialisation who described the challenges of combining motherhood and careers. Most of the women view their careers as their primary role and therefore possess a strong career orientation.

The women have been supported in their careers by informal mentoring relationships, especially with foreign decision-makers, which were characterised by their mutually beneficial nature.

Informal mentoring relationships have played a role in the careers of most of the women. They reported how they, as women, were trusted more than men by their mentors (who were often from abroad). The women described how potential mentors regarded Chinese men as being prone to rivalries or as being less adaptable, and so tended to distrust them. In contrast to the findings of various studies (Tharenou, 2007), the Chinese women found it easier to develop mentoring relationships with foreign decision-makers than their male Chinese counterparts. Unlike traditional mentoring relationships described in the literature, the mentoring relationships in this study were characterised by mutual dependence. A good term for the relationship is "mutually beneficial alliance". The mentors, generally foreign male or female GMs, were dependent on trusted Chinese subordinates with local market knowledge and language skills, and preferred women to men because they believed them to be more trustworthy. The female executives needed the foreign mentors to rise up the corporate ladder and to gain access to the head office, the centre of power in multinational companies, to further their own career progression. They also needed the mentor to exercise their intercultural advantage. The interviewees believe that at multinational companies women have a clear advantage over men on this front.

> *The biggest strength of female Chinese executives in multinational companies is their intercultural competence, which allows them to "move between cultures". The women posses global mindsets and are Chinese global leaders.*

The women's individual descriptions reveal exceptional levels of intercultural competence, which manifest in their ability to "move between cultures". They are able to adapt both to local Chinese culture and management styles and to one or more Western ones as required, depending on context, and are able to operate within different socio cultural frameworks. The women believe their intercultural skills are stronger than those of most Chinese men and foreign executives. These skills can be regarded as one of the women's most important assets, alongside the other capacities described in the research.

An economy that continues to become more and more globalised requires managers able to use differences in culture positively to increase efficiency for the benefit of their companies. In his much-debated book *The Clash of Civilizations*, Huntington (1997) describes "fault line conflicts" that can appear wherever there is a lack of cultural affinity. Besides cultural, social, religious and political differences, another core element is certainly the lacking ability to communicate confidently in the others' language. Thus far, scarcely any foreign managers are able to speak Chinese well enough to conduct negotiations in the language. The interviewed women's particular skill is their ability to "move between the cultures" in a sensitive, adaptive and assertive way, guiding staff, teams and their superiors safely through the "fault line conflicts" that are more or less inevitable in culturally mixed businesses in which China seems very remote to many staff. Besides their linguistic advantage, the women also have the ability to create lacking the "affinity" through their strong interest, curiosity, and desire to understand, ensuring their success in the respective context through adaptation and transformation.

> *Female Chinese senior executives at multinational companies are well educated, possess strong professional skills and have exceptional achievement orientation. Their personalities are marked by high self-confidence and a*

> *strong capacity to adapt to situations and people they encounter in the context
> of their careers.*

The women in this group have a high level of education. They have all completed university degrees and almost all have an MA or equivalent qualification. They also possess strong language skills. A third of the women have studied abroad. This study group lends further support to the correlation between career success and level of education claimed by Ragins (1998).

The women's descriptions of their personalities demonstrate high achievement orientation, an open and very positive attitude towards competition and a high willingness to assume responsibility and act as a role model. The majority of women in the group have high leadership motivation combined with a positive attitude towards exercising power, as evidenced in the strong influence they exert on other people and social situations. With regard to conflicts, the group is divided into women who described themselves as dealing with conflict in a very direct way and a smaller group who generally try to avoid conflict. The latter group must be viewed against the cultural backdrop of a "striving for harmony" and a desire to "save face". The women appear to be exceptionally flexible. The Chinese women have a strong capacity to adapt to situations and people they encounter in the context of their careers. In this connection, they described being very open to change – both in terms of relocating to new places and with respect to changes in their work, roles and experiences. It is striking how self-confident the women are overall. In the interviews, this self-confidence was observable in their natural, effortless, innate authority, while in their self-descriptions it was highlighted by their strong belief in their own achievements.

The women's leadership styles are predominantly transactional and democratic in nature, which is consonant with findings in the literature on female leadership styles (Stanford et al., 1995). However, a quarter of women in the group categorised themselves as having a more autocratic style. According to King et al. (2014), such styles appear to be more accepted in China than in the West. The women described themselves as being more empathetic and sensitive towards employees' needs than male executives. This reflects their application of Confucian traditions to modern management practices. All the women have a high team orientation, and the core of their leadership consists in cultivating interpersonal relationships and supporting other people. They aim to be the "first among equals" and lead accordingly.

The female Chinese executives have a high career orientation and strive for objective and subjective success criteria in equal measure. For them, financial reward and status are the basis of success. Subjective success means challenging, interesting and fulfilling work in an international setting. The women plan their careers in an autonomous, proactive and goal-focused way, and described themselves as engaged in continuous learning. Most of them have internal career loci.

These Chinese women have a high career motivation. They work strategically towards executive roles and plan how they can advance to the next position on the career ladder. Career success is defined in terms of both objective factors, such as reaching senior positions, and subjective ones, such as a sense of fulfilment and enjoyment of their work. Overall, most of the women tend to associate the notion of success with their careers. Most of the interviewed women have internal career loci: they plan their careers in a proactive, self-reliant way, rather than their career paths primarily being determined by chance or external influences (as is the case with an external career locus). This was shown by the various strategic plans for achieving their career goals that the women described. Overall, an analysis of the women's career paths shows that most of them adapted proactively to unanticipated occurrences such as the Asian financial crisis in ways that promoted their personal career goals.

Most of the women expressed a positive view of their current work-life balance. It is notable that they regard long working hours, temporary spikes in their workloads and frequent travel as the norm. All the women still work long hours but less than they did at the start of their careers now that they have progressed to higher positions.

The conditions in which the women began their careers varied considerably. Most of them started during the period of China's economic reforms and expansion. A total of 17 of the women started in state-assigned jobs. They remained in these jobs for varying lengths of time before choosing to switch to a multinational company. Eighteen of the women chose their first job themselves, with eight of them beginning their careers abroad. For the women without a Shanghai *hukou* (local residence permit), the choice of first job was primarily driven by the desire to obtain a *hukou* for a city where they would be able to pursue a career at a multinational company. Twenty-six of the thirty-five women have worked abroad. The other women, especially the ones who did not have a Shanghai *hukou* at the start of their careers, exhibited a high level of mobility within China. There was a connection between overseas experience (working or studying abroad) and reaching the most senior level in companies, such as president or GM.

The majority of women's career paths are marked by changes of company and can be classified as unbounded careers. The main motivation for changing companies was a desire for more challenges combined with hierarchical progression.

Most of the women in the Shanghai Women's Career Lab have unbounded career paths that are not bound to a single company, and they have changed companies four to five times on average. Over half the women have experience in a variety of department types, while others have pursued careers in one specific field: most commonly HR, followed by controlling and finance. Around a third of the interviewees have switched between corporate roles and positions at service providers such as consultancies or agencies.

The main motivation for changing companies was a desire for challenges and career progression. Many of the women have also changed companies at later stages in their careers, including during the Asian financial crisis, with the goal of further advancement. There is little evidence of strong ties to particular companies. The births of children were factored into existing decisions and plans and were pretexts, rather than reasons, for changing companies or taking career breaks. Criteria for selecting positions included the degree of challenge offered by the roles and whether companies and general managers had a good image.

When asked about possible alternatives to the career choices they actually made, the most common answer was that they could have worked abroad, which several women had chosen not to do for family reasons. According to the women, the combination of generally very good and supportive family networks and affordable household help that liberates them almost completely from duties within their families in China cannot be transferred abroad. By contrast, mobility within China (which in some cases involves travelling or relocating similarly great distances) poses no problem for this group.

The female Chinese executives see international private Chinese companies as offering one possible avenue for their future. They are working towards further hierarchical advancement. Chinese companies that will go more global in the future seem to be an alternative career path as there are no barriers to executives with Chinese nationality achieving General Manager status.

Two specific tendencies can be identified in this group with regard to future career plans: hierarchical advancement and professional development. Only five of the thirty-five women expressed a desire to leave the corporate world or did not have any specific goals, which once again indicates that the group has a high career orientation within the framework of the corporate system, including with respect to the future. However, the women tend to regard private international Chinese companies as the future market for their careers, especially due to their belief that they could become GMs at such companies as Chinese women.

The career paths of female Chinese senior executives at multinational companies can be categorised into five types with a majority of unbounded paths and internal career loci.

The criterion of career paths, certain other sub criteria and the determinants that enabled the sharpest possible distinctions to be drawn were selected for the career path typology (Catyp-FCE) developed for this group. This yielded five types, three of which dominated in numerical terms: "unbounded global", "flexible hoppers" and "stop and go". These career paths are all unbounded as defined here and have internal career loci. Differences arise with respect to mobility and the impact of the determinants.

All the subgroups represent an upward managerial track. However, lateral phases occurred in one group in particular, the "stop and go" group, due to the women taking account of aspects of life other than traditional work. Only 22% of the women from the overall group belong to this subgroup. The "stop and go" group comes closest to the findings of Kaleidoscope Career theory developed by Mainiero et al. (2005), according to which most women prioritise family over career. Family matters only play a subordinate role, or do not play any role at all, for the career decision-making of the other four types in this study.

The "flexible hoppers" group strategically plan their career progression within China, choosing positions that they believe will offer the greatest challenge and variety. They are not bound to particular organisations. These women are very self-confident and have a high achievement orientation and desire to learn. These features are also present in the other groups, but based on the women's self-descriptions are especially pronounced in this subgroup. This group seems to be more affected by changes in labour market conditions. Furthermore, they faced unanticipated effects and risks related to changing companies more than the other groups, which were evident in lateral phases before they moved to a higher hierarchical level.

Women in the "bounded global" and "unbounded global" groups, who developed their intercultural competencies in different countries, have attained the highest senior management positions. The intercultural skills of the women in these groups have been enhanced by their experience of living, studying and working outside of China. The "unbounded global" women worked abroad once or several times, changed employer several times and used this experience in a targeted manner to advance their careers in China. The "bounded global" women, who were fewer in number, display a greater need for security and reliability and made the more conservative choice of working only in one company. They all worked for German companies.

The smaller group of "lean on and move up" women showed an increase in the described "mutual benefit alliances" in their mentor relationships. These women followed their mentors several times when they changed companies, displayed strong personal loyalty and at times made themselves dependent on their mentors' success or lack of success. They are the only group to have an external career locus.

The typology developed here is not identical to any of the existing typologies of women's careers found in the literature. The determinants that have influenced the careers of Chinese women and the resultant career patterns represent distinctive profiles. Further research would be required to identify any commonalities with other female populations in China or in other countries.

Seven conclusions about Chinese women's careers in top management

The preceding chapters have provided a comprehensive picture of the career trajectories and most important influences on the careers of female Chinese executives in multinational companies in China. The findings of the Shanghai Women's Career Lab thus contribute to a better understanding of how women in China rise to top management levels. Seven main conclusions can be drawn from the findings:

(1) The Chinese female executives describe their social and cultural environment as largely positive for their career trajectories, in contrast to many of the accounts given in the literature. It is striking that they see themselves as completely equal and partly even superior to men within multinational companies. They also feel completely accepted in their roles by society as a whole. The oft-described image of the disadvantaged, criticised Chinese career woman is not reflected in this study. This result also mirrors the author's personal experiences of executive coaching and of seminars with Chinese women and men. In general, the topic of gender is

not mentioned. Women take professional careers for granted, handling their professional lives in a very self-confident manner.

China is very culturally diverse. Overly simplified depictions of social and traditional influences on women risk showing only part of the country's realities. For example, the women of the Mosuo, one of the world's rare quasi-matriarchal cultures, are just as much part of the cultural influence as the described Confucian traditions. The Mosuo women have legitimate authority over their family, administrate its wealth and decide with which man they want to have children to carry on their bloodline (Namu and Mathieu, 2007; Coler and Giersberg, 2009). It is easier to find parallels with the women of the Shanghai Women's Career Lab than with the picture of the oppressed Chinese woman often (as described above) painted in publications on women in management.

(2) Socialisation through women and grandmothers with full-time careers in a society that strongly encourages gender equality shapes women's positive attitude towards their own career roles. The strong family orientation of women promoted in many Western societies is not a model that these women see as an option for themselves. Far from it. Descriptions along the lines of "I don't want to be a parasite in society" or "It is not enough for me to be a man's ornament" show how having their own professional lives, self-responsibility and independence are the norm for these women.

(3) Their socialisation also shapes their understanding of their role as mother. Bringing up children is seen as the task of an extended family system and not as their own primary role. In this, the women differ markedly from women in many Western societies such as Germany, for example. From the point of view of the Chinese women, recognition of their career achievements by society and their families predominates and does not conflict with their role as mothers. The women's partners also recognise the women's career ambitions and support them in this. In the interviews, uncertainty about how to reconcile their role as mothers with their role as managers was only voiced very seldom. Based on the author's personal experiences of working with many women from various countries as an executive coach, Chinese women have a very different view of this matter than women from other parts of the world. While German, American and Japanese women, for example, brought up the difficulty of reconciling these roles in every executive coaching session, this topic did not occur with Chinese women. The image of the *Rabenmutter* that throws German women with a strong career orienta-

tion into such inner turmoil is non-existent among these female Chinese executives.[17]

(4) The women proactively search for informal foreign mentors and superiors who support them and create mutually beneficial alliances. The relationship between these mentors and the women really merits a new name as it is shaped more strongly by mutual benefit than traditional mentor relationships. Accordingly, one could speak of "mutually beneficial alliances". The mentor benefits more strongly in these cases than in traditional mentor relationships, as he or she usually lacks local knowledge, local business connections and knowledge of the language. In her book *Lean In* (2015), Sanders describes the advantages that mentors gain through their role. In her view, the most important of these are useful information from the grassroots level and an emotional sense of pride. However, the Chinese women become the foreign managers' extended arm, as it were, reaching into their organisation and into the market, achieving far more than a simple transfer of knowledge. The foreign bosses prefer Chinese women to men in these alliances as the women are able to adapt better, have less fear of losing face and display high intercultural skills overall. Trust and loyalty are at the core of this alliance. Here, the women definitely have an advantage over their male colleagues and one could even go as far as to speak of male discrimination. The women's loyalty is more to their mentor's person than to the business, which is also reflected in career decisions where women follow their mentor to another company. After the move, the "mutual benefit alliance" again operates successfully in the new business.

(5) The female Chinese executives exhibit the attitudes and traits that are necessary to pursue careers in multinational companies and to attain high-level positions.

The women exhibit exceptional achievement motivation and a positive attitude towards competition and exercising power, which they do mainly through influencing and persuasion. They have a high willingness to assume responsibility and are very self-confident. The women are also exceptionally flexible: not just with regard to their work, roles and experiences, but also with regard to geographical mobility. Many described themselves as seeking out and welcoming change. They are demonstrably willing to take on career challenges, and display the characteristics

---

[17]   The term *Rabenmutter* is used in Germany to refer to a woman who does not take good enough care of her children, casting them out of the nest like a raven. This German term is not found anywhere else in the world and gives expression to the traditionally high expectations of German women in their roles as mothers.

and behaviours which Helgensen and Goldsmith (2018) describe as favourable to career advancement.

(6) The women are "Chinese global leaders" with global mindsets and the particular ability to "move between cultures". The women have the gift of being able to adapt their leadership and communication to the culture in question – regardless of whether their respective context requires a local form of management and communication, the dominant Western style, or a hybrid form. This is the women's greatest competitive advantage, setting them apart from both male colleagues and foreign bosses. Their strength consists of the weakness of others who fulfil global roles, but are forced to remain "Western leaders" due to a lack of language skills and local knowledge. The analysis has shown that the Chinese women possess the four factors – savvy, character, perspective and inquisitiveness – that, according to Black and Morrison (2014), define global leaders. Lewis (1996) refers to global leaders as individuals who are able to "move between cultures". Accordingly, these are not necessarily leaders holding global positions. Lewis sees problems above all with the so-called "Big Five", the world's biggest economies: the USA, Japan, Germany, the UK and France. According to Lewis, companies from these countries have been particularly insensitive in their handling of intercultural issues. With their cultural sensitivity and openness and their language and market knowledge, the Chinese women in this study offer the kind of support urgently needed in order to operate successfully in China. They "move in all necessary directions", deeper into their own culture or into Western culture; astonishingly, the women are also able to distinguish well between the individual Western cultures. According to the women, their male colleagues are less talented at this and have less interest in doing so. The roots of this talent lie in their genuine interest and delight in foreign cultures.

(7) The typology of career patterns reveals that while the Chinese women's career patterns do not follow a single type, they are mainly unbounded and focused upon rising within the hierarchy. The five different types differ from other career typologies for women in management in the literature, both in regard to the career paths themselves as well as in regard to the influence of certain determinants overall. The women plan their careers actively and independently of individual organisations. Only one of the five types, the "stop and go" women, come close to descriptions from the literature, according to which women focus mostly on relational aspects when planning their careers. The "unbounded global" and "bounded global" groups of women show that overseas experience plays a special role in the development of careers at multinational companies. GM or President level tended

to be achieved more frequently in these two groups. The career paths of the "flexible hoppers" show these women rising locally by frequently changing company, manoeuvring themselves flexibly through shifting risks and market changes.

Drawing conclusions from the findings described, it is possible to identify which factors have had an influence on these women's successful rise to senior management level. The recipe for success in the "Shanghai Women's Career Lab" is complex, consisting of multiple factors. The main insight derived from the women's descriptions is that there is an interplay in this group between individual success mechanisms and highly supportive external factors conducive to a career in management. This results in well-planned career paths, which are characterised by stringent advances and the strategic development of positions. One of the most striking observations was the discrepancy between the women's accounts of gender equality and social acceptance and the many publications presenting a more pessimistic picture of the situation of women in top management in China. The Shanghai Women's Career Lab paints a predominantly positive picture, optimistically encouraging women to aim high when planning a career in management. The Chinese women demonstrate impressively that "women can do it if they want to". It remains to be seen to which extent a future stronger orientation towards Western patterns in China might change social expectations of women's roles, for example concerning the upbringing of children.

Key findings concern, on the one hand, the special context of the transformation of the Chinese economy with its kind of "gold rush" atmosphere, which the women have utilised shrewdly for their own purposes. This particular situation is unique in kind and cannot be transferred one to one to women's careers in other economic contexts. Furthermore, while the special family support system in China offers a possible model, it has no socially and culturally embedded parallel in many Western societies. The Chinese women's pronounced career motivation in connection with their own high expectations of their performance are determinants that can be transferred to women everywhere in the world. In particular, the ability "to move between cultures" is something that women in other global contexts can develop and cultivate as a competitive advantage. However, thus far this factor seems not to have taken root sufficiently as a career instrument. The encouragement of genuine cultural adaptation and transformation in managers, going beyond simple deployments abroad or an experience of company mergers, is recommended as an HR tool. Here, intercultural executive coaching to develop global mindset can play an important role.

The Shanghai Women's Career Lab encourages the discussion of its findings with women all over the world planning a career in management, with decision-makers in companies wanting to support women, as well as opinion leaders in societies who want to support more women in top management.

Implications for women planning their careers in top management

The findings of the Shanghai Women's Career Lab are helpful to women making decisions on their path into top management levels. As has been shown, women's careers are more strongly influenced by certain determinants than men's. So for women who want to reach top-level management, it is very important to consider both external and individual determinants that can influence careers. It is recommended that the findings of this study from China be used as the basis for personalised career coaching. The results presented here can help women to critically rethink their own career strategies (process that a professional executive coach can support them with). The following main conclusions are of particular relevance:

(1) The Shanghai Women's Career Lab wants to give encouragement to other women. The example of female Chinese executives shows that careers in senior management should be possible for more women and that they are also compatible with having a family. However, for this, women need to have a strong career orientation and reflect on and respond to their own concepts of their different roles at an early stage. The Chinese women in this study group possess this clear career orientation. Women across the globe aiming to pursue a career in management are recommended to use the Chinese model for their own guidance.

(2) The Chinese women's specific socialisation as full-time professionals could be taken as basis for further discussions on which norms a society needs to support women in executive functions. Young women raised in other countries with a socialisation that includes full-time home-maker roles for women need to clearly identify which family model they want to pursue at an early stage. Gaining a clear idea of their own wishes and ideas concerning the compatibility of roles is a prerequisite of successful career planning for women in particular, and thus forms a fixed component of coaching for women in management careers.

(3) The example of the Chinese women shows that it can benefit women's careers if they choose a partner who will provide emotional support for their professional lives. Many of the women in this study group have partners who are less career-oriented and support their spouses in their career focus. Based on this study group, this constellation seems to be a possible successful model for women who wish to

rise to senior management positions. The approach of Schwan (2014), who called for equal concepts of partnership in which both partners are able to achieve their career ambitions, is not reflected in these findings.

(4) Most of the Chinese women found it easier to pursue careers with one child rather than two. They believe that the number of children they have could have an impact on their careers. China's one-child policy encouraged this family model for many years. This finding suggests that women who wish to have several children alongside pursuing a career in senior management need to be very good at planning childcare. However, besides the questions of feasibility and of how support is to be financed, the women's personal attitude to their role was once again decisive. A strong career orientation is necessary for a career in senior management, as the interviewed women show very clearly. This orientation is embedded in the women's own value systems and affects the way they live their role within the family.

(5) The research analyses which abilities and character traits were beneficial to the Chinese women on their career paths. In addition to a good education and strong management skills they showed a very high achievement motivation, a positive attitude to competition and a strong leadership motivation. The women were flexible about relocating or doing different types of work. These are particularly important individual factors that supported career development in this group. The Chinese women were also very team-oriented and supportive of others. Their high intercultural competency, based on a curiosity about other cultures and a desire to learn from them, is a distinguishing feature of this study group that could act as an incentive for other women to hone their own cultural skills. Cultural skills here include both the ability to operate successfully in international settings and within different corporate cultures. The Chinese women have demonstrated that they understand how to use their cultural skills to benefit themselves and their career development. A strong inner belief in one's own abilities and the resulting self-confidence, a desire to learn continuously and strong networking (similar to Chinese *guanxi* principles) appear to be other factors that supported the success of the women in this research in a corporate environment.

HR strategies for increasing women's participation in senior management

Farrell and Grant (2005) point out a looming shortage of home-grown talent for both multinational companies in China and Chinese companies with global ambitions. Answering the question of how to attract, develop and retain qualified female executives could be part of a solution to this growing problem. According to

Ventolini and Mercier (2015), managing careers is of essential strategic importance for organisations to ensure that employees who hold essential skills for the company's success stay motivated. The research has shown that these Chinese women are highly motivated to rise to the top level of senior management and at present on the whole still favour multinational companies as employers. Multinational companies are faced with the challenge of how to retain and develop talented women in future.

Some of the women in this research regard international private Chinese companies as an alternative offering them future career progression prospects. State-owned Chinese companies are not a viable alternative for these women, as they see no fit regarding company culture and have not built up the network of relations that forms a precondition for careers in state-owned companies. The main reasons given for their consideration of private Chinese companies were the vision of some Chinese owners as well as the lack of a nationality barrier to Chinese nationals becoming GMs of these companies. In light of the intensifying competition for the best executives due to the increasing internationalisation of private Chinese companies, on the basis of this study's findings the following specific recommendations can be made for HR departments of companies in China that wish to retain and promote female executives. One way to do so would be to provide more support for the advancement of local Chinese women to General Manager or President level. Some of the women described a kind of glass ceiling for Chinese in multinational companies. Hence it is recommended to encourage local female talent more strongly than hitherto, supporting women in moving up to the highest hierarchical levels in particular.

One of the main wishes of the interviewed women who had not worked abroad was to gain professional experience overseas. For some of the interviewees, this was a kind of lifelong dream. Furthermore, this study showed that overseas experience tended to be useful for making the step to a general manager position. However, overseas assignments are particularly hard to reconcile with women's family situations. Moreover, in the majority of cases most women are uncertain whether moving abroad will guarantee an attractive position in China on their return. Accordingly, measures for motivating and gaining women's loyalty could include programmes that enable Chinese women at multinational companies to gain experience abroad or at the company headquarters, with a long-term plan for further career progression in China. Programmes limiting the duration of the time spent abroad would be ideal for some of the "flexible hoppers" and "lean on" types. It would also make sense to plan positions for the women to return to in China before they move abroad.

The exciting visions and sense of new beginnings perceived in private Chinese companies could be complemented with a stronger involvement of female executives in the adaptation of the multinational companies' global business visions. If more women were involved in the vision programmes, the advantage could be double: the women would be encouraged and challenged equally, as it were. For one, they would be able to develop their visionary potential, would face exciting challenges and thus feel motivated. Secondly, this involvement would ensure that companies' visions are adapted to and communicated with the local context, rendering them more attractive to local staff.

Implementing individual executive coaching for women as an integral part of a development strategy is a highly effective way for HR departments to support women who want to get into management, since coaching can be tailored to women's individual needs. Women will benefit tremendously from executive coaching that specifically addresses issues linked to the determinants analysed in this research and helps them to clarify their personal strategies for success. At the start of their careers, individual coaching will help them to answer key questions around career orientation and work-life challenges. In later stages, women will benefit from coaching that is tailored to their specific needs as female executives, because at higher hierarchical levels different questions and challenges will arise in connection with career progression. The Female Career Model can serve as a framework for coaching tailored to female executives.

A further aspect of Human Resource initiatives is related to business communication concerning strategies to encourage and support women. It is recommended that multinational companies communicate individually, or even better in conjunction with one another, which advantages they offer for women in management in China and how they support them specifically. This could be an incentive to set themselves apart from local global companies longer-term and retain women as management talent. For this to happen, programmes for the promotion of women need to become a fixed part of company culture in local business branches to a greater degree than hitherto, and this culture needs to be promoted by company decision-makers. Here, taking account of intercultural equality is of particular importance, as the feeling that Chinese staff are at a latent disadvantage was found throughout the entire study group. The strategy of stronger promotion of good local female executives could have a variety of benefits for organisations. Given the high costs of expatriations into China (Foster, 2000), more support for local women to advance to senior levels combined with the option of shorter rotations at the head office could be a good way for companies to retain their edge when competing with global Chinese companies to attract and retain the best female executives.

Supportive environments for career women (and their children)

By contrast with what might have been expected based on the literature, the Chinese women reported a very supportive social environment which makes it easier for them to succeed in upper management as they feel accepted and respected. They gave a very positive assessment of equality of opportunities for women, of women's image in society and of the support they receive to combine work and family. In many cases, they even reported having advantages over men during their careers at multinational companies. Social attitudes towards women in senior executive roles and towards managers who are also mothers can have either a positive or negative impact on women's careers. In order for women to be able to pursue senior management careers on an equal footing with men, it helps if they are supported by the external determinants described above. However, these factors alone do not guarantee women will make it to management level, since (as shown by the results) this also crucially depends on the women's individual competencies and personality traits. In terms of external conditions, it is recommended that societies work on giving equal recognition to women and mothers in leadership roles. Since China's history cannot be transposed to other countries, every society needs to find its own ways to establish equal acceptance of female managers throughout society and to break down stereotyped views of women. The aim should be to reach the state described by one of the Chinese women in the interviews: "Gender is not an issue". One crucial issue is how a society supports women with childcare. The Chinese women's extended family system, with grandparents taking care of their children, is one possibility offering positive social benefits that go beyond simply supporting women's careers. In China, older generations play a meaningful role and stay actively involved in the extended family system. However, it is questionable whether this culturally rooted form of strong familial support could be transposed to other countries. Scandinavian and Eastern European countries offer alternative models for how a state can provide full-time care for children and thus pave the way for greater equality of opportunities for women in the workplace. Other countries, such as Germany, continue to struggle to expand full-time childcare provision due to a combination of traditional values and mothers' predominant role in raising children. Currently there is debate in China on whether the significant involvement of grandparents in children's upbringing may not also entail some disadvantages. While possible disadvantages were not mentioned by the participants in this study group, the question does arise of how long the Chinese system currently supporting women in their careers will remain sustainable, given the increase in Western influence. The right way to support women with their careers may vary for different countries. However, it is clear that without high-quality childcare tailored to the needs of a management career – whether it is provided by families, the state or private providers – all other policies to support women will have a diminished impact. The example of the Chinese women shows that they were able to concentrate on their careers because they were relieved of a significant portion of the childcare burden. None of the interviewees reported having any problems with childcare. The participants in the Shanghai Women's Career Lab said that they were able to pursue their careers on an equal footing with men. In their career orientation, the Chinese women adapt to circumstances, make plans and act in the same way as their male colleagues. Sociocultural structures provide them with strong support that helps them to combine their two roles. The general recommendation arising from the findings here would be that societies should create equal external conditions for women as a fundamental basis for them to pursue careers.

10. Conclusion: Chinese women as worldwide role models for top management careers

Contra De Mente, the women interviewed in the Shanghai Women's Career Lab do not see themselves as being "the moon reflecting the sunlight" – that is to say, as primarily serving a supportive role for men, as most literature still suggests. Rather, it is Mao Zedong's words "Women can hold half the sky" that are clearly reflected in the perceptions and career experiences of the Chinese women in senior management at multinational companies in China who were interviewed for this study. They also share the attitude of "Whatever men can do, women can do" (Wang, 1997) in relation to senior management. Current discussion in China is dominated by the demand to involve mothers more strongly in their children's upbringing and the debate on the disadvantages of involving grandparents too strongly. Future research will need to assess to which extent increased globalisation and thus increased Western influence and further changes in the economy, such as the globalisation of private Chinese companies in China, will have an effect on the role of women in senior management.

Are Chinese women suited to be global role models for women's careers? The answer here is a resounding yes. The analysis of the interviews reveals various ways in which external conditions have positively impacted on these women's careers. These external determinants are country-specific and culturally moulded, and the question of whether and how they can be transposed to other countries opens up new perspectives and avenues for discussion. The most significant results to come out of the Shanghai Women's Career Lab are those concerning the women's individual traits. It is above all the combination of individual strengths exhibited by the women in the Shanghai Women's Career Lab – for example, their strong career orientation, high flexibility and intercultural competencies – that have a role model character capable of offering guidance to other women throughout the world. Continuous learning, cultivating management skills and honing relevant personality traits offer ways for women across the world to follow the Chinese women to the top levels of companies.

The 35 women who gave up their time and thus showed their solidarity with this research project could be trailblazers for women across the globe – or could prove to be exceptional phenomena as framework conditions change over time. The best-known Chinese gender theorist, Xiaojiang Liu, remarked in her 2014 speech at the German Consulate in Shanghai "that Chinese women already hold more than half the sky".[18] The debate about the significance of Chinese women's strong career orientation for Chinese society as a whole has begun.

The solidarity of the Chinese women in the Shanghai Women's Career Lab, which was what made the research for this book possible in the first place, undeniably has "global role model" character, since it is based on the idea of helping and supporting other women to achieve their goals.

---

[18]   See the full authorised quotation in the section on assessments of equality of opportunity.

Figures and Tables

Figures

Tables

Appendix

Determinant	Author
1. Socio cultural	Gangrose (2007), Li (2000), Frank (2001), Liu (2013), Korabik (1993), Yung (2011)
Confucian traditions	Blanchard (2010), Lin (1939), Ko (1994), Woo (1998), Mann (1997)
Confucian traditions and management	Arthur (2001), Hall (1976), Li (2013)
gender equality in China	Li (2000), Cooke (2001), Keith (1997), Jiang (2000),Wang (1997), Stockmann (1994)
	Potter (1999), Xi (1985)
image of female managers	Powell (2011), Frank (2011), Rajerison (1996), Korabik (1993), Judd (1990)
	Schein (2007, 1996, 1989,1994), Eagly (2007), Doge (1996), Benner (1989)
2. Labour market context (socioeconomic)	Tagscherer (1999), Fernandez (2006), Taubmann (1994), Yeung (2004), Cho (1995)
	Nyaw (1996), Wie (2005), Staiger (2006), Leung (2002), Bosse (1998)
market data	Lam (2013), McKinsey (2012), Thornston (2014), Catalyst (2014), Hays (2015)
glass ceiling	Henn (2012), Liu (2013), Ragins (1998), Gangrose (2005), Yun (2011), Congbin (2009)
	Frank (2001), Eagly (2007)
equality	Croll (1995), Chi (2008), Gustafsson (2000), Huges (2002), Jiang (2000), Ding (2009)
	Guo (2009), Whyte (1984)
3. Family	Bourdie (1977, 1982), Hartmann (1996), Fietze (2011), Rescht (2014), Schnitzer (1998)
social origin	Whiston (2004), Mayrhofer (2005), Trusty (1997), Riley (1994), Yang (1986)
	Wong (2010), Evans (2007), Schellhorn (2014)
family influences	Powell (2010), Law (2002), Hall (1976), Eagly (2007), Yan (2000), Henn (2012),
	Hewlett (2006), Cheung (2010), Holst (2013), Budig (2001), Thompson (1999),
	Choi (2006), Mennino (2002), Friedmann (2000), Spector (2004), Aryee (1999),
	Chen (2010),Kim (2010), Cong (2008), Whyte (2003), Ling (2001),
husbands attitudes	Gilbert (1988), Lin (2000), Halpern (2008, Powell (2011)
4. Mentoring &Networking	Rastetter (2012), Ragins (1989, 1997), Allen (2004), Kram (1985), Levinson (1978)
	Headlam-Wells (2005), Leck (2012), Tharenou (2007), Lyness (2000), Weber (1972),
Guanxi networks	Reiners (2008), Kanter (1977), Yeung (1996), Li (2000), Harrison (2014), Yang (1986)

	Oi (1989), Pye (1985), Leung (2000, 2002), Peng (1997), Boisot (1988)
5. Education	Tharenou (1994), Judge (1995), Mayrhofer (2005), Reilly (1982), Kraiger (1985),
	Johnes (1990), Meulemann (1990), Hayes (1998), Kirchmeyer (1998), Lyness (2000)
6. Competences	Boyatzis (2011), Henn 82012), Regnet (2014), Spiess (1998), Jokinen (2005),
	Tucker (2014), Rosinski (2003), Chen (2001), Hinterhuber (1977), Senge (1996)
	Korabik (1992), Bischof-Köhler (1993), Kanter (1977), Kanning (2005)
7. Personality	Mayrhofer (2005), Catell (1986), Rothmann (2003), Ayman (2010), McClelland (1982)
	Miner (1993, 1991, 1978), Chen (1991), Hofstede (1996, 1998, 2005), Yu (1997)
	Powell (1993), Korabik (1994), Dolecheck (1987), Chen (1997), Ebrahimi (1991, 1997)
	Chow (1995), Hossiep (2003, 2000), Gough (1990), Markman (2003), Borkenau (1993)
	Snyders (1974), Williams (1997), Tokar (1998)
8. Female Leadership	Hogan (1994), Friedel-Howe (1990), Powell (2011), Eagly (2003), Judge (2004),
	Rosner (1990), Tannenbaum (1973), Ayman (2010)

Figure 5: Career determinants for female executive careers in China (Al-Sadik-Lowinski, 2017, selected from the author)

Bibliography

Aaltio, I. & Huang, J. 2007. Women managers' careers in information technology in China: high flyers with emotional costs? *Journal of Organizational Change Management*. 2007

Aberle, A. 1994. *Karriereorientierungen angehender Akademikerinnen und Akademiker*. Bielefeld

Adler N.J. 1999. Global leaders: Women of influence. In G. Powell (Ed.), *Handbook of gender in organizations*: 239–261, Thousand Oaks, CA: Sage.

Adler, N. J., Izarelis, D.N. 1988. *Women in management worldwide*. New York: M. E. Sharpe.

Allen, T. D., Eby, L. T., Poteet, M. L., Lentz, E. & Lima, L. 2004. Career benefits associated with mentoring for protégeé: a meta-analysis, *Journal of Applied Psychology*, 89: 127–136.

Arthur, M. B., Hall, D. & Lawrence, B. S. 1996. *Handbook of career theory*. (5th ed.). Melbourne: Cambridge University Press.

Arthur, M. B., Rousseau, D. M. 1996 and 2001. *The boundaryless career*. New York: Oxford University Press.

Aryee, S., Field, D., Luk, V. 1999. A cross-cultural test of a model of work-family interface, *Journal of Management*. 25, pp. 491–511

Astin, H. S. 1984. The meaning of work in women's lives: A sociopsychological model of career choice and work behavior. *The counseling psychologist*.

Ayman, R. & Korabik, K. 2010.*Leadership: Why Gender and Culture Matter*. American Psychologist. 65: 157–170.

Auer, M. 2000. Vereinbarungskarrieren. *Eine karrieretheoretische Analyse des Verhältnisses von Erwerbsarbeit und Elternschaft*. Hampp: München/Mehring.

Barbuto, J. 2005. *Motivation and transactional, charismatic, and transformational leadership: A test of antecedents*. Journal of Leadership and Organizational Studies, 11: 26–40.

Barrick, M. R., Mount, M. K., & Judge, T. A. 2001. Personality and performance at the beginning of the new millennium: What do we know and where do we go next?. *International Journal of Selection and assessment*, 9(1-2), 9–30.

Becker, F. G. 1993. Explorative Forschung mittels Bezugsrahmen – ein Beitrag zur Methodologie des Entdeckungszusammenhangs. *Zeitschrift für Personalforschung*, pp.111–127.

Betz, N. E., & Fitzgerald, L. F. 1987. *The career psychology of women*. Academic Press.

Bischof-Köhler, D. 1993. Self object and interpersonal emotions. Identification of own mirror image, empathy and prosocial behavior in the 2nd year of life. *Zeitschrift für psychologie mit Zeitschrift für angewandte Psychologie. 202*(4). pp. 349–377.

Blanchard, D. A., Warnecke, T., Button, L. S., Italiana, V., Demirbas, G., Auth, D., & Murphy, M. P. 2010. *Women in China, between Confucius and the market.*

Bloemer, V. 2005. *Patchwork-Karriere.* Aufl., Walhalla Fachverlag, Regensburg ua.

Boisot, M., & Child, J. (1988). The iron law of fiefs: Bureaucratic failure and the problem of governance in the Chinese economic reforms. *Administrative Science Quarterly*, 507–527.

Borkenau, P., & Ostendorf, F. 1993. *NEO-Fünf-Faktoren Inventar: (NEO-FFI); nach Costa und McCrae.* Hogrefe.

Bosse, F., Schüller, M. 1998. Ausländische Direktinvestitionen in der VR China: Neuere Entwicklungen in den 90er Jahren und die besondere Rolle Japans. *China Aktuell*, 12/98, 1320–1333.

Bourdieu, P. 1977. *Outline of a Theory of Practice* (Vol. 16). Cambridge university press.

Bourdieu, P. 1982. Die feinen Unterschiede. *Kritik der gesellschaftlichen Urteilskraft. Frankfurt aM: Suhrkamp, 164.*

Bowen, C.-C., Wu, Y., Hwang, C. & Scherer, R. F. 2007. Holding up half of the sky? Attitudes toward women as managers in the people's republic of China.*The International Journal of Human Resource Management*, 18: 268–283.

Boyatzis, R. E. 2011. Managerial and leadership competencies: A behavioural approach to emotional, social and cognitive intelligence. *Vision*, 15: 91–100.

Brenner, O.C., Tomkiewicz, J, Schein, V.E. 1989. The relationship between sex rolestereotypes and requisite management characteristics revisited. *Acadamy of Managment Journal*, Vol 32, pp.662–669

Briscoe, J. P, Hall, D. T. 2006. The interplay of boundaryless and protean careers: Combinations and implications. *Journal of Vocational Behavior*, 69, S. 5–19.

Budig, M. J. 2012.The motherhood penalty in a cross national perspective. *Social Politics*, 19: 163–193.

Budig, M. J. & England, P. 2001. The wage penalty for motherhood. *American Sociological Review*, 66: 204–25.

Budig, M. J., Misra, J., & Boeckmann, I. 2012. The motherhood penalty in cross-national perspective: The importance of work-family policies and cultural attitudes. *Social Politics: International Studies in Gender, State & Society, 19*(2), 163–193.

Burke, R. J. &McKeen, W. 1990. Mentoring in organizations: Implications for women. *Journal of Business Ethics*, 9: 317–332.

Catalyst, 2016: *The world databank* 2016: Labor force participation rate, female, estimated China 2014 (available at: http://www.catalyst.org/knowledge/women-workforce-china)

Cattell, R. B. 1986. The 16 PF personality structure and Dr. Eysenck. *Journal of Social Behavior and Personality*, *1*(2), 153.

Caligiuri, P. M., & Cascio, W. F. 1998. Can we send her there? Maximizing the success of western women on global assignments. *Journal of World Business*, *33*(4), 394–416.

Chak-keung Wong, Simon & Gloria Jing Liu. 2010. "Will parental influences affect career choice? Evidence from hospitality and tourism management students in China." *International Journal of Contemporary Hospitality Management*. 22.1: 82–102.

Chen, Feinian, Guangya Liu & Christine A. Mair. 2011. "Intergenerational ties in context: Grandparents caring for grandchildren in China." *Social Forces, 90.2*: 571–594.

Chen, C. C., Yu, K. C., & Miner, J. B. 1997. Motivation to manage: A study of women in Chinese state-owned enterprises. *The Journal of Applied Behavioral Science*, *33*(2), 160–173.

Cheung, F. M. & Halpern, D. F. 2010. Women at the top: Powerful leaders define success as work and family in a culture of gender.*American Psychologist*, 65: 182–193.

Chi, W. & Li, B. 2008. Glass ceiling or sticky floor? Examining the gender earnings differential across the earnings distribution in urban China, 1987–2004. *Journal of Comparative Economics*, 36: 243–263.

Chin, C. O., Gu, J., & Tubbs, S. L. 2001. Developing global leadership competencies. *Journal of Leadership & Organizational Studies*, *7*(4), 20–31.

China daily, September 2013, 13, Chinadaily.com.cn. Source: State Administration for Industry and Commerce

China Daily. Xinhuet. 2001. March 6

Cho, H. 2005. Chinas langer Marsch in die neoliberale Weltwirtschaft. *PROKLA. Zeitschrift für kritische Sozialwissenschaft*, 35: 601–618.

Choi, J. & Chen, C. C. 2006. Gender differences in perceived work demands, family demands, and life stress among married Chinese employees. *Management & Organization Review*, 2: 209–229.

Coler, R., & Giersberg, S. 2009. *Das Paradies ist weiblich: eine faszinierende Reise ins Matriarchat*. Berlin: Kiepenheuer.

Cong, Z., & Silverstein, M. 2008. Intergenerational time-for-money exchanges in rural China: Does reciprocity reduce depressive symptoms of older grandparents?. *Research in Human Development*, *5*(1), 6–25.

Cooke, F. L., Xiao, Y. 2013. Gender roles and organizational HR practices. *Human Resource Management*, 53: 23–44.

Cooke, F. L. 2012. *Human resource management in China: New trends and practices*. London, UK: Routledge.

Cooke, F. L. 2009. A decade of transformation of HRM in China. *Asia Pacific Journal of Human Resources*, 47: 6–40.

Cooke, F. L. 2005. Women's managerial careers in China in a period of reform. *Asia Pacific Review*, 11: 149–162.

Cooke, F. L. 2001. Equal opportunity? The role of legislation and policies in women employment in China. *Women in Management Review*, 16: 334–348.

Credit Suisse Research Institute, 2014. Table 1: Percentage of women on boards by country. China. *The CS Gender 3000: Women in senior leadership*: p.8

Creswell, J. W. 2014. *Research design – Qualitative, quantitative and mixed methods approaches* (4th ed.). London: Sage.

Croll, E. 1995. *Changing identities of Chinese women: Rhetoric, experience, and self-perception in twentieth century China*. London: Zed Books.

De Fillippi, R. J. & Arthur, M. B. 1994. The boundaryless career: A competency-based perspective. *Journal of organizational behavior*, *15*(4), 307–324.

De Jonge, A. 2014. The glass ceiling that refuses to break: Women directors of listed firms in China and India. *Women's Studies International Forum*, 4: 326–233.

DeLong, T. J. (1982). Reexamining the career anchor model. *Personnel*, *59*(3), 50–61.

De Mente, B.L., 1999, Women in new China, *Asia Parcific Management Forum*, January, 1999

Devillard, S., Graven, W., Lawson, E., Paradise, R., & Sancier-Sultan, S. (2012). *Women Matter 2012*. Making the Break through. McKinsey & Company.

Digman, J. M. (1990). Personality structure: Emergence of the five-factor model. *Annual review of psychology*, *41*(1), 417–440.

Ding, S., Dong, X.-Y. & Li, S. 2009. Women's employment and family income inequality during China's economic transition. *Feminist Economics*, 15: 163–190.

Doge, K.A., Gilroy, F.D., Fenzel, L.M, 1995, Requisite management characteristics revisited: two decades later, in: Struthers, N. (ed.), Gender in the Workplace, Vol. 10, Journal of Social Behavior and Personality, pp. 253–64

Dolecheck, M. M., & Dolecheck, C. C. 1987. Business ethics: a comparison of attitudes of managers in Hong Kong and the United States. *Hong Kong Manager*, *1*, 28–43.

Du, X. (2016). Does Confucianism reduce board gender diversity? Firm-level evidence from China. *Journal of Business Ethics*, *136*(2), 399–436.

Eagly, A. H. 2007. Female leadership advantage and disadvantage: Resolving the contradictions. *Psychology of Women Quarterly*, 31: 1–12.

Eagly, A. & Carli, L. 2007. *Through the labyrinth – the truth about how women become leaders*. Boston, MA: Harvard Business School Press.

Eagly, A. & Carly, L. 2003. The female leadership advantage: An evaluation of the evidence. *The Leadership Quarterly*, 14: 807–834.

Ebrahimi B. P. 1997. Motivation to manage in Hong Kong: modification and test of miner sentence completion scale-H. *Journal of Managerial Psychology*, 12: 401–414.

Ebrahimi, B., & Miner, J. B. 1991. The cultural dynamics of managerial motivation among students from pan-pacific basin countries. *Journal of Global Business*, 2(1), 87–98.

Eddelston, K. A.; Baldridge, D. C. &Veiga, J. F. 2004. Toward modeling the predictors of managerial career success: Does gender matter? *Journal of Managerial Psychology*, 19: 360–385.

Ehrich, L. C. 2008. Mentoring and women managers: Another look at the field. *Gender in Management: An International Journal*, 23: 469–483.

Evans, Harriet. 2007. *The subject of gender: daughters and mothers in urban China*. Rowman & Littlefield Publishers

Farmer, H. 1985. Model of career and achievement motivation for women and men. *Journal of Counseling Psychology*, 32: 363–390.

Farrell, D. & Grant, A. 2005. China's looming talent shortage. *McKinsey Quarterly*, 5: 70–79.

Feng, Xu, 2014, Opportunities and challenges of Shanghai women's participation in social governance, *2014 Shanghai International Forum on Women's Development*

Fernandez, J. A. & Underwood, L. 2006. *China CEO: Voices of experience from 20 international business leaders*. Singapore: Wiley.

Fischlmayr, I. C. & Puchmüller, K. M. 2016. Married, mom and manager – how can this be combined with an international career? *The International Journal of Human Resource Mangement*, 27: 744–765

Fietze, S., Holst, E., & Tobsch, V. (2011). Germany's next top manager: Does personality explain the gender career gap?. **Management revue**, 240–273.

Fitzgerald, L. F., & Weitzman, L. M. 1992. Women's career development: Theory and practice from a feminist perspective. *Adult career development: Concepts, issues and practices*, 125–157.

Flick, U. 2014. *An introduction to qualitative research*. (5th ed.). Los Angeles: Sage,

Fondas, N. (1996). Feminization at work: Career implications. *The boundaryless career: A new employment principle for a new organizational era*, 282–293.

Forster, N. 2000. The myth of the 'international manager'. *International Journal of Human Resource Management*, *11*(1), 126–142.

Forrier, A., Sels, L., & Verbruggen, M. 2005. Career counseling in the new career era: a study about the influence of career types, career satisfaction and career management on the need for career counseling.

Frank, E.J. 2001. Chinese students' perceptions of women in management: will it be easier? *Women in Management Review*, 16: 316–324.

Friedel-Howe, H. 1990. Zusammenarbeit von weiblichen und männlichen Fach- und Führungskräften. *Weibliche Fach- und Führungskräfte. Wege zur Chancengleichheit. Stuttgart: Schäffer*, 16–34.

Friedmann, S.D., Greenhaus, J.H., 2000, *Work and Family – Allies or Enemies? What happens when business professionals confront life choices*, New York, NY: Oxford University Press

Gallos, J. V. 1989. Exploring women's development: Implications for career theory, practice, and research. Handbook of career theory, *110*, 132.

Ganrose, C. S. 2007. Gender difference in career perception in the People's Republic of China. *Career Development International*, 12: 9–27.

Ganrose, C. S. (Ed.). 2005. *Employment of women in Chinese cultures: Half the sky*. Cheltenham, UK and Northampton, MA: Edward Elgar.

Gasteiger, R. M. 2007. *Selbstverantwortliches Laufbahnmanagement: Das proteische Erfolgskonzept*. Hogrefe Verlag.

Gersick, C. J. G. & Kram, K. E. 2002. High-achieving women at midlife: An exploratory study. *Journal of Management Inquiry*, 11: 104–127.

Gilbert, L. A. 1993. *Two careers/one family: The promise of gender equality*. Sage Publications, Inc.

Gough, H. G. 1990. *The California Psychological Inventory*. Lawrence Erlbaum Associates, Inc.

Guan, Y., Zhen, W., Dong, Z., Liu, Y., Yue, Y., Haiyan, L., Zhou, W. & Liu, H. 2013. Career locus of control and career success among Chinese employees: A multidimensional approach. *Journal of Career Assessment, 21: 295–310.*

Guo, C. B., Tsang, M., & Ding, X. H. (2007). Gender difference in the education and employment of science & engineering students in HEIs [J]. *Journal of Higher Education, 11*, 021.

Guide, H. A. S. 2013. HAYS Survey Highlights Impact of the Skills Shortage. *HAYS Global Report*.

Gunkel, M., Lusk, E J., Wolff, B. &Fank, Li. 2007. Gender-specific effects at work: An empirical study of four countries. *Gender, Work & Organization*, 4: 56–79.

Guo, H.M., 2000, "Gender discrimination in women's employment and the completion of relevant laws and regulations, paper presented at the International Seminar on the legal Protection of women's employment Rights, Shanghai, April

Gustafsson, B. & Li, S. 2000. Economic transformation and the gender earnings gap in urban China.*Journal of Population Economics*, 13: 305–329.

Hackett, G. & Betz, N. E. 1989. A self-efficacy approach to the career development of women. *Journal of Vocational Behavior*, 18: 326–339.

Hartmann, M. & Kopp, J.(2001) *Koelner Zeitschrift für Soziologie und Soziale Psychologie* 53: 436. doi:10.1007/s11577-001-0074-6

Hayes, C. 1998. *World class learning*. Black Enterprise, 28 (10): 85–89

Hall, D. T. 1976. *Careers in Organizations*. Santa Monica: Addison-Wesley.

Hall, D. T. 2004. The protean career: A quarter-century journey. *Journal of vocational behavior*, 65(1), 1–13.

Hall, D. T. & Mirvis, P. H. (1996): The new protean career: psychological success and the path with the heart. In: Hall, D. T. (Ed.): *The career is dead, long live career. A relational Approach to Careers*. San Francisco, S. 15–45.

Halpern, D.F. & Cheung, F. M. 2008.*Women at the top: Powerful leaders tell us how to combine work and family*. New York: Wiley Blackwell.

Hannum, E. C., Yupin, Z. &Meian, W. 2013. Why are returns to education higher for women than for men in urban China? *The China Quarterly*, 215: 616–640.

Harrison, R. T., Scott, J. M., Hussain, J., & Millman, C. (2014). The role of guanxi networks in the performance of women-led firms in China. *International Journal of Gender and Entrepreneurship*, 6(1).

Hays Asia Salary guide. 2015. *HAYS Salary Report*, www.hays.cn/salary-guide

Hau-Siu Chow, I. 1995. Career aspirations, attitudes and experiences of female managers in Hong Kong. *Women in management review*, 10(1), 28–32.

Headlam-Wells, J., Gosland, J. & Craig, J. 2005. 'There's magic in the web': E-mentoring for women's career development. *Career Development International*, 10: 444–459.

Helgesen, S, Goldsmith, M., 2018, *How women rise*, London, Random House

Henn, M. 2012. *Die Kunst des Aufstieges: Was Frauen in Führungspositionen kennzeichnet*. Frankfurt/Main: Campus.

Hennig, M., & Jardim, A. 1987. *Frau und Karriere: Erwartungen, Vorstellungen, Verhaltensweisen*. Rowohlt.

Hewlett, S. A. 2006. Executive women and the myth of having it all. *Harvard Business Review*, 80(4): 66–73.

Hildebrandt, H. W. & Liu, J. 1988. Chinese women managers: A comparison with their U.S. and asian counterparts. *Human Resource Management*, 27: 291–314.

Hinterhuber, H. H. (1977). *Strategische Unternehmungsführung*. W. de Gruyter.

Hofstede, G. 1996. Gender stereotypes and partner preference of Asian women in masculine and feminine cultures. *Journal of Cross-Cultural Psychology, 27: 533–546.*

Hofstede, G. 1998. The cultural construction of gender. In G. Hofstede (Ed.). *Masculinity and feminity: The taboo dimension of national culture*: 75–105. Thousand Oaks, CA: Sage.

Hofstede G. J. 2005. *Lokales Denken, globales Handeln*. München: DTV.

Hogan, R., Curphy, G. J., & Hogan, J. 1994. What we know about leadership: Effectiveness and personality. *American psychologist, 49*(6), 493.

Holland, J. L. 1987. Current status of Holland's theory of careers: Another perspective. *The Career Development Quarterly*, *36*(1), 24–30.

Holst, E., Busch-Heizmann, A., & Wieber, A. 2001. *Führungskräfte-Monitor 2015*. Update, 2013.

Hossiep, R., Paschen, M. 2003. *Das Bochumer Inventar zur berufsbezogenen Persönlichkeitsbeschreibung: BIP*. Hogrefe, Verlag für Psychologie.

Huang, Q., & Sverke, M. 2007. Women's occupational career patterns over 27 years: relations to family of origin, life careers, and wellness. *Journal of vocational behavior, 70*(2), 369–397.

Hughes, J. & Maurer-Fazio, M. 2002. Effects of marriage, education and occupation on the female/male wage gap in China. *Pacific Economic Review*, 7: 137–56.

Hui, C. H. Pak, S. T. & Cheng, K. H. 2009. Validation studies on a measure of overall managerial readiness for the Chinese. *International Journal of Selection and Assessment*, 17: 127–41.

Huntington, S. P. 1997. *The clash of civilizations and the remaking of world order*. Penguin Books India.

International Monetary Fund. 2015. World Economic outlook – China. www.imf.org/external/pubs/ft/weo/2015/02/

Jackson, L. A., Hodge, C. N., & Ingram, J. M. 1994. Gender and self-concept: A reexamination of stereotypic differences and the role of gender attitudes. *Sex roles, 30*(9), 615–630.

Jiang, Y.P., 2000, State intervention in the employment of urban women, *paper presented at the international Seminar on the legal protection of women's employment rights*, Shanghai, April

Jokinen, T. 2005. Global leadership competencies: a review and discussion. *Journal of European Industrial Training*, *29*(3), 199–216.

Jones, E. B., & Jackson, J. D. 1990. College grades and labor market rewards. *The Journal of Human Resources*, *25*(2), 253–266.

Judd, E.R., 1990, "Men are more Able": Rural Chinese Women's Conception of Gender and Agency, *Parcific Affaires*, 63, pp.40–61

Judge, T. A., Cable, D. M., Boudreau, J. W. & Bretz, R. D., Jr. 1995. An empirical investigation of the predictors of executive career success. *Personnel Psychology*, 48: 485–519.

Judge, T. A., & Ilies, R. 2002. Relationship of personality to performance motivation: a meta-analytic review. *Journal of applied psychology*, *87*(4), 797.

Judge, T. A., & Piccolo, R. F. 2004. Transformational and transactional leadership: a meta-analytic test of their relative validity. *Journal of applied psychology*, *89*(5), 755.

Tan, J. 2008. Breaking the "bamboo curtain" and the "glass ceiling": the experience of women entrepreneurs in high-tech industries in an emerging market. *Journal of Business Ethics*, *80*(3), 547–564.

Kanning, U. P. 2005. *Soziale Kompetenzen: Entstehung, Diagnose und Förderung* (Vol.10). Hogrefe Verlag.

Kanter, R. M. (1977). *Men and women of the corporation*. New York: Basic Books.

Keith, R., 1997, Legislating women's and children's rights and interests in the PRC, *The China Quarterly*, Vol. 149, pp. 29–55

Kerlinger, F. N. 1986. *Foundations of Behavioral Research*. Holt, Rinehart and Winston, New York, NY.

Kim, S.W., Fong, V. L., Yoshikawa, H., Way, N., Chen, X. Y., Deng, H. H. & Lu, H. Z. 2010. Income, work preferences and gender roles among parents of infants in urban china: A mixed method study from Nanjing. *China Quarterly*, 204: 939–959.

Kimberly, A., Eddleston, D. C.; Baldridge, J. F. &Veiga, J. F. 2004. Toward modeling the predictors of managerial career success: does gender matter? *Journal of Managerial Psychology*, 19: 360–85.

King, P. & Wei, Z. 2014. Chinese and western leadership models: A literature review. *Journal of Management Research*, 6(2), 1–21.

Kirchmeyer, C. 1998. Determinants of managerial career success: Evidence and explanation of male-female differences. *Journal of Management*, 24: 673–692.

Kirchmeyer, C. 2002. Gender differences in managerial careers: Yesterday, today, and tomorrow. *Journal of Business Ethics*, 37: 5–24.

Klenner, W., 2006, *Chinas Finanz- und Währungspolitik nach der Asienkrise: Bilanz und Perspektiven der Reformpolitik*. Vol. 6. Lucius & Lucius DE

Ko, Dorothy, 1994, Teacher of the inner Chambers: women and Culture in the seventeenth-Century China, *Stanford University Press*, Stanford,, CA,

Korabik, K. 1992. Women hold up half the sky: The status of managerial women in China.In W. Wedley (Ed.), *Advances in Chinese industrial studies*: 197–211. Greenwich, CT: JAI Press.

Korabik, K. 1993. Women managers in the People's Republic of China: Changing roles in changing times. *Applied Psychology: An International Review*, 42:353–363.

Korabik, K. 1994. Managerial women in the People's Republic of China: The long march continues. In N. J. Adler & D. N. Israeli (Eds.), *Competitive frontiers: Women managers in the global economy*: 114–126. Cambridge, MA: Blackwell.

Korabik, K. 1993. Managerial women in the People's Republic of China: The long march continues. *International Studies of Management and Organization*, *23*: 47–56.

Kraiger, K., & Ford, J. K. 1985. A meta-analysis of ratee race effects in performance ratings. *Journal of applied psychology*, *70*(1), 56.

Kram, K.E., 1985, *Mentoring at Work*, Developmental Relationships in Organisational Life, Scott Foresman, Glenview, II

Kram, K. E., Lynn A. I., 1985, "Mentoring alternatives: The role of peer relationships in career development." *Academy of management Journal* 28.1: 110–132.

Kumar, R. 2014. *Research methodology. A step-by-step guide for beginners*. (4th ed.). Los Angeles: Sage.

Lam, K. C., McGuinness, P. B. &Vieto, J. P. 2013. CEO gender, executive compensation and firm performance in Chinese-listed enterprises. *Pacific-Basin Finance Journal*, 21: 1136–1159.

Law, B. F. &Meijers, W. G. 2002. New perspectives on career and identity in the contemporary world. *Journal of Guidance and Counseling*, 30: 431–449.

Leck, J. D., Elliott, C. &Rockewell, B. 2012. E-mentoring women: Lessons learned from a pilot program. *Journal of Diversity Management*, 7: 84–96.

Lehnert, C. J. 1996. Folgerungen für die Planung von Karriereverläufen. *Neuorientierung der betrieblichen Karriereplanung. Deutscher Universitätsverlag*. pp. 177–203

Lepine, I. 1992. Making their way in the organization: women managers in Quebec. *Women in Management Review*, *7*(3).

Leung, A. S. 2000. Gender differences in guanxi behaviours: An examination of People's Republic of China state-owned enterprises. *International Review of Women and Leadership*, *6*(1), 48–59.

Leung, A. S. M. 2002. Gender and career experience in mainland Chinese state-owned enterprises. *Personnel Review*, 31: 602–619.

Levinson, D. 1978, *The seasons of a Man's life*; New York, Knopf

Lewis, R. D. 1996. *When culture collide*. London, UK: Nicholas Brealey.

Li, C. 2000. Confucianism and feminist concerns: Overcoming the confucian "gender complex". *Journal of Chinese Philosophy*, 27: 187–199.

Li, J., & Wright, P. C. 2000. Guanxi and the realities of career development: a Chinese perspective. *Career Development International*, 5(7), 369–378.

Li, Y. 2000. Women's movement and change of women's status in China. *Journal of International Women's Studies*, 1: 30–40.

Liang, Z. & Zhondong, M. 2004. China's floating population: New evidence from the 2000 census.*Population and Development Review*, 30: 467–488.

Lin, N. 2000. Inequality in social capital. *Contemporary sociology*, 29(6), 785–795.

Lin, Y, 1939, *My country and My people*, New York, the John Day Company, p.139

Ling,Y. &Powell, G.N. 2001. Work-family conflict in contemporary China: Beyond an American-based model.*International Journal of Cross Cultural Management*, 1: 357–373.

Liu, S. 2013. A few good women at the top: The china case. *Business Horizons*, 2013, 56: 483–490.

Liu, Xiaolang. 2014. *The situation of women in China and implications for female careers*. Presentation at Salon Yongfu, German Consulat, Shanghai

Lyness, K. S. & Thompson, D. E. 2000. Climbing the corporate ladder: Do female and male executives follow the same route? *Journal of Applied Psychology*, 85: 86–101.

Mainiero, L. A., & Sullivan, S. E. 2005. Kaleidoscope careers: An alternate explanation for the "opt-out" revolution. *The Academy of Management Executive*, 19(1), 106–123.

Mann, S., 1997, Precious Records: Women in China's Long Eighteenth Century, Stanford, CA, *Stanford University Press*, pp. 222–223

Markman, G. D., & Baron, R. A. 2003. Person-entrepreneurship fit: why some people are more successful as entrepreneurs than others. *Human resource management review*, 13(2), 281–301.

Mayrhofer, W., Meyer, M. & Steyrer, J. 2005. *Macht? Erfolg? Reich? Glücklich?: Einflussfaktoren auf Karrieren*. Wien: Linde Verlag.

Mayrhofer, W., Meyer, M., Steyrer, J., Iellatchitch, A., Schiffinger, M., Strunk, G. & Mattl, C. 2002. Einmal gut, immer gut? Einflussfaktoren auf Karrieren in, neuen Karrierefeldern. *German Journal of Human Resource Management: Zeitschrift für Personalforschung*, 16(3), 392–414.

Mayring, P. 2010. *Qualitative Inhaltsanalyse: Grundlagen und Techniken*. (11. Aufl.). Weinheim: Beltz.

Maxwell, J. A. (2012). *Qualitative research design: An interactive approach: An interactive approach*. Sage.

McClelland, D. C. &Bovatzis, R. E. 1982. Leadership motive pattern and long-term success in management. *Journal of Applied Psychology*, 67: 737–743.

Melamed, T. 1996. Career success: An assessment of a gender-specific model. *Journal of Occupational and Organizational Psychology*, 69: 217–242.

Mennino, S. F. &Brayfield, A. 2002. Job-family trade-offs: The multidimensional effects. *Gender, Work and Occupation*, 29: 226–56.

Meulemann, H. 1990. Studium, Beruf und der Lohn von Ausbildungszeiten. *Zeitschrift für Soziologie, 19*(4), 248–264.

Miles, M. B., Huberman, A. M., & Saldana, J. 2013. *Qualitative data analysis: A methods sourcebook*. SAGE Publications, Incorporated.

Miner, J. B. 1993. *Role motivation theories*. London: Routledge.

Miner, J. B. 1978. Twenty Years of Research on Role-Motivation Theory of Managerial Effectiveness. *Personnel Psychology*, 31: 739–760.

Miner, J. B., Chen, C. & Yu, K. C. 1991. Theory testing under adverse conditions: Motivation to manage in the People's Republic of China. *Journal of Applied Psychology*, 76: 343–349.

Mirvis, P.H., Hall, D.T. 1996: Psychological Success and the Boundaryless Career. In: Arthur, M. B./Rousseau, D. M. (Hrsg.): *The Boundaryless Career*. New York/Oxford, S. 237–255.

Morehead Dworkin, T., Maurer, V. & Schipiani, C. A. 2012. Career mentoring for women: New horizons / expanded methods. *Business Horizons*, 55: 363–372.

Namu, Y. E., & Mathieu, C. 2007. *Leaving mother lake: A girlhood at the edge of the world*. Little, Brown.

Naughton, B. 1995.Growing out of the plan: Chinese economic reform, 1978–1993. New York: *Cambridge University Press*, 1995.

Ng, C. W., & Pine, R. (2003). Women and men in hotel management in Hong Kong: perceptions of gender and career development issues. *International Journal of Hospitality Management, 22*(1), 85–102.

Noe, R. A. 1988. Women and mentoring: A review and research agenda. *The Academy of Management Review*, 13: 65–78.

Nyaw, M. 1996: Investment Environment Perceptions of Overseas Investors of Foreign-funded Industrial Firms. In: Yeung, Y.; Sun, Y. (Ed.): Shanghai. *Transformation and Modernisation under China's Open Policy*. Hong Kong, 1996, S. 249–272.

O'Brien, K. E., Biga, A., Kessler, S. R. & Allen, T. D. 2008. A meta-analytic investigation of gender differences in mentoring. *Journal of Management*, 36: 537–554.

Oi, J. (1989). Market reforms and corruption in rural China. *Studies in Comparative Communism*, 22, 221–234. Pasternak, B.

O'Leary, J. 1997. Developing a new mindset: the "career ambitious" individual. *Women in Management Review*, 12: 91–99.

O'Neil, D. A., Bilimoria, D., & Saatcioglu, A. 2004. Women's career types: attributions of satisfaction with career success. *Career Development International*, 9(5), 478–500.

O'Neil, D., Hopkins, M. M. &Bilimoria, D. 2008. Women's careers at the start of the 21st century: patterns and paradoxes. *Journal of Business Ethics*, 80: 727–743.

O'Neill, D. A. & Hopkins, M. M. 2013. Patterns and paradoxes in women's careers. In: W.Patton (Ed.): *Conceptualising women's working lives: Moving the boundaries of discourse:* 63–79. Rotterdam et al.: Sense Publishers.

Ortiz-Walters, R., Eddleston, K.-A. & Simione, K. 2010. Satisfaction with mentoring relationships: does gender identity matter. *Career Development International*, 15: 100–120.

Osipow, S. H., & Fitzgerald, L. F. (1996). *Theories of career development*. Allyn and Bacon. Needham Heights.

Patterson V. 1997. Breaking the Glass-Ceiling: What's holding women back? *Wall Street Journal*, 14 December 1997

Patton, W., & McMahon, M. 2014. *Career development and systems theory: Connecting theory and practice* (Vol. 2). Springer.

Patton, W.; McMahon, M. 2014. Theories of career development. In W. Patton & M. McMahon (Eds.), *Career development and systems theory: Connecting theory and practice*. (3rd ed.): 135–181. Rotterdam et al.: Sense Publishers.

Peng, M. W. (1997). The importance of guanxi (connections) in China. Chow et al. (Eds), *Business Strategy*, an Asia-Pacific Focus, Prentice-Hall, New York, NY.

Peus, C., Braun, S. &Knipfer, K. 2015. On becoming a leader in Asia and America: Empirical evidence from women managers. *The Leadership Quarterly*, 26: 55–67.

Poole, M. E., Langan-Fox, J., Ciavarella, M.,& Omodei, M. (1991).A contextual model of Professional attainment: Results of a longitudinal study of career paths of men and women. *The Counseling Psychologist*, 19, 603–624.

Potter, P., 1999, The Chinese legal system: continuing commitment to the primacy of state power, *The China Quarterly*, Vol 159, pp.673–683

Powell, G. N. 2012. Six ways of seeing the elephant: the intersection of sex, gender, and leadership. *Gender in Management: An International Journal*, 27: 119 141.

Powell, G. N. 2011. *Women and men in management*. (4th ed.). Los Angeles: Sage.

Powell, G.N. and Butterfield, D.A. , 1989, The "good Manager": did androgyny fare better in the 1980s?, *Group & Organization Studies*, Vol. 14, pp. 216–33

Powell, G. N., Francesco, A. M., & Ling, Y. (2009). Toward culture-sensitive theories of the work-family interface. *Journal of Organizational Behavior*, 30(5), 597–616.

Powell, G. N., & Mainiero, L. A. (1993). Getting ahead – in career and life. *Women and men in management*, 186–224.

Pye, L. 1985. *Asian power and politics*. Cambridge, MA: Belknap/Harvard University Press

Ragins, B. R. 1998: Gender gap in the executive suite: CEOs and female executives report on breaking the glass ceiling.*Academy of Management Executive*, 12: 28–42.

Ragins, B. R. 1989. Barriers to mentoring: The female manager's dilemma. *Human Relations*, 42: 1–22.

Ragins, B. R. 1997. Diversified, mentoring relationships in organizations: A power perspective. *The Academy of Management Review*, 22: 482–521.

Rajerison, N., 1996, Women Managers in China, *ESU Online Management Journal*, Emporia State University (http://academic.emporia.edu/smithwil/)

Rajshekhar, G. J., Scherer, R., Sánchez, C., Pradenas, L., Rojas, V., Daza, Parada, Hwan, C. & Yan, W. 2011. A comparative analysis of the attitudes toward women managers in China, Chile, and the USA. *International Journal of Emerging Markets*, 6: 233–253.

Ranker, G., McLeod, M., Global mindset coaching, 2017

Rastetter, D., Cornils, D. 2012. „Networking: aufstiegsförderliche Strategien für Frauen in Führungspositionen." *Gruppendynamik und Organisationsberatung* 43.1 (2012): 43–60.

Reichel, A., Chudzikowski, K., Schiffinger, M., & Mayrhofer, W. (2010). Mehr Unabhängigkeit im neuen Karrierekontext? Der Kampf um Arbeit und die rosa Brille der Karriereforschung. In *Der Kampf um Arbeit* (pp. 379–402). VS Verlag für Sozialwissenschaften.

Reiners, F. (2008). Networking in Organisationen. I n O. Neuberger (Hrsg.), *Schriftenreihe Organisation & Personal*, Bd. 19. München: Hampp Verlag

Reichel, A., Chudzikowski, K., Schiffinger M. & W. Mayrhofer. 2010. Mehr Unabhängigkeit im neuen Karrierekontext? Der Kampf um Arbeit und die rosa Brille der Karriereforschung. In G. Schweiger & B. Brandl, *Der Kampf um Arbeit: Dimensionen und Perspektiven:* 401–424. Wiesbaden: VS Verlag für Sozialwissenschaften.

Reilly, R. R., Chao, G. T. 1982. Validity and fairness of some alternative employee selection procedures. *Personnel Psychology*, 35(1), 1–62.

Resch, Katharina. 2014. „Ungleiche Karrieren. Erklärungsansätze für den Einfluss der sozialen Herkunft auf Karrieren." *Karriereverlaufe in Forschung und Entwicklung: Bedingungen und Perspektiven im Spannungsfeld von Organisation und Individuum*: 34.

Richardson, M. S. 1974. The dimensions of career and work orientation in college women. *Journal of Vocational Behavior*, 5(1), 161–172.

Richardson, M. S. (1996). **From career counseling to counseling/psychotherapy and work, jobs, and career.**

Riley, N. E. (1994). Interwoven lives: Parents, marriage, and Guanxi in China. *Journal of Marriage and the Family*, 791–803.

Rosener, J. B. 1990. Ways women lead: The command-and-control leadership style association with men is not the only way to succeed. *Harvard Business Review*, 68 (6): 119–125.

Rosinski, P. 2003. *Coaching across cultures: New tools for leveraging national, corporate, and professional differences*. London: Nicholas Brealey Publishing.

Rothbath, N. P. 2001. Enriching or depleting? The dynamics of engagement in work and family roles.*Administrative science quarterly*, 46: 655–684.

Rothmann, S. Coetzer E. P. 2003. The big five personality dimension and job performance. *Journal of Industrial Psychology*, 29: 68–74.

Rump, J. 2003. Wandel in der Arbeitswelt – Herausforderungen für Mensch und Organisation. *Human Resource Management*, Köln.

Sandberg, S. 2013. *Lean in: Women, work, and the will to lead*. Random House.

Schein, V. 2007. Women in management: reflections and projections. *Women in Management Review*, 22: 6–18.

Schein, V.E., Mueller, R.,Lituchy, T.& Liu, J. 1996. Think manager – Think male: A global phenomenon? *Journal of Organizational Behavior*, 1996, 17: 33–41.

Schellhorn, H. 2014. *Welche Auswirkungen hat die Erwerbstätigkeit von Müttern auf die Sozialisation ihrer Kinder*

Schwan, Gesine. 2014. *Partnership between spouses – a concept to support female careers*. Presentation at Salon Yongfu, German Consulat, Shanghai

Senge, P. M. 1996. *Die fünfte Disziplin: Kunst und Praxis der lernenden Organisation. 3. Aufl., Stuttgart.*

Sincoff, M. Z., Owen, C. L. & Coleman, J. W. 2009. Women as managers in the United States and China: A cross-cultural study. *Journal of Asia-Pacific Business*, 10: 65–79.

Snyder, M. 1974. Self-monitoring of expressive behavior. *Journal of personality and social psychology*, *30*(4), 526.

Sonnenfeld, J., Kotter, S.L, 1982, The maturation of career theory. *Human Relations*, 35: 19–46

Spector, P.E., Cooper, C.L., Poelsmas, S., Allen, T.D., O'Discoll M., Sanchez, J.I., Lu.L., 2004, A cross-national comparative study of work-family stressors, working hours, and well-being: China and Latin America versus the Anglo World, *Personnel Psychology*, 57, 119–142

Stanford, J. H., Oates, B. R. & Flores, D. 1995. Women's leadership styles: a heuristic analysis. *Women in Management Review*, 10: 9–16.

Spiess, E. 1998. „Das Konzept der Empathie", in E. Spiess (Ed.), *Formen der Cooperation: Bedingungen und Perspektiven* (pp. 53–62), Hogrefe, Göttingen.

Stockmann, N., Bonney, N., Sheng, X.W., 1995, *Women's work in the east and West: The dual burden of Employment and Family Life*, London: UCL Press Ltd.

Sturges, J. 1999. What it means to succeed: Personal conceptions of career success held by male and female managers at different ages. *British Journal of Management*, 10: 239–252.

Süssmuth-Dyckerhoff, C., Wang, J. & Chen, J. 2012. *Women matter: An Asian perspective – harnessing female talent to raise corporate performance*. McKinsey.

Sullivan, S. E. 1999. The changing nature of careers: A review and research agenda. *Journal of management*, 25(3), 457–484.

Super, D. E. 1980. A life-span life-space approach to career development. *Journal of Vocational Behavior*, 16: 282–298.

Tagscherer, U. 1999. *Mobilität und Karriere in der VR China – Chinesische Führungskräfte im Transformationsprozess*. Heidelberger Geographische Arbeiten, Geographisches Institut der Universität Heidelberg. Heidelberg: Ruprecht-Karls-Universität Heidelberg

Tan, J. 2008. Breaking the "bamboo curtain" and the "glass ceiling": The experience of women entrepreneurs in high-tech industries. *Journal of Business Ethics*, 80: 547–564.

Tannenbaum, R., & Schmidt, W. H. 1973. *How to choose a leadership pattern* (pp. 3–12). Boston, MA: Harvard Business Review.

Tatli, A., Vassiopoulou, J. & Özbilgin, M. 2013. An unrequited affinity between talent shortages and untapped female potential: The relevance of gender quotas for talent management in high growth potential economies of the Asia Pacific region. *International Business Review*, 22: 539–553.

Taubmann, Wolfgang. 1994. Shanghai – Chinas Wirtschaftsmetropole. Gormsen, E., Thimm, A., (Ed.)*Megastädte in der Dritten Welt.*, Mainz: 45–71.

Taylor, F. W. 1913. Die Grundsätze wissenschaftlicher Betriebsführung, Original: *The principles of scientific management* (1912), deutsch von R. *Roesler, München*.

Tharenou, P. 1997. Explanations of Managerial Career Advancement. *Australian Psychologist*, 32: 19–28.

Tharenou, P., Donohue, R., & Cooper, B. (2007). *Management research methods* (p. 338). Melbourne: Cambridge University Press.

Tharenou, P., Latimer, S. & Conroy, D. 1994. How do you make it to the top? An examination of influences on women's and men's managerial advancement. *The Academy of Management Journal*, 37: 899–931.

The World Economic Forum. 2015. *The global gender gap report 2015*: p. 140–141

Thompson, C. A.; Bauvais, L. L. & Lyne, K. S. 1999. When work-family benefits are not enough: The influence of work-family culture on benefit utilization. *Journal of Vocational Behavior*, 54: 392–415.

Thornton, G. 2014. Women in Business: From classroom to boardroom. *Grant Thornton International Business Report*.

Tokar, D. M., Fischer, A. R., & Subich, L. M. 1998. Personality and vocational behavior: A selective review of the literature, 1993–1997. *Journal of Vocational Behavior*, 53(2), 115–153.

Tu, H. S., Forret, M. L. & Sullivan, S. E. 2006. Careers in a non-western context: An exploratory empirical investigation of factors related to the career success of Chinese managers.*Career Development International*, 11: 580–593.

Tucker, M. F., Bonial, R., Vanhove, A., & Kedharnath, U. 2014. Leading across cultures in the human age: an empirical investigation of intercultural competency among global leaders. *SpringerPlus*, 3(1), 1.

Turner, Y. 2007. Swinging open or slamming shut? The implications of China's open door policy for women, educational choice and work. *Journal of Education and Work*, 19: 47–65.

Underhill, C. M. 2006. The effectiveness of mentoring programs in corporate settings: A meta-analytical review of the literature. *Journal of Vocational Behavior*, 68: 292–307.

Ventolini, S., & Mercier, S. 2015. Le gestionnaire de carrière ressuscité?. *Management & Avenir*, (6), 115–133.

Vinkenburg, C. J., & Weber, T. 2012. Managerial career patterns: A review of the empirical evidence. *Journal of Vocational Behavior*, 80(3), 592–607.

Wang, Zheng, 1997, Maoism, Feminism, and the UN Conference on Women: Women's studies research in Contemporary China, *Journal of Women's history*, V 8, n4, pp. 126–153

Warner, M. 1996: Economic reform, industrial relations and human resources management in China in the early 1990s. In: Bettignies, H.-C. de (Hrsg.): *Business transformation in China*. London u.a.O., 133–152

Weber, M. (1972). *Wirtschaft und Gesellschaft – Grundriss der verstehenden Soziologie*. Tübingen: Mohr.

Wegmann, G., & Ruviditch, I. 2015. Analyse historique du concept de performance en Chine. Un regard occidental. *Prospective et stratégie*, (6), 43–55.

Wei, Y.D. Leung, C.K., 2005: Development Zones, Foreign Investment, and Global City Formation in Shanghai. In: *Growth and Change*, Vol 36, Heft 1, pp. 16–40.

Whiston, S. C., & Keller, B. K. 2004. The influences of the family of origin on career development a review and analysis. *The Counseling Psychologist, 32*(4), 493–568.

White, B. 1995. The career development of successful women.*Women in Management Review*, 10(3): 4–15.

Whyte, M.K., 1984, "Sexual inequality under socialism: the Chinese case in perspective", in: Watson, J., (ed.) *Class and Social Stratification in Post-Revolution China*, Cambridge University Press, Cambridge

Whyte, M. K., & Xu, Q. 2003. Support for aging parents from daughters versus sons. *China's revolutions and intergenerational relations*, 167–196.

Williams, S. 1997. Personality and Self-Leadership. *Human Resource Management Review*, 7 (2): 139–155.

Woo, T., 1998, Confucianism and Feminism, in *Feminism and World Religions*, Edited by Arvind Sharma and Young, K., Albany, State University of New York Press, pp.110–147

Xi, L., 1985, Are Women Intellectually Inferior to Men? *Women of China*, Jan. 1985, p. 37

Xian, H., & Woodhams, C. (2008). Managing careers: Experiences of successful women in the Chinese IT industry. *Gender in Management: An International Journal, 23*(6), 409–425.

Xiu, L. & Gunderson M. 2013. Gender earning differences in China, Base, transformation and total pay. *Contemporary Economic Policy*, 31: 235–254.

Yan, N. & Chan, C. C. 2000. Sources of work-family conflict: A Sino-US comparison of the effects of work and family demands. *Academy of Management Journal*, 43: 113–123.

Yang, K. S. 1986. Chinese personality and its change.

Yeung, I. Y., & Tung, R. L. 1996. Achieving business success in Confucian societies: The importance of guanxi (connections). *Organizational Dynamics, 25*(2), 54–65.

Yeung, Y., Shen, J., 2004. Developing china's west: A critical path to balanced national development. *Chinese University Press*, 2004.

Yin, R. K. 2014. *Case study research: Design and methods*. (5th ed.). Los Angeles et al.: Sage.

Young, M. Y., Cady, S. & Foxon, M. J. 2006. Demystifying gender differences in mentoring: theoretical perspectives and challenges for future research on gender and mentoring *Human Resource Development Review*, 5: 148–175.

Yuan, L. (2013). *Traditional Chinese Thinking on HRM Practices: Heritage and Transformation in China*. Springer.

Yun, Y. 2011. Gender and engineering career development of hotel employees in China. *Systems Engineering Procedia*, 1: 365–371.

Zahidi, S. & Ibarra, H. 2010. *The corporate gender gap report 2010*, Geneva: The World Economic Forum.

Zhang, J., Han J., Liu, P.-W. & Zhao, Y. 2008. Trends in the gender earnings differential in urban China: 1988–2004.*Industrial & Labor Relations Review*, 61: 224–243.